Communications in Computer and Information Science 2537

Series Editors

Rationale

The CCIS series is devoted to the publication of proceedings of computer science conferences. Its aim is to efficiently disseminate original research results in informatics in printed and electronic form. While the focus is on publication of peer-reviewed full papers presenting mature work, inclusion of reviewed short papers reporting on work in progress is welcome, too. Besides globally relevant meetings with internationally representative program committees guaranteeing a strict peer-reviewing and paper selection process, conferences run by societies or of high regional or national relevance are also considered for publication.

Topics

The topical scope of CCIS spans the entire spectrum of informatics ranging from foundational topics in the theory of computing to information and communications science and technology and a broad variety of interdisciplinary application fields.

Information for Volume Editors and Authors

Publication in CCIS is free of charge. No royalties are paid, however, we offer registered conference participants temporary free access to the online version of the conference proceedings on SpringerLink (http://link.springer.com) by means of an http referrer from the conference website and/or a number of complimentary printed copies, as specified in the official acceptance email of the event.

CCIS proceedings can be published in time for distribution at conferences or as post-proceedings, and delivered in the form of printed books and/or electronically as USBs and/or e-content licenses for accessing proceedings at SpringerLink. Furthermore, CCIS proceedings are included in the CCIS electronic book series hosted in the SpringerLink digital library at http://link.springer.com/bookseries/7899. Conferences publishing in CCIS are allowed to use Online Conference Service (OCS) for managing the whole proceedings lifecycle (from submission and reviewing to preparing for publication) free of charge.

Publication process

The language of publication is exclusively English. Authors publishing in CCIS have to sign the Springer CCIS copyright transfer form, however, they are free to use their material published in CCIS for substantially changed, more elaborate subsequent publications elsewhere. For the preparation of the camera-ready papers/files, authors have to strictly adhere to the Springer CCIS Authors' Instructions and are strongly encouraged to use the CCIS LaTeX style files or templates.

Abstracting/Indexing

CCIS is abstracted/indexed in DBLP, Google Scholar, EI-Compendex, Mathematical Reviews, SCImago, Scopus. CCIS volumes are also submitted for the inclusion in ISI Proceedings.

How to start

To start the evaluation of your proposal for inclusion in the CCIS series, please send an e-mail to ccis@springer.com

Łukasz Tomczyk
Editor

New Media Pedagogy: Research Trends, Methodological Challenges, and Successful Implementations

Third International Conference, NMP 2024
Kraków, Poland, November 28–29, 2024
Revised Selected Papers

Springer

Editor
Łukasz Tomczyk
Jagiellonian University
Kraków, Poland

ISSN 1865-0929 ISSN 1865-0937 (electronic)
Communications in Computer and Information Science
ISBN 978-3-031-95626-3 ISBN 978-3-031-95627-0 (eBook)
https://doi.org/10.1007/978-3-031-95627-0

This Springer imprint is published by the registered company Springer Nature Switzerland AG
The registered company address is: Gewerbestrasse 11, 6330 Cham, Switzerland

Preface

It is with great pleasure that we present to you the publication summarising the international conference New Media Pedagogy – NMP 2024, which took place on 28–29 November 2024 at the Jagiellonian University in Krakow (Poland). The event brought together researchers, teachers, education experts and new technology enthusiasts to explore the current challenges and opportunities associated with the transformation of education in the digital age.

The book is divided into two main parts, reflecting the leading topics of the conference. Part I – Innovative ICT Applications in Education – focuses on the practical and theoretical aspects of using information and communication technologies in various educational contexts. The articles in this section address topics such as digital competence, early childhood education, the use of VR, brain-computer interfaces and the role of critical pedagogy in shaping the new digital education.

Part II – Artificial Intelligence in Education – presents a wide range of research and reflections on the impact of AI-based tools on didactic processes, teaching practices and student experiences. The authors analyse both the theoretical framework of education in the age of AI and the practical implications of using generative artificial intelligence in education at various levels – from primary schools to higher education.

The international character of the conference is particularly noteworthy – the authors of the papers include representatives from as many as 16 countries: Belgium, China, Italy, Portugal, Poland, Slovakia, the Czech Republic, Greece, the UK, Morocco, Slovenia, Austria, Indonesia, Chile, Australia and Germany. This global perspective enables a better understanding of common challenges and local contexts of education in a digital world, as well as the exchange of best practices and educational inspiration.

The book contains 23 chapters, carefully selected from 72 submissions sent to the conference in a double-blind review process with three reviews per submission. This means an acceptance rate of 31.94%, which testifies not only to the reliable and responsible work of the Scientific Committee, but above all to their attention to the high substantive quality of the articles presented. The papers were selected with the aim of maintaining high standards of research into the digitalisation of education. In an era of overproduction of analyses of information and communication technologies (ICT) in education, methodological consistency, logical reasoning and adequate anchoring in social science theories take on particular importance. I would like to take this opportunity to thank all the reviewers who helped select the best texts and provided a number of valuable comments for the authors. Without your support, it would not have been possible to finalise the NMP 2024 conference in the form of a book.

The papers presented here show the diverse approaches, methods and cultural perspectives that together form a panoramic picture of contemporary media pedagogy. The NMP 2024 conference and this publication are not only intended to document progress in the field of digital education, but above all to inspire further research, innovation and activities for the conscious, critical and inclusive use of new media in the educational process.

We would like to thank all authors, reviewers and conference participants for their contribution to the development of this important field and at the same time invite you to participate in the next edition, NMP 2025, which, as every year, will be organised by the Institute of Pedagogy at the Jagiellonian University. More information about the event is available at: www.ict-education.pl

April 2025 Łukasz Tomczyk

Organization

General Chair

Łukasz Tomczyk	Jagiellonian University, Poland

Program Committee

Michał Apollo	University of Silesia in Katowice, Poland
Małgorzata Bogunia-Borowska	Jagiellonian University, Poland
Cesar Alberto Collazos	Universidad del Cauca, Colombia
Ludvik Eger	University of West Bohemia, Czech Republic
Maria Amelia Eliseo	Universidade Presbiteriana Mackenzie, Brazil
Francisco David Guillen-Gamez	University of Málaga, Spain
Nataliia Demeshkant	Pedagogical University of Krakow, Poland
Valeria Farinazzo-Martins	Universidade Presbiteriana Mackenzie, Brazil
Laura Fedeli	University of Macerata, Italy
Ismar Frango Silveira	Universidade Presbiteriana Mackenzie, Brazil
Akhmad Habibi	University of Jambi, Indonesia
Anna Gaweł	Jagiellonian University, Poland
Leen d'Haenens	KU Leuven, Belgium
Agnieszka Iwanicka	Adam Mickiewicz University, Poland
Vicente J. Llorent	University of Córdoba, Spain
Pierpaolo Limone	Pegaso Telematic University, Italy
Anthi Karatrantou	University of Patras, Greece
Therese Keane	La Trobe University, Australia
Janina Kostkiewicz	Jagiellonian University, Poland
Bård Ketil Engen	Oslo Metropolitan University, Norway
Michał Klichowski	Adam Mickiewicz University, Poland
Daniel Mara	"Lucian Blaga" University of Sibiu, Romania
Gemma Martinez	Universidad del País Vasco, Spain
Maria Lidia Mascia	University of Sassari, Italy
Haris Memisevic	Sarajevo University, Bosnia & Herzegovina
Regina Motz	Universidad de la República, Uruguay
Anders D. Olofsson	Umeå University, Sweden
Julio Ruiz Palmero	University of Málaga, Spain
Piotr Plichta	University of Wrocław, Poland
Katarzyna Potyrała	Cracow University of Technology, Poland

Jacek Pyżalski	Adam Mickiewicz University, Poland
Roberta Renati	University of Cagliari, Italy
Hasan Saliu	AAB College, Kosovo
Natale Salvatore Bonfiglio	University of Cagliari, Italy
Elma Selmanagić-Lizde	University of Sarajevo, Bosnia and Herzegovina
Fazilat Siddiq	University of South-Eastern Norway, Norway
Francisco Simões	CIS-IULCentro de Investigação e de Intervenção Social (ECSH), Portugal
Piotr Siuda	Kazimierz Wielki University in Bydgoszcz, Poland
Siri Sollied Madsen	UiT the Arctic University of Norway, Norway
Solomon Sunday Oyelere	Luleå University of Technology, Sweden
Lazar Stošić	Union – Nikola Tesla University, Serbia
Arthur Tatnall	Victoria University, Australia
Hüseyin Uzunboylu	Near East University, Northern Cyprus
Natalia Walter	Adam Mickiewicz University, Poland
Michał Wierzchoń	Jagiellonian University, Poland
Ewa Ziemba	University of Economics in Katowice, Poland

Additional Reviewers

Abdelmajid el Hajaji
Alessandro Biraglia
Alessandro Soriani
Antony Hoyte-West
Armand Faganel
Beata Cieśleńska
Carolina Matamala
Charlene James
Christopher Walker
Daniel Raichvarg
Davide Cino
Emanuele Bardone
Fedor de Beer
Franca Rossi
Gabriela Špinarová
Gıyasettin Demirhan
Ingrid Forsler
Jan Beseda
Jan Zahorec
Jolanta Szempruch
Lenka Flikingerová
Lucie Rohlikova
Magdalena Wędzińska
Markéta Košatkova
Maunel Leon
Michal Radošinský
Michal Zemko
Milan Klement
Mirko Markič
Nektarios Moumoutzis
Ngenge Ransom Tanyu
Panagiota Babatsouli

Paola Molina
Paolo Bonafede
Pavol Prokop
Polixeni Arapi
Rachid Boudri
Radovan Savov
Ryan Worn
Sara Martins
Simona Cakirpaloglu
Sudi Mungkasi
Tina Štemberger
Veronika Růžičková
Whitney Bevill
Žaneta Gužíková
Zuzana Halakova

Contents

AI in Education

Innovative ICT Applications in Education

Report-Based Interpretation of 2024 Digital Literacy and Skills in China and the EU: Status, Differences, and Future Directions

Chao Wang[1,2] and Leen d'Haenens[1(✉)]

[1] Media Culture and Policy Lab, Faculty of Social Sciences, KU Leuven, Leuven, Belgium
leen.dhaenens@kuleuven.be

[2] School of Information Management, Sun Yat-sen University, Guangzhou, China

Abstract. This paper provides a comparative analysis of China's *National Digital Literacy and Skills Development Survey Report 2024* and the EU's *State of the Digital Decade 2024* report, examining the current state, challenges, and future strategies for fostering digital skills in both regions. In China, the data shows progress in digital skills among both adults and youth, attributed to the centralized and ambitious government-led initiatives such as nationwide digital literacy campaign and targeted training programs in rural areas. These efforts, aligned with China's broader digital transformation goals, aim to equip citizens with essential skills for participation in an increasingly digital economy. However, challenges persist, particularly in addressing the urban-rural digital divide and ensuring equal access to high-quality digital education across all provinces. The EU presents a more fragmented landscape. While many member states are striving to achieve universal basic digital skills by 2030, progress varies significantly across the region. The disparity stems from differences in educational systems, funding allocations, and national priorities, which create both challenges and opportunities. This article explores how China and the EU can learn from one another to address their unique challenges and leverage their respective strengths. By comparing the successes, obstacles, and forward-looking strategies outlined in the two reports, it identifies key areas for collaboration and mutual learning. Despite their divergent political and economic contexts, both regions share the potential to jointly build a digitally inclusive society capable of adapting to rapid technological changes.

Keywords: Digital Literacy and Skills · Report-based Analysis · Comparative Analysis · European Union (EU) · China

1 Introduction

In the 21st century, digital literacy is key to development. It helps people use technology and contribute to society [1]. As digital change speeds up, cultivating people digital skills supports innovation, strong economies, and social fairness. Digital literacy is now essential for adapting to new technology and closing gaps [2]. Governments are making digital education a priority to prepare citizens for the digital world [3, 4].

Ł. Tomczyk (Ed.): NMP 2024, CCIS 2537, pp. 3–18, 2025.
https://doi.org/10.1007/978-3-031-95627-0_1

This paper looks at how China and the EU tackle digital literacy development. It focuses on best practices, common challenges, and ways to work together. Drawing on data from China's *National Digital Literacy and Skills Development Survey Report 2024* [5] and the EU's *State of the Digital Decade 2024* [6], it compares their strategies. China employs a centralized, government-driven model, while the EU adopts a decentralized approach, reflecting regional diversity. As these reports reflect only the self-assessment of the regions studied, this constitutes a limitation. By analyzing the data, the paper reviews progress, identifies challenges, and offers practical insights. It also links findings to global trends, providing value for policymakers, educators, and stakeholders.

2 Background

2.1 Definition

Digital literacy means being able to use digital technologies effectively and critically [7]. It includes basic skills like using digital devices, accessing online services, and staying safe online. It also involves advanced skills like analyzing data, coding, and using digital platforms ethically [8]. The European Commission defines it as the skills needed to use digital tools in daily life, education, and work, based on its Digital Competence Framework (DigComp 2.2) [9]. United Nations Educational, Scientific and Cultural Organization (UNESCO) views digital literacy as a lifelong skill that helps people and reduces the digital divide [10].

In China, digital literacy is part of the goal to improve 'national digital capabilities.' This includes digital awareness, knowledge, and practical skills. China focuses on education on how to use digital technologies safely, ethically, and effectively. It also aims to help citizens adapt to new technologies like AI and big data. A key goal is to promote digital inclusion and narrow the digital divide, so everyone can take part in the digital society [11].

Both the EU and China see digital literacy as key in modern society. The EU uses a detailed framework to teach specific skills for the digital age. China takes a broader approach, linking digital literacy to national goals and focusing on practical use and ethics. Understanding these differences helps analyze their policies and programs. It also shows how each region handles the challenges and opportunities of digital transformation. While both regions recognize digital literacy as vital in modern society, their approaches differ. The EU adopts a detailed framework for skill development, whereas China links digital literacy to national goals, prioritizing practical applications. This divergence reflects the varying cultural and policy contexts shaping their strategies.

2.2 Policy Context

China uses a centralized, policy-driven approach to improve digital literacy. National strategies ensure inclusiveness and broad impact [12]. The *Education Informatization 2.0 Action Plan* [13] and *Digital China Initiative* [14, 15] provide a clear framework for teaching digital skills. Policies focus on three main goals: (1) Improve digital infrastructure in rural and underserved areas; (2) Add digital literacy to school curricula with an emphasis on new technologies; (3) Run public campaigns to promote responsible digital use. China's 2024 report shows progress in reducing the rural-urban digital gap. Programs like the *Rural Broadband Project* [16] and training for elderly and low-income groups have played a key role.

The EU's digital literacy strategy follows the *Digital Compass 2030* [17] and the *European Skills Agenda* [18]. It aims to ensure basic digital skills for everyone by 2030. Unlike China, the EU uses a multi-level system where member states create and run programs under EU guidelines [19]. Key parts of the strategy include: (1) The *Digital Education Action Plan*, which supports new teaching methods and digital training for teachers; (2) Funding programs like Erasmus + [20] and the Digital Europe Program [21] to reduce regional gaps; (3) Events like EU Code Week [22] to encourage citizens to build digital skills. Despite these efforts, the EU faces challenges due to its regional diversity. These include uneven funding, different implementation speeds, and varying educational priorities among member states.

2.3 Current Status

Digital literacy is a key focus for both China and the EU, though their methods and progress differ. In China, over 60% of adults and 64.7% of minors have basic digital skills. This aligns with national goals, emphasizing both basic skills and advanced abilities like problem-solving and creativity. The EU aims for universal basic digital skills by 2030 under its Digital Compass 2030 plan [17]. By 2024, 55.6% of the EU population has these skills, over 2.1 million Europeans have joined digital training programs through the Recovery and Resilience Facility (RRF), and digital services like eID and online health records have also improved. While progress is steady, the current pace raises concerns about meeting the 2030 goal.

China has made quick progress in digital literacy through strong policies and programs. However, regional gaps remain [23]. Eastern provinces have higher literacy rates (63.2% of adults and 71.6% of minors) compared to western regions (56.9% and 59.3%). Urban areas also perform better than rural ones, with 65.9% literacy in cities compared to 50.6% in rural areas. The EU faces similar challenges with differences among member states. Northern and western countries lead in literacy, while southern and eastern regions lag due to varied education systems, funding, and policies.

Furthermore, both regions have strategies to improve digital skills, but their methods reflect different social and cultural needs. China's *National Action Plan for Improving Digital Literacy and Skills* [24] is a key policy. It includes digital skills in education and focuses on training teachers. Platforms like the *National Smart Education Platform* [25] and programs for rural residents, the elderly, and workers aim to reduce disparities. Infrastructure projects, like expanding broadband in underserved areas, also help close the gap between urban and rural regions. The EU focuses on improving digital skills through its Digital Compass 2030 framework [17] and funding programs like the RRF. It works to close the Information and Communications Technology (ICT) skills gap and improve digital public services [26]. Key initiatives include advancing eID systems, online healthcare records [27], and cross-border digital tools [28]. The EU also promotes cloud computing, data analytics, and AI use, especially among small and medium businesses [29].

3 Research Questions and Methodology

3.1 Research Questions

This study compares how China and the EU develop digital literacy, looking at their policies, challenges, and successes. It focuses on two main questions:

- What are the key differences and similarities in how China's centralized governance model and the EU's multi-level governance structure promote digital literacy?
- How do political and regulatory frameworks influence digital literacy initiatives in each region, and what lessons can they learn from each other to improve digital skills and reduce digital gaps?

By answering these questions, the study aims to show how different government approaches affect digital literacy and what strategies work best.

3.2 Methodology

To explore these questions, the study uses a comparative analysis based on official reports, policy documents, and academic research. The main sources of information are China's *National Digital Literacy and Skills Development Survey Report 2024* and the EU's *State of the Digital Decade 2024*. These reports provide detailed data on digital literacy levels, government programs, and policy goals. In addition, studies from organizations like UNESCO, Organization for Economic Co-operation and Development (OECD), and the World Economic Forum (WEF) are used to place the findings in a global context.

The research follows three main steps. First, it looks at government policies and strategies to understand how digital literacy is promoted in each region. Second, it identifies key challenges and success factors, such as differences in education, infrastructure, and access to technology. Third, it compares China's top-down approach reflecting its broader political model, where state-driven policies and strategic national planning shape digital literacy initiatives, with the EU's multi-level governance framework, balancing EU-wide directives with national and regional policies often shaped by public-private partnerships, showing how each system impacts digital literacy progress.

The study relies on content analysis to examine policy reports and other documents. It also includes some official statistics to support the findings. However, there are limitations. Since the study mainly uses government reports, the data may reflect political priorities rather than the full picture or a neutral assessment of digital literacy needs. Moreover, as digital policies change quickly, some findings might become outdated as new programs are introduced. Finally, the study does not include direct interviews or surveys, which means it does not capture personal experiences with digital literacy programs.

Despite these limitations, this approach provides a clear and structured way to compare digital literacy in China and the EU. By highlighting what works well and what challenges remain, the study offers useful insights for policymakers, educators, and researchers looking to improve digital skills and promote equal access to technology in different parts of the world.

4 Comparative Analysis

Both China and the EU face challenges despite their progress. In China, regional economic differences affect access to digital literacy resources [30]. Rural residents are still at a disadvantage, even with programs like training for farmers and small entrepreneurs. Age also plays a role, with young adults (18–29 years) having higher skills (75.8%) than older adults (36.2% for those aged 60–69). In the EU, progress varies widely among member states. Northern and western regions are ahead, while southern and eastern areas are lagging. Rural and remote areas face infrastructure gaps, making it hard to develop digital skills. Small and medium enterprises (SMEs) struggle to use advanced technologies due to limited resources [31]. Cultural factors also affect progress. Older adults and low-income groups are slower to adopt digital tools, and many people lack awareness of digital rights, reducing engagement with digital programs [32].

4.1 Report Overview and Limitations

Insights from China's 2024 National Digital Literacy and Skills Development Survey. The *2024 National Digital Literacy and Skills Development Survey Report*, led by the Cyberspace Administration of China, gives a detailed look at the digital skills of the country's population. The report uses data from 2.72 million samples across 31 provinces, covering adults (18–69 years) and minors (12–17 years). It measures digital literacy in three areas: digital understanding, skills, and critical thinking. Key findings include: (1) Over 60% of adults and 64.7% of minors have basic digital skills, and 16.26% of adults have advanced skills; (2) Eastern provinces perform better than central and western regions; (3) Urban residents and younger people have higher digital skills than rural and older groups. The report highlights China's efforts to close the digital gap with policies like training centers, national education platforms, and adding digital skills to job standards. It helps policymakers find gaps, focus on key groups, and improve digital skills across the country.

While the report shows progress, it does not clearly define what "basic" or "advanced" digital skills mean. Without this explanation, it is hard to know if people are truly skilled or just familiar with basic technology. The report does not fully explore whether certain groups, like rural residents or older adults, have difficulties accessing digital training. Large-scale surveys provide useful trends, but without independent checks or long-term tracking, it is unclear if these improvements lead to real benefits in daily life or work. Future studies could include performance tests and real-world examples to better understand how people use digital skills. In addition, the report does not pay enough attention to AI. It only mentions the need to enhance the recognition and understanding of concepts such as AI in the part on digital concept cognition, but does not elaborate on it, nor does it mention the latest content such as AI literacy.

Key Findings from the EU's State of the Digital Decade 2024. The *State of the Digital Decade 2024* report by the European Commission reviews the EU's progress toward 2030 digital goals. It focuses on digital infrastructure, skills, and public services. The report uses key performance indicators (KPIs) to measure progress in areas like basic digital skills, business use of digital tools, and public services. Key findings include: (1)

Only 55.6% of the EU population has basic digital skills, with large differences between regions; (2) Progress on 5G and fiber-optic coverage is slow, especially in rural areas; (3) Businesses, especially SMEs, face barriers in adopting advanced technologies like AI and data analytics. The EU report highlights the challenges of regional differences among member states. It stresses the need for joint and flexible strategies to meet 2030 goals. It also mentions laws like the *Digital Services Act* and *Digital Markets Act*, which aim to improve digital safety, fairness, and innovation.

The report relies on KPIs to measure digital skills but lacks clarity on whether they include critical thinking and cybersecurity awareness or just basic technology use. It highlights regional digital literacy gaps without fully exploring causes like education, infrastructure, and policy differences, making it hard to assess program effectiveness. While the *AI Act* promotes responsible AI use, it may burden startups and SMEs with compliance challenges. The report also lacks concrete data on AI-driven sustainability efforts and their impact, raising concerns that the EU's approach could hinder international AI collaboration.

Both reports show the importance of digital skills in building strong and inclusive societies that can adapt to fast technological changes. They help track progress, find gaps, and guide policies. China uses a centralized approach with strong national coordination, while the EU's decentralized model shows the challenges of uniting diverse regions. These reports offer insights into regional strategies and opportunities for learning and cooperation.

4.2 Achievements

Both China and the EU have made progress in digital literacy through different approaches. Their efforts reflect their governance styles, economic goals, and cultural backgrounds. Both have worked to close digital gaps, including digital skills in policies, and promote innovation [30, 33].

Strategic Frameworks and Policy Implementation. China's centralized approach, shown in the *National Action Plan for Improving Digital Literacy and Skills*, has boosted digital skills in many groups. Over 60% of adults and 64.7% of minors now have basic digital literacy, showing the success of government-led programs. The EU, meanwhile, has worked to create a fair and safe digital space with laws like the *Digital Services Act* and *Digital Markets Act* [34]. These laws aim to ensure fair practices and protect citizens.

Inclusive Programs for Bridging Digital Divides. Targeted programs have helped reduce digital gaps in both regions. In China, training for rural residents, older adults, and workers has lowered differences between urban and rural areas and across age groups [35]. In the EU, funding from the Recovery and Resilience Facility (RRF) has supported digital training for over 2.1 million people, showing a focus on inclusion and workforce skills [36].

Embedding Digital Literacy in Education and Public Services. Education systems in both regions play a key role in promoting digital literacy. In China, digital literacy is part of the national curriculum, with strong teacher training and education platforms supporting early skill development [12]. In the EU, progress in digital public services, like eID systems and e-health services, has improved access to essential resources [37].

Support for Innovation and Businesses. Both China and the EU support businesses in adapting to the digital age. China focuses on helping industries become more creative and flexible, allowing workers to adjust to digital environments. The EU, through programs like Digital Europe and Horizon Europe, promotes innovation and technology use in SMEs. Progress has been made in areas like cloud computing and data analytics, but more efforts are needed to speed up SME digital transformation.

4.3 Challenges

China and the EU face many challenges in developing digital literacy and skills. Both struggle with regional gaps and fast-changing technology. However, their different economic conditions and governance systems create unique problems [38].

Common Challenges Facing China and the EU. Both China and the EU face regional gaps in digital literacy and infrastructure. In China, rural and western areas lag behind urban and eastern regions due to uneven development and resources. In the EU, northern and western countries lead in digital adoption, while southern and eastern regions progress more slowly due to funding and system issues [39].

Older adults, low-income groups, and rural communities in both regions face challenges in learning digital skills. These barriers to inclusion are often due to poor access to digital infrastructure, programs that are not well-suited to their needs, and low digital awareness. These factors contribute to ongoing gaps in inclusion [40, 41].

Fast changes in AI, big data, and quantum computing put pressure on skill training systems. Both regions need to update education and training programs regularly to keep up with technology and prepare people for these advancements. This requires planning and flexibility [39, 42].

Unique Challenges. Despite its strong national policies, China faces challenges due to its large population and economic differences between regions [43]. These gaps make it hard to apply the same policies everywhere. The rural-urban digital divide is a major issue, with rural areas having much lower digital literacy and access to technology [44].

The EU's decentralized governance makes it harder to implement unified policies across member states [45]. Some states lead in digital skills, while others fall behind due to different priorities, resources, and capacities. Relying on voluntary participation slows progress toward the EU's 2030 goals [46]. SMEs also face challenges, such as limited resources and technical expertise, which make it difficult for them to use advanced digital tools effectively.

4.4 Strategies

China and the EU use different but complementary methods to promote digital skills. Their strategies show the importance of strong coordination, regional flexibility, and teamwork across sectors to meet diverse digital needs.

Governance Models: Centralized vs Collaborative Approaches. China's centralized policies show the benefits of a top-down approach. Programs like the *Digital Literacy and Skills Improvement Platform* allow fast a17ction and resource distribution nationwide. This helps bring digital literacy programs to remote and underserved areas.

The EU uses a collaborative approach, with member states working together under plans like the *Digital Compass 2030* []. This allows countries to pursue common goals while creating programs that fit their specific needs. It supports targeted and flexible solutions for different regions.

Inclusive and Targeted Programs. Both regions focus on inclusion through targeted efforts. In China, training programs for rural residents, workers, and other groups aim to close digital gaps. These programs meet the specific needs of underserved groups, ensuring fair access to digital education and tools.

The EU supports regional flexibility with programs like EU Code Week and Digital Innovation Hubs. These initiatives help member states create local programs that fit their needs. This approach allows the EU to tackle regional challenges while working toward shared digital literacy goals.

Infrastructure Development and Cross-Sector Partnerships. Infrastructure development is key to China's strategy [47]. Expanding broadband and improving digital education in rural areas ensure that digital literacy programs reach more people and can grow effectively.

The EU focuses on public-private partnerships to promote innovation and share resources [48]. Collaboration between governments, businesses, and civil groups has improved digital literacy. Programs like Horizon Europe support innovation and digital skill-building.

5 Future Directions

5.1 Learning from the EU's Experience

China can learn from the EU's focus on flexible and inclusive policies. The Digital Compass 2030 [17] shows how decentralized governance can address local needs while meeting shared goals. Adding more regional flexibility to China's centralized system could improve its digital literacy programs across provinces. The EU's emphasis on digital rights, such as privacy, fairness, and inclusion, in the *Digital Services Act* and *Digital Markets Act* [49, 50], offers ideas for ethical practices. These principles could help build trust and inclusivity in China's digital ecosystem.

China could strengthen public-private partnerships, taking inspiration from programs like Digital Europe [21] and Horizon Europe [51]. Partnerships between governments and private companies could speed up the creation of digital tools, share resources, and improve technology access for underserved groups.

5.2 Insights from China for the EU

The EU can learn from China's ability to scale and quickly implement large programs. The National Smart Education Platform [25] shows how centralized planning can rapidly deliver digital initiatives, especially in underserved areas. Adopting parts of this approach could help the EU improve infrastructure and digital literacy in its weaker regions.

China's focus on skill development for groups like the elderly and rural workers provides a useful model for the EU. Programs tailored to the needs of vulnerable groups could help reduce gaps and improve digital inclusion. China's centralized resource allocation, which ensures efficient execution of nationwide programs, could also inspire the EU to better coordinate efforts across member states for greater impact.

5.3 Opportunities for Collaboration

China and the EU face similar challenges in closing digital gaps and keeping up with fast-changing technologies. This creates opportunities for cooperation. Joint research on technologies like AI, quantum computing, and big data could address issues such as data privacy and cybersecurity while encouraging innovation [52]. Exchange programs for policymakers, educators, and tech developers could promote knowledge sharing. Chinese officials could learn about the EU's regulatory systems, while EU officials could study China's methods for large-scale digital education [53].

Another area for cooperation is creating standardized digital literacy curricula. China's experience with centralized curriculum design and the EU's focus on inclusivity and flexibility could combine to develop strong programs. These programs could meet the needs of different groups and align with global standards. Additionally, China and the EU could work together to improve AI literacy, helping people understand and use AI responsibly. As AI becomes a bigger part of everyday life, both sides could develop training programs to teach citizens how AI works, its benefits, and its risks, such as biased algorithms or data privacy concerns. By sharing knowledge and resources, they could create learning materials that promote critical thinking and ethical awareness when using AI. This cooperation would also support discussions on AI policies and regulations, making sure people are better prepared for an AI-driven world.

5.4 Global Leadership in Digital Literacy

As leaders in digital development, China and the EU can shape global digital literacy. They could work with UNESCO and International Telecommunication Union (ITU) to set global standards that align with the Sustainable Development Goals (SDGs). Creating shared resources, like digital tools, best practices, and research, would help other countries benefit from their expertise.

Joint efforts to provide affordable and accessible technologies in developing regions could help close the global digital divide [54]. Both regions should also prepare their populations for future technologies by creating AI-based learning tools and analyzing skill gaps [55]. These steps will keep their workforces flexible and competitive in a digital world. By sharing strengths and working together, China and the EU can tackle common challenges, improve digital literacy programs, and help create a more inclusive and innovative global digital future.

To further strengthen global digital literacy, China and the EU could help people better understand how new technologies, including AI, shape the way information is accessed and used. Teaching critical thinking and transparency in digital environments would help individuals make informed decisions and adapt to changing digital landscapes. Developing accessible learning tools and resources would also support people in different regions, ensuring that technological advancements are widely shared while addressing challenges like misinformation and digital fairness.

6 Discussion

6.1 Implications

The 2024 reports from China and the EU provide key insights for improving digital literacy and skills programs. In China, centralized planning and government-led efforts have quickly boosted digital literacy [56]. However, the data shows a need for more flexible, local strategies to address gaps in rural areas and among older populations. In the EU, decentralized governance supports flexibility and inclusivity. Still, better coordination and accountability are needed to ensure steady progress toward 2030 goals [57]. Increased investment in public-private partnerships and SME digitalization could further accelerate progress in the EU. Additionally, targeted intervention programs are crucial for vulnerable population groups, such as NEETs (not in education, employment, or training), parents with lower socioeconomic status and literacy levels, and individuals with a migration background who are at risk of exclusion.

Integrating digital literacy into formal education through technology offers a valuable way to personalize learning and foster lifelong skills. Incorporating digital competencies into curricula and enhancing teacher training equips learners with both foundational and advanced skills essential for the digital age. This approach not only benefits young students but also supports lifelong learning to keep pace with technological advancements. Targeted training programs are crucial for bridging digital divides, particularly among marginalized groups such as the elderly, rural populations, and low-income communities. Practical, accessible solutions can empower these groups, enabling their participation in the digital economy [58]. Customized programs are vital to addressing barriers and ensuring equitable access to digital resources.

Investing in digital infrastructure is crucial. Expanding broadband and improving connectivity in rural and remote areas is key to closing the digital divide. As noted by IEEE Connecting the Unconnected (CTU), such investments allow individuals and communities to access digital platforms and services, promoting inclusion [59]. Strengthening education, offering tailored programs, and improving infrastructure are essential for advancing digital literacy and creating an inclusive digital future. These actions follow global best practices and support fair digital transformation.

6.2 Research Gaps

Despite progress, China and the EU still face research gaps in digital literacy. These gaps limit understanding and solutions for challenges in this field. Future studies should explore detailed areas to improve strategies and support long-term digital resilience.

Studying how digital literacy connects with factors like gender, disability, and income is important to understand the barriers people face. Such analysis can uncover overlapping challenges and help create more inclusive policies and programs [60]. Long-term studies are also needed to track changes in digital literacy over time. These studies can show how current policies affect economic and social outcomes and provide insights into the success of digital literacy strategies [61]. Both regions should study how to include new technologies like AI, quantum computing, and blockchain in digital literacy programs. These technologies are changing the digital world, and training must keep up. Comparative studies of groups, such as rural and urban populations, can help create tailored programs and share successful strategies across different areas. Recent reviews by d'Haenens et al. highlight the need for tailored interventions in media literacy and digital skills to improve educational and civic outcomes, while emphasizing data literacy as a critical, inclusive competency for navigating ethical and societal challenges in a datafied world [62].

Another key topic is the link between digital ethics and literacy. Studying how knowledge of digital rights, privacy, and inclusivity affects the use of digital tools can improve strategies for ethical digital adoption [63]. This research can help ensure that digital literacy supports broader societal values. Closing these gaps will help China and the EU improve their digital literacy programs. It will lead to more inclusive, adaptable, and resilient approaches. Expanding research in these areas is key to addressing current challenges and creating fair and effective digital literacy frameworks.

7 Conclusion

7.1 Key Insights

The comparison of China's 2024 Digital Literacy Report and the EU's State of the Digital Decade 2024 shows their strengths and common challenges in improving digital skills. Both have made progress but still face barriers, highlighting the need for learning and collaboration.

China's centralized system has helped over 60% of its population achieve basic digital skills. This success comes from strong national policies and training programs for different groups. The EU's decentralized system allows regional flexibility. Programs like the Recovery and Resilience Facility and Digital Europe Program support digital governance, SME digitalization, and skills training. But digital divides exist across regions, income levels, and age groups. In China, gaps between urban and rural areas are significant. In the EU, differences are clear between northern, western, southern, and eastern states. Rapid changes in technologies like AI and quantum computing also require constant updates to digital literacy programs.

Therefore, China could adopt the EU's focus on digital rights, public-private partnerships, and flexible regional governance [64]. These practices support inclusivity and ethical digital growth. The EU could learn from China's centralized resource allocation and scalable training models to improve progress in slower regions. The digital age offers a chance for global cooperation. By using their strengths, China and the EU can tackle shared challenges and lead progress in digital skills. Joint efforts, such as researching new technologies, creating inclusive digital literacy programs, and developing shared digital rights frameworks, can drive innovation and fairness [65]. These collaborations could set an example for other countries, helping build a resilient and inclusive global digital society.

7.2 Call to Action

Digital literacy is key to building a strong and resilient society. Policymakers should create flexible and inclusive strategies to close digital gaps and ensure fair access to resources, especially for underserved regions and vulnerable groups. Educators should include digital skills in school programs at all levels, promoting lifelong learning to help people adapt to changing technology [66]. Policymakers should support user-friendly, customizable toolkits with best practices, adaptable curricula, and evaluation guidelines, while promoting knowledge sharing to adapt successful strategies across regions and sectors [67].

Collaboration among public and private sectors, civil society, and global partners is vital to expand digital literacy efforts. Public-private partnerships and international cooperation can drive innovation, share resources, and create scalable solutions [68]. Joint work between China and the EU in research, curriculum development, and digital rights could set a global standard for improving digital literacy and skills. By learning from each other and working together, China and the EU can lead the world in using digital literacy to empower people, strengthen economies, and promote fairness. This can set an example for other countries to follow.

It is important to keep learning about AI to understand both its benefits and risks. Reports from the OECD and UNESCO show that people need to know how AI works and what problems it might cause, such as unfair decisions and lack of transparency. For example, Amazon once used an AI system to review job applications, but it unfairly rated female candidates lower, so the company had to stop using it [69]. In some U.S. courts, AI systems have been used to predict crime risks, but studies found they often gave higher risk scores to minority groups, leading to unfair treatment [70]. Large AI programs, like those from OpenAI and Google, have also been found to repeat stereotypes about race and gender [71]. These cases show why it is important to question AI decisions and make sure AI is used fairly.

China's Social Credit System (SCS) is another example of how AI and digital tools are used in society. The SCS is not a single system but a group of programs that rate the trustworthiness of businesses, organizations, and people [72]. In finance, it works like a credit score in many other countries, helping banks decide who can get a loan. Supporters believe this system makes businesses more honest and improves transparency, but others worry about too much government control, privacy risks, and unclear decision-making. Some studies suggest that using AI in social policies can lead to unfair results, especially if there is no clear process to correct mistakes [73]. Understanding how such systems work in different countries helps people think critically about the role of AI in society and its impact on fairness and personal rights.

References

1. Jacqueline, A.A.: Digital literacy in the 21st century: preparing students for the future workforce. Res. Output J. Arts Manage. **3**(3), 40–43 (2024)
2. Audrin, C., Audrin, B.: Key factors in digital literacy in learning and education: a systematic literature review using text mining. Educ. Inf. Technol. **27**, 7395–7419 (2022)

3. Organisation for Economic Co-operation and Development (OECD): digital strategies in education across OECD countries (2020). https://doi.org/10.1787/33dd4c26-en, Accessed 11 Nov 2024
4. Gabriel, F., Marrone, R., Van Sebille, Y., et al.: Digital education strategies around the world: practices and policies. Irish Educ. Stud. **41**(1), 85–106 (2022)
5. Cyberspace Administration of China (CAC): National Digital Literacy and Skills Development Survey Report (2024). https://www.gov.cn/lianbo/bumen/202410/P020241028320648229592.pdf, Accessed 11 Nov 2024
6. European Commission (EC): Report on the state of the Digital Decade 2024 (2024a). https://digital-strategy.ec.europa.eu/en/library/report-state-digital-decade-2024, Accessed 11 Nov 2024
7. UNESCO Institute for Statistics (UIS): A global framework of reference on digital literacy skills for indicator 4.4.2 (2018). http://uis.unesco.org/sites/default/files/documents/ip51-global-framework-reference-digital-literacy-skills-2018-en.pdf, Accessed 11 Nov 2024
8. Symbio6: Digital literacy: Definition and meaning (2024). https://symbio6.nl/en/definition/digital-literacy, Accessed 11 Nov 2024
9. European Commission (EC): Shaping Europe's digital future - Digital skills (2024b). https://digital-strategy.ec.europa.eu/en/policies/digital-skills, Accessed 11 Nov 2024
10. United Nations Educational, Scientific and Cultural Organization (UNESCO): Information literacy for lifelong learning (2017). https://unesdoc.unesco.org/ark:/48223/pf0000245577, Accessed 11 Nov 2024
11. Cyberspace Administration of China (CAC): Action Plan for Improving Digital Literacy and Skills for All (2021). https://www.cac.gov.cn/2021-11/05/c_1637708867754305.htm, Accessed 11 Nov 2024
12. Ministry of Education of the People's Republic of China (MOE): Deepening digital transformation, building a bright future of education (2023). http://en.moe.gov.cn/features/2023WorldDigitalEducationConference/KeynoteSpeech/202302/t20230214_1044654.html, Accessed 11 Nov 2024
13. Ministry of Education of the People's Republic of China (MOE): Notice on the issuance of the Education Informatization 2.0 Action Plan (2018). http://www.moe.gov.cn/srcsite/A16/s3342/201804/t20180425_334188.html, Accessed 11 Nov 2024
14. Xinhua News Agency: Full text of Xi Jinping's speech at the opening ceremony of the Second World Internet Conference. Chinese Government (2015). https://www.gov.cn/xinwen/2015-12/16/content_5024712.htm, Accessed 11 Nov 2024
15. Xinhua News Agency: The Central Committee of the Communist Party of China and the State Council issued the Overall Layout Plan for the Construction of Digital China (2023). https://www.gov.cn/zhengce/2023-02/27/content_5743484.htm, Accessed 11 Nov 2024
16. People's Daily: The State Council issues the 14th Five-Year Plan for Digital Economy Development (2022). https://www.gov.cn/xinwen/2022-01/04/content_5666254.htm, Accessed 11 Nov 2024
17. European Commission (EC): Europe's Digital Decade: digital targets for 2030 (2024c). https://commission.europa.eu/strategy-and-policy/priorities-2019-2024/europe-fit-digital-age/europes-digital-decade-digital-targets-2030_en, Accessed 11 Nov 2024
18. European Commission (EC): European Skills Agenda (2020a). https://ec.europa.eu/social/main.jsp?catId=1223&langId=en, Accessed 11 Nov 2024
19. Organisation for Economic Co-operation and Development (OECD): Shaping digital education: Enabling factors and policies (2023). https://doi.org/10.1787/849af8d0-en, Accessed 11 Nov 2024
20. European Commission (EC): Erasmus+ (2014). https://erasmus-plus.ec.europa.eu/, Accessed 11 Nov 2024

21. European Commission (EC): Digital Europe Programme. European Commission (2021a). https://commission.europa.eu/funding-tenders/find-funding/eu-funding-programmes/digital-europe-programme_en, Accessed 11 Nov 2024
22. European Commission (EC): EU Code Week (2013). https://codeweek.eu/, Accessed 11 Nov 2024
23. Pick, J., Ren, F., Sarkar, A.: Digital inequalities in China in 2020: spatial and multivariate analysis. Appl. Sci. **14**(13), 5385 (2024)
24. Global Times: China launches initiative to boost national digital literacy (2024). https://www.globaltimes.cn/page/202402/1307467.shtml, Accessed 11 Nov 2024
25. Ministry of Education of the People's Republic of China (MOE): Compulsory Education Curriculum Plan and Curriculum Standards (2022 Edition). http://www.moe.gov.cn/jyb_xwfb/s5147/202204/t20220406_614072.html, Accessed 11 Nov 2024
26. European Commission (EC): European Interoperability Framework: Commission presents new guidance for digital public services (2017). https://digital-strategy.ec.europa.eu/en/news/european-interoperability-framework-commission-presents-new-guidance-digital-public-services, Accessed 11 Nov 2024
27. European Commission (EC): Electronic cross-border health services (2019a). https://health.ec.europa.eu/ehealth-digital-health-and-care/electronic-cross-border-health-services_en, Accessed 11 Nov 2024
28. NCP Flanders: Interoperable Europe Act enters into force (2024). https://ncpflanders.be/index.php/news/interoperable-europe-act-enters-into-force, Accessed 11 Nov 2024
29. European People's Party (EPP): Shaping policies for Europe's digital decade (2022). https://www.epp.eu/files/uploads/2022/02/Digital_Policy_7_February_Paper_Website_Template.pdf, Accessed 11 Nov 2024
30. Zhang, H., Li, X.: Digital literacy and skills development in China and the European Union: a comparative analysis. Mar. Policy **150**, 105127 (2023)
31. Kergroach, S.: SMEs going digital: policy challenges and recommendations (2021). https://goingdigital.oecd.org/data/notes/No15_ToolkitNote_DigitalSMEs.pdf, Accessed 11 Nov 2024
32. Elena-Bucea, A., Cruz-Jesus, F., Oliveira, T., Coelho, P.S.: Assessing the role of age, education, gender and income on the digital divide: evidence for the European Union. Inf. Syst. Front. **23**(4), 1007–1021 (2021)
33. Wu, D., Wang, J., Che, Z.: Digital education: connotation, pathway, and trend. Front. Digit. Educ. **1**(1), 59–68 (2024)
34. European Commission (EC): Digital Markets Act (DMA) (2020b). https://digital-markets-act.ec.europa.eu/index_en, Accessed 11 Nov 2024
35. China Daily: Forum highlights global impact of China's socialist modernization (2023). https://global.chinadaily.com.cn/a/202304/03/WS642a27e1a31057c47ebb7f83.html, Accessed 11 Nov 2024
36. European Commission (EC): Recovery and Resilience Facility (2020c). https://commission.europa.eu/business-economy-euro/economic-recovery/recovery-and-resilience-facility_en, Accessed 11 Nov 2024
37. Troitiño, D. R., Mazur, V.: E-Governance in the European Union: strategies, tools, and policies. In: E-Governance in the European Union, pp. 1–22 (2024)
38. Ben, S., Bosc, R., Jiao, J., Li, W., Simonelli, F., Zhang, R.: Digital infrastructure: overcoming the digital divide in China and the European Union (2017). https://ssrn.com/abstract=3075161, Accessed 11 Nov 2024
39. Szeles, M.R., Simionescu, M.: Regional patterns and drivers of the EU digital economy. Soc. Indic. Res. **150**(1), 95–119 (2020)
40. Vassilakopoulou, P., Hustad, E.: Bridging digital divides: a literature review and research agenda for information systems research. Inf. Syst. Front. **25**(3), 955–969 (2023)

41. Zhang, Y.: Measuring and applying digital literacy: Implications for access for the elderly in rural China. Educ. Inf. Technol. **28**, 9509–9528 (2023)
42. Holl, A., Rama, R.: Spatial patterns and drivers of SME digitalisation. J. Knowl. Econ. **15**(2), 5625–5649 (2024)
43. An, Z., He, E., Du, X., Sun, B.: Path analysis of regional logistics and economy coordinated development: an fsQCA approach. PLoS ONE **19**(2), e0297441 (2024)
44. Fong, M.W.L.: Digital divide between urban and rural regions in China. Electron. J. Inf. Syst. Dev. Countries **36**(1), 1–12 (2017)
45. Arnaoutoglou, N.-B.: Institutions and cohesion policy in the European Union (2022). https://mpra.ub.uni-muenchen.de/113543/1/MPRA_paper_113543.pdf, Accessed 11 Nov 2024
46. European Commission (EC): Reflection paper: towards a sustainable Europe by 2030 (2019b). https://www.dotaceeu.cz/getattachment/f60231f1-c341-4df0-a2c8-453239753a11/Reflection-paper_Towards-a-sustainable-Europe-by-2030.pdf.aspx?lang=cs-CZ&ext=.pdf, Accessed 11 Nov 2024
47. Zou, L., Shen, H., Zhang, J., Lee, C.-C.: What is the rationale behind China's infrastructure investment under the Belt and Road Initiative? J. Econ. Surv. **36**(3), 675–700 (2022)
48. Carbonara, N., Pellegrino, R.: The role of public private partnerships in fostering innovation. Constr. Manag. Econ. **38**(2), 140–156 (2019)
49. European Union (EU): Regulation (EU) 2022/2065 of the European Parliament and of the Council of 19 October 2022 on a Single Market for Digital Services (Digital Services Act) and amending Directive 2000/31/EC (2022a). https://eur-lex.europa.eu/legal-content/EN/TXT/?uri=CELEX%3A32022R2065, Accessed 11 Nov 2024
50. European Union (EU): Regulation (EU) 2022/1925 of the European Parliament and of the Council of 14 September 2022 on contestable and fair markets in the digital sector (Digital Markets Act) (2022b). https://eur-lex.europa.eu/legal-content/EN/TXT/?uri=CELEX%3A32022R1925, Accessed 11 Nov 2024
51. European Commission (EC): Horizon Europe: The EU research and innovation programme (2021–2027) (2021b). https://research-and-innovation.ec.europa.eu/funding/funding-opportunities/funding-programmes-and-open-calls/horizon-europe_en, Accessed 11 Nov 2024
52. European Commission (EC): The EU and China have signed an administrative arrangement to support cooperation (2022). https://research-and-innovation.ec.europa.eu/news/all-research-and-innovation-news/eu-and-china-have-signed-administrative-arrangement-support-cooperation-2022-04-26_en, Accessed 11 Nov 2024
53. European Commission (EC): EU-China: Commission and China hold second High-level Digital Dialogue (2023). https://digital-strategy.ec.europa.eu/en/news/eu-china-commission-and-china-hold-second-high-level-digital-dialogue, Accessed 11 Nov 2024
54. United Nations Department of Global Communications (DGC): Widening digital gap between developed, developing states threatening to exclude world's poorest from next industrial revolution, speakers tell Second Committee (2023). https://press.un.org/en/2023/gaef3587.doc.htm, Accessed 11 Nov 2024
55. Bakhshi, H., Downing, J. M., Osborne, M. A., Schneider, P.: The future of skills: employment in 2030 (2017). https://futureskills.pearson.com/research/assets/pdfs/technical-report.pdf, Accessed 11 Nov 2024
56. Wang, C., Si, L.: The intersection of public policy and public access: digital inclusion, digital literacy education, and libraries. Sustainability **16**(5), 1878 (2024)
57. European Commission (EC): Digital Education Action Plan (2021–2027) (2020d). https://education.ec.europa.eu/focus-topics/digital-education/action-plan, Accessed 11 Nov 2024

58. United Nations Development Programme (UNDP), United Nations Educational, Scientific and Cultural Organization (UNESCO): Resources for, and needs of vulnerable and marginalized young people on digital literacy, safety and participation (2022). https://www.undp.org/publications/resources-and-needs-vulnerable-and-marginalized-young-people-digital-literacy-safety-and-participation, Accessed 11 Nov 2024
59. IEEE Connecting the Unconnected (CTU): Solutions to the digital divide: Moving toward a more equitable future (2023). https://ctu.ieee.org/blog/2023/02/03/solutions-to-the-digital-divide-moving-toward-a-more-equitable-future/, Accessed 11 Nov 2024
60. Naples, N.A., Mauldin, L., Dillaway, H.: From the guest editors: gender, disability, and intersectionality. Gend. Soc. **33**(1), 5–18 (2019)
61. Arias-López, M.D.P., et al.: Digital literacy as a new determinant of health: a scoping review. PLOS Digit. Health **2**(10), e0000279 (2023)
62. d'Haenens, L., Vissenberg, J., Puusepp, M., et al.: Fostering media literacy: a systematic evidence review of intervention effectiveness for diverse target groups. Media Commun. **13**, Article 8901 (2024). https://www.cogitatiopress.com/mediaandcommunication/article/view/8901
63. Giannoumis, G.A., Skjerve, R.A.: Digital accessibility and intersectional discrimination. In: Stein, M. A., Lazar, J. (eds.) Accessible Technology and the Developing World, pp. 174–190. Oxford University Press (2021)
64. American Library Association (ALA): Digital equity through literacy: Framing the conversation (2022). http://www.ala.org/sites/default/files/advocacy/content/diversity/Digital%20Equity%20Through%20Literacy_Framing%20the%20Conversation_5.31.22.pdf, Accessed 11 Nov 2024
65. United Nations Development Programme (UNDP): From access to empowerment: Digital inclusion in a dynamic world (2024). https://www.undp.org/sites/g/files/zskgke326/files/2024-05/undp_digital_inclusion_in_a_dynamic_world.pdf, Accessed 11 Nov 2024
66. Erwin, K., Mohammed, S.: Digital literacy skills instruction and increased skills proficiency. Int. J. Technol. Educ. Sci. (IJTES) **6**(2), 323–332 (2022)
67. d'Haenens, L.: REMEDIS Policy Brief 2 (2025). https://zenodo.org/records/14603957
68. Buckup, S.: How public-private cooperation can connect and empower the 'Global South' (2024). https://www.weforum.org/stories/2024/01/public-private-cooperation-can-connect-and-empower-the-developing-world/, Accessed 11 Nov 2024
69. Dastin, J.: Insight: amazon scraps secret AI recruiting tool that showed bias against women (2018). https://www.reuters.com/article/world/insight-amazon-scraps-secret-ai-recruiting-tool-that-showed-bias-against-women-idUSKCN1MK0AG/
70. Feiner, L.: Judges are using algorithms to justify doing what they already want (2024). https://www.theverge.com/2024/10/30/24281924/pretrial-risk-assessment-algorithms-research
71. MIT Technology Review: OpenAI's big model tends to generate images of white men? Research finds that many AI models have racial and gender biases (2023). https://www.mittrchina.com/news/detail/11744
72. Shen, K.: The legal approach to building a social credit system (2019). https://fzzfyjy.cupl.edu.cn/info/1035/11343.htm
73. Zhou, T.L., Walsh, M.: In Depth: How Chinese Companies Can Get Off Social Credit Blacklists (2020). https://www.caixinglobal.com/2020-05-27/in-depth-how-chinese-companies-can-get-off-social-credit-blacklists-101559282.html

The Use of Technology by Children Aged 0–6: A Study on Educational Models, Attitudes, and Media Behaviors of Educators and Teachers in the Context of the "New Normal."

Ilaria Bortolotti[1(✉)], Franca Rossi[1], and Alessandro Biraglia[2]

[1] Sapienza University of Rome, 00185 Rome, Italy
ilaria.bortolotti@uniroma1.it
[2] Leeds University Business School, Leeds LS2 9JT, UK

Abstract. In today's increasingly digitalized world, formal educational contexts play a critical role in shaping young children's relationship with technology. In nurseries and preschools, educators introduce children aged 0–6 to digital tools that can support their development. This study, conducted during the "new normal" (2022–2023), surveyed 164 Italian educators using an anonymous questionnaire to examine the use of digital devices, including touch-based and internet-connected tools, in early childhood education. The study explored educators' attitudes, the presence and use of digital tools, and their perceived self-efficacy in technology use. Results reveal limited enthusiasm for digital devices post-pandemic, especially for children under three, with a greater acceptance of technology for children aged 3–6, particularly in educational settings. While common digital activities with children include listening to music, stories, educational videos, and using apps, more complex tasks like research and media editing are less frequent. Despite their interest in integrating technology into teaching, educators report low confidence in their digital skills, with the Intrapersonal Technology Integration Scale revealing low self-efficacy. Respondents are doubtful about technology's potential to enhance teaching effectiveness or job satisfaction. These findings highlight the need for professional development to enhance educators' technological competencies and optimize digital tool integration in early childhood education.

Keywords: Media Education · Pre-alphabetized children · Educators' perspective

1 Introduction

Over the years, digital technology has evolved continuously, enabling an increasing number of people to access services such as the Internet [1] and devices of varying costs that combine substantial computing power with user-friendly interfaces, such as smartphones and tablets. The ease of use of these tools has facilitated their adoption at an earlier age, particularly in developed countries, with children aged 0–6 years [2] also making use of them. This trend was further accelerated by the Covid-19 pandemic, which

Ł. Tomczyk (Ed.): NMP 2024, CCIS 2537, pp. 19–32, 2025.
https://doi.org/10.1007/978-3-031-95627-0_2

shifted educational and socialization activities online, replacing face-to-face interactions in formal educational settings such as nurseries and preschools [3].

In this context, it is increasingly important not only to investigate which devices are available in family and educational settings and the type of use permitted for preschool children but also, more crucially, to understand the skills and attitudes of the adults who mediate the relationship between children and digital technologies. These adults include parents and caregivers as well as educators and teachers, who guide and support children's development within formal educational contexts.

Indeed, the importance of these "internal" elements of educators and teachers in influencing the introduction of digital devices into educational activities has been highlighted by several authors. [4, 5].

A key question in the field of digital media is how educational experiences should be organized to incorporate digital devices effectively. Educational contexts increasingly recognize that introducing digital technologies in preschool settings (e.g., smartphones, projectors, digital cameras) naturally leads to the emergence of a new language, offering both children and teachers new opportunities. Consequently, a new didactic model has emerged, in which children's engagement with digital technologies is integrated into their everyday cognitive activities [6].

Families play a crucial role in managing access to electronic devices, employing parental mediation strategies that range from restrictive to more active and participatory approaches [7, 8]. Restrictive mediation (e.g., authoritarian style; [9, 10]) focuses on setting rules, limiting screen time, and controlling access to content available to children. This category also includes technical mediation, such as using applications to restrict access to specific types of content. Conversely, participatory approaches (e.g., authoritative style; [9, 10]) involve adults engaging in active mediation, characterized by discussions and shared content experiences with the child. Finally, permissive mediation (e.g., permissive style; [9, 10]) represents a style in which children are free to explore and use devices without guidance or control from adults.

These studies further indicate that the mediation styles parents adopt do not differ significantly from those employed when managing children's access to television, a more "traditional" technological device. As a result, no distinction is made based on the specific device children use. While numerous studies have explored parental mediation between children and digital devices, there is a notable lack of research on the mediation styles expected or desired by educators and teachers. This gap represents a critical dimension of the school-family relationship, which has the potential to serve as a formative influence, offering guidance to families.

2 Methods

2.1 Research Questions

The study presented in this paper is part of a broader research project on the topic of Media Education in early childhood (children aged 0–6 years) within the Italian context. Specifically, the overarching aim of the study is to analyze, through the responses of preschool teachers and nursery educators, the characteristics of the use of new digital devices with touch technology and Internet-connected devices among pre-literate children, in relation to the access opportunities provided by preschools and nurseries.

The study addresses several gaps in the existing literature, particularly the lack of empirical data on the actual use of digital technologies in early childhood education settings in Italy. Furthermore, little is known about the views and attitudes of educators and teachers, the types of digital activities offered to children, and the expectations placed on families regarding their role. Finally, the influence of individual and contextual factors - such as self-efficacy and digital competence - on professional attitudes toward digital technologies has been only partially explored so far.

The responses collected from nursery educators and preschool teachers made it possible to outline an overview of the digital resources available in educational institutions, the type of use made of these resources for and with children, and the mediation styles between children and digital technologies that educators and teachers expect families to adopt at home.

A more specific aim of the study is to understand respondents' attitudes toward the use of digital technologies in early childhood and to analyze internal factors related to respondents and the educational context that may influence these attitudes.

The study addresses the following Research Questions (RQs):

- RQ1: What devices are available in the educational institutions where the respondents work?
- RQ2: What types of activities are carried out by educators and teachers *for* and *with* their children in the educational setting?
- RQ3: What are the attitudes of educators and teachers toward the use of digital devices by children aged 0–3 and 3–6 Years in educational and family contexts?
- RQ4: What parental mediation behaviors between digital technologies and children aged 0–6 are considered desirable by the respondents?
- RQ5: What are the levels of Teacher Self-Efficacy [11], Computer Self-Efficacy [12], as well as Self-Efficacy, Performance Outcome Expectations, Self-Evaluative Outcome Expectations, and Interest in educational digital technologies [13] among the respondents?
- RQ6: Are there differences in all the variables and indices investigated to answer the previous RQ based on the educational level at which the respondents work?
- RQ7: Do Teaching Self-Efficacy [11], Computer Self-Efficacy [12], as well as Self-Efficacy, Performance Outcome Expectations, Self-Evaluative Outcome Expectations, and Interest in educational digital technologies [13] influence the attitudes of educators and teachers toward the use of digital devices by children aged 0–3 in school and at home, and by children aged 3–6 in school and at home?

2.2 Tool and Data Analysis

The data collection tool used in this study was developed by modifying an instrument originally designed by the research group and colleagues in a previous study.

The modified questionnaire addressed to nurseries educators and preschool teachers is divided into different sections focusing on several aspects:

- Socio-demographic characteristics;
- Types of digital tools available in the educational institution;
- Ways the respondent uses the available digital devices in general and for educational purposes, either individually or with the children they work with in the institution;
- Respondents' attitudes toward digital teaching;
- Teaching self-efficacy, and Computer self-efficacy of the respondents. The scales used were adapted from the Ohio State Teacher Efficacy Scale (OSTES, [11]) and the Computer Self-Efficacy Scale (CSE, [12]);
- Teachers'/educators' Self-Efficacy (SE), Performance Outcome Expectations (POE), Self-Evaluative Outcome Expectations (SEOE), and Interest (INT) regarding the use of digital technologies in educational practices, investigated through the Intrapersonal Technology Integration Scale (ITIS, [13]);
- Respondents' beliefs about the attitude they think parents of preschool children should adopt regarding their children's use of digital media. These beliefs were measured using a reduced version of the Style Internet Parenting Scale (IPSI, [14, 15]);
- Attitudes toward the use of technological devices within the educational institution, and in the family context, based on the age of the preschool children (0–3 years and 3–6 years);
- General opinions and considerations on the topic, collected through an open-ended question.

The questionnaire, created online using Google Forms, was administered from the second half of April 2023 to the first half of July 2023. Participation was preceded by the provision of informed consent concerning data processing and storage, in accordance with the GDPR (EU Regulation 2016/679). The information regarding the study and consent for data processing were developed in accordance with the guidelines provided by the Transdisciplinary Research Ethics Committee of the University of Rome Sapienza and the Italian Association of Psychology.

The sampling was convenience-based, using a snowball method: educators and teachers working in educational institutions across the national territory, who had already been in contact with the research group, responded to the questionnaire. These participants then helped disseminate the request for completion among their own networks.

Quantitative analyses were conducted on the data through Microsoft Excel to obtain descriptive statistics related to the investigated dimensions. Additionally, a series of ANOVAs and regression analyses using SPSS (version 28) to identify any statistically significant differences between variables, as well as potential relationships among them, in relation to the research questions (RQs) were performed.

2.3 Participants

The study included 164 Italian educators and teachers, the majority of whom were women (99.4%; men = 0.6%), with an average age of approximately 38 years (mean = 37.65). The participants were evenly divided based on their workplace, with 49.4% employed in nurseries and 50.6% in preschools.

Geographically, the distribution was varied, with most participants concentrated in central Italy (87.2%), followed by respondents from Southern Italy (10.36%), while northern Italy represented only a small minority (2.44%) (Table 1).

Table 1. Geographical distribution of the respondents.

Geographical area	f% (f)
Central Italy	87.20% (143)
Southern Italy	10.36% (17)
Northern Italy	2.44% (4)
Total	100.00% (164)

In terms of professional experience, 39.02% of respondents reported having between 1 and 5 years of experience in the field, while 23.78% indicated 6 to 10 years of experience (Table 2).

Table 2. Professional experience of the respondents.

Region	f% (f)
1 to 5 years of experience	39,02% (64)
6 to 10 years of experience	23.78% (39)
21 to 25 years of experience	9.76% (16)
16 to 20 years of experience	7.93% (13)
11 to 15 years of experience	6.71% (11)
26 to 30 years of experience	6.10% (10)
More than 30 years of experience	3.66% (6)
No experience	3.05% (5)
Total	100.00% (164)

3 Results

The main results will be presented following the Research Questions (RQs) outlined in the Methods section.

3.1 RQ1: What Devices are Available in the Educational Institutions Where the Respondents Work?

Regarding the devices available in the educational institutions where the respondents work (Fig. 1), a certain variety emerges, with a predominance of PCs (63.09%) and printers, including 3D printers (56.38%).

Tablets are less common (32.21%), as are TVs (23.49%) and cameras (22.82%). Some of these nurseries and preschools also feature more advanced devices, such as multimedia stations (8.72%) and programmable robots (5.37%).

The "Other" category includes projectors, microscopes, stereo systems, and Bluetooth speakers (7.38%). Notably, 3.36% of respondents reported that no technological devices are available in their institution.

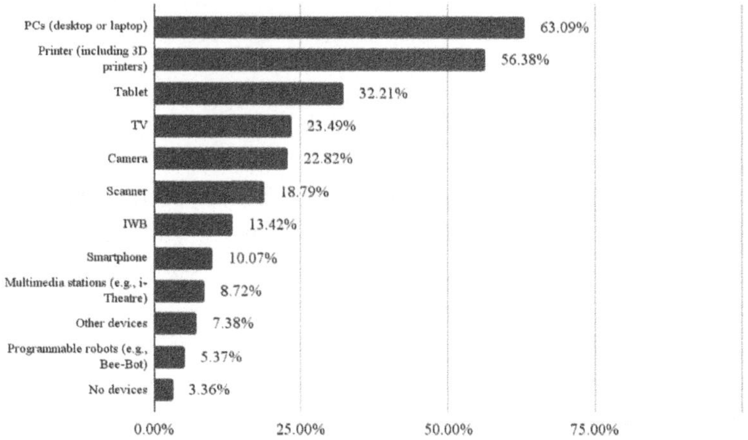

Fig. 1. Devices available in the educational contexts in which the respondents work.

3.2 RQ2: What Types of Activities are Carried Out by Educators and Teachers *for* and *with* their Children in the Educational Setting?

The distinction between activities conducted *for* children and *with* children is noteworthy as it underscores a continuity in the "educational" use of digital resources both within and beyond educational institutions. It also highlights a professional dynamic that extends into "private" time - an overlap traditionally resisted and limited by schools.

The data indicate that the primary activities carried out *for* children by the participants include the preparation of educational materials (67.07%) and tasks aimed at researching and deepening educational content (64.63%). In addition, respondents report engaging in other daily practices, such as exchanging materials with colleagues (55.49%), watching videos (45.12%), downloading music and videos (29.27%), consulting forums (25.61%), and participating in online meetings with parents (24.39%) (Fig. 2).

With regard to activities performed directly *with* children, as shown in Fig. 3, listening to music stands out as the most frequently reported daily activity, involving 65.24% of participants. Other common activities include storytelling (38.41%), watching cartoons or movies (15.24%), and viewing videos of experiences created in educational settings (14.02%). Furthermore, a considerable proportion of respondents indicate engaging in more complex activities with children on a daily basis, such as searching for information or materials (41.46%) and producing multimedia content, including photos and videos (37.80%). Finally, 20.73% of respondents report involving children in the use of educational apps, reflecting a more active and engaging integration of technologies into their practices.

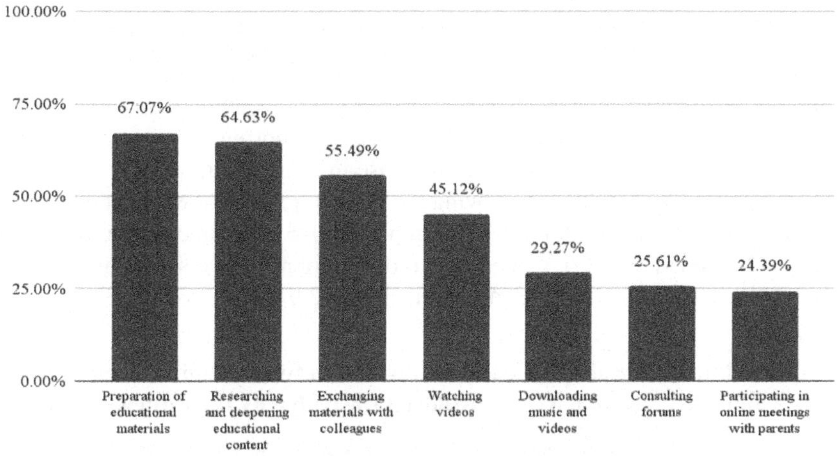

Fig. 2. Activities performed *for* children by respondents.

The range of activities with children and the varying intensities of digital tool usage reveals a dual impact of digital devices in educational activities. On one hand, these tools enhance traditional activities that are already prevalent and considered essential for this age group, such as exposure to musical language and narrative thinking, as Bruner emphasized in his work on the role of culture and storytelling in cognitive development [16]. On the other hand, they serve as tools that provide opportunities for less common experiences, such as searching for information, gathering materials, and producing multimedia content.

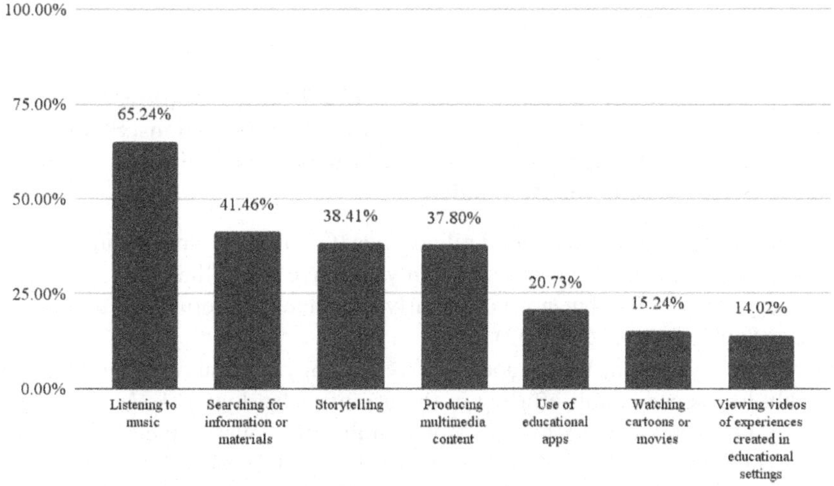

Fig. 3. Activities performed *with* children by respondents.

3.3 RQ3: What are 4 and Teachers Toward the Use of Digital Devices by Children Aged 0–3 and 3–6 Years in Educational and Family Contexts?

The attitudes of educators and teachers towards the use of technology in both educational and domestic environments during this period of 'new normality' appears ambivalent. Respondents did not report a substantial increase in openness to the use of technology in schools by preschool children following the pandemic (M = 2.89[1]). They were more critical of the use of digital devices by children aged 0–3 years in daycare settings (M = 2.20) and at home (M = 2.24), while being more supportive of children aged 3–6 using technology at school (M = 3.05) and at home (M = 2.91).

3.4 RQ4: What Parental Mediation Behaviors Between Digital Technologies and Children Aged 0–6 Are Considered Desirable by the Educators/Teachers?

Analyzing the responses regarding the mediation behaviors parents should adopt - particularly in the context of fostering continuity of actions and collaboration between families and educational institutions - two distinct parenting styles emerge as significant: authoritarian and authoritative [9, 10].

Respondents consider it highly important for parents to block access to specific websites and content (M = 4.71, authoritarian style) and to explain the rules for device usage (M = 4.72, authoritative style) once they have been established (M = 4.68, authoritarian style). Additionally, parents are expected to be present while children use these tools (M = 4.65, authoritative style) and while they play (M = 4.41, authoritative style), to assist them in case of problems (M = 4.45, authoritative style), and to use devices together with their children (M = 4.3, authoritative style).

The two actions deemed less important are blocking access to devices (M = 3.44, authoritarian style) and encouraging the child's independent exploration of digital devices (M = 2.38, permissive style) (Fig. 4).

3.5 RQ5: What Are the Levels of Teacher Self-Efficacy, Computer Self-Efficacy, as Well as Self-Efficacy, Performance Outcome Expectations, Self-Evaluative Outcome Expectations, and Interest in Educational Digital Technologies (ITIS Scale) Among the Respondents?

All the multi-item measures had good reliabilities (Cronbach's alpha values from .65 to .95). Participants perceive themselves as highly effective in fulfilling their role (Teaching Self-Efficacy, M = 4.04) but not particularly competent in terms of computer skills (Computer Self-Efficacy, M = 2.32).

A deeper analysis using the Intrapersonal Technology Integration Scale (ITIS) reveals a relatively low sense of self-efficacy in the use of technology (SE, M = 2.29) and a perception that using technology does not significantly enhance their effectiveness as educators (POE, M = 2.93) or their job satisfaction (SEOE, M = 2.91). However, they exhibit a notable level of interest in the integration of technology in education (INT, M = 3.42).

[1] All mean values presented in the Results paragraph are calculated on a 5-point Likert scale, where the theoretical mean is 2.50, representing the central value of the scale.

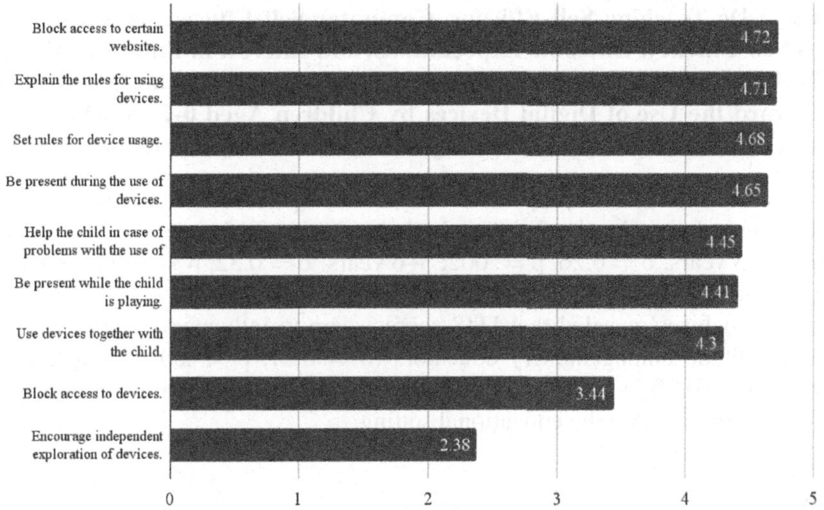

Fig. 4. Parental actions for mediating the relationship between children and digital technologies as expected by the respondents.

3.6 RQ6: Are there Differences in all the Variables and Indices Investigated to Answer the Previous RQ Based on the Educational Level at which the Respondents Work?

From the analyses conducted, it emerges that the group of nursery educators differs from that of preschool teachers across some of the variables. Specifically, preschool teachers report a significantly higher number of years of service ($M = 13.66$) compared to nursery educators ($M = 7.02$; $F (1, 163) = 21.78$, $p < .001$).

Statistically significant differences are also observed in the types of activities conducted for and with the children. Preschool teachers engage more frequently, and in a statistically significant manner, in activities *for* their children such as downloading music and applications/apps, watching videos, and preparing teaching materials (all p values $< .01$). Similarly, this group of teachers also engages more often than nursery educators in activities *with* their children such as listening to and/or watching stories, viewing movies/cartoons, using educational games, creating immersive/virtual environments, watching videos of experiences created within the educational context, and connecting with children from other preschools or nurseries (p values between .026 and $< .001$).

The analyses also reveal that the group of preschool teachers scores significantly higher across two of the ITIS subscales: POE (Preschool: $M = 3.18$, Nursery: $M = 2.67$, $F (1, 163) = 10.98$, $p = .001$); and INT (Preschool: $M = 3.60$, Nursery: $M = 3.24$, $F (1, 163) = 4.74$, $p = .031$). Furthermore, they exhibit a more positive value attribution toward digital tools (Preschool: $M = 3.23$, Nursery: $M = 2.88$, $F (1, 163) = 8.14$, $p = .005$). Conversely, nursery educators are statistically more inclined to perceive themselves as effective in their role (Teacher Self-Efficacy) (Preschool: $M = 3.97$, Nursery: $M = 4.13$, $F (1, 163) = 4.08$, $p < .05$).

3.7 RQ7: Do Teaching Self-Efficacy, Computer Self-Efficacy, as Well as Self-Efficacy, Outcome Expectations, and Interest in Educational Digital Technologies (ITIS Scale) Influence the Attitudes of Educators and Teachers Toward the Use of Digital Devices by Children Aged 0–3 in School and at Home, and by Children Aged 3–6 in School and at home?

In general, the ITIS Scale [13] appear to be a significant predictor of participants' attitudes toward the use of digital technologies in both age groups (0–3 years and 3–6 years) both at home (0–3 years: $b = 0.26$, $p = .002$; 3–6 years: $b = 0.32$, $p < .001$) and in school (0–3 years: $b = 0.38$, $p < .001$; 3–6 years: $b = 0.51$, $p < .001$).

Further analyses revealed that ITIS scores seem to influence a significantly more favorable attitude among nursery educators ($b = 0.57$, $p < .001$) compared to the preschool ($b = 0.20$, $p = .19$) toward the use of digital technologies by children in the 0–3 age group within the educational setting.

4 Discussion

The results show that educational settings where educators and teachers who participated in the survey work are equipped with a substantial number of digital devices. These include "classic" devices (>50%) such as PCs and printers, including 3D printers, as well as more accessible devices for pre-literate children (>20%), such as tablets, which use touch technology, and TVs, which provide a more passive fruition of the tool. More advanced technologies such as smartphones, IWB, Multimedia stations and programmable robots are not so widespread (>10%).

Educators use these devices daily to prepare and research materials, collaborating with colleagues (>50%) and planning complex educational activities for children (>25%). Notably, in the educational practice with children there is significant engagement beyond mere content music (>65%) or cartoons (≃15%) or experience video (≃14%) consumption, with a considerable proportion of educators supporting children in storytelling activities (>38%) content searching and material production (>37%), and, in some cases, playing digital games through applications (>20%).

Activities vary according to the children's age groups: preschool teachers seem to more frequently engage children in complex and "active" activities compared to nursery educators. This difference likely reflects the need to align with children's developmental processes and their progressive acquisition of cognitive and manipulative skills, which become increasingly sophisticated with age and let them use more sophisticated digital devices such as Pcs.

This extensive and varied use of digital devices highlights the importance of understanding educators' and families' attitudes toward technology to optimize its integration into early education.

The participants' opinions and attitudes toward the use of digital devices by preliterate children indicate a low inclination to support the use of such devices for children aged 0–3 years in both educational and family contexts. However, there is a more positive attitude toward the use of digital devices by children aged 3–6 years, with a preference for their application in formal educational settings.

In the domestic context, participants expect parental mediation actions consistent with authoritative and authoritarian parenting styles. These include a greater usefulness perceived for actions like blocking inappropriate websites and content (authoritarian) and setting rules, explaining them, being present when the child uses devices, helping children in case of problems and using devices with them (authoritative). Conversely, actions such as encouraging autonomous exploration of devices by children or blocking the access to such tools are perceived as less useful.

These findings highlight the importance of collaboration between educators and families to establish consistent mediation strategies that align with educational goals.

In light of this, the study also suggests the need to support families in developing educational digital and media competences that are consistent with early childhood pedagogical models. Educators and teachers tend to favor parental mediation strategies aligned with authoritative and, to a lesser extent, authoritarian styles - such as setting and explaining rules, co-using devices, supervising media activities, and blocking inappropriate content - while discouraging permissive behaviors like unsupervised exploration. These expectations reveal a clear postulate for parent education: to promote active, supportive, and developmentally appropriate mediation practices. Preschools and nurseries can play a key role in this process by fostering school-family dialogue and offering opportunities for parents to reflect on their media practices. At the same time, institutions and policymakers in Italy should invest in structural initiatives that support both educators and families, ensuring coordinated and informed digital education from the earliest years.

The attitude toward digital technologies - significantly more positive among preschool teachers than nursery educators - appears to be influenced by a set of internal variables examined through the ITIS Scale [13]. Higher levels of Self-Efficacy (SE), Performance Outcome Expectations (POE), Self-Evaluative Outcome Expectations (SEOE), and Interest (INT) regarding the use of digital technologies in educational practices - although generally low across the respondent group, except for interest in the application of technology in education - are associated with more positive value attributions to digital technologies and greater openness to their use in both formal educational and family settings by children aged 0–6 years. Preschool teachers scored significantly higher than nursery educators across all subscales of the ITIS. These higher ITIS scores among preschool teachers suggest that their greater confidence and interest in technology integration may enable them to explore different methods and technologies to engage children in more active and complex activities, particularly with older age groups.

Further analysis revealed that nursery educators with high scores on ITIS factors (SE, POE, SEOE, INT) [13] tend to have a more favorable attitude toward the use of digital technologies by the children in their educational target group within their workplace. Consistent with findings in the literature (see Introduction), Teaching Self-Efficacy [11] and Computer Self-Efficacy [12] were also examined to verify any connection between them and teachers' attitudes toward digital technologies and digital tool use. Teaching self-efficacy was notably high, particularly among nursery educators, who differed significantly from preschool teachers. In contrast, computer self-efficacy was relatively low across the entire respondent group. However, neither factor appeared to influence participants' attitudes toward the use of digital devices by pre-literate children.

The results provide insight into the practices, opinions, and attitudes of educators and teachers working with children aged 0–6, contributing to the limited body of research on this theme in the Italian context. However, it is necessary to highlight some limitations of the study presented in this contribution, which reflect the inherent challenges of conducting research in this field.

The sampling method used to identify the research participants, for example, did not allow for the inclusion of a representative sample of the national population of nursery and preschool educators and teachers. Future research can address this limitation by reaching educational institutions well-distributed across the national territory through institutional networks that can disseminate the research instrument. However, this aspect remains challenging in the Italian context, where educators and teachers are often engaged in multiple responsibilities and, as a result, frequently unable to participate in research activities, even when these require completing a relatively simple instrument.

Another limitation of the study lies in its reliance on self-reported data, which may introduce biases into participants' responses. Future research could incorporate observational or netnographic methods to validate these findings and further explore the role of ITIS factors, but also Teacher Self-Efficacy, in shaping educators' attitudes toward technology use in early childhood education.

5 Conclusion

This study contributes to understanding the integration of digital technologies in early childhood education by providing insights into the practices, attitudes, and challenges of a group of educators and teachers working with children aged 0–6.

A notable finding is the limited accessibility, in the context of respondents, to digital tools specifically designed for this age group, such as multimedia stations or touch-based devices like tablets, which are more suitable for pre-literate children. While certain "classic" technologies, such as PCs and printers, are widely available, their suitability for younger children remains questionable.

The findings also reveal significant differences between nursery educators and preschool teachers in their use of and attitudes toward technology. Preschool educators are more likely to engage children in active and complex digital activities, aligning with the developmental milestones of their age group. However, a stronger emphasis on equipping nursery educators with appropriate tools and training is needed to ensure equitable access and use across age groups.

The study underscores the importance of aligning technology use with the developmental needs of young children while fostering active and meaningful engagement. It also highlights the crucial role of collaboration between educators and families in defining consistent and effective mediation strategies for technology use, particularly in the domestic sphere.

Despite limitations such as non-representative sampling, and reliance on self-reported data, the research provides a valuable foundation for future studies. These should aim to address the accessibility and appropriateness of digital tools for young children, explore their role in supporting developmental goals, and validate findings through observational methodologies and netnographic studies. Furthermore, future research may investigate how different parental styles (following Baumrind's or alternative classification) impact the uptake of the use of digital technologies by parents.

In this regard, it will also be essential to consider how educational institutions can actively support families in developing digital and media competences aligned with early childhood educational goals, promoting consistent mediation practices between home and school. Institutional and policy-level interventions could strengthen this effort by providing resources and frameworks for family-school cooperation in the digital domain.

In conclusion, ensuring broader access to age-appropriate digital technologies and fostering professional development opportunities for educators are essential steps toward enhancing the integration of digital tools in early childhood education. By addressing these gaps, future research and policy initiatives can support a more inclusive and effective use of digital technologies, ultimately benefiting both educators and children in this critical developmental stage.

Acknowledgments. The authors would like to thank the research team that developed the original research tool and contributed to the data collection process. Special thanks to Professors Renata Metastasio and Donatella Cesareni for their valuable collaboration and support in the design and execution of the study. While the authors have written the paper, the contributions of the research team were essential in shaping the original research instrument revised for this study and gathering the data.

References

1. Castells, M.: The Rise of The Network Society. Wiley-Blackwell, USA (2000)
2. Balbinot, V., Toffol, G., Tamburlini, G.: Tecnologie digitali e bambini: un'indagine sul loro utilizzo nei primi anni di vita. Medico e bambino **35**(10), 631–636 (2016)
3. Metastasio, R., Bortolotti, I.: Tecnologie digitali e prima infanzia- Una sfida per famiglie e scuole tra rischi e opportunità. Della Rocca Editore, Viterbo (2024)
4. Ertmer, P.A.: Addressing first- and second-order barriers to change: strategies for technology integration. Educ. Technol. Res. Dev. **47**(4), 47–61 (1999)
5. Mueller, J., Wood, E., Willoughby, T., Ross, C., Specht, J.: Identifying discriminating variables between teachers who fully integrate computers and teachers with limited integration. Comput. Educ. **51**(4), 1523–1537 (2008)
6. Ludwiczak, J., Maj, A.: The dialogue between children and digital technologies – from the experience of reggio emilia preschools. Elementary Educ. Theor. Pract. **15**(1), 39–59 (2020)
7. Nikken, P., Jansz, J.: Developing scales to measure parental mediation of young children's internet use. Learn. Media Technol. **39**(2), 250–266 (2014)
8. Symons, K., Ponnet, K., Emmery, K., Walrave, M., Heirman, W.: A factorial validation of parental mediation strategies with regard to internet use. Psychologica Belgica **57**(2), 93–111 (2017)
9. Baumrind, D.: The influence of parenting style on adolescent competence and substance use. J. Early Adolesc. **11**(1), 56–96 (1991)
10. Maccoby, E.E., Martin, J.A.: Socialization in the context of the family: parent–child interaction. In: Mussen, P.H. (Series ed.), Hetherington, E.M. (Vol. ed.) (eds.) Handbook of Child Psychology, 4th edn. Socialization, Personality, and Social Development, vol. 4, pp. 1–101. Wiley, New York (1983)

11. Tschannen-Moran, M., Hoy, A.W.: Teacher efficacy: capturing an elusive construct. Teach. Teach. Educ. **17**(7), 783–805 (2001)
12. Sang, G., Valcke, M., Van Braak, J., Tondeur, J.: Student teachers' thinking processes and ICT integration: predictors of prospective teaching behaviors with educational technology. Comput. Educ. **54**(1), 103–112 (2010)
13. Benigno, V., Chiorri, C., Chifari, A., Manca, S.: Adattamento italiano della Intrapersonal Technology Integration Scale, uno strumento per misurare gli atteggiamenti degli insegnanti nei confronti delle TIC. G. Ital. Psicol. **40**(4), 815–838 (2013)
14. Van Rooij, T., Van den Eijnden, R.J.J.M.: Monitor Internet en Jongeren 2006 en 2007: Ontwikkelingen in internetgebruik en de rol van opvoeding. IVO, Rotterdam (2007)
15. Valcke, M., Bonte, S., De Wever, B., Rots, I.: Internet parenting styles and the impact on Internet use of primary school children. Comput. Educ. **55**(2), 454–464 (2010)
16. Bruner, J.: Acts of meaning. Harvard University Press, Cambridge (1990)

Brain-Computer Interfaces and Educational Inclusion: The Potential of BCI for Learners with Additional Support Needs (NAS)

Filipe T. Moreira(✉), Rui Oliva Teles, and José Oliveira

Escola Superior de Educação, Instituto Politécnico do Porto, Rua Dr. Roberto Frias 602, 4200-465 Porto, Portugal
filipemoreira@ese.ipp.pt

Abstract. Communication is a fundamental human right that enables the transmission and reception of information, essential for social and educational inclusion. However, children and young people with additional support needs, due to neurological or motor diseases, face severe communication barriers. Technologies such as Augmentative and Alternative Communication (AAC) and Brain-Computer Interfaces (BCI) offer solutions to overcome these barriers, providing alternative means of expression and interaction. This chapter presents the concept of BCI and explores how spontaneous brain activity in response to stimuli can be used to develop effective communication methods for individuals facing severe communication difficulties due to neurological conditions such as cerebral palsy and multiple sclerosis. The study adopts an action-research approach, using the Unicorn Hybrid Black Speller system. The results indicate that, although there are technical challenges in calibrating and using the systems, there is significant potential for their application in educational and social contexts, improving the autonomy and quality of life of users.

Keywords: Brain-Computer Interface (BCI) · Augmentative and Alternative Communication (AAC) · Additional Support Needs (ASN) · Special Education

1 Introduction

Brain-Computer Interfaces (BCIs) are innovative technological systems that enable direct communication between the human brain and external devices, bypassing traditional motor pathways. These interfaces work by capturing brain activity, which is translated into commands to control equipment or perform tasks. According to Vidal [1], a pioneer in the concept of BCI, the main objective is to establish a direct connection between the brain and machines, opening unprecedented possibilities for human-computer interaction.

In recent years, the development of BCIs, especially non-invasive ones based on electroencephalography (EEG), has allowed significant advances in educational contexts and in assisting people with additional support needs (ASN). Such technologies represent great potential for promoting inclusion, particularly for individuals with severe motor or

Ł. Tomczyk (Ed.): NMP 2024, CCIS 2537, pp. 33–50, 2025.
https://doi.org/10.1007/978-3-031-95627-0_3

communication limitations, such as those caused by cerebral palsy, multiple sclerosis, or spinal muscular atrophies [2, 3].

In the educational field, the relevance of BCIs is amplified by their ability to provide alternative means for expression and interaction, helping to overcome barriers that limit the active participation of learners with ASN in their school communities [4]. This technology not only increases the autonomy of these individuals but also contributes to a more inclusive education by offering solutions that meet their specific communication and learning needs.

1.1 Justification of the Study

Communication is a fundamental human right and an essential pillar for educational inclusion. The United Nations Convention on the Rights of Persons with Disabilities [5] highlights the importance of ensuring communication accessibility so that individuals with disabilities can fully exercise their human rights. However, people with ASN often face significant communication challenges due to limitations imposed by neurological or motor conditions [6].

The use of assistive technologies, such as BCIs, is essential to overcome these barriers and promote the active participation of these individuals in educational environments. The integration of BCI systems into pedagogical practices can facilitate access to quality education, a crucial element for the holistic development of learners with ASN.

Despite the promised benefits of BCIs, there is a significant gap between technological innovations and the effective implementation of these solutions in educational contexts. Issues such as the need to adapt technologies to the individual characteristics of learners, the complexity of system calibration and use, and associated costs represent challenges that need to be addressed for the potential of BCIs to be fully explored [7, 8].

Therefore, the study and development of BCIs aimed at the educational context are crucial not only to improve the quality of life of individuals with ASN but also to promote a more equitable and inclusive education. The research presented in this chapter seeks to contribute to the advancement of this area by exploring the impact of BCIs on the communication and learning of individuals with severe limitations and offering insights for their effective application in school environments.

2 Human Communication

Communication is one of the fundamental pillars of human development, allowing individuals to express thoughts, feelings, and needs while building interpersonal and social connections. Classical theoretical models, such as the linear model by Shannon and Weaver [9], provide an initial understanding of communication as a transfer of information. However, more contemporary approaches, such as the transactional model [10], recognise the interactive and collaborative nature of this process. For Lasswell [11], communication also performs essential functions, such as environmental surveillance, correlation of societal parts, and transmission of cultural heritage.

On an individual level, communication is not only a means of expression but also a process of identity and autonomy construction. Pearson et al. [12] highlight that the ability to communicate effectively promotes emotional and social well-being, as well as facilitating problem-solving and decision-making.

Communication is the foundation upon which personal, social, and professional life is built [12]. The study of communication is essential as it improves how we see ourselves and how others see us. Through communication, we learn about human relationships and the most important life skills. The study of communication helps people feel confident in expressing and defending their opinions and creates space to give voice to others.

Despite that, language processing involves a complex interaction between different areas of the brain. For example, when we hear a sentence, auditory information is processed in the superior temporal cortex and transmitted to Wernicke's area for comprehension. If we want to respond, Broca's area plans and organises the response, which is then articulated with the help of the cerebellum. The dorsolateral prefrontal cortex (DLPFC) oversees the entire process, managing attention, working memory, and pragmatic aspects of communication [13].

However, not all individuals are able to express themselves in the same way, due to different limitations. To help minimise this problem, different augmentative and alternative communication (AAC) techniques have been developed over the decades. Without AAC resources, many citizens would be excluded from society and prevented from expressing themselves or learning, for example.

Augmentative and Alternative Communication represents a set of strategies and technologies designed to support individuals with communication difficulties. According to Elsahar et al. [14], these tools can be categorized into three levels of complexity: no-technology (e.g., sign language), low-technology (e.g., communication boards), and high-technology (e.g., speech-generating devices). AAC seeks to value the strengths of each individual, offering personalized solutions to meet their specific needs [15]. This approach is especially relevant in educational contexts, where the inclusion of students with NAS often depends on technological solutions that guarantee their active participation and their right to communication. Light and McNaughton [16] highlight that the integration of AAC technologies in schools promotes not only personal expression, but also engagement. Although there is a basis for considering BCI in the context of AAC [7], current practice does not utilise BCI in existing AAC structures.

3 Brain-Computer Interface

Brain-Computer Interface (BCI), according to Lotte et al. [17] are systems that translate a measurement of a user's brain activity into messages or commands for an application.

J. Vidal [1] was the first to use the term BCI, in an article entitled "Toward Direct Brain-Computer Communication" published in the Annual Review of Biophysics and Bioengineering. In the article, the author mentions the possibility of using brain-computer interfaces (BCI) to establish direct communication between the human brain and external devices.

Brain-Computer Interface (BCI) systems represent an interdisciplinary field of research at the intersection of neuroscience, medicine, and engineering. These technologies have the potential to transform human-computer interaction by enabling direct communication between the brain and external devices.

Simply put, BCIs function as shortcuts, allowing the brain to control devices without the need for muscle movement [18]. Imagine moving a cursor on a computer just by thinking about it or operating a robotic prosthesis directly through neural activity—these are the possibilities offered by BCI technology.

Among the different BCI approaches, electroencephalography (EEG)-based BCIs have experienced exponential growth due to their non-invasive nature and wide range of applications. One of the most impactful uses of BCI is in facilitating communication for individuals with severe motor impairments.

BCI technology is particularly crucial for individuals in a state of complete lock-in syndrome (CLIS)—a condition in which a person loses all voluntary motor control but remains fully conscious. For these individuals, BCI may serve as the only available means of communication with the outside world.

Understanding the anatomy and physiology of the brain is essential to designing effective BCIs. The location of specific areas of the brain associated with different cognitive functions guides the strategic placement of electrodes and sensors. Furthermore, knowledge of neuronal physiology allows for the proper interpretation of captured brain signals [19].

In the brain there are regions with a high concentration of neuron cell bodies and regions with a high concentration of neuron extensions, mainly axons. Neurons are made up of a cell body (perikaryon) and two types of extensions: dendrites (short and branched) and axons (generally single and with constant thickness, branching at the end) [20].

The plasticity of our brain, that is, the ability to adapt and switch between different brain wave frequencies, is essential for dealing with stress, concentrating on tasks and getting restful sleep. An imbalance in the production of any of the five types of brain waves can negatively affect their functioning [21].

Brain waves are the result of the synchronized electrical activity of large groups of neurons. When one neuron communicates with another, it generates a small electrical impulse. When millions of neurons fire simultaneously, these impulses together create the oscillatory patterns that characterize brain waves. The frequency of these waves depends on the speed at which neurons fire and the strength of the synaptic connections between them [22].

Brain waves are classified into five categories: Delta (1–3 Hz), associated with deep sleep and unconscious processes; Theta (4–7 Hz), related to creativity, intuition and REM sleep; Alpha (8–12 Hz), predominant in a state of relaxation, light sleep and during meditation; Beta (13–30 Hz), associated with alertness, concentration, problem solving and active thinking; and, finally, Gamma (above 30 Hz), related to demanding cognitive processes, such as learning, memory, attention and consciousness [23].

To understand how BCI systems work, it is important to delve into the basic principles that form the basis of this technology. At the basis of BCIs are, as we have seen, the neurophysiological principles that guide the formation and transmission of electrochemical signals that occur in the human brain.

BCIs can use several technologies, some invasive and others non-invasive. There are a variety of neuroimaging techniques that can be used in a research context. These are categorized to measure different brain activities, including electrical, magnetic, and metabolic. Brain electrical activity can be measured using EEG (Electroencephalogram),

ECoG (Electrocorticogram) and intracortical neuron reading (INR), and magnetic activity can be measured using Magnetoencephalogram (MEG), while brain metabolic activity can be measured using imaging by functional magnetic resonance imaging (fMRI), near infrared spectroscopy (NIRS), Positron Emission Tomography (PET), Diffuse Optical Imaging (DOI), Computed Axial Tomography (CAT) and Event Related Optical Signal (EROS) techniques [24].

The choice between invasive and non-invasive techniques depends on the research objective and the specific needs of each application. Invasive techniques such as ECoG and INR offer greater resolution and accuracy in measuring neuronal activity but involve surgical risks and are generally used in specific clinical contexts or in animal research. Non-invasive techniques, such as EEG, MEG, fMRI, NIRS, PET, DOI, TAC and EROS, in turn, are safer and widely used in research, but may have limitations in terms of spatial or temporal resolution.

Thus, three categories emerge: non-invasive, incorporated and intracranial. Non-invasive BCIs, like EEG, are those that do not enter the body. The embedded ones go a step further, being placed under the scalp or inside the skull, but without crossing the protective membrane of the brain. Finally, intracranial BCIs are those that penetrate this membrane, and can even be placed inside the brain tissue, as is the case with "neural dust" implants [25].

Regarding assessments of brain functions, electrical measurement techniques, despite having a high level of noise, provide high temporal resolution, while metabolic signals, although providing high spatial resolution, require many resources (such as large and expensive scanners), machines, etc.), have low time resolution and require a high level of computational complexity. Therefore, among these approaches, EEG-based BCIs are the most widely used as they are portable, non-invasive, reasonable, and have high temporal resolution [24].

For this reason, in this work we focus on non-invasive BCIs and, within these, electroencephalogram (EEG).

3.1 No-Invasive BCI

The operating principle of BCIs (e.g. Unicorn Hybrid Black by G-Tec - medical engineering GmbH, Austria) is to establish communication between the brain and an external device (computer or other) by translating specific EEG stimuli into commands [26].

In addition to the basic principles already discussed, understanding brain activity in response to external and internal stimuli is essential for the development of effective BCI systems. As we have seen, EEG allows the electrical activity of the brain to be recorded non-invasively. The analysis of these signals, however, requires specific techniques to extract relevant information about cognitive processes. Two types of EEG signals widely used in BCIs are Event-Related Potentials (ERP) and Steady-State Visual Evoked Potentials (SSVEP) [27].

Event-related potentials (ERPs) are electrophysiological responses of the brain to sensory, motor, or cognitive stimuli. These responses are transient and occur within milliseconds of stimulus presentation. ERPs are characterized by a series of positive and negative deflections in the EEG waveform, which vary in amplitude and latency depending on the type of stimulus and the cognitive task. Different components of

ERPs are associated with different cognitive processes, such as attention, perception, and decision-making [28].

Another widely investigated approach involves event-related potentials (ERPs), which measure the time-locked brain response to a specific stimulus or event. For example, a P300-based BCI speller uses the ERP response to an infrequent stimulus to control communication applications. ERP-based paradigms are commonly used in reactive BCIs, which rely on external stimuli to elicit brain responses [29].

SSVEP is a brain signal that generates a response to a visual stimulus with a specific frequency. In the context of a BCI, multiple visual stimuli with different frequencies are presented to the user. When the user fixates their gaze on a specific stimulus, the brain generates an oscillatory response at the same frequency as the visual stimulus. This response can be detected and analyzed through EEG, allowing us to determine which of the stimuli the user is focusing their attention on. SSVEP has been widely used in BCIs, particularly in communication and control systems, due to its high information transfer rate, relatively low variability between users, strong versatility, and short training time [30].

The combination of different EEG paradigms of hybrid BCIs represents a significant advance in this area. By integrating multiple data sources, these systems can offer greater accuracy, flexibility, and robustness compared to single BCI systems. This approach has great potential to improve the quality of life of people with NAS. The main goal of hybrid BCIs is to improve BCI performance through multimodal signal inputs, for example, combinations of different brain signals, BCI paradigms, and/or other external devices.

There are other Event-Related Evoked Potentials, which, due to the diversity of stimuli to which the brain is exposed, generate a wide range of electrophysiological responses. In addition to the ERP and SSVEP already mentioned, other evoked potentials have been explored in BCIs, each with its own specific characteristics and applications. Contingency Negative Variation (CNV) [31] is related to stimulus anticipation and decision making. Mismatch Negativity (MMN) reflects the detection of deviations in auditory or visual patterns. Somatosensory Evoked Potentials (SEPs) originate in response to tactile stimulation and can generate evoked potentials that can be used to control a BCI. Auditory Evoked Potentials (AEPs) are brain responses to auditory stimuli and can be used to control devices through sound stimuli. Illusion-Induced Visual Evoked Potential (VEP) explores the brain's ability to respond to illusory stimuli, revealing aspects of visual perception and processing that go beyond the simple detection of physical stimuli [32].

3.2 BCI in the Educational Context

In this section we present an overview of the potential, limitations and ethical challenges of using BCI in educational contexts.

3.2.1 Potential Applications of BCI in Education

There are many benefits and potentialities of using BCI technology in an inclusive school environment.

Promoting autonomy and independence in students with NAS is essential for their integral development. By encouraging communication and expression, we facilitate not only social inclusion, but also the development of new skills and abilities, increasing their possibilities and preparing them for a more autonomous and participatory life [33].

Considering BCIs with educational objectives, the earlier they are used, the greater the likelihood of success. Using them in playful/pedagogical game contexts can also be an added value, as the student is more motivated to use them and begins to train the skills that are necessary for their effectiveness, as early as possible [34].

A review of 22 significant studies by Xu & Zhong [35] investigated the application of wearable BCI technology in educational contexts. Their findings identified seven key research areas:

a) Reading processes;
b) Learning material design;
c) Interactive behavior analysis;
d) Education and entertainment;
e) Online learning;
f) Motor skill acquisition;
g) Learning performance optimization.

These areas demonstrate the diverse potential of BCI in enhancing education through cognitive and motor skill support.

Based on the theory of diffusion of technological innovations, Jiang et al. [36] proposed crucial strategies for the adoption of BCI in educational settings. The authors highlight four primary application areas:

a) Attention detection and intervention;
b) Emotion recognition and regulation;
c) Science popularization and research;
d) Movement function.

According to their study, these key areas serve as the main drivers for BCI dissemination and implementation in schools, ensuring the technology is aligned with educational objectives.

The selection of an appropriate BCI depends on the support needs of a child or young person in combination with their learning goals. BCI devices can enhance communication and improve functionality across various aspects of life for individuals with NAS, particularly in education.

Despite these benefits, current BCI technology faces limitations, especially regarding typing speed. Existing systems have restricted information transfer rates, but new non-invasive technologies under development may allow users to communicate at speeds of up to 100 words per minute by directly translating thoughts into text.

However, little is known about commercially available BCI products due to high development costs and limited transparency in corporate research. Nevertheless, these advancements are technologically feasible and could revolutionize learning strategies for all individuals, with and without NAS.

3.2.2 Limitations to the Success of its Use

Cristopher Wegemer [8] states that a coordinated effort between education researchers and BCI researchers is necessary, in addition to an in-depth analysis of the social, economic and educational implications of the technology, identifying six main areas of research:

1. Technological challenges: Solving technical problems related to the operation of BCIs and ensuring their effectiveness and accessibility.
2. Partnerships: Establishing collaborations between education researchers and BCI researchers to address the different aspects of the technology.
3. Historical analysis: Comparing BCIs with previous innovations in education to understand their potential and impact.
4. Equity: Studying how BCIs can affect equality of educational opportunities.
5. Economic analysis: Developing strategies to integrate and test BCIs in educational environments.
6. Implementation: Developing strategies to integrate and test BCIs in learning environments [8].

3.2.3 Ethical and Social Aspects

According to Proverbio [37], the use of Event-Related Potentials (ERPs) to study language offers several advantages in the educational context. One of the key benefits is the early detection of language difficulties, such as dyslexia. Specific ERP components, like N170 (related to orthographic analysis) and N400 (associated with semantic integration), can identify anomalies in processing. This enables early intervention and the development of personalized strategies to support students with learning difficulties.

Additionally, ERPs allow for a detailed assessment of reading and writing processes, as they can track, in milliseconds, the different stages of brain processing. This information is valuable for understanding how students manage spelling, phonology, and syntax, providing essential insights for adapting teaching methods more effectively.

ERPs also facilitate in-depth analysis of semantic and syntactic processing. Components such as N400 and P600 serve as indicators of students' ability to integrate word meanings and process grammatical structures. This data can be used to enhance school curricula, optimizing strategies to improve these specific skills.

Another important application is the study of biases and stereotypes in language. ERPs can reveal how these implicit factors influence comprehension, offering critical insights for promoting inclusive education. By leveraging this knowledge, educators can develop strategies to reduce inappropriate behaviors and foster a more equitable learning environment [37].

4 Empirical Study

The study presented here is characterized by a case study and a qualitative action research. This methodology was chosen because it does not intend to burden the volunteers with any type of formal evaluation, avoiding them feeling embarrassed about being evaluated due to past experiences. Action research offers the advantage of being a flexible approach, allowing adjustments throughout the research process, which is essential to respond to different needs and situations that arise during the research.

The application of the action research methodology to the study focuses on continuous cycles of planning, action, observation and reflection. The objective is not only to understand, but also to improve the use of BCI. Interventions are planned based on the challenges identified, carried out in practical sessions, and the results are observed to collect qualitative data. Observing the participants while using the system at different moments of communication allows us to identify the aspects that need adjustments or improvements. Based on this analysis, new actions are planned for the next cycle, promoting an interactive process of continuous improvement of the system and the methodology used. This approach aims to ensure that participants feel comfortable, and that the data collection process occurs naturally, without imposing formal assessments, favoring a progressive adaptation to their needs.

4.1 Participants and Context: Characterisation of the Sample

Volunteer R is male, 27 years old and has the following diagnoses supported by medical reports: Spinal Muscular Atrophy Type II or also called Neuromuscular Degenerative Disease Type II (age of onset and severity of symptoms Type I < 6 months, Type II $> 6 < 18$ months and Type III > 18 months), Bronchiectasis, Scoliosis, Gastric stasis, Hemoptysis, Renal lithiasis, Asymmetric tetraparesis. I had no experience when using BCI-EEG for the first time. Has good communication and understanding skills, but a perspective of progressive loss of skills due to degenerative disease.

Volunteer C is a 50-year-old female with the following diagnoses supported by medical reports: Multiple Sclerosis, Spastic tetraparesis with pancerebellar symptoms (causes weakness, muscle stiffness and coordination problems throughout the body, due to problems in the cerebellum and part of the brain), Neurogenic bladder with suprapubic cystostomy, Intrathecal baclofen pump, Renal lithiasis, PEG, Urostomy. I had no experience when using BCI-EEG for the first time. Has the ability to communicate and understand, but a perspective of progressive loss of skills due to degenerative disease.

4.2 BCI Equipment and Intervention Context

The study used the Unicorn Hybrid Black Speller BCI system (g.tec medical engineering GmbH) to collect EEG data from participants. The system consists of a wearable head-mounted EEG device (wearable EEG headset) and spelling software (speller) and a biosignal amplifier connected to a personal computer via Bluetooth (2.1). The EEG device has 8 dry electrodes (conductive gel can also be used for electrodes - hybrid electrodes). With the eight channels (one per electrode) EEG data is captured at a sampling rate of 250 Hz per channel and an input sensitivity range of approximately 750 mV (millivolt), at the following electrode positions by the standard 10–20 - Fz, C3, Cz, C4, Pz, P07, Oz and PO8. Furthermore, ground and reference EEG electrodes were attached to the participants' mastoids to allow better noise (interference) reduction and improved reference of the electrodes placed on the scalp. It should also be noted that the device and all its components have been tested and found to comply with the electromagnetic compliance limits of Directive 2014/53/EU (Radio Equipment Directive, RED).

Unicorn Suite Hybrid Black (version 1.24.00) was installed on a personal computer. In this suite there are several windows with applications (Unicorn: Recorder, Speller, Painting, Blondy Check, Brainbuddy, Platformer and Puzzel Game), in another window there are development tools (Unicorn: C API – C/CC++,.NET API – C#, Python API, Simulink – MATLAB, LSL – Labstreaminglayer library, UDP - protocol and Unity – game engine). Another window is for managing usage licenses and another manages connections between the personal computer and the BCI via Bluetooth.

Spelling software (Speller) features a variety of spelling boards with letters, numbers, and control characters. This works on the principle of the P300, which uses the ERP response to an infrequent stimulus to select a character.

The place used to carry out the sessions with the BCI was a room measuring 5 m long by 3.5 m wide. In the space there were 4 tables, each with a computer and its monitor. The space is characterized by having two windows through which natural light enters one side and on the other side a door leading to the corridor. In relation to human resources, only the researcher and the volunteer were in the space to carry out the communication session. The sessions were held during a period when there was no noise or movement in the location and its surroundings.

4.3 Procedures: Detailed Description

With the intention of evaluating the viability of BCI as a communication tool for people with NAS, we proposed to the institution's technical team that experimental sessions be carried out. The choice of this institution, for logistical and accessibility reasons, allowed us to start testing with a pre-defined group of participants.

The procedures for putting on the Unicorn Hybrid Black EEG helmet in preparation for the BCI sessions were:

Environment Preparation:
Ensure an environment with soft lighting, avoiding direct reflections on the screen. Make sure the person is sitting comfortably in their own chair, with their neck and eyes aligned with the screen and their shoulders relaxed as much as possible. Minimize visual and audio distractions to optimize concentration during the session.

EEG Helmet Preparation:
Clean the EEG helmet with a soft cloth and a suitable cleaning product, following the manufacturer's instructions. Check that all devices are connected correctly: computer and EEG helmet (Bluetooth and software). Make sure the EEG helmet has enough battery power to carry out the sessions.

EEG Helmet Placement:

1. Check that the EEG helmet fits snugly, comfortably, and securely on the person's head.
2. Hybrid electrodes (of the equipment) combining characteristics of dry and gel electrodes. It allows you to choose which one is most suitable for each person and which one has the best signal.
3. Positioning of the Sensors – electrodes (we will use the anatomical markers of the head (inion, nasion, pre-auricular) to assist in the precise location of the electrodes).

Placement of the 8 electrodes (Fz, C3, Cz, C4, Pz, PO7, Oz and PO8 - solid circles) according to the international 10–20 system as a reference to ensure standardization and comparability of results. Make sure the frontal sensors are positioned correctly on the person's head, usually in the midline of the forehead and above the eyebrows, with the occipital sensors positioned at the back of the head, on the bony protuberance. Place the Reference electrodes (Ref.): on the mastoids (behind the ears) – Fig. 1.

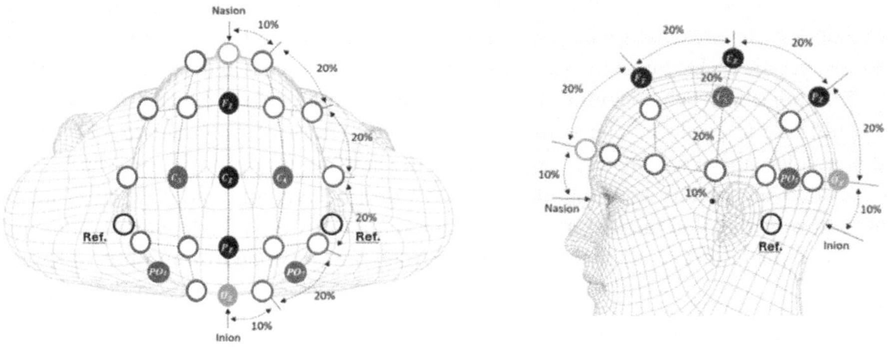

Fig. 1. Top and side view of electrode positioning according to the international 10–20 system (adapted from BITalino (r)evolution Lab Guide) – image retrieved from device guidelines

To guarantee the reliability of the data to be collected, we carried out preliminary tests with two members of the institution's technical team. These tests allowed us to evaluate the effectiveness of the equipment and the clarity of the procedures, in addition to serving as practical training for carrying out sessions with volunteers. In addition to enlightening the team, these preliminary tests served to validate the choice of study participants and adjust, if necessary, the research protocols. On May 15, 2024, volunteer R was asked if he could perform two sessions with BCI and presented with the Free and Informed Consent Form (original copy attached), which was duly signed by him.

The session with volunteer R (05/22/2024) began with the placement of the EEG helmet. Before starting the main task, a rigorous check of the EEG signal quality was performed using G-Tec's Unicorn Bandpower module. This tool allowed each electrode to be analyzed individually, ensuring that the data collected was reliable and free from artifacts such as noise or interference and that the electrodes had good contact with the scalp. Volunteer R used the G-Tec speller module, a brain-based orthographic speller system (EEG-based text generation module) based on the P300 paradigm. After selecting a target word, the volunteer was able to spell the first letter. However, errors occurred in subsequent letters, although it was possible to correct the errors using the system's backspace feature. After four attempts, and observing signs of discomfort and frustration on the part of the volunteer, the session was ended.

The Unicorn Hybrid Black suite has been updated to version 1.24.00 Beta. In addition to algorithmic improvements, three new game modules have been incorporated: Brainbuddy, Platformer and Puzzle Game. The Brainbuddy and Platformer games include an initial calibration procedure based on the SSVEP paradigm, known for its speed and lower susceptibility to artifacts.

The session with volunteer C (05/22/2024) began with the placement of the EEG helmet. Several calibration attempts were made, adjusting the electrodes, allowing signal to be obtained in only 5 of the 8 electrodes (using the Unicorn Bandpower module). To evaluate the quality of the calibration, the new games from the Unicorn suite were used, but without success. An additional attempt was made with the Speller module, aiming to spell the volunteer's name, but also without positive results.

In order to prepare the second session, a meeting was held with volunteer R on June 12, 2024. At this meeting, the objectives of the session, called 'Communication Moments', were presented with the reading of the protocol. These moments consisted of three specific tasks: answering a question, expressing a wish and expressing a feeling.

Thinking about what would most interest the volunteer, we asked him what topic he would like to explore. The volunteer chose the history of Cantanhede and asked to watch a video about it. This choice served as the starting point for the session.

A video on the city of Cantanhede was chosen beforehand and a PowerPoint presentation was made on the history of the municipality of Cantanhede with 5 slides and a question at the end. The correct answer to the question was one of four options (Fig. 2).

Fig. 2. Video and speller visualisation by Volunteer R - Communication moments (picture by the autors)

On June 13, 2024, during the session (Communication Moments), the EEG helmet was placed on volunteer R, the signal quality was checked, and the Unicorn Hybrid Black system was calibrated. All procedures were performed according to the protocol. Subsequently, using the Unicorn Bandpower module, response tests were performed to different stimuli: visual (change in the state of the eyes) and auditory (rapid verbal stimulation), with the aim of analyzing the variability of brain activity.

After watching the video lasting 2 min and 59 s, the volunteer expressed his appreciation, using the spelling tool to write the word "Lindo" (that means beautiful). Then, a sequence of five slides about the history of the municipality of Cantanhede was shown. At the end of the presentation, an assessment was carried out in which the volunteer had to choose the correct answer from four alternatives. The volunteer selected option "A". Finally, when asked about his wishes, the volunteer used the speller and wrote "FINA", demonstrating the intention of writing "final".

5 Data Analysis: Methods Used

The variability observed between volunteers R and C suggests that individual factors, such as hair density, previous experience with technology, and possible genetic differences or pre-existing medical conditions, may influence both signal quality and system performance. These aspects highlight the importance of adapting BCI technologies to users' physiological and cognitive characteristics.

In this context, calibration proved to be crucial. Volunteer C faced significant difficulties during the process, obtaining a signal in only 5 out of 8 electrodes. This underscores the need for accurate calibration procedures to ensure the proper functioning of the system and improve usability for individuals with diverse physical conditions.

On the other hand, system limitations became evident through spelling errors made by volunteer R, even after correction attempts. Additionally, volunteer C struggled to obtain consistent results, pointing to gaps in the system's accuracy and robustness. These findings suggest that further improvements in signal processing and adaptive calibration techniques are necessary to enhance BCI performance.

The interaction of the volunteers was also analyzed. Volunteer R exhibited a higher level of engagement, expressing appreciation for the video and successfully spelling words. In contrast, volunteer C faced more difficulties and showed lower motivation, which may indicate that user experience varies based on individual cognitive and technical adaptability.

Moreover, frustration and discomfort were recorded, particularly with volunteer R, whose session had to be interrupted after four attempts at the last letter due to signs of fatigue and frustration. This suggests that the spelling task, which lasted approximately one hour, can be mentally and physically demanding for some participants. Future research should explore strategies to reduce cognitive load and optimize session duration to improve user experience. Also regarding the volunteers' feedback, the expression "LINDO" (means beautiful), used by volunteer R to describe the video, reveals a positive experience and a level of satisfaction with the task. Regarding the effectiveness of the tasks, the spelling activity was challenging for both volunteers, who made frequent mistakes and had difficulty maintaining concentration. However, the tasks of responding to visual and auditory stimuli were successful in the case of volunteer R, which demonstrates the system's ability to capture different brain responses. The relevance of the tasks was also discussed, with the task of answering questions about a video and a presentation proving to be more motivating for the volunteer than the task of spelling random words, which proved to be more abstract.

Finally, difficulties and limitations in the system were also identified, namely the technical difficulties associated with obtaining a quality EEG signal and calibrating the system. The BCI system used showed limitations in terms of accuracy, speed and flexibility, and individual factors, such as previous experience with technology and cognitive characteristics, influenced the volunteers' performance and the effectiveness of the system.

Furthermore, this research highlighted several challenges associated with the use of non-invasive BCI systems, with particular emphasis on inter-individual variability and observed technical limitations. This variability, resulting from factors such as biological characteristics and differences in cognitive responses, requires a more personalized approach in the design and implementation of such systems. However, the analysis also revealed important opportunities to optimize the user experience, namely through the personalization of tasks and the use of more intuitive interfaces adapted to the individual capabilities and preferences of each user.

It is therefore recommended to carry out a preliminary study that includes the detailed analysis of the EEG metrics of each participant, in order to adjust the parameters of the BCI system more effectively. In addition, the adoption of more advanced signal processing technologies, such as artificial intelligence and machine learning algorithms, could significantly contribute to noise reduction and increased measurement accuracy. Exploring the potential of immersive technologies, such as virtual and augmented reality, represents another promising area, allowing to create more engaging and effective learning environments.

The integration of non-invasive BCI systems into the educational context can have a major impact on teaching practices, paving the way for the creation of highly personalized learning experiences tailored to the cognitive and emotional needs of each student. These technologies allow teaching to be adapted in real time, based on students' brain responses, thus enhancing their performance and engagement.

Given the highly technical and specific nature of neurotechnology, and considering the rapid pace of its evolution, it makes sense for the implementation and maintenance of these systems, as well as the interpretation of the resulting data, to be managed by specialized services through outsourcing. This approach would not only ensure the constant updating of technological solutions but would also allow educational institutions to focus on their main objective: providing quality education adapted to the demands of a rapidly changing world.

6 Conclusions

The main objective of this research was to examine the feasibility and applicability of non-invasive brain-computer interfaces (BCIs) based on electroencephalography (EEG) for individuals with Additional Support Needs (NAS) who face, or have the potential to develop, severe limitations in communication, especially in social and educational contexts. The research aimed to explore the use of patterns of spontaneous, stimulus-induced brain activity as an alternative form of communication, in line with the principles established by Brumberg et al. [38], who describe EEG as a tool to capture brain responses and facilitate communicative interaction in people with NAS.

The sessions carried out with volunteers R and C allowed to gain significant knowledge about the use of the BCI speller system based on the P300 paradigm, highlighting challenges and advances throughout the interventions. During the initial session with volunteer R, the importance of rigorous calibration and high quality of the EEG signal for the success of the tasks was verified. The use of the Unicorn Bandpower module proved to be essential to ensure data reliability by identifying artifacts and interference in the electrodes. Although the volunteer managed to spell the first letter of the target word, subsequent difficulties arose, resulting in errors that led to frustration and the end of the session after four attempts.

On the other hand, the session with volunteer C revealed problems in the initial calibration, with quality signals being obtained in only 5 of the 8 electrodes. The attempt to use the new games in the Unicorn suite to validate the calibration was unsuccessful, and the application of the speller module also did not produce the expected results.

To create greater motivation for the sessions, we introduced the "Communication Moments" approach, with the aim of increasing the volunteer's interest and providing an experience closer to situations encountered in teaching and in real contexts. During the second session with volunteer R, the "Communication Moments" were organized into three specific tasks: answering a question, expressing a wish and expressing a feeling.

The choice of the theme on the history of Cantanhede served to motivate the volunteer and contextualize the activities. After watching a video about the municipality, the volunteer was able to use the speller to express the word "LINDO", which indicated a successful interaction with the system. In the final stage, the volunteer had to select the correct answer from a presentation, managing to complete the task, despite errors in specific letters.

These results indicate that the BCI speller system has the potential to support communication, but there are significant challenges, such as the accuracy of the electrodes and participant discomfort, which must be addressed to optimize performance and user experience. The research demonstrated the need for more interactive interventions, adjusting the methodology based on feedback and data obtained, central characteristics of action research.

Comparing the results with the literature, such as the studies by Sun et al. [39] and Chen et al. [40], there is a convergence regarding the need for precise calibrations and personalized interventions to improve the effectiveness of BCIs. However, the presence of difficulties in calibration and the impact of discomfort are aspects that vary according to the protocol used and the participants' familiarity with the technology, highlighting the importance of continuous adjustments in the process.

6.1 Implications for Practice: Potential Application of ICBs

The integration of BCI and AAC requires a personalized and evidence-based selection process. Assessing individual characteristics and comparing different BCI methods are essential to ensure that the chosen system represents the specific needs of each individual. Choosing the most technologically advanced device does not guarantee the best solution; it is essential to consider the compatibility between the BCI and the user's capabilities [7].

A major limitation of this study is the small sample size, which prevents the generalization of the results to larger populations. For future research, it would be important to consider a more diverse and representative sample in order to obtain more robust and comprehensive data.

In addition, difficulties in calibrating BCI devices were observed, which limited the effectiveness of the system, especially in participants with anatomical variations or specific medical conditions. Future studies should focus on improving calibration techniques and improving the accessibility of systems for users with different physical and neurological characteristics.

Another factor to consider is cognitive fatigue, which can occur with prolonged use of non-invasive BCI systems, compromising task performance. It would be beneficial to explore strategies to minimize the mental and physical load on users during longer sessions, thus ensuring their effectiveness over time.

The diversity of tasks was another limitation observed. The communication moments performed were limited in terms of variety and context. For future research, it would be advisable to include a wider range of practical scenarios, especially in real classroom contexts, to better assess applicability in educational and social settings.

The use of BCI technology also raises ethical concerns related to the privacy of users' brain data, especially in vulnerable populations such as children and young people with NAS. Future research should include a more in-depth analysis of the ethical implications and develop robust data protection measures.

Finally, the current study was based on a limited period of training for users, but the effectiveness of BCI systems could be increased with more extensive and structured training programs. Further research should investigate the impact of more intensive training to maximize the effectiveness of technology on users.

References

1. Vidal, J.J.: Toward Direct Brain-Computer Communication. Annu. Rev. Biophys. Bioeng. **2**(1), 157–180 (1973). https://doi.org/10.1146/annurev.bb.02.060173.001105
2. Birbaumer, N.: "Your Thoughts are (were) Free! ": Brain-Computer-Interfaces, Neurofeedback, Detection of Deception, and the Future of Mind-Reading. Appl. Psychophysiol. Biofeedback (2024). https://doi.org/10.1007/s10484-024-09648-z
3. Nam, C. S., Choi, I., Wadeson, A., Whang, M.: Brain–Computer Interface. In: Brain–Computer Interfaces Handbook, pp. 11–52. CRC Press (2018). https://doi.org/10.1201/9781351231954-1
4. Hill, K., Huggins, J., Woodworth, C.: Inter-professional practitioners' opinions on features and services for an Augmentative and Alternative Communication-Brain-Computer Interface device. PM&R (2020). https://doi.org/10.1002/pmrj.12525
5. United Nations: Convention on the rights of persons with disabilities (2006). Retrieved from https://www.un.org/development/desa/disabilities/convention-on-the-rights-of-persons-with-disabilities.html
6. Cabero-Almenara, J., Guillén-Gámez, F.D., Ruiz-Palmero, J., Palacios-Rodríguez, A.: Teachers' digital competence to assist students with functional diversity: Identification of factors through logistic regression methods. Br. J. Edu. Technol. (2021). https://doi.org/10.1111/bjet.13151
7. Pitt, K.M., Brumberg, J.S.: Guidelines for Feature Matching Assessment of Brain-Computer Interfaces for Augmentative and Alternative Communication. Am. J. Speech Lang. Pathol. **27**(3), 950–964 (2018). https://doi.org/10.1044/2018_ajslp-17-0135
8. Wegemer, C.: Brain-computer interfaces and education: the state of technology and imperatives for the future. Int. J. Learn. Technol. **14**(2), 141–161 (2019). https://doi.org/10.1504/ijlt.2019.101848
9. Shannon, C. E., Weaver, W.: The mathematical theory of communication. University of Illinois Press (1964). (Original work published 1949)

10. Canossa Dias, J., Mineiro, A., Damen, S.: A new intervention to prevent social isolation in people with complex communication needs. Scientific Reports 14(1) (2024). https://doi.org/10.1038/s41598-024-63519-5
11. Lasswell, H.D.: The structure and function of communication in society. In: Bryson, L. (ed.) The communication of ideas, pp. 37–51. Harper and Row, New York (1948)
12. Pearson, J. C., Nelson, P. E., Titsworth, S., Hosek, A. M.: Human Communication 6e (Kean Univ. College of Communication, Media and Journalism COMM 1402). McGraw Hill Education (2017)
13. Tremblay, P., Brambati, S. M.: A historical perspective on the neurobiology of speech and language: from the 19th century to the present. Frontiers in Psychology 15 (2024). https://doi.org/10.3389/fpsyg.2024.1420133
14. Elsahar, Y., Hu, S., Bouazza-Marouf, K., Kerr, D., Mansor, A.: Augmentative and Alternative Communication (AAC) Advances: A Review of Configurations for Individuals with a Speech Disability. Sensors **19**(8), 1911 (2019). https://doi.org/10.3390/s19081911
15. Beukelman, D.R., Mirenda, P.: Augmentative and alternative communication: Supporting children and adults with complex communication needs, 4th edn. Brookes Publishing, Paul H (2013)
16. Light, J. C., Beukelman, D. R.: Augmentative & Alternative Communication: Supporting Children and Adults with Complex Communication Needs. Brookes Publishing (2020)
17. Lotte, F., Nam, C. S., Nijholt, A.: Introduction: Evolution of Brain-Computer Interfaces. In: Brain-Computer Interfaces Handbook: Technological and Theoretical Advances. Taylor & Francis Group (2018)
18. Schuh, A. R.: Interface cérebro-computador híbrida e colaborativa no processo de tomada de decisão. Pontifícia Universidade Católica do Rio Grande do Sul (2017). http://tede2.pucrs.br/tede2/handle/tede/7711
19. Nunez, P. L.: Electric and Magnetic Fields Produced by the Brain. In: Brain–Computer Interfaces Principles and Practice, pp. 46–64. Oxford University Press (2012). https://doi.org/10.1093/acprof:oso/9780195388855.003.0003
20. Watson, C., Kirkcaldie, M., Paxinos, G.: Nerve cells and synapses. In: The Brain, pp. 1–10. Elsevier (2010). https://doi.org/10.1016/b978-0-12-373889-9.50001-2
21. Kaczmarek, B.L.J.: CURRENT VIEWS ON NEUROPLASTICITY: WHAT IS NEW AND WHAT IS OLD? Acta Neuropsychologica **18**(1), 1–14 (2020). https://doi.org/10.5604/01.3001.0013.8808
22. Li, R., Yang, D., Fang, F., Hong, K.-S., Reiss, A.L., Zhang, Y.: Concurrent fNIRS and EEG for Brain Function Investigation: A Systematic. Methodology-Focused Review. Sensors **22**(15), 5865 (2022). https://doi.org/10.3390/s22155865
23. Khosla, A., Khandnor, P., Chand, T.: A comparative analysis of signal processing and classification methods for different applications based on EEG signals. Biocybernetics and Biomedical Engineering **40**(2), 649–690 (2020). https://doi.org/10.1016/j.bbe.2020.02.002
24. Samal, P., Hashmi, M. F.: Role of machine learning and deep learning techniques in EEG-based BCI emotion recognition system: a review. Artificial Intelligence Review 57(3) (2024). https://doi.org/10.1007/s10462-023-10690-2
25. Leuthardt, E. C., Moran, D. W., Mullen, T. R.: Defining Surgical Terminology and Risk for Brain Computer Interface Technologies. Frontiers in Neuroscience 15 (2021). https://doi.org/10.3389/fnins.2021.599549
26. Pontifex, M. B., Coffman, C. A.: Validation of the g.tecUnicorn Hybrid Black wireless EEG system. Psychophysiology (2023). https://doi.org/10.1111/psyp.14320
27. Pan, J., Li, Y.: Hybrid Brain–Computer Interfaces and Their Applications. In: Brain–Computer Interfaces Handbook, pp. 525–548. CRC Press (2018). https://doi.org/10.1201/9781351231954-27

28. Miranda, P., Cox, D., Alexander, M., Danev, S., Lakey, R. T.: Event-related-potential (ERP) markers of traumatic brain injury (TBI) severity and cognitive function – Understanding how the brain works and thinks post TBI. Journal of Systems and Integrative Neuroscience 6(3) (2020). https://doi.org/10.15761/jsin.1000225
29. Leung, J., Chau, T.: Mindset – A General Purpose Brain-Computer Interface System for End-users. IEEE Access 1 (2024). https://doi.org/10.1109/access.2024.3441382
30. Kim, H., Won, K., Ahn, M., Jun, S.C.: Comparison of recognition methods for an asynchronous (un-cued) BCI system: an investigation with 40-class SSVEP dataset. Biomed. Eng. Lett. (2024). https://doi.org/10.1007/s13534-024-00357-4
31. O'Reilly, J.A., Wehrman, J., Sowman, P.F.: A Guided Tutorial on Modelling Human Event-Related Potentials with Recurrent Neural Networks. Sensors **22**(23), 9243 (2022). https://doi.org/10.3390/s22239243
32. Li, R., Zhao, X., Wang, Z., Xu, G., Hu, H., Zhou, T., Xu, T.: A Novel Hybrid Brain-Computer Interface Combining the Illusion-induced VEP and SSVEP. IEEE Transactions on Neural Systems and Rehabilitation Engineering 1 (2023). https://doi.org/10.1109/tnsre.2023.3337525
33. Jamil, N., Belkacem, A. N.: Advancing Real-Time Remote Learning: A Novel Paradigm for Cognitive Enhancement Using EEG and Eye-Tracking Analytics. IEEE Access 1 (2024). https://doi.org/10.1109/access.2024.3422926
34. Spüler, M., Krumpe, T., Walter, C., Scharinger, C., Rosenstiel, W., Gerjets, P.: Brain-Computer Interfaces for Educational Applications. In: Informational Environments, pp. 177–201. Springer International Publishing (2017). https://doi.org/10.1007/978-3-319-64274-1_8
35. Xu, J., Zhong, B.: Review on portable EEG technology in educational research. Comput. Hum. Behav. **81**, 340–349 (2018). https://doi.org/10.1016/j.chb.2017.12.037
36. Jiang, Y., Huang, Q., Li, Y.: Application Strategies of Brain-computer Interface in Education from the Perspective of Innovation Diffusion Theory. Brain-Apparatus Communication: A Journal of Bacomics 3(1) (2024). https://doi.org/10.1080/27706710.2024.2376368
37. Proverbio, A. M.: EEG and ERPs in the Study of Language and Social Knowledge. In: Social and Affective Neuroscience of Everyday Human Interaction, pp. 195–212. Springer International Publishing (2022). https://doi.org/10.1007/978-3-031-08651-9_12
38. Brumberg, J.S., Pitt, K.M., Mantie-Kozlowski, A., Burnison, J.D.: Brain-Computer Interfaces for Augmentative and Alternative Communication: A Tutorial. Am. J. Speech Lang. Pathol. **27**(1), 1–12 (2018). https://doi.org/10.1044/2017_ajslp-16-0244
39. Sun, Q., Zheng, L., Pei, W., Gao, X., Wang, Y.: A 120-target brain-computer interface based on code-modulated visual evoked potentials. J. Neurosci. MethodsNeurosci. Methods **375**, 109597 (2022). https://doi.org/10.1016/j.jneumeth.2022.109597
40. Chen, Y., Yang, C., Ye, X., Chen, X., Wang, Y., Gao, X.: Implementing a calibration-free SSVEP-based BCI system with 160 targets. J. Neural Eng. (2021). https://doi.org/10.1088/1741-2552/ac0bfa

VR, Online, Hybrid or Traditional Training? Cyber Threats Training Preferences and needs from the Perspective of Polish and British Teachers - A Comparative Study

Dorota Siemieniecka(✉) and Kamila Majewska

Nicolaus Copernicus University in Toruń, Toruń, Poland
{dsiemien,majewska}@umk.pl

Abstract. The aim of the research was to determine the training needs of Polish and British teachers in the field of cyber threats and the preferred forms of training. The research was conducted between 2023 and 2024 and covered 824 teachers (431 Polish and 393 from the UK). The selection of the sample was purposive. The research used an author's survey questionnaire. Mann-Whitney U tests were used in the research analysis. The obtained values were interpreted using the Stanisz scale. The results showed that Polish teachers have a better knowledge of areas related to cyber threats, which may be the result of their greater activity in creating educational materials. The survey showed that, on average, 64% of Polish teachers and 49% of British teachers receive further training once a year, while 23% of Polish teachers and 12% of British teachers declared a lack of interest in the subject. Both groups indicated the need for training on cyberbullying, malware, identity theft, accessing inappropriate content, inappropriate contacts, data security and online fraud, gaming/Internet addiction, e-gambling, outing, cyberstalking, flaming, as well as mobile device management, as used in the BYOD model.

Teachers' preferences for forms of training include hybrid training (the need was reported by 75.41% of Polish and 45.55% of British teachers), synchronous online training (indicated by 19.72% of Polish, 7, 38% of British teachers), training with artificial intelligence and VR goggles (0.70% of Polish, 36.39% of British). Teachers emphasize the need to implement training based on useful and practical content, offering them suggestions for solutions and assistance. An important issue is the need of teachers regarding contact with the lecturer.

Keywords: Cyber threats · Teacher training · Online safety · Teachers' knowledge of cyber threats

1 Teachers' Knowledge of Cyber Threats

The problem of cyber threats in the field of education affects both individuals and institutions. The 2022 report *The Cyber Threat to Education and Academy Trusts in the UK* stated that "*the education sector is more likely to experience a data breach or cyber*

Ł. Tomczyk (Ed.): NMP 2024, CCIS 2537, pp. 51–67, 2025.
https://doi.org/10.1007/978-3-031-95627-0_4

attack, than the typical UK business or organization, and the size of the educational establishment directly correlates with the likelihood of a breach or attack" [22]. The authors consider the issue of threats from the perspective of the school as an institution, pointing out that schools have been "*struck by more than 70 ransomware attacks during the pandemic*" [22]. Educational institutions, therefore, face the challenge of disseminating up-to-date knowledge among teachers on how to protect against potential attacks targeting schools as institutions [22, 35], as well as how to identify and respond to cyber threats in situations where students may be victims or perpetrators.

Despite the introduction of effective preventive measures in schools (as seen in the UK) against PDNS (*Protective Domain Name System*) threats such as phishing, malware, or ransomware attacks [23], the issue remains unresolved.

In the *Guidance Essential Digital Skills Framework*, developed by the UK Department for Education (2019 and also included in 2018 by Crown), authors put attention to digital competencies in online security [25]. The document recommends enhancing skills in the following areas: digital foundation skills, communication, handling information and content, transacting, problem-solving, and staying safe and legal online [25, 37]. The authors emphasize these skills through practical examples, underscoring the importance of implementing organizational security procedures in both everyday life and the workplace (skills for life, additional skills for work, life examples and work examples) [25].

The findings of the *Tech4Teachers White Paper* (2024) state that "*Policymakers should focus on activity to provide greater incentivisation for teachers to develop their digital skills. This may include integrating digital skills into initial teacher training (ITT) and as part of the requirements to obtain qualified teacher status (QTS)*" [18]. In security studies, it is emphasized that the weakest link in security is always the human factor.

The issue of cyber threats in the context of school reality is highly significant. Available data show that the number of unpleasant incidents affecting both students and teachers is steadily increasing.

The research conducted by Lukasz Tomczyk and Katarzyna Potyrata found that "*at least once in their lives, 17.5% of teachers had encountered a situation where someone had published insulting or demeaning comments about their professional competence, 10.8% had received digital messages intended to provoke negative emotions, 8.3% had experienced account hacking and impersonation of a teacher, 6.8% had suffered the unfavorable publication of their image without consent, 6.4% had received threats via electronic communication channels, 5.9% had their personal data disclosed, 5.5% had to deal with a situation where a fake account was set up with their private data, 5.3% were subjected to fake news about themselves, 4.9% were provoked to behave strangely and this material was then made available in cyberspace, 4.3% had to deal with their school mail or electronic diary being hacked, and 3.9% experienced a situation where a fake website was set up to discredit them because of their profession*" [1]. Teachers are also witnessing cyber threats in the school space affecting their students [2]. This issue is gaining importance, and raising awareness is an important factor in combating it [3, 4]. This task is not easy, due to the dynamic nature of the cyber threats, and the ever-increasing number of problems entering its field. Research conducted in 2021–2022 by Dorota Siemieniecka and Kamila Majewska showed that Polish teachers' knowledge of cyber threats is insufficient. It can be noted that *"the responses show that teachers assess their knowledge of cyber threats as: - Very good - 31.9%, Good - 47.8%, Satisfactory - 17.1%. 3.2% of the respondents rated their knowledge lower than satisfactory. In fact, every fifth teacher is not able to give specific examples of threats related to students and the space of the Internet, using the general term 'cyber threat'. 11.16% of the respondents mentioned only one known threat when commenting on cyber threats. 53.38% mentioned two examples of threats, and 15.14% mentioned three or more. One of the respondents replied that she did not know any threats lying in wait for students in the Internet space (0.4%)*"[5]. When comparing the knowledge of Polish and British teachers about cyber threats, it turns out that the former group demonstrates higher competence in this area. This is undoubtedly influenced by the greater independence and initiative of Polish teachers in preparing preventive materials for parenting lessons [6]. Research conducted by Pragya Kumari and Nimisha Srivastava (published in 2021) [7] showed that only 15.59% of future teachers (N=186) show a positive attitude towards cybercrime. Only 18.82% have a high level of awareness on the subject, while the majority (66.66%) demonstrate an average level of awareness. Additionally, 14.52% of the group have a low level of awareness of cybercrime. Women characterized by a higher average awareness (125.62) compared to men (124.77) regarding cybercrime. Authors used: *Self constructed and validated Cyber Crime Attitude Scale* and *Cyber Crime Awareness Scale* developed by S. Rajeshker (CCAS) [7]. The level of awareness among teachers depends on the region in which they live. Teachers and students residing in rural areas present a lower awareness of threats [7, 9]. This relationship is indicated by research: K. Rajender, S. Bikram, Y. Mukesh (2017) [8] and Yodida Bhutia and Evahunlang R Passah (2019) [9]. Some studies indicate an insufficient level of knowledge among teacher candidates. Teachers do not possess knowledge about the methods and techniques for combating cybercrime [10]. Research findings highlight differences in knowledge and awareness among future teachers in the context of gender and the amount of time spent using computers [10]. Generally, a higher level of awarness is characteristic of women; however, men studying STEM fields and individuals who spend more than eight hours online also demonstrate a higher level of knowledge [10]. Awareness of cyber threats is also linked to a higher frequency of password changes, participation in IT courses, experience with online banking and shopping, and the type of software they use [10]. However, it is worrying that, as the authors state, "*most teacher candidates do not take a course in information technology*" [10].

In the literature, attention is drawn to the limited number of studies on the effectiveness of training programs for teachers in relation to their teaching activities [22, 30]. There is a lack of research regarding teachers' knowledge in a comparative context and their training needs in the area of cyber threats.

In 2021, research conducted by Andy Phippen revealed advantages and also weaknesses in the current teacher training system in the United Kingdom. Phippen says: "*Without well trained staff we cannot be confident that online safety education will be delivered consistently and effectively, and without knowledgeable scrutiny from governing bodies, we cannot have any assurance that schools are receiving effective challenge on the online safety practices or a clear steer on how they might improve them*" [20]. The implementation of training programs is being proposed.

An author states that the school's governing body is responsible for training in child safety and protection, including online safety. Various initiatives were analyzed, including The Department for Education's *Keeping Children Safe in Education* (KCSiE). According to the document, there is a need to update the content of these training sessions and implement recommendations from cybersecurity experts, including companies and specialists. Information on child safety and protection should be disseminated via email, newsletters, and organized meetings. It is essential that this information reaches teachers regularly. Additionally, the document emphasizes that the governing body should acknowledge the competencies and qualifications acquired by teachers in this field. This underlines the need to involve active teachers in shaping child protection policies [20]. The report states that "*There are two fundamental areas of concern here given our evaluation. Firstly, as stated above, over 40% of schools have no staff training in place. Therefore, we can show that just over 40% of schools are failing their statutory duties around ensuring staff training (covering online safety) is being addressed. However, there are wider concerns with this – while we have stated above that Online Safety Education is delivered in the vast majority of schools, the guidance states that governors and proprietors are responsible for ensuring the education programme is delivered and how it is discharged. We would suggest that untrained staff delivering online safety education will not result in the education delivered being effective. Furthermore, we know that the Impact of Online Safety Policy and Practice is a consistently weak aspect, therefore we can state confidently that the majority of schools will not know if, for example, their education programme is effective because they do not evaluate or evidence impact*" [20].

Despite the fact that two-thirds of English teachers have undergone cybersecurity training, 66% of trained teachers found the training useful [26].

The results of a study of a group of British teachers presented in the *Tech4Teachers White Paper* show that there are barriers to cybersecurity education. Teachers are unable to engage in additional training due to an overload of responsibilities and lack of time [18, 19]. At the same time, attention is drawn to the existence of accompanying problems: "*In the U.K., teachers are under pressure due to staff shortages, funding issues, pupil hardship, and worsening behaviour, meaning that investing in cyber security measures and staff training are often not a top priority. Tight budgets also mean schools often still run legacy software and cannot employ security experts to train staff or protect their systems*" [27].

The document *Teacher Digital Skills* (2024) describes the current requirements for teachers' digital competences. Unfortunately, the programme does not include content on cyberthreat response skills. The authors only referred to the safe use of devices and accounts by teachers, covering cyber hygiene, information assessment skills and awareness of the risks associated with social media [21]. However, they can be found on the Department for Education's website dedicated to education about cyber threats. This document is entitled *Guidance Teaching online safety in schools*. According to it, cyber threats affect various areas of the curriculum. The aim of education is to prepare pupils for safe use of the Internet. This requires the implementation of several aspects. The first of these is online safety. Pupils should use technology in a safe and responsible way, and be able to show respect for others [28]. They should know where to look for help if problems arise [28]. An important issue is recognising threats, which requires the acquisition of skills in identifying fake websites, recognising fraud via e-mails, persuasion techniques used by criminals, and knowledge about the risks associated with sharing personal data [28]. The education against cyber threats according to the recommendations [28] includes the critical analysis of website content and the recognition of disinformation and manipulation.

Social competencies, such as respect for others, empathy, and risk management, are also important. Other important issues are privacy protection and risk management [28]. According to the document [28], the teacher's role is to tailor content to the age and developmental level of students, educate and support them in challenging situations, provide information on where to seek help, and foster a supportive community [22, 28]. The document identifies various risks, including abuse, dangerous challenges, harmful content, fake profiles, grooming, live streaming, pornography, and unsafe communication [28].

Similar problems concerning cybersecurity education and the issues addressed in the documents of the ministries responsible for education in Poland and the United Kingdom can be observed. Certainly, education about cyber threats requires coordination in the field of teacher training, digital security and the development of infrastructure available at school [30]. The Polish core curriculum introduces the concepts of 'digital competence', 'shaping students' digital skills' and 'problem solving' [30]. These competences should be acquired at different educational stages and during the implementation of various subjects [30]. The issues raised in the aforementioned British reports are present in Polish ministerial documents, such as: *Resolution No. 98 of the Council of Ministers of 12 September 2024 on the adoption of a public policy called the "Digital Transformation of Education Policy"* (Uchwała nr 98 Rady Ministrów z dnia 12 września 2024 r. w sprawie przyjęcia polityki publicznej pod nazwą "Polityka Cyfrowej Transformacji Edukacji" 33) *Safe School* (Bezpieczna Szkoła). Threats and recommended preventive measures in the field of physical and digital safety of students - a guide from the Ministry of National Education and research: *Digital School 4.0* (Cyfrowa Szkoła 4.0), NASK reports and others.

2 Teachers' Preferences Regarding the Nature and Delivery of Training

The 2024 study showed that Polish teachers are more likely to supplement their knowledge of cyber threats than British teachers do. The collected data indicate that on average 64% of Polish teachers and 49% of British teachers receive further training on the subject once a year. Training on cyber threats and cyber security is carried out once in five years by 13% of Polish teachers and 39% of British teachers, while a total lack of interest in the above topics was declared by 23% of Polish teachers and 12% of British teachers [6].

Regarding the form of training, online training is gaining popularity today. Research conducted by Librus in 2021 (during the pandemic) showed that *"97.4% of respondents confirm that they are already participating in online training and the vast majority of them declare (86.7%) that they will do so when the pandemic ends"* [11]. Convenience and time savings are cited among the benefits of this form of education. However, in the context of online training, concerns have been raised about its potential lower effectiveness compared to other forms. Sanjana Kumari, Hitender Gautam, Neha Nityadarshini, Bimal Kumar Das, and Rama Chudhry, in their research summary, point out that *"there is a general consensus that no technology can replace face-to-face teaching in real because in this, there will be visual as well as verbal discussion*" [12].

The governmental documents and research results presented clearly show the areas important for education and take the form of programme elements that teachers should implement. Sample lessons are posted on the websites of the Polish and British ministries of education. However, there is a noticeable lack of proposals using the educational technologies (such as VR, AR). This is particularly evident in accessible learning or teaching materials where participants do not have the opportunity for direct interaction with the teacher. It is not enough to provide even the best instructional materials. Personal experience and learning based on simulated or real situations are important for safety education [38]. Learning that combines direct knowledge and the presence of a teacher allows for a combination of group work and individual experience, increases the level of motivation and influences the development of appropriate habits and reactions to difficult situations, and can also be immediately developed. The learner must interact with the learning material and experience and solve a real problem. The basis for the design of the training programme is a knowledge assessment and diagnosis of the needs.

3 Research Methodology

The presented survey was carried out in the period from February 1, 2023 to January 20, 2024, among Polish and British teachers. The sampling for the study was purposive.

Among other things, the research goal was to identify quantitative differences between the study groups, as well as the strength and direction of the relationship between variables in the study groups. The researchers focused on identifying the training needs of Polish and British teachers in the field of cyber threats. The study sought to identify areas of knowledge and skills that require training, as well as their preferred forms, taking into account traditional and modern educational methods. An original survey questionnaire, prepared in Polish and English, was used to operationalize the variables. The questionnaire in the planning phase and the development of the research procedure was subjected to a standardization and normalization procedure. In addition to closed questions, the questionnaire included open-ended questions that helped to determine training needs, both in terms of the content of cyber threats and the forms of their implementation. The survey was online and was developed using Google Forms. Sheets were sent individually to teachers with an invitation and assurances about: the anonymity of the survey, its purpose, topic, course of action, the time needed to complete the questionnaire, and the researchers' ability to use the data. The mailing addresses came from community groups dedicated to teachers, available on Facebook. The questionnaire was sent to a total of 1,100 teachers (550 Polish teachers and 550 British teachers). The return rate of the sheets fluctuated around 75%, as a result, 824 people - 431 Polish teachers and 393 British teachers - completed the survey. Most of the survey participants were women, which is a direct result of the feminization of the teaching profession. The characteristics of the respondents are presented in Figure 1.

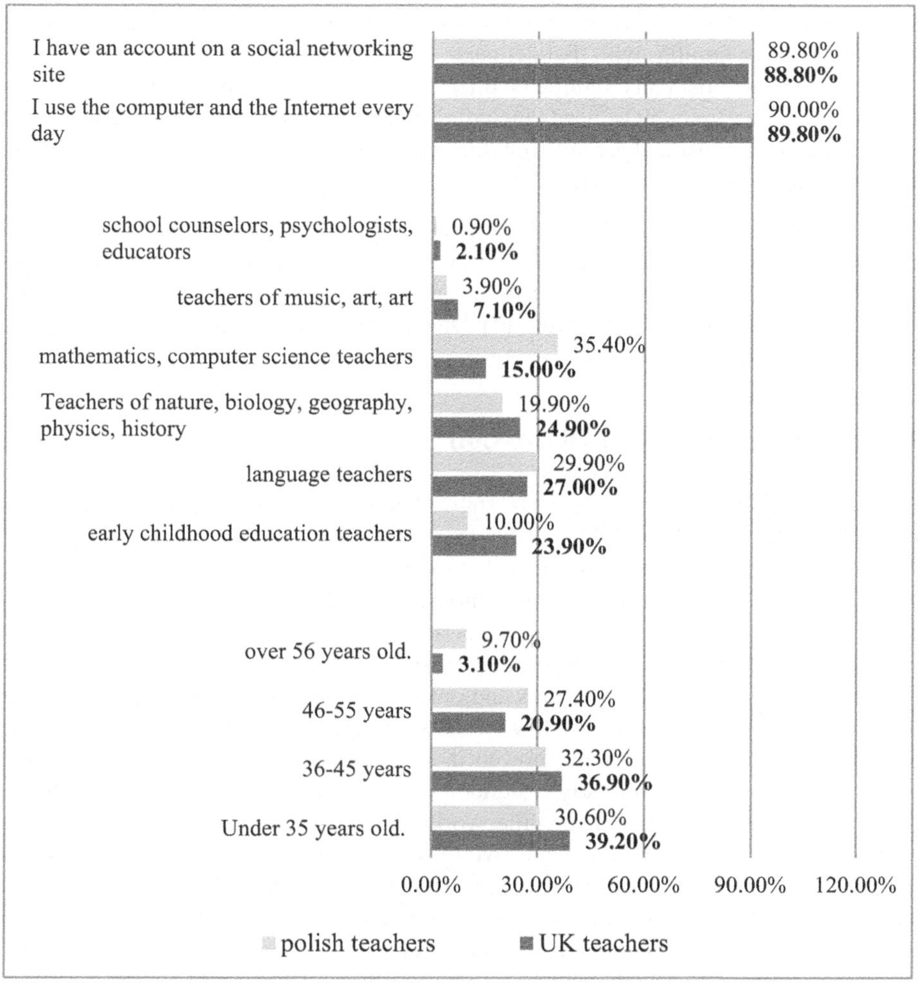

Fig. 1. Characteristics of the surveyed teachers.

The research objective was to identify the training needs of Polish and British teachers in the context of cyber threats, as well as the forms of training in this area that interest them. To this end, the following research questions were formulated:

1. Are there statistically significant differences between teachers' backgrounds and the areas they are familiar with that delineate cyberthreat issues?
2. Are there statistically significant differences between teachers' backgrounds and their individual assessment of needs including further training on cyber threats?
3. Are there statistically significant differences between teachers' backgrounds and their preferred forms of cyber threat training?

Based on an analysis of the available literature, it was assumed that:

H1. There are no statistically significant differences between teachers' backgrounds and the areas they are familiar with that delineate cyber threats.
H2. There are no statistically significant differences between teachers' backgrounds and their individual assessment of needs including further training on cyber threats
H3. There are no statistically significant differences between teachers' backgrounds and their preferred forms of cyber threat training.

Mann-Whitney U tests were used in the research analysis. The obtained values were interpreted using the Stanisz scale. The choice of tests was a direct result of the nature of the variables, the lack of normal distribution of the dependent variables, as well as the lack of equality of the studied groups [13]. Due to space limitations, the authors decided to omit statistical tabulations [6][1].

4 Reseach Results and Discussion

Data collected from knowledge tests showed that there are significant differences between teachers' backgrounds and the areas they know that delineate cyber threats ($U = 60271.50$; $p < 0.05$), which means that should reject hypothesis H1. Knowledge of more areas related to cyber threats was demonstrated in Polish teachers. The researchers linked this phenomenon to the greater experience of Polish teachers due to their age. The higher knowledge of this group may also have been a consequence of personal experience, as 27% of Polish teachers and only 7% of British teachers reported having school-aged children, which may have a direct bearing on their interest in the topic. In addition, as the collected data showed in the group of British teachers, 14% more people were associated with early childhood education (children aged 7 to 10) than in the group of Polish teachers. Meanwhile, working with children, analyzed in the context of cyber threats, is not a factor conducive to further education in this area, due to the false sense of cyber security of the youngest students. Better knowledge of cyber threats emerging from different areas may also be due to the fact that Polish teachers are more often working independently on educational materials in this area. Indeed, the survey found that teaching materials for educational activities planned with students are prepared independently by 80% of Polish and 60% of British teachers. The above activities are conducive in expanding cognitive activity, which further justifies the higher level of knowledge (in this area) of Polish teachers.

The present study found that among Polish teachers, the threats mainly known were those located in the area related to: cyberbullying (66.3%), addiction to online games and gambling (17.2%), access to inappropriate content (19.9%), contact with inappropriate people (9.7%), identity theft (15.5%), malware and DDOS attacks (9.5%), data security and online fraud (3.7%). For British teachers, it was cyberbullying (64.6%), online gaming and gambling addiction (41.5%), accessing inappropriate content (18%), contact with inappropriate people (11.9%), and identity theft (7.4%) (Fig. 2).

[1] Other research areas analyzed in the procedure undertaken are described in the article: [6] D. Siemieniecka, K. Majewska, "Knowledge of Polish and British Teachers about Cyber Threats - A Comparative Study". *The New Educational Review* (2024).

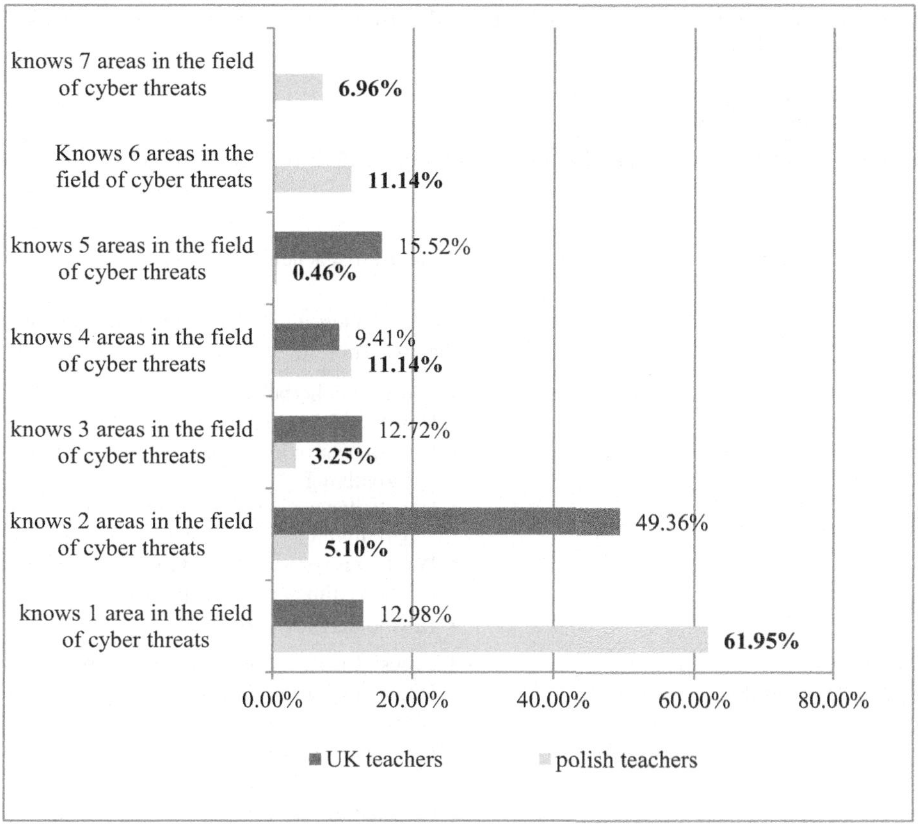

Fig. 2. Number of areas related to cyber threats known to Polish and British teachers.

Interestingly, none of the teachers thought about the possible risks that could arise from managing the mobile devices brought by students and the BYOD model used in schools [14].

Despite the differences between Polish and British teachers in the level of knowledge about cyber threats and related areas, it turned out that the individual assessment of needs covering further education topics in the field of cyber threats is similar between them. As a result, the calculations performed showed that there are no statistically significant differences between teachers' backgrounds and their individual assessment of needs including further training on cyber threats ($U= 82213.50$; $p= 0.062$), so there is no basis for rejecting the H2 hypothesis. It is worth noting that 23% of Polish teachers and 12% of British teachers have never received further training on cyber threats and cyber security topics. Nonetheless, these groups unanimously agreed that if it were necessary to participate in training on cyber threats, they would want it to include information on: cyberbullying in the broadest sense, malware and hacking attacks, identity theft, accessing inappropriate content, inappropriate contacts, data security and online fraud, gaming/internet addiction, e-gambling, outing, cyberstalking, flaming, as well as mobile device management, as used in the BYOD model. In the context of these issues, teachers would expect (Table 1):

- To expand and update their knowledge,
- get practical tips for action,
- guidelines on where to seek help and how to provide it for a specific problem.

Table 1. Cyber threats and issues of interest to teachers in this context.

problem	issues of interest to teachers in the context of the problem
Cyberbullying	• Forms of cyberbullying, • How to talk to students about cyberbullying, • How to behave in case of being a victim of cyberbullying, • How to behave in case of witnessing cyberbullying, • What consequences cyberbuying can cause for the victim and for the perpetrator, • How to defend yourself,
Malware and hacking attacks	• Types of malware and hacking attacks, • How to defend against malware and hacking attacks, • Preventive measures, • Which antivirus software to choose and how to install it,
Identity theft	• Reasons, • Contributing factors, • How to prevent and how to defend, • What to do in case of being a victim, • The consequences of the phenomenon for the victim and the perpetrator,
Access to inappropriate content	• How to secure computer devices so that students do not encounter inappropriate content, • How to respond if inappropriate content is displayed during class, • How to talk to students when encountering inappropriate content,
Access to inappropriate contacts	• How to protect students from inappropriate contacts, • To which children in particular should be sensitized, • How to talk to parents about the problem,

(*continued*)

Table 1. (*continued*)

problem	issues of interest to teachers in the context of the problem
Data security and fraud online	• How to set passwords on your computer/smartphone, etc. and how often to update them to keep them secure, • How to take care of data security, what to watch out for, • What online fraud is and what form it can take, • How to protect yourself from online scams, • What to do and when to do it to minimize the consequences of online fraud,
Addiction to games/internet, e-Gambling	• Which children are included in the risk group, • How to talk to parents about children's addiction to games/Internet, e-gambling, • How to know your child's addiction problem, • Where to seek help, • What preventive measures are effective,
Outing	• How to respond when personal information is made public, • Where to seek help, • What to do, as a witness to the situation, • How to talk to students about the problem and the consequences of the phenomenon,
Cyberstalking	• forms of the phenomenon, • Where to seek help, • How to defend yourself against a stalker,
Flaming	• How to react while being a victim, • What to do, as a witness to the situation, • How to talk to students about the problem and the consequences of the phenomenon,
Mobile device management, which is used in the BYOD model	• What to pay attention to in order to stay safe.

It should be noted that due to the social nature of the problem, teachers would expect contact with a lecturer (who could explain the doubts that arise), and not just with the educational material. As a result, 62% of Polish teachers and 88.6% of British teachers, given a choice between asynchronous and on-site remote classes, would choose the latter. The situation is slightly different when teachers have a greater variety of training choices. The results of the survey showed that there are significant differences between teachers' backgrounds and their preferred forms of cyber threat training ($U= 58319.50$; $p< 0.05$), which means that hypothesis H3 should be rejected. The answers given suggest that teachers, given a choice of training: traditional, asynchronous online, synchronous online, hybrid, or using artificial intelligence and VR goggles, at the present moment are most likely to choose hybrid training - providing contact with the learning content, with the lecturer, and partly allowing customization of delivery times. Wanting to look at the numerical values and declared preferences, it should be noted that Polish teachers would be most willing to participate in hybrid training, which 75.41% of them declared. This was followed by Polish teachers indicating: synchronous online training (19.72%), traditional training (2.55%), asynchronous online training (1.62%), training with artificial intelligence and VR goggles (0.70%). For British teachers, the indications were as follows: hybrid training (45.55%), training with artificial intelligence and VR goggles (36.39%), online synchronous training (7.38%), traditional training (6.87%), online asynchronous training (3.82%) (Fig. 3).

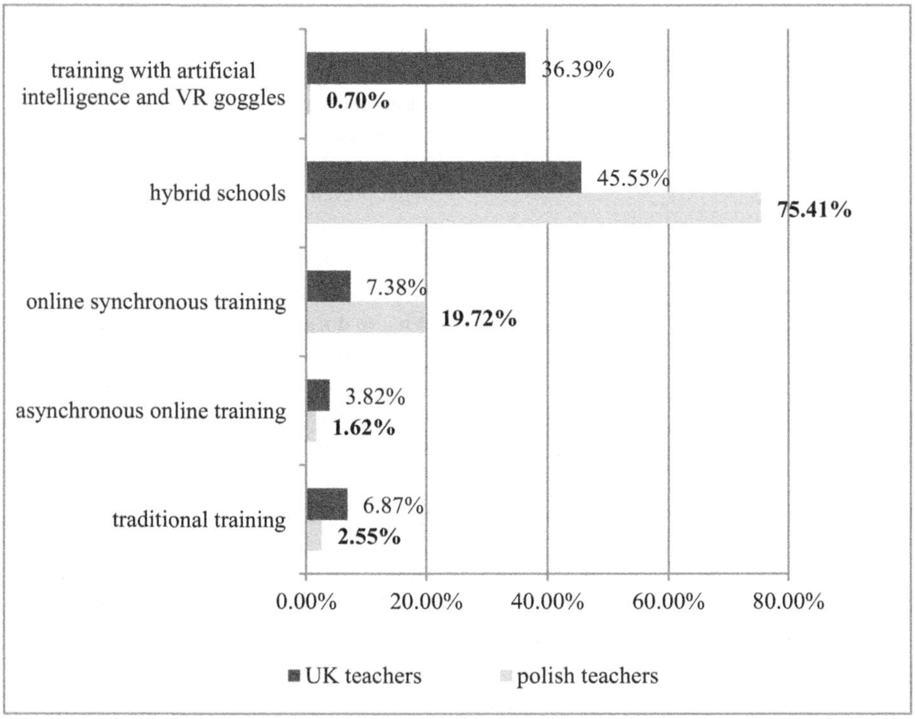

Fig. 3. Teachers' preferences for cyber threat training.

The area of teacher training is not limited to the phenomenon of cyberbullying; it is necessary to support teachers in the use of teaching methods based on new technologies [34]. In literature, it is recommended that effective education uses project methods [30, 31].

In contrast, in the 2024 Report entitled *Digital School 4.0* Joanna Waszkowska proposes: education based on the search for new contexts (real situations and media form the basis of analyses), engaging in dialogue at the level of global phenomena (SDGs), education based on student experience, simulations, gamification, Erasmus projects, eTwinning, iEARN [32]. Marek Grzywna emphasises that good communication between students and teachers is the key to effective teaching [32].

Teaching solutions can be developed at the university level. This issue is addressed by the UK Department for Education in the text *Realising the potential of technology in education: A summary report*. It draws attention to the following objectives: "*Supporting teachers so that they can develop and learn more flexibly. (...) Demonstrate how technology can support schools and teachers to diagnose their development needs and to support more flexible CPD*" [24]. The report shows the role of universities in developing examples of good practice in education and implementation. The aim of the institution is to "*Provide guidance on monitoring, filtering, data security and cyber security (...) Encourage EdTech suppliers to follow 'Cyber Essentials' minimum standards and the Code of Practice for Consumer Internet of Things Security*" [24]. However, it should not be forgotten that today's teachers are both digital natives and digital immigrants. It is worth noting that the requirements of expanding cybersecurity qualifications can cause anxiety and resistance among teachers, especially those with lower digital competence.

5 Conclusions

The data collected in the knowledge tests showed that there are significant differences between teachers' educational backgrounds and the areas they are familiar with that determine the issue of cyber threats. Higher competence in this area was demonstrated by Polish teachers, who, when preparing for educational classes on cyber threats and cyber security, in the vast majority (80%) complete and develop the above materials on their own. This does not change the fact that the individual needs assessment for further training on cyber threats for Polish and British teachers was similar, and the tests did not show statistically significant differences in this respect. Teachers are overburdened with responsibilities, which is a barrier to improving knowledge and skills in the field of cyber threats [18–20]. This requires proper planning of responsibilities so that the requirements are achievable.

Although teachers declared a similar interest in the general content and specific issues that should be covered in cyberbullying courses, they expressed different opinions on the forms of training they expected. The aforementioned differences were so significant that the calculations carried out showed statistically significant differences between teachers' education and their preferred forms of cyber threat training.

In this context, new opportunities are offered by technologies such as simulations (VR, AR), real-life examples, case studies, MOOCs, gamification, and cooperative learning, which can connect teachers to experiential learning.

In the literature, solutions targeting the development of cybersecurity competences are proposed [15, 16, 20]. Implementing these solutions in teacher education requires addressing three dimensions: knowledge, skills and their applications. Regarding knowledge, consistent actions are needed at the education level in the EU (and other countries), targeting curriculum development, open forms of education [16, 20] and open access teaching materials. It is also necessary to cooperate in educational research and to strengthen the cooperation of the education sector with experts (from the field of cyber security, but also psychologists and psychotherapists) and companies. Work is needed on this educational offer aimed at groups with diverse needs and levels of advancement [16, 36]. Continuing education on cyber threats requires motivation. One way of doing this is to formally recognise qualifications and reward them financially in the career advancement system [20]. Courses should have different levels of difficulty due to the complexity of cybersecurity issues. The course content should be directly linked to the teaching practice of teachers and the content of the curriculum. Media and the problems arising from their use will be a permanent part of social reality. Cyber threats is an interdisciplinary area and concerns not only technical and IT problems, but also psychological, social, legal and ethical aspects. In this context, the knowledge and pedagogical skills involved in getting to know students and diagnosing the problems they may face are equally important. Teachers must be also prepared for it. The next issue is to support parents. Media and cyber threats have an impact on mental health of children [17]. The psychological safety and well-being of students are further challenges that it is up to the teacher to create a safe environment [39] in which every member of the community is 'visible' and can count on support and help. We are touching on issues of personal and social security here. An important issue is to build trust between all the links related to education (institutions, teachers, parents, children). It is important to develop universal solutions and good practices while evaluating effectively and level of knowledge. The volatility inherent in the development of new technologies and the associated risks requires constant updates. As mentioned before this implies space for closer cooperation between schools and teacher training institutions with universities (researchers, academic teachers focused on teaching methods and EdTech) [24]. Putting knowledge into practice requires continuous evaluation of the effectiveness of educational projects, factors influencing efficiency of education [24] but also to identify existing barriers. These activities may take the form of bottom-up initiatives, e.g. at the level of a voivodeship (provincial, city), but it is difficult to imagine comprehensive institutional, educational and social activities without the mobilisation of appropriate financial resources (e.g grants, competitions). Developing solutions requires the implementation of international comparative research on teachers' knowledge of cyberthreats and their training needs (there are many reports available on teacher education). The proposals for educational content presented in the text can provide a draft for the development of a thematic outline for teacher training. A diagnosis of the state of education should be the first step to creating training systems oriented on cyber threats designed for teachers. It is also worth considering directing students' interests towards the area of cybersecurity. In literature [29], attention is drawn to the necessity of educating and retaining highly qualified people in the field of cybersecurity (by increasing the number of students choosing computer science in exams). The education system should be geared towards training future qualified personnel and should consider these competences as important in the context of future professions created in the education space [29]. Inspiring students today requires well-prepared teachers [29]. Therefore, it can be agreed that the foundation for change is the development of society [29], and the main goal is safety.

Disclosure of Interests. The authors have no competing interests to declare that are relevant to the content of this article.

References

1. Tomczyk, Ł., Potyrała, K.: How often are Polish teachers attacked online? Int. Rev. Victimology 1–15 (2024)
2. Wójcik, S.: Zagrożenia dzieci i młodzieży związane z używaniem Internetu. In: Sajkowska, M., Szredzińska, R. (eds.), Dzieci się liczą 2022. Raport o zagrożeniach bezpieczeństwa i rozwoju dzieci w Polsce. Fundacja Dajemy Dzieciom Siłę (2022).
3. Pyżalski, J.: Doświadczanie przemocy elektronicznej a naruszenie praw młodych ludzi w środowisku online. In: Dojrzeć do praw. Raport z monitoringu praw i podmiotowości dziecka w Polsce w dobie społeczeństwa informacyjnego, pp. 82-88. Orange Foundation, Warsaw (2023)
4. Jaskulska, S., et al.: Bullying and cyberbullying victimization and associated factors among adolescents in six European countries. Sustainability **14**(21), 14063 (2022)
5. Siemieniecka, D., Majewska, K.: The state of knowledge of teachers and educators in primary and secondary education on cyber threats challenging students on a daily basis - proposal of prevention and training areas. In: Chova, L.G., López Martínez, A., Lees, J. (eds.) ICERI2022 Proceedings, pp. 2781–2789. IATED Academy, Spain (2022)
6. Siemieniecka, D., Majewska, K.: Knowledge of Polish and British Teachers about Cyber Threats - A Comparative Study. The New Educational Review (2024)
7. Kumari, P., Srivastava, N.: Attitude and awareness towards cyber crime among perceptive teachers. J. Res. Educ. **9**(1), 85–96 (2021)
8. Rajender, K., Bikram, S., Mukesh, Y.: A study of cyber crime awareness among B. Ed. And M. Ed. Students of Sirsa District. J. Econ. Manage. Perspect. **11**(3), 74–84 (2017)
9. Bhutia, Y., Passah, E.R.: Cyber crime awareness among student-teacher of B. Ed in Relation to Internet Usage. Learn. Commun. **10**(1), 17–27 (2019)
10. Topal, A., Geçer, A., Akkaya, O., Güzel, Y., Of, M.: Examining of teacher candidates' knowledge levels about Cyber Crimes. Pamukkale Üniversitesi Eğitim Fakültesi Dergisi - Pamukkale Univ. J. Educ. **45**, 159–174 (2019)
11. Librus. How teachers gain knowledge. http://portal.librus.pl/szkola/artykuly/jak-nauczyciele-zdobywaja-wiedze, Accessed 26 Mar 2025
12. Kumari, S., Gautam, H., Nityadarshini, N., Das, B.K., Chudhry, R.: Online classes versus traditional classes? Comparison during COVID-19. J. Educ. Health Promot. **10**(1), 457 (2021)
13. Predictive Solutions. https://en.predictivesolutions.pl/en, Accessed 26 Mar 2025
14. Iskierka, S., Krzeminski, J., Weżgowiec, Z.: Technologia BYOD w polskich szkołach (BYOD technology in Polish schools). Dydaktyka Informatyki **10**, 80–89 (2015)
15. Caena, F., Redecker, C.: Aligning teacher competence frameworks to 21st century challenges: the case for the European digital competence framework for educators (DigCompEdu). Eur. J. Educ. **54**, 356–369 (2019)
16. Kuzminykh, I., Yevdokymenko, M., Yeremenko, O., Lemeshko, O.: Increasing teacher competence in cybersecurity using the EU security frameworks. Int. J. Modern Educ. Comput. Sci. **6**, 60–68 (2021)
17. Siemieniecka, D., Jarczyńska, J.: Relationship between social media use and adolescent mental health - a systematic review. Int. J. Pedagogy Innov. New Technol. 10/1 (2023)
18. Tech4Teachers white paper. Improving access and digital skills for teachers:challenges and opportunities, January 2024. https://digitalpovertyalliance.org, Accessed 26 Mar 2025
19. Krille, C.: Teachers' Participation in Professional Development: A Systematic Review. Springer, Germany (2020)

20. Phippen, A.: UK Schools Online Safety Policy & Practice Assessment. Annual Analysis of 360 degree safe self review data covering schools and colleges in England2021. https://swgfl.org.uk/assets/documents/uk-schools-online-safety-policy-and-practice-assessment-2021.pdf, Accessed 26 Mar 2025
21. Teacher Digital Skills, Education Scotland, Foghlam Alba. Available from: https://education.gov.scot/media/fdaf4yxe/teacher-digital-skills-draft2-011123.pdf, Accessed 26 Mar 2025
22. The cyber threat to education and academy trusts in the UK, Moore CleanComm. Available from: https://mooreks.co.uk/wp-content/uploads/2022/10/Cyber-Threat-to-Education.pdf?utm_medium=Insight+utm_medium=Insight+download&utm_campaign=Cyber-Threat-to-Education, Accessed 26 Mar 2025
23. National Cyber Secure. All UK schools offered free cyber service to protect against online threats. https://www.ncsc.gov.uk/news/all-uk-schools-offered-free-cyber-service-to-protect-against-online-threats, Accessed 26 Mar 2025
24. DfE. Realising the potential of technology in education: a strategy for education providers and the technology industry. https://assets.publishing.service.gov.uk/media/5f92bd1fe90e077afc99d48f/Realising_the_potential_of_technology_in_education_summary_report.pdf, Accessed 26 Mar 2025
25. Guidance Essential digital skills framework, Department for Education. https://www.gov.uk/government/publications/essential-digital-skills-framework/essential-digital-skills-framework, Accessed 26 Mar 2025
26. Ofqual. poll highlights value of cyber security training in schools. https://www.gov.uk/government/news/ofqual-poll-highlights-value-of-cyber-security-training-in-schools, Accessed 26 Mar 2025
27. Jackson, F.: One-Third of UK Teachers Lack Cybersecurity Training, While 34% Experience Security Incidents, TechRepublic. https://www.techrepublic.com/article/uk-teachers-cybersecurity-training/, Accessed 26 Mar 2025
28. Guidance Teaching online safety in schools, Department for Education: Updated 12 January 2023. https://www.gov.uk/government/publications/teaching-online-safety-in-schools/teaching-online-safety-in-schools, Accessed 26 Mar 2025
29. National Cyber Strategy 2022 Pioneering a cyber future with the whole of the UK. https://assets.publishing.service.gov.uk/media/6201326a8fa8f5388f444f1a/national-cyber-strategy-large-print.pdf, Accessed 26 Mar 2025
30. Polityka Cyfrowej Transformacji Edukacji. Diagnoza.https://www.google.com/url?sa=t&source=web&rct=j&opi=89978449&url=https://www.gov.pl/attachment/02cc2285-f376-4222-b185-2923278aadf1&ved=2ahUKEwj19K6cp6eMAxXdFxAIHQwiI5sQFnoECCAQAQ&usg=AOvVaw2nRtNr5svTZl4BqQgzd8v6, Accessed 26 Mar 2025
31. Liontas, J., i Karagoz, I.: Digital pedagogy. A look forward. In: Sözler, S. (eds.), Digital Transformation in EFL Settings - An Open and Distance Learning Perspective, pp. 189-212. Nobel Akademik Yayıncılık (2023)
32. Cyfrowa szkoła 4.0, Raport Związku Cyfrowa Polska. https://cyfrowapolska.org/wp-content/uploads/2024/03/Raport_Cyfrowa_Szkola_4.pdf, Accessed 26 Mar 2025
33. Rada Ministrów, Uchwała nr 98 Rady Ministrów z dnia 12 września 2024 r. w sprawie przyjęcia polityki publicznej pod nazwą "Polityka Cyfrowej Transformacji Edukacji". Monitor Polski. Dziennik Urzędowy Rzeczypospolitej Polskiej, 12 września 2024.https://dziennikustaw.gov.pl/M2024000081201.pdf, Accessed 26 Mar 2025
34. Majewska, K.: Virtual reality, interactive whiteboard lessons or traditional education? Analysis of the degree of acceptance of individual forms of activity by students at the level of early school education. Edukacja Elementarna w Teorii i Praktyce 18, **2**(69), 55-71 (2023)
35. Amankwa, E.: Relevance of cybersecurity education at pedagogy levels in schools. J. Inf. Secur. **12**, 233–249 (2021)

36. Hean, S.: Strengthening the links between practice and education in the development of collaborative competence frameworks (2015)
37. Essential digital skills framework, Crown (2018). https://assets.publishing.service.gov.uk/media/5b9246d4e5274a4236952309/Essential_digital_skills_framework.pdf, Accessed 26 Mar 2025
38. How simulation in Education Benefits Students and Patients.https://www.usa.edu/blog/simulation-in-education/Accessed 26 Mar 2025
39. Reeves, M. A., Kanan, L. M., Plog, A. E.: Comprehensive planning for safe learning environments: A school professional's guide to integrating physical and psychological safety – Prevention through recovery. New York, NY: Routledge (2010)

The Role of Critical Pedagogy in Searching for a New Model of Digital Education in Poland

Konrad Ciesiołkiewicz(✉)

Korczak University, Warsaw, Poland
konrad.ciesiolkiewicz@gmail.com

Abstract. The analysis indicates that the dominant models of digital education in today's educational practices in Poland do not adequately address all the needs and challenges faced by children and youth in the new media environment. There is a need to explore a more holistic approach, emphasizing a comprehensive understanding of competence and maintaining the proper balance between its components: attitude, knowledge, and skills. The undervalued source for the new integrated model presented in this paper is the stream of critical pedagogy, viewed as a necessary condition for enhancing the agency of individuals and social groups, as well as promoting the democratization of society.

Keywords: digital education · digital media · new media · critical pedagogy

1 Introduction

In public discourse, there is a noticeable conviction that institutions responsible for formal, non-formal, and informal education are failing to keep pace with the rapid technological advancements and the dynamic social transformations occurring under the influence of pervasive digital media. There is no doubt that it is necessary to search for new approaches to digital, information, and media education offered to young people in the education system, but also in the activities of non-governmental organizations and popular culture in general. This task is even more urgent as we observe a growing penetration of services offered by digital platform and messaging service providers, including among minors who are not officially eligible to use them. An increasing number of young people are being influenced by algorithm-based recommendation systems, the mechanisms of which they are not even aware of.

2 Background

As part of the analysis in question, it is necessary to outline the key characteristics of the contemporary socio-political ecosystem and socio-economic context, which serve as the foundation for developing an integrated model that promotes the acquisition of competences essential for democratic citizenship. The profile can be defined by four fundamental characteristics.

Ł. Tomczyk (Ed.): NMP 2024, CCIS 2537, pp. 68–80, 2025.
https://doi.org/10.1007/978-3-031-95627-0_5

The first characteristic is the pervasive influence of information technology on social, economic, and political life, which is described in the literature through various approaches, depending on the adopted research framework and axiological perspective. The starting point should be the intense mediatization of public life, understood as "the process of media mediation in the understanding of the world, the influence of media on the perception of reality inaccessible to direct experience, along with the consequences of such mediation: shaping the image of the entire social reality and even comprehensive social experiences under the influence of media constructions" [1]. According to Magdalena Szpunar, new media – digital media – "are entering almost all spheres of human activity with force, transforming labor relations, communication processes, the nature of interpersonal relationships, leisure time, and even the sphere of spirituality" [2]. The most commonly used categories to describe these transformations include "electronic republic" [3], "media democracy" [4], "media policy" [5], "teledemocracy", "electronic democracy", "cyberdemocracy", and "electronic democratization" [1]. Importantly, most of these categories also express a certain degree of hope placed in the development of new media as a means of strengthening the agency of individuals and social groups, as well as processes of democratization. Different beliefs have recently begun to emerge within public discourse. These perspectives are advocated, for example, by Shoshana Zuboff, who highlights the social costs of "surveillance capitalism" [6]; Yanis Varoufakis, who labels the contemporary economic system as harmful "technofeudalism" [7]; and Christian Fuchs, who identifies the dominance of "digital authoritarianism", rooted in the concept of authoritarian leadership, nationalism, acceptance of violence, and a Manichean worldview that divides people into "us - friends" and "them - enemies" [8]. All of them draw on critical theory, albeit to varying degrees.

The second characteristic is a noticeable tendency to challenge the values of the democratic system. According to the think tank Economist Intelligence Unit, which monitors the political systems of countries and publishes the annual Democracy Index, in 2023, only 8 percent of societies lived in full democracies, 40 percent in authoritarian regimes, and nearly the same percentage in flawed democracies. The authors of the report state that existing democracies and the institutions they have established are struggling to cope with strong tendencies toward conflict, violence, and the increasingly widespread use of authoritarian methods [9]. Given the Polish context of the analysis, it should be noted that Poland is once again classified as a flawed democracy. Over the past few years, it has experienced declines in the media freedom index published by the "Reporters Without Borders" organization. In the ranking of 180 countries, it fell from 18th place in 2015 to 66th place in 2022 [10]. The 2023 Liberties Media Freedom Report also highlighted difficulties in accessing public information in Poland and the absence of systemic solutions to tackle the growing problem of hate speech [11].

Another distinguishing factor of the modern socio-political ecosystem is the low level of social trust. According to the latest IPSOS research, an average of 30 percent of people worldwide believe that others can be trusted. The vast majority maintains a significant distance. Poland ranks among the countries with the lowest levels of trust globally. In Poland, only 16 percent of respondents answer affirmatively when asked whether other people can be trusted [12]. The low level of trust, leading to deficits in social capital, has persisted in Poland for many years.

Particular attention should be given to the mental health crisis among minors, which has been exacerbated by the COVID-19 pandemic. It is estimated that over 13% of children globally suffer from depression [13]. Sadness is an emotion experienced by as many as 17 percent of second-grade primary school students in Poland. Another study found that the three most commonly experienced difficult emotions among high school students are agitation and irritability (72 percent), discouragement and fatigue (62 percent), and helplessness (57 percent) [14].

According to official police data in Poland, six teenagers attempt suicide each day. Additionally, between 2012 and 2023, an increase in suicide attempts among children and adolescents was reported [15]. In the report by the "Life Worth Talking About" organization, which focuses on this phenomenon, the key direct and indirect risk factors associated with the internet were identified and described. The first group includes exposure to content related to suicidal behaviors, the influence of algorithms on social media, the possibility of forming suicide pacts with other users, online incitement to suicide, descriptions of detailed suicide methods and attempts, as well as the romanticization and glorification of suicidal death. The indirect risk factors identified include: the impact of social media on lowered self-esteem among teenagers, peer violence online, the phenomenon of loneliness in the digital space, desensitization to aggression in online games and media reports, addiction to internet and social media usage, practically unlimited access to pornography, which contributes to the brutalization of teenagers' sexual lives, and the deprivation of needs caused by constant comparisons with others on social media [15].

The final characteristic of the contemporary socio-political ecosystem worth highlighting is the phenomena emerging within the digital environment. Being aware of the limitations related to their selective selection and frequent emphasis on risky aspects, highlighting some of them appears essential for further discussion. It should be noted that digital media, operating within a commercial paradigm, do not inherently prioritize the best interests of the child. As a result, this space becomes a breeding ground for abuse, domination, aggression, and violence against young people. For 68.4% of Polish teenagers, hate speech is a significant problem on the internet. Nearly half of them report exposure to antisocial content on social media, 43.7% believe that it is impossible to distinguish between true and false information online, and 49.9% are not concerned with the credibility of profiles and their authors on social media. Loneliness in this environment affects as many as 53.9% of respondents, while 4 out of 10 teenagers report low self-esteem [16]. According to the international Youth Skills study, Polish youth is the most exposed to harmful content and hate speech online compared to five other countries [17]. Sonia Livingstone highlights that a higher level of practical digital skills does not necessarily lead to a higher level of well-being among young people. A higher level of digital skills, particularly in content creation, is accompanied by an increased risk of exposure to harmful materials, including discriminatory, racist, self-harm, and anorexia-related content, among others [18]. A relatively new phenomenon studied in relation to children and youth is disinformation and conspiracy theories. According to American research, 80 percent of teenagers who use social media have encountered conspiracy narratives. In turn, 81 percent of them tend to believe in certain conspiracy theories [18]. Jan Kreft observes that digital platforms, while promising an experience of agency, in practice marginalize social control and objectify users, resulting in the paradox of controlled agency [19]. An example of the negative impact of algorithms is the "rabbit hole" phenomenon, where users become trapped by continuously following recommendations generated by social media recommendation systems. The report on the experiment involving minors was documented by the international organization Amnesty International. In the document titled "Driven into the Darkness", Amnesty International demonstrated how quickly TikTok's algorithms suggest increasingly harmful content affecting minors' mental health, including material related to mental illnesses, suicide instructions, and the glamorization of death [20].

The Polish socio-economic context in this regard is, to some extent, reflected in the Digital Economy and Society Index (DESI), which has been conducted in the European Union since 2014, as well as in the local characteristics of socio-digital exclusion. DESI monitors 32 indicators across four areas, based on which it determines the level of digital maturity. These include human capital (including digital competences), connectivity (infrastructure), the digital transformation of enterprises, and the scale and quality of public service digitalization. In the overall ranking, Poland is below the EU average, placing 24th. In terms of digital competences, the EU average among individuals aged 16–74 is 54%, while in Poland, it stands at 43% [21]. Social inequalities in Poland have been growing faster than in other countries. According to the report by the European Bank for Reconstruction and Development, social inequality in Poland has been growing slightly faster than in other countries. While in 2016, 40% of income inequality was determined by factors beyond citizens' control (including family background), by 2022, such independent factors accounted for as much as half. In Poland, parental status accounts for 77% of the total inequality of opportunities, while place of birth contributes 18% [22]. Considering the aspect of social inequalities, it should be noted that, according to the Organization for Economic Co-operation and Development (OECD), the phenomenon of digital exclusion is an integral part of the discussion on inequalities among individuals, households, enterprises, and regions. There are two types of digital exclusion. The first type is related to access to infrastructure, devices, software, and digital services. The second type of exclusion considers aspects of competence, motivation, and exclusion based on how new technologies are used [23]. Therefore, the term that better describes the author's area of interest is socio-digital exclusion, understood as the phenomenon "of the permanent structural limitation of the life chances of individuals and local communities due to the overlapping and mutually reinforcing effects of unfavorable social and economic conditions and deficits related to the ability to use digital services. The fundamental mechanism here is the feedback loop, in which the infrastructural, income, cultural, mental and competence conditions for using technology cause and are simultaneously shaped by social and economic inequalities (income disparities, educational inequalities, differences in cultural capital)" [23]. When creating the Local Exclusion Index for the needs of educational projects, the team, which also included the author, took into account 30 indicators in four dimensions of exclusion: social exclusion (low social capital, intensity of the problem of poverty and unemployment), economic exclusion (local economy, activity of enterprises), digital exclusion (disparities in access to telecommunications infrastructure), educational exclusion (differences in the education of children's parents, educational results in primary schools). According to the aforementioned index, approximately 20% of Polish municipalities have been identified as being at high risk of social and digital exclusion [23]. The low performance of Polish students in the global PISA (Programme for International Student Assessment) [24] studies on social and emotional competences is a cause for concern. Polish teenagers scored significantly below average in emotional control, stress resistance, assertiveness, empathy, cooperation, curiosity, and perseverance [25].

To summarize this part of the argument, it is important to highlight a certain paradox within pedagogical practice in Poland, as well as in many other countries. This concerns the lack of inclusion of digital media issues in school curricula, particularly regarding social media platforms, recommendation systems, and the impact of algorithms.

The scope of digital education in the core curricula is almost exclusively limited to the subject of computer science. Other elements important from the perspective of these considerations are implemented selectively through voluntary programs, often carried out in cooperation with non-governmental organizations. Moreover, the still dominant lecture-based methods of knowledge transmission in schools are compounded by a lack of readiness to address new challenges, such as those related to the digital environment. In the most recent EU Kids Online study, 64.5% of teenagers reported that they are not being engaged at school in conversations about their online activities, what concerns them (56.4%), or why some internet content is positive while other content is harmful (45.5%) [26].

3 Research Hypothesis and Method

Considering the socio-political conditions outlined above, the author proposes the following hypothesis: critical pedagogy of digital media constitutes a key component of a new integrated model of informational, digital, and media education and serves as a necessary condition for strengthening individual agency, empowering social groups, and fostering the democratization of society. To verify this, selected models and their characteristic approaches to digital, information, and media competences will be analyzed and interpreted through the perspective of critical media pedagogy. For this purpose, the author will use selected subject literature on digital education, media education, media pedagogy, literature from the canon of critical pedagogy, as well as official documents of international organizations, including the European Union and UNESCO, which outline competency models related to digital education. All of them have been indicated in Sect. 4. Based on this, a new integrated model will be presented, characterized by its distinctive features and incorporating the most significant aspects of the currently prevailing approaches to education in this field.

4 Review of Dominant Approaches to Education and Digital Media

Based on the literature on the subject, including the European Digital Competence Framework (DigComp) [27], the Council of Europe's reference framework for competencies supporting democratic culture [28], UNESCO's ICT competence framework [29], the Catalog of Media, Information, and Digital Competencies of the Modern Poland

Foundation [30], the analyses of Douglas Kellner and Jeff Share [31], David Buckingham [32], Len Masterman [33], Canadian critical educators Lorayne Robertson and Joli Scheider-Benns [34], as well as Paulo Freire [35], Henry Giroux [36], and Tomasz Szkudlarek [37], the following three dominant approaches to education in the field of digital, informational, and media competencies can be identified: techno-pessimistic, artistic, and technocratic. The following description of each takes into account the general attitude toward digital media, the key values affirmed, and the role of the teacher.

The techno-pessimistic trend is defined by a negative perception of digital media and their prevailing influence. The key value emphasized in this approach is the need to protect and ensure the safety of the youngest individuals. The role of the teacher is primarily to act as a guardian and an instructor in the field of safety knowledge. On the other hand, the artistic approach, focuses on the opportunities for creative development created by new media. In this approach, self-expression, creativity, and individualism are highly valued. The teacher serves as a mentor, and the relationship with the students can be described as a master-student dynamic. According to the third and most commonly encountered approach—the technocratic approach—the development of digital media is primarily centered on economic opportunities, career advancement, and the enhancement of social status. The axiology of this trend is defined by individual success and efficiency, with the teacher being perceived as a technological expert.

In this context, attention should be paid to the diverse approaches to competence and the lack of a coherent definition of this concept. Paradoxically, the most striking example can be found in the European Digital Competence Framework [27], which serves as the foundational document for the public policies of European Union countries. Competencies are perceived there as a set of precisely formulated skills—abilities in performing various activities at different levels. This is an approach typical of the technocratic trend. It is easy to notice that in the artistic trend, we also find a similar understanding of competencies. In this approach, individual creative abilities, although motivated by a slightly different axiology, are also perceived, with a focus mainly on the sphere of praxis – the final cultural product. For the purpose of this analysis, competencies will be understood as attitudes (closely related to axiology), knowledge, and practical skills [38].

The term "digital education" is also used imprecisely. In public discourse, this concept is usually understood in a technocratic way and strongly linked to technical skills. Using the catalog created by the Modern Poland Foundation, it can be pointed out that digital education encompasses informational, media, and digital competencies, which are inextricably linked. The list includes the following thematic areas: using information, the individual in the media environment, the language of media, creativity in using media, ethics, security, law, economic aspects, media actions, digital skills, mobile security [30].

An addition to the dominant approaches to education is the field of critical pedagogy. Its source is the critical theory of the Frankfurt School, whose main representatives were Max Horkheimer, Theodor Adorno, Herbert Marcuse, and Erich Fromm. They subjected mass media to thorough criticism, which they referred to as the "culture industry", emphasizing that culture becomes one of many commodities and is excessively subject to economic laws that objectify the public sphere, civic values, and the recipients themselves, who are drawn into a consumerist trance, unaware of the processes and actual intentions behind the media system [39]. This trend is currently developed, among others, by Henry Giroux and Tomasz Szkudlarek, whose observations will be referenced later in the discussion.

The basic assumptions of critical pedagogy can be based on three pillars. First, the task of theory is to describe and analyze educational and social processes, taking into account all conflicts. In this context, the analysis of power, located in various parts of the political and media system, is very important. The second aspect is the need for social change. It is dependent on having a distinct ethical compass—an axiological system—in which values such as equality, emancipation, social justice, community, and empowerment hold a central place. In this context, education is synonymous with liberation from a state of ignorance. The last pillar is taking appropriate actions in an inclusive, dialogical, and participatory manner [37]. This issue is related to the rejection of the banking concept of education, referred to by Paulo Freire as "depository education" [35], in which the teacher is presented as the one who knows everything, and the student is seen through the lens of deficits. The role of the second one is merely to listen and follow the instructions of the instructor. Freire and other critical educators oppose this approach with authentic dialogue. However, for it to exist, love for the world and people, humility, faith in people, and hope for social change are needed [35]. In dialogue, students and the instructor together "name the world", give it meaning, and humanize it [40].

As part of agency (both individual and within social groups), which is one of the fundamental goals of the digital, informational, and media education process, the need for special reflexivity is emphasized—defined as "readiness and ability for deep reflection on one's own actions" [40]. This includes communicative agency, purposeful action, a sense of distinctiveness and identity, and the pursuit of balance between external expectations and one's personal agenda. The opposing state is alienation and disempowerment [41]. The educational process is a conscious form of empowerment, driven by the conviction of the need for social change in favor of disadvantaged individuals and the undertaking of activities that strengthen and equalize conditions, provide power and increased autonomy, and lead to the reduction of dominance and the balancing of power [42].

Critical pedagogy, by its nature and its emphasis on balancing power, must remain responsive and address the most profound problems and conflicts of contemporary societies [36]. Critical pedagogy opposes an educational practice that focuses solely on adapting to existing socio-political conditions, arguing that such an approach perpetuates social structures that uphold and deepen inequalities. The task is not to reproduce existing structures but to drive systemic transformations within the public sphere.

Two concepts deserve particular emphasis. One is related to the civic sphere. Masterman considers media education an integral part of democratic education, striving to "transform the relationship between teacher and student by providing both sides with objects for reflection and dialogue. [...] By its very nature, it is activating and requires participation, enhancing the development of a more open and democratic pedagogy. He encourages students to take greater responsibility for the learning process" [33]. Tomasz Szkudlarek, in turn, introduces the category of "pedagogy of distance" as the essence of critical media education. In his view, it must serve a dual role, "affirming the meanings constructed by young people during the process of media reception, while also teaching them to maintain distance from these constructed meanings" [43]. The role of the teacher in this process is distinctive, as they must personally engage with pressing social and political issues, viewing their work as a challenge to involve others in the public sphere. They cannot be limited solely to the execution of technically defined tasks. The teacher must be loyal to the group and society while remaining self-critical of the methods employed. They should demonstrate exceptional civic courage by speaking out publicly in support of the vulnerable and striving to transform social structures. Their key task is not so much the didactic transmission of knowledge, but organizing a space for dialogue and communal work, in which they themselves are not the holder of the only truth. Giroux refers to this style of work and the public role of the teacher as the "transformative intellectual" [44].

To summarize this part of the discussion, it is important to emphasize that critical pedagogy introduces a fourth approach to education and digital media, which, for the purposes of this analysis, the author refers to as the reflective-critical approach. He maintains a distanced and, to some extent, ambivalent attitude towards the development of digital media, conditioning it by many factors, primarily the structure of the media system that creates the digital environment and its impact on a specific community. The aforementioned axiology encompasses values such as equality, social justice, democracy, individual agency, and community. In this paradigm, the teacher is not, unlike in other approaches, a master to imitate and listen to, nor a disciplining guardian, but rather a facilitator of the educational process, focusing on addressing inequalities and advocating for the unheard.

5 The Proposed Model of Digital Education

Taking into account that all the previously discussed trends play an important role, as they address social needs, the author of the article proposes a new, integrated, three-component model of digital education (see Fig. 1). All its components should be interpreted through the prism of competencies – attitudes, knowledge, and practical skills. In the area of attitudes, the field of critical pedagogy complements other approaches with the previously mentioned values. It combines elements of information, media, and digital education.

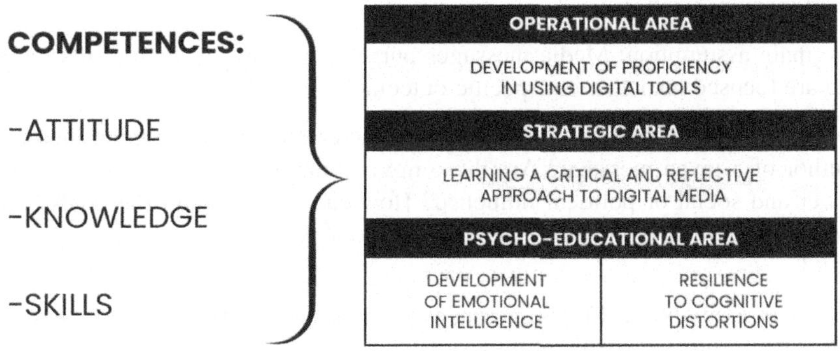

Fig. 1. Integrated model of digital education

The first area of the model includes psychoeducation, which assumes the development of emotional intelligence and the cognitive sphere in terms of awareness and the ability to recognize basic cognitive distortions. Emotional intelligence refers to the ability to accurately recognize one's own emotions and those of others, to feel empathy, to express feelings, and to regulate emotions – using emotions to better understand complex social reality, learning, and development [45]. Emotional intelligence is also called social intelligence, as it forms the basis for the development of social competencies such as assertiveness, cooperation, relationship building, social resilience, and prosocial behavior [46]. In the development of emotional intelligence, particularly as a prevention of all forms of violence in the digital media environment, the key seems to be the use of programs that foster empathy, recognized as the most effective protective factor, as exemplified by the research-based Impact program [47]. In building resilience to cognitive distortions, it is important to teach the distinction between controlled and automatic thinking, that is, simplified and trap-generating thinking that leads to far-reaching social consequences—such as susceptibility to misinformation, strong polarization, online violence, hate speech, and many other actions that meet the criteria of radicalization. An example of an intervention could be the Precobias program for teachers and social workers working with youth, created at the request of the European Commission. It provides knowledge about the most common cognitive distortions and exercises that enable their recognition. The discussed distortions include: the authority effect, the in-group and out-group effect, the confirmation bias, positive retrospection, the negativity bias, the foot-in-the-door technique, the hostile media effect, the superiority of image over content effect, the humor effect, and the oversleeping effect [48].

The second area of the proposed model of digital education, which is the strategic one, involves learning a critical and reflective approach to digital media. Below is an example of a methodological framework used to conduct classes in the form of a dialogue with students. It was built based on the critical experiences of Canadian educators [34] and the guidelines of Kellner and Share [49].

- The main assumption: All media messages are constructed in such a way as to provide us with a limited, narrowed version of reality.

Questions: What version of reality does a given media message present? To what extent does it reflect your reality and experiences? How can you compare it to your own world of meanings and values?

- The main assumption: Media messages pursue persuasive goals towards recipients and are focused on achieving specific outcomes.

Questions: What could be the intention of the creators of a particular medium and the author of a given message? Are these more commercial goals or are they related to power and social or political influence? How can you interpret the goals behind a message or a particular medium? What could your reaction be, and what can you do about it?

- The main assumption: Media messages are not neutral. They always carry certain values and promote specific attitudes.

Questions: What values and points of view do the analyzed messages represent? What points of view are missing in the given material? How would you supplement this material?

- The main assumption: Media and their messages are designed to influence a selected audience, reaching them in various ways.

Questions: For which social groups was this message constructed? What is the basis for this assumption? How might other individuals and social groups perceive this message, for example, from the perspective of gender, ability/disability, health status, age, poverty, sexual and religious minorities, and others? What could be the response of these groups to the given message? What could be your response?

- The main assumption: Media messages are often based on stereotypes, either by portraying or mocking them. Stereotypes are usually harmful.

Questions: What stereotypes are present in the given message, and which ones have been avoided? To what extent do the characteristics attributed to certain individuals and social groups align with your personal experiences with such people? How can you influence the change of harmful perceptions of others? How would you change the structure of the message to avoid harming stigmatized social groups?

- The main assumption: As an independent critic of digital media, you can modify content and replace it with a positive and empowering message.

Questions: How would you modify the given message? What could you say, write, or record and produce to create a constructive message?

- The main assumption: Digital media (including social media) rely on algorithms and artificial intelligence, building knowledge about your preferences, trapping you in bubbles of your own interests, communities, and content that often confirm your point of view and beliefs.

Questions: To what extent do you try to step outside your own social media bubbles, seeking sources, social groups, and content that are not automatically suggested to you? How do you search for information and knowledge on the internet? How often do you switch your social media accounts to chronological mode? What distortions can arise, and what stereotypes can be reinforced during the creation of algorithms?

The third area of the integrated model of digital education involves developing skills and proficiency in using tools. To a large extent, this component is visible in the models developed within the techno-pessimistic, artistic, and technocratic approaches.

6 Conclusions

By incorporating the constitutive elements of critical pedagogy and holism, the new integrated model of digital education can address the most pressing social needs, including intensive processes of mediatization, anti-democratic tendencies, low levels of social trust, the crisis of mental health in children and youth, and concerning phenomena in the digital environment, such as the influence of algorithms on human behavior. Its inclusion in the public education system would also make it an instrument for reducing social inequalities. However, it is only a preliminary proposal that requires further research.

References

1. Prędkowicz, D.: E-demokracja. Zastosowanie nowych technik informacji i komunikacji w życiu publiczno-politycznym – początkiem nowej ery demokracji. Służba Cywilna **10**, 79–85 (2005)
2. Szpunar, M.: Czym są nowe media – próba konceptualizacji. Studia Medioznawcze **4**(35), 31–40 (2008)
3. Grossman, L.: Republika elekroniczna. In: Szczupaczyński, J. (ed.) Władza i społeczeństwo, part 2, pp. 285–293. Scholar, Warsaw (1998)
4. Michalczyk, S.: Demokracja medialna. Teoretyczna analiza problem. Wydawnictwo Adam Marszałek, Torun (2010)
5. Castells, M.: Władza komunikacji. Wydawnictwo Naukowe PWN, Warsaw (2013)
6. Zuboff, S.: Wiek kapitalizmu inwigilacji. Wydawnictwo Zysk i S-ka, Poznan (2020)
7. Varoufakis, Y.: Technofeudalizm. Co zabiło kapitalizm? Wydawnictwo Glowbook, Sieradz (2024)
8. Fuchs, C.: Social media. A critical introduction. 3th edn. Sage, London (2021)
9. Economist Intelligence: Democracy Index 2023, https://www.eiu.com/n/campaigns/democracy-index-2023/, Accessed 27 Jan 2025
10. Wikipedia: Wskaźnik wolności prasy, https://pl.wikipedia.org/wiki/Wska%C5%BAnik_wolno%C5%9Bci_prasy, Accessed 27 Jan 2025
11. Civil Liberties Union for Europe: Liberties Media Freedom Report 2023, https://dq4n3btxmr8c9.cloudfront.net/files/lurkq7/Liberties_Media_Freedom_Report_2023.pdf, Accessed 27 Jan 2025
12. Ipsos: Interpersonal Trust Across The World, https://www.ipsos.com/sites/default/files/ct/news/documents/2022-03/Global%20Advisor%20-%20Interpersonal%20Trust%202022%20-%20Graphic%20Report_1.pdf, last accessed 2025/01/27
13. UNICEF Poland: Kryzys zdrowia psychicznego, https://unicef.pl/chce-pomoc/nasze-akcje/ratowanie-zycia-dzieci/kryzys-zdrowia-psychicznego, Accessed 27 Jan 2025
14. Tomaszewska, K., Ciesielska, A.: Zdrowie psychiczne dzieci i młodzieży. Przyczyny kryzysu, https://www.gov.pl/web/cyfryzacja-badania-i-projektowanie/zdrowie-psychiczne-dzieci-i-mlodziezy, Accessed 27 Jan 2025
15. Witkowska, H., Kicińska, L., Palma, J., Łuba, M.: Zrozumieć, aby zapobiec 2024 – zachowania samobójcze wśród dzieci i młodzieży. II edycja raportu na podstawie danych KGP i serwisu www.zwjr.pl, Serwis Życie Warte Jest Rozmowy, Warsaw (2024)
16. Lange, R., et al.: Nastolatki 3.0. Raport z ogólnopolskiego badania uczniów i rodziców. NASK, Warsaw (2023)
17. d'Haenens, L., Joris, W., Bossens, E.: Syntehis of ySKILLS results, https://www.hf.uio.no/imk/english/research/center/children-media/publications/reports/yskills/d7.1---synthesis-of-yskills-results.pdf, last accessed 2025/01/27
18. Livingstone, S., Stoilova, M., Rahali, M.: Respect, protect, fulfil: how digital literacy enables the realisation of children's rights, https://yskills.eu/respect-protect-fulfil-how-digital-literacy-enables-the-realisation-of-childrens-rights/, Accessed 27 Jan 2025
19. Amnesty International: Driven into Darkness: How TikTok's 'For You' Feed Encourages Self-Harm and Suicidal Ideation, https://www.amnesty.org/en/documents/pol40/7350/2023/en/, Accessed 27 Jan 2025

20. Kreft, J.: Władza platform. Za fasadą Google, Facebooka i Spotify. Univeristas, Krakow (2022)
21. Komisja Europejska: Indeks gospodarki cyfrowej i społeczeństwa cyfrowego (DESI), https://digital-strategy.ec.europa.eu/pl/policies/desi, Accessed 16 Mar 2025
22. Siemionczyk, G.: Polska nie jest już krajem równych szans. Sytuacja się pogarsza, https://www.money.pl/gospodarka/polska-nie-jest-juz-krajem-rownych-szans-sytuacja-sie-pogarsza-7077421308767200a.html, Accessed 16 Mar 2025
23. Bartol, A., Herbst, J., Pierścińska, A.: Wykluczenie społeczno-cyfrowe w Polsce. Stan zjawiska, trendy, rekomendacje. Fundacja Stocznia i Fudacja Orange, Warsaw (2021)
24. PISA: Badanie PISA., https://pisa.ibe.edu.pl/, Accessed 16 Mar 2025
25. Konczal, M.: Ekspert pokazał wyniki polskich uczniów. Te kompetencje są na najniższym poziomie, https://strefaedukacji.pl/ekspert-pokazal-wyniki-polskich-uczniow-te-kompetencje-sa-na-najnizszym-poziomie-znacznie-ponizej-sredniej/ar/c5-18271077, Accessed 16 Mar 2025
26. Pyżalski, J., Zdrodowska, A., Tomczyk, Ł., Abramczuk, K.: Polskie badanie EU Kids Online 2018. Najważniejsze wyniki i wnioski. Wydawnictwo Naukowe UAM, Poznan (2019)
27. DigComp: Europejskie Ramy Kompetencji Cyfrowych w Polsce. https://www.digcomp.pl/, Accessed 27 Jan 2025
28. Paush, M., Hladschik, P., Pazderski, F., Nagem, R.: Odporność na tendencje antydemokratyczne przez edukację. Poradnik dla pracowników socjalnych i osób pracujących z młodzieżą. Rada Europy – Instytut Spraw Publicznych, Salzburg–Strasbourg–Toulouse–Vienna–Warsaw (2021)
29. UNESCO: UNESCO ICT Competency Framework for Teachers, https://unesdoc.unesco.org/ark:/48223/pf0000265721, Accessed 27 Jan 2025
30. Budzisz, W., et al.: Katalog kompetencji medialnych, informacyjnych i cyfrowych (2014). https://edukacjamedialna.edu.pl/media/chunks/attachment/Katalog_kompetencji_medialnych_2014_EudBrrI.pdf, Accessed 27 Jan 2025
31. Kellner, D., Share, J.: Critical media literacy is not an option. Learn. Inquiry **1**, 59–69 (2007)
32. Buckingham, D.: The Media Education Manifesto. Polity Press, Cambridge (2019)
33. Ogonowska, A.: Współczesna edukacja medialna: teoria i rzeczywistość. Wydawnictwo Naukowe Uniwersytetu Pedagogicznego, Krakow (2013)
34. Robertson, L., Scheider-Benns, J.: Critical media literacy as a transformative pedagogy. Literacy Inf. Comput. Educ. J. **7**(1), 2247–2253 (2016). Freire, P.: Pedagogy of the Oppressed. Penguin Random House (2017)
35. Freire, P.: Pedagogy of the Oppressed. Penguin Random House (2017)
36. Giroux, H.: On critical pedagogy. Bloomsbury Academic, London–New York–Oxford–New Dehli–Syndey (2020)
37. Szkudlarek, T.: Pedagogika krytyczna. In: Kwieciński, Z., Śliwerski, B. (eds.) Pedagogika. Podręcznik akademicki, pp. 574–575. PWN, Warsaw (2019)
38. Witkowski, J.: Zrozumieć kompetencje. Praktyki i podejścia sprzyjające systematycznemu rozwijaniu kompetencji w szkole, https://ceo.org.pl/zrozumiec-kompetencje/, Accessed 27 Jan 2025
39. Mersch, D.: Teorie mediów. Wydawnictwo Sic!, Warsaw (2010)
40. Mizerek, H.: Refleksja krytyczna w edukacji i pedagogice. Impuls, Krakow (2021)
41. Ciesiołkiewicz, K.: Kondycja dialogu społecznego i podmiotowości komunikacyjnej instytucji na przykładzie Rady Dialogu Społecznego. Newsline, Rzeszów (2023)
42. Szarfenberg, R.: Empowerment. In: Rysz-Kowalczyk, B., Szatur-Jaworska, B. (eds.) W kręgu pojęć i zagadnień współczesnej polityki społecznej, pp. 99–100. Wydawnictwo Uniwersytetu Warszawskiego, Warsaw (2016)
43. Szkudlarek, T.: Media. Szkic z filozofii i pedagogiki dystansu. Impuls, Krakow (2009)

44. Giroux, H.A.: Teachers as intellectuals. Bergin & Garvey, Wesport–Connecticut–London (1988)
45. Gerrig, R.J., Zimbardo, P.G.: Psychologia i życie. PWN, Warsaw (2009)
46. Matczak, A., Martowska, K.: Profil kompetencji społecznych. Podręcznik. Pracowania Testów Psychologicznych Polskiego Towarzystwa Psychologicznego, Warsaw (2013)
47. Impact: Interdyscyplinarny Model Przeciwdziałania Agresji i Cyberprzemocy Technologicznej, https://impact.fdds.pl/, Accessed 27 Jan 2025
48. Bouko, C., Krempaska, A., Kucińska, A.: Stop radykalizacji. Jak uodpornić młodych ludzi na treści ekstremistyczne w sieci? Krytyczne myślenie i świadomość roli błędów poznawczych w procesie radykalizacji, https://www.precobias.eu/toolkit/teachers/PRECOBIAS-Toolkit-for-teachers-PL.pdf, Accessed 27 Jan 2025
49. Kellner, D., Share, J.: Toward Critical Media Literacy: Core concepts, debates, organizations, and policy. Disc. Stud. Cult. Polit. Educ. **26**, 374–377 (2005)

Beyond Tools: Navigating Pedagogical Innovation in Postdigital Classrooms

Martina Manna(✉) and Maka Eradze

University of L'Aquila, Viale Nizza 14, 67100 L'Aquila, Italy
{martina.manna,maka.eradze}@univaq.it

Abstract. Nowadays, emerging technologies are not simply tools to facilitate learning but are becoming an integral part of how knowledge is created, shared, and experienced. Defining pedagogical innovation in such a complex landscape is not an easy task. Traditionally, two instrumentalist perspectives have guided the conceptualization of pedagogical innovation: it can be either driven by technology or by pedagogy. To move beyond this binary vision, Fawns (2019) proposed the idea of entangled pedagogy, which serves as a foundation for envisioning future classrooms as environments where technology is intricately woven into the sociotechnical landscape. Consequently, pedagogical innovation is not solely a matter of incorporating technological tools; rather, it involves reimagining teaching and learning in settings where the digital and non-digital are fully integrated, and it might shape and be shaped by collective imaginaries of how future classrooms should look like. However, anticipated futures of postdigital classrooms include a vague concept of pedagogical innovation, which remains blurred if not concretized in specific case-in-point. Therefore, focusing on the specific case of gen-AI, the authors of this paper collaborated with students of a teacher training program to go through the speculative production, enactment, and negotiation of future postdigital classrooms. Building on an integration of speculative methods and scenario design, the authors exploited the uncertainty as a prompt to inform visions of the future direction of education. The speculative practice helped to concretize the shape that pedagogical innovation may achieve in the postdigital era.

Keywords: Pedagogical innovation · Postdigital Classrooms · Collective Imaginaries

1 Introduction

1.1 Pedagogical Innovation, How Do We Get There in the Postdigital Era?

The idea of rethinking and enhancing education comes with the same collective sense of wonder on how emerging technologies should transform education that ancient mythology expressed towards the Chimera, a fearsome and fantastical creature, which was often depicted as a symbol of something unattainable or illusory. Remaining on the ancient

Ł. Tomczyk (Ed.): NMP 2024, CCIS 2537, pp. 81–94, 2025.
https://doi.org/10.1007/978-3-031-95627-0_6

logic of metaphors, allegories and similitudes to understand the world and its new phenomena, in Plato's Allegory of the Cave, prisoners were chained in a cave, only able to see shadows cast on a wall, which they believe to be the entirety of reality. When one prisoner was freed and exposed to the outside world, he realized the shadows were mere reflections of a broader, more complex reality. If thought carefully, this allegory can be useful to understand how the concept of pedagogical innovation has been traditionally conceived in education, on the one hand, and the shape it could achieve in the contemporary sociotechnical reality, on the other.

As several scholars underlined [1–4] traditional visions of potential futures, tools, and pedagogical innovations were primarily instrumentalist, focusing narrowly on either technological tools or pedagogical methods without considering the broader, interconnected context. Among the authors which tried to move beyond this dichotomy [3–5]. Fawns (2019) [6] introduced the concept of entangled pedagogy, which integrates technology seamlessly within the sociotechnical context [7]. These traditional, technology-driven or pedagogy-driven views of educational innovation can be seen as the shadows on the wall of the Plato cave; limited perspectives that do not fully capture the whole potential of what innovation can mean for education. Fawns' concept of entangled pedagogy parallels the freed prisoner's realization of a more comprehensive reality. Just as the freed prisoner understands the true nature of the world beyond the cave, entangled pedagogy encourages to move beyond simplistic dichotomies. This approach recognizes the complex interplay between technology, pedagogy, and the social and cultural environment, leading to a richer, more nuanced understanding of educational possibilities.

The abandonment of the instrumentalist and solutionist views of pedagogical innovation leads to embrace the postdigital and sociomaterial perspectives on education [8, 9] which means to exit the cave and to accept to be, at least initially, blinded by a new reality to be discovered, just like the prisoner who is blinded, at first, by the sunlight he had never known. As Jandrić et al.[1] highlighted, indeed: 'The postdigital is hard to define; messy; unpredictable; digital and analog; technological and non-technological; biological and informational. The postdigital is both a rupture in our existing theories and their continuation' (p.3) and again 'The postdigital' is a guiding idea, rather than an absolute or definitively bounded concept' (p. 4). Therefore, if we embrace the postdigital perspective we can assume that pedagogical innovation is about re-thinking how the teaching and learning experience happens in the sociotechnical environment [2] which means that pedagogical innovation shapes and is shaped by individual imaginations and/or collective imaginaries of how future classrooms should look like. It is, henceforth, through the study of those imaginaries that we will be able to move forward, to explore and to understand the direction that pedagogical innovation should follow to undertake the most valuable decisions in relation to the new reality which is unfolding in front of us.

However, it must be underlined that anticipated futures [10] of postdigital classrooms include a vaguely defined concept of pedagogical innovation which could remain blurred if not concretized in specific cases-in-point [11, 12]. Considering the impact of Generative Artificial Intelligence (GenAI) and Large Language Models (LLMs) on future educational policy and practices [13] the authors of this study focused on their crucial role as catalysts for reimagining the postdigital classroom, as well as on the consequences of this role on the envision of future imaginaries and on the collective creation of knowledge. By collaborating with students of a teacher education programme to go through the phases of speculative production, enactment, and negotiation of future postdigital classrooms and by building on speculative methods and design [14, 15] the authors exploited the uncertainty as a prompt to inform visions of the future direction of education [16], in general, and of pedagogical innovation, specifically, to understand the shape that this last one could reach in the postdigital era.

2 Methodological Notes

Conducting research on imaginaries of future classrooms to understand the direction that pedagogical innovation could undertake in the postdigital environment implies the embracement of what Catherine Hasse [17] defines as "Socratic Ignorance". According to the scholar, recognizing one's own ignorance is a fundamental prerequisite for creating a deeper understanding of how knowledge is produced, distributed, and interpreted in the postdigital era. Moreover, as Jandrić et al. (2023) highlighted, in conducting research from a postdigital perspective there are no marked paths. "We, the Postdigital Science and Education community, make our own path by researching. But there are no right or wrong paths; the process is much more important than the results" [1] (p.24).

From a methodological perspective, therefore, the uncertainty of the phenomena related to the study of the postdigital could represent an issue, if we assume that traditional methodological approaches could not be "enough" to approach a new (and unknown) realty. On the other hand, however, the Allegory of the Cave and the teachings from the past come to our aid again, also from a methodological perspective. In their manifesto for teaching and learning with AI, Bozkurt et al. [11] underline how the idea of metaphors to understand reality has always accompanied the development of humanity. "The future is filled with unknowns, mysteries, and alternative possibilities. When faced with uncertainty, humans write stories, create myths, or use metaphors to better comprehend emerging phenomena. These stories become reified in the tools and practices we invent" ([11] p.488). Building on the assumption that metaphors have historically served as means for humanity to grasp complex and emerging phenomena, it becomes evident that these narrative tools are not just reflective but also formative. As Bozkurt et al. [11] articulate, metaphors and stories help us navigate the uncertainties of the future, embedding themselves in the very fabric of our technological and pedagogical practices. Moreover, Ernst & Schröter [18] underline how emerging technologies are ontologically constructed as "diegetic objects", which means that they are identifiable in the broader context of certain visions and narratives that construct education futures.

This conceptual framework aligns seamlessly with the principles of sociotechnical perspectives [7], which advocates for an integrated approach to understanding the interplay between society and technology. To truly innovate in the postdigital classroom, it is necessary to transcend traditional methodologies and adopt an entangled perspective that considers both the social and technical dimensions of education. Consequently, the speculation on collective visions of desirable futures [7] could bring to the development of pedagogical strategies that are not only adaptive and personalized but also deeply rooted in the collective creation of knowledge and in the dynamic realities of the postdigital age. Moreover, speculative approaches can be particularly impactful for students who have not found their identities or needs represented in mainstream media, such as fiction and film, prevailing curricula, or technology design and they could, therefore, lead to more inclusive practices [19].

Considering the reflections conducted so far and the surge in popularity that speculative approaches are experiencing as a form of pedagogy, especially in the context of the development and application of GenAI [19], it is clear that these methodologies offer a unique lens through which to explore and shape the future of education. Speculative approaches, by embracing uncertainty and fostering imaginative thinking, enable educators and students to envision and co-create alternative educational futures that are more inclusive, equitable, and responsive to the complexities of the postdigital age. Henceforth, the authors of this study suggest and adopted an integrated approach to the study of the postdigital, based on the integration of Scenario-based Research (SBR) with Persona Design (PD) from the field of human-computer interaction [21], on the one hand, and Speculative Design Methods [14, 22], on the other. The specific features adopted from each individual approach and the ways in which these were integrated in the methodological framework of this study will be presented in the following paragraphs.

2.1 Scenario-Based Research with Persona Design

John Rheinfrank and Shelley Evenson [23] highlighted the power of "stories of the future" in developing conceptually complex interactive systems [21] (p. 103). Similarly, John Carroll [24] has extensively explored scenario-based design. Narrative techniques are particularly effective for visually depicting interactive products, as interaction design fundamentally involves the design of behaviour over time. Consequently, combining a narrative structure with fast and flexible visualization tools, such as the humble whiteboard, is ideal for motivating, envisioning, representing, articulating and validating interaction concepts. SBR with Persona Design is a methodological approach that leverages narrative and scenario-based techniques to explore and develop innovative educational tools and practices. Narrative, one of humanity's oldest creative methods, is particularly powerful in imagining and communicating new possibilities. By constructing stories about personas—detailed representations of possible users with specific goals and behaviours—researchers can envision how these individuals might interact with educational technologies in future classrooms [25]. In the article "Thinking with heritage: past and present in lived futures", Sandford [26] talks about "lived future" to refer to the ways in which individuals and communities experience and enact their futures in everyday life. This concept emphasizes the practical, lived aspects of future-making, focusing on how people integrate their heritage and present circumstances to shape their anticipated futures. Sandford explores how heritage—understood as the legacy of cultural, social, and material aspects from the past—interacts with present actions to influence the formation of these lived futures. The author suggests that by engaging with heritage, individuals can navigate and negotiate their future paths, making heritage a dynamic component in the continuous process of future-making.

Therefore, SBR may not only enhance creativity, but it also facilitates the sharing of ideas among stakeholders, making the design process more comprehensible and engaging since students and teachers co-participate in the design itself, envisioning themselves as future users of the artifacts and the practices they are imagining and, henceforth, designing [27]. SBR involves creating detailed narratives that describe how personas achieve their goals using a product or service. These scenarios are developed iteratively, starting with high-level context scenarios that explore how the product can best serve the personas' needs. As the design process progresses, these scenarios are refined into key path scenarios that detail specific user interactions and validation scenarios that test the design in various situations [21]. By focusing on the narrative structure and using flexible visualization tools, such as digital boards, researchers and participants can quickly and effectively develop and validate interaction concepts.

In the context of pedagogical innovation, SBR with PD allows for the exploration of speculative imaginations, enabling students to engage in creative and critical thinking about the future of education. This approach is particularly helpful not only in understanding students' and teachers' needs and behaviours, but also in designing educational experiences that are inclusive, adaptive, and responsive to the evolving postdigital landscape. Considered the main features of SBR with PD and the role that future imaginaries play in the context of GenAI implementation in education, the authors of this study deemed it necessary to integrate this approach with speculative methods, both for the reasons expressed in the previous paragraph and for a deeper analysis of the speculative scenarios designed by the participants. Therefore, the main characteristics of speculative approaches are detailed afterwards.

2.2 Speculative Methods

Speculative methods, characterized by their non-representational, complexity-informed, and inventive qualities, offer a unique approach to exploring and developing innovative educational tools and practices [14]. These methods engage with the future as a space of uncertainty, using this uncertainty creatively in the present to envision or craft futures that may not yet exist [16]. In educational research, speculative methods have been employed to investigate the social and ethical implications of datafication, challenge the invisibility and inevitability of data-driven practices, and foster critical imagination among participants [14]. For instance, data walking [28] a speculative method, involves participants exploring their environment to document encounters with data, thereby sensitizing them to invisible data practices and prompting ethical reflection. Another speculative approach, thinking otherwise, encourages participants to imagine alternative futures by considering what they would change about their current educational context [29]. Additionally, design fiction workshops, where participants create AI-powered solutions to educational problems, reveal the socio-material effects of emerging technologies and question the equity effects of educational technology [15]. The use of speculative methods in educational research has several significant implications, including prompting ethical reflection and critical thinking, fostering inclusivity and diversity, stimulating innovation and creativity, and challenging dominant discourses [14]. However, these methods also present challenges such as ambiguity and uncertainty, discursive closures, ethical considerations, and balancing creativity with practicality. To overcome such possible issues, in the context of this study, the authors focused on providing clear guidance, attempting to create a safe environment for exploration. Moreover, the integration of speculative methods with other research approaches is considered a powerful strategy to ensure outcomes are both imaginative and actionable [15]. Henceforth, by integrating speculative methods with SBR and PD, this study aimed to trigger speculative imaginaries among students, enabling them to engage in the collective creation of knowledge and envision more inclusive, equitable, and responsive educational futures.

2.3 The Power of Narrative as a Design Tool

Considering the methodological implications discussed so far, the authors of this paper worked with students from a teacher education program to shape ideas of future postdigital classrooms. By leveraging speculative methods and design, uncertainty was implemented as a catalyst to shape visions of the future trajectory of education. The 78 students organized themselves into 20 groups with a minimum of 3 and a maximum of 5 people per group. After an open discussion with the entire classroom on the implications of GenAI for education and on the meaningful strategies to interact with it, each group worked independently based on the guidelines provided. The task was divided into three sub-steps and each step was followed by an open discussion. The aim of separating the task was to scaffold the speculative production of future imaginaries, since the authors of the study considered that the speculative activity on possible educational futures could consist of a puzzling exercise for some students if not gradually supported during the development of the task. Henceforth, as a first step, students were asked to interact with a GenAI platform to design learning activities which had to include the use of GenAI as well. Afterwards, some groups presented their learning design to the classroom, sharing with their peers reflections on the modalities in which they integrated GenAI according to specific educational purposes, on the criteria they identified to choose a specific GenAI platform instead of another, and on the ways in which they think the use they made of GenAI in (and for the design of) the learning activities could enhance the teaching and learning processes.

In the second step of the activity, students developed scenarios based on the principles of the Persona Design. Examples were given to support students, as well as step by step guidelines to include several details such as the age and education of the persona designed in the scenario, the cultural and social environment of the classroom or specific teaching objectives, challenges and issues. This step was deemed necessary to start to trigger the process of speculative production of future imaginaries. Scenarios were shared with the entire classroom, as for the previous step. The aim of the open discussions after each step was to further stimulate creativity and imagination, prompting critical thinking and fostering innovative thoughts through the sharing of ideas. Students were encouraged to think out of the box, consequently the open discussions supported the creation of a more relaxed and friendly environment, which was deemed crucial to stimulate and trigger students' imagination.

The third and last step of the activity consisted of the truly speculative exercise, during which the different groups developed their imaginaries of future postdigital classrooms as well as of future artifacts to implement in such classrooms, based on what they had designed and developed in the two previous steps. Henceforth, the design of GenAI based educational activities of the first step was integrated with the scenario and Persona Design of the second step. Consequently, the learning activities and the scenario were included by students into the imaginary of future classroom in the third and last step. Students where free to implement any digital tool to support the development of their ideas, and they mainly worked with Microsoft Word, as well as with Miro and Genially platforms, using both written narratives and images. The resulting products were presented to the classroom through verbal narrative and with the support of a digital board, they were stored in the private Team platform of the course (therefore shared with the entire classroom online as well), and analyzed by the authors of this study implementing narrative inquiry as a guiding approach, as it will be described in the next section.

3 From Stories to the Design: Reflections on Students' Imaginaries

Narrative inquiry is particularly suited for the purpose of analyzing the scenarios and the speculative imaginaries produced by students, as it allows for a deep exploration of personal and contextual experiences through stories. This methodology is grounded in the understanding that individuals make sense of their lives and experiences through narratives, which are collected and analyzed to uncover underlying themes and meanings [30]. The approach emphasizes relational engagement, fostering a collaborative environment between the researcher and the participants, which was crucial in the context of this study for capturing the nuanced perspectives of students and to foster their imagination [31]. By considering the three-dimensional space of interaction (personal and social), continuity (past, present, and future) and situation (place), narrative inquiry provides a comprehensive framework for understanding the complexities of the students' speculative imaginaries [32]. Considering that narrative research engages with small groups of participants to deeply explore the meaning that individuals attributed to their experiences [32], as well as the limitations of this contribution, the authors of the study decided to focus on the analysis of one single product, to provide more meaningful insights into the potential of speculative narrative as a guiding tool to understand the direction that educational content and practices, policies and physical spaces (among other aspects) should take in the future postdigital classrooms. Ethical considerations, such as confidentiality and informed consent, were meticulously observed to respect the personal nature of the narratives.

Below are presented the activities developed by the group of students considered, translated from Italian into English, in the order they were assigned as previously described.

STEP 1: Learning Design

Subject: Science
Lesson Topic: Leaves
Grade Level: Primary School
Objectives and Goals: Learning the structure of a leaf and critically using GenAI platforms
Methodological Approach: Cooperative learning and laboratory activities
Classroom Setting: "Parco del Sole" and the classroom
Tools and Technologies Needed for Activity Development: Interactive whiteboard, tablets or phones, AI apps: PlantNet, ChatGPT, Copilot
Activity Development Phases and Expected Time: 3 phases.
Phase 1: School Trip; Phase 2: Comparison between textbooks and GenAI contents; Phase 3: Discussion on the findings from the comparison and what was learned by using AI.
Expected length: 2 lessons
Assessment Method: Evaluating interest and participation
Expected outcome: By comparing information obtained from textbooks and using GenAI from their devices, students are encouraged to develop critical thinking and the ability to critically assess the information obtained. Moreover, students are expected to learn content related to the structure of the leaf.

STEP 2: Scenario and Persona Design

Name: Maria Lucia
Occupation: Graduate in Primary Education Sciences
Age: 33
Education: Maria Lucia has a five-year degree in Primary Education Sciences. She has been teaching in a primary school for 5 years. She is passionate about mathematics and science, as well as technology, and tries to use the latter in her classrooms, especially to help students who have difficulties in the subject.

Teaching Environment: Maria Lucia works with children aged 6 to 8 years. Her goal is to develop critical thinking using tools such as artificial intelligence in an appropriate and suitable manner.
Challenges and Difficulties: Maria Lucia's students do not show particular interest in the subject because they find it boring. The challenge she sets for herself is to raise greater awareness and interest in the subject.

STEP 3: Imaginaries of Future Classroom

"The School of the Future"

Imagine a classroom with walls that can become interactive surfaces. Children can draw, interact with images, and write on them. The chairs and tables will be mobile, allowing them to be moved as desired, and they can even shrink. This is to ensure that students have constantly changing spaces that do not hinder learning.
Referring to the previous scenario, imagine having a tool that allows real-time analysis of leaf characteristics. It is a small, portable, and easy-to-use device. Its main features include: a high-resolution camera, a sensor for chemical analysis of leaves, Bluetooth connectivity to link the device to a phone and its application, and AI features to quickly collect and analyze data.
The tool is shaped like a pen, and by bringing it close to a leaf, it acquires all the data in a few seconds. The data will be transcribed onto the App on the phone, and students can read and save the collected data to study or to continue with other educational activities.

The "Step-1" educational activity designed by the students aligns well with the postdigital vision of education, which emphasizes the seamless integration of digital and physical learning environments [1]. The incorporation of different GenAI tools, such as PlantNet, ChatGPT and Copilot, and the use of interactive whiteboards and mobile devices in both the classroom and outdoor settings (*Parco del Sole*) exemplifies the blend of digital and physical spaces, fostering an engaging and dynamic learning experience. Moreover, the activity employs GenAI platforms not only to search for content and information on the structure of leaves, but it also aims to develop critical thinking skills and the ability to critically assess the information acquired through these platforms.

This dual focus underscores the participants' awareness of the necessity for educating younger generations on the proficient and ethical use of GenAI. By integrating GenAI tools into the learning design, the activity encourages students to engage in a comparative analysis between traditional textbooks and AI-generated content. This process fosters critical thinking by prompting students to evaluate the reliability, accuracy, and relevance of the information provided by GenAI, thereby enhancing their ability to discern and synthesize knowledge from multiple sources. The emphasis on critical thinking aligns with current educational discourse, which highlights the importance of preparing students for a future where AI technologies are ubiquitous [33]. Moreover, the ability to critically engage with AI-generated content is crucial in mitigating potential biases and inaccuracies inherent in these technologies [27].

The activity's design reflects a forward-thinking approach, recognizing that a specific education in the use of GenAI is essential for equipping future students with the skills needed to navigate and thrive in a postdigital world. The participants of the study demonstrated, henceforth, a proactive stance towards integrating advanced technologies in pedagogical practices. This approach is supported by the growing body of literature advocating for the responsible and informed use of GenAI in education [34]. As such, the activity not only addresses immediate learning objectives but also contributes to the broader goal of fostering a generation of learners who are able to use GenAI tools critically and ethically. Moreover, the design of an activity which include the contemporary implementation of GenAI both for content creation and for orientating students on its critical use, seems to suggest that a meaningful manner to incorporate GenAI in the future classroom could be by including training on the effective use of GenAI in the development of the learning activities.

The following two steps of the activity (the scenario creation with persona design and the future classroom exercise), illustrate more clearly the speculative methodological approach. By creating a detailed persona, Maria Lucia, and, afterwards, by envisioning a future classroom with interactive walls and mobile furniture, the students engaged in SBR and speculative thought, which stimulated their creative thinking and their imagination of future possibilities. The approach encouraged students to think beyond current limitations and to explore innovative ways to innovate future educational practices, as it can be observed in the idea of shrinking tables and chairs that can be easily moved in order to guarantee a faster adaptation of the physical space to the needs and the development of the lesson. In the framework of a future postdigital landscape, such an imaginary could be interpreted as a necessity to provide future schools with smart furniture (interactive walls, shrinking tables and chairs), which adapt to the ongoing teaching and learning needs that unfold during the development of a lesson.

Less meaningful in terms of future visions, maybe, can be considered the GenAI specific artifact that students designed (a tool shaped like a pen that, if pointed to a leaf, acquires data to transmit them to the related mobile App). This more simplistic speculation, closer to smart devices and applications which already exist, could be explained in relation to the cognitive load of the speculative exercise itself. It is possible that students focused and spent more time on the design of the educational activity, the persona, the scenario, and the overall imaginary of future classroom than on the design of a future GenAI artIfact. However, smart furniture and interactive walls imply the integration of AI, and they can, therefore, be considered as future AI based artIfacts themselves as well.

The narrative inquiry approach allows for a deeper and comprehensive analysis of the students' narratives by focusing on the three-dimensional space of interaction (personal and social), continuity (past, present, and future), and situation (place) [32]. In the context of the three-steps activity, the interaction dimension examines both personal and social aspects of the participants' experiences. For instance, the persona of Maria Lucia highlights passion for mathematics, science, and technology, as well as attention for the social role of a teacher which feels responsible for engaging her students. By analyzing the narratives, it is possible to understand how individual motivations and social dynamics influenced the development of the tasks. The cooperative learning approach and the implementation of GenAI tools in group settings fostered social interaction, allowing students to share their insights and collaborate, thereby enriching their collective speculative experience.

The continuity dimension focuses on the temporal aspects of participants' experiences. The overall activity was scaffolded in three different steps with related classroom discussions, from the design of a GenAI based educational activity to the development of an imaginary of the future, reflecting a progression over time. By examining the narratives, it is possible to observe how students' understanding evolved from the initial design of a learning activity to the elaboration of a future imaginary. Additionally, the speculative scenario of the future classroom encouraged students to project their current learning experiences into future possibilities, bridging their past and present knowledge with future innovations. This temporal analysis helps identify how students' reflections and ideas on GenAI use may change, and improve, over time the more they perform activities like those proposed in this study.

The situation dimension relates to the physical and contextual settings of participants' experiences. For this dimension, the settings that participants imagined for their future classroom may reflect the ways in which different physical environments can impact the engagement and learning outcomes of the participants themselves, showing, therefore, not only possible needs of future students, but also theirs. The activities take place in several environments, such as the *Parco del Sole* and the classroom, each offering unique learning opportunities. For example, the outdoor setting of the school trip provides a hands-on, immersive experience, while the classroom setting allows for structured analysis and discussion. The imagined future classroom with interactive walls and mobile furniture further expands the situational context, illustrating how innovative environments can enhance learning. By analyzing these situational elements, it is possible to gain insights into how different physical spaces influence students' interactions with GenAI and AI based tools. Therefore, in structuring our ideas of possible educational futures the learning experience must be considered from a holistic perspective, where the innovative, changing and adaptable environments seem to be more than necessary.

4 Conclusions and Future Research

With this study the authors aimed to conceptualize pedagogical innovation by moving beyond the traditional, instrumentalist vision of a technology-pedagogy dichotomy towards Fawns' perspective of an entangled pedagogy by embracing postdigital and sociomaterial views on education [1]. The shift towards the idea that pedagogy and technology are entangled within the socio-technical components of the teaching and learning environment, and therefore, that pedagogical innovation it is not solely a matter of incorporating technological tools but it shapes and it is shaped by individual imagination and collective imaginaries of how future education should look like, implies embracing uncertainty and taking distances from traditional methodological approaches, exactly as the prisoner of the Plato's myth of the cave that, by stepping out of it, understands the true nature of the world beyond the cave itself even if he is first blinded by it.

Therefore, the authors leveraged uncertainty as a catalyst to inform visions of the future of education [16], focusing on a speculative collaborative exercise to structure future visions of postdigital classrooms through a scaffolded activity and by employing a speculative methodological approach, that integrated Scenario-Based Research from human-computer interaction [21] with Persona Design and Speculative Design methods [15]. In the first step of the speculative exercise, students were asked to design a GenAI based learning activity, in the second step they developed a scenario with a Persona, which was designed on the previous activity they elaborated. In the third and last step students structured their imaginaries of future postdigital classrooms, leveraging the two previous steps of the activity as a support and a trigger to develop their visions. The authors analyzed the students' outcome considered in the context of this paper through the approach of narrative inquiry, which provided a rich foundation for understanding and outlining the shapes that pedagogical innovation may acquire to structure the future of education.

The case presented here demonstrates the efficacy of the combined methodological approach implemented for the purpose of defining pedagogical innovation. By triggering students' imagination and creative thinking and through leveraging the power of narrative as a design tool during the analysis of the outcomes, the authors derived information that may consists of practical guidelines for the future direction of education, especially if supported by further studies. For instance, from the study emerged the idea of educating future generations on the correct use of GenAI by incorporating guiding exercises within learning activities that include GenAI itself.

Furthermore, findings suggest that the school of the future may feature smart furniture and buildings that adapt swiftly to the needs of teaching and learning processes *in itinere*, such as shrinking desks and chairs. From a methodological perspective, the scaffolding of the imaginaries activity proved to be a valuable strategy for structuring students' reasoning, as well as creative and critical thinking, as evidenced by the results of the three-dimensional analysis of the narrative inquiry approach [32].

For future research, it would be beneficial to allocate more time for students to develop more detailed scenarios and artifacts. Encouraging participants to exchange and build upon each other's work could further stimulate creative thinking and enhance design outcomes as well. Furthermore, collecting data through structured observations and interviews during the design activities could provide deeper insights into the visions and the specific characteristics of the innovations being designed. Lastly, recognizing that design is an iterative process, the authors aim to present, discuss, and refine the designed artifacts and scenarios with in-service teachers through a recursive and iterative co-design practice. This collaborative effort may help us explore new directions to achieve meaningful advancements in defining pedagogical innovation and in shaping the future of education. It is time to exit the cave.

References

1. Jandrić, P., MacKenzie, A., Knox, J.: (eds.). Postdigital research: genealogies, challenges, and future perspectives. Springer (2023)
2. Forsler, I., Bardone, E., Forsman, M.: The future Postdigital classroom. Postdigital Sci. Educ. (2024)
3. Eradze, M., Bardone, E., Tinterri, A., Dipace, A.: Self-initiated online communities of teachers as an expanded meso space. Professional development in education, pp. 1–19 (2023)
4. Bardone, E., Mõttus, P., Eradze, M.: Tinkering as a complement to design in the context of technology integration in teaching and learning. Postdigital Sci. Educ. **6**, 114–134 (2024). https://doi.org/10.1007/s42438-023-00416-6
5. Oliver, M.: Technological determinism in educational technology research: some alternative ways of thinking about the relationship between learning and technology: educational technology and determinism. J. Comput. Assist. Learn. **27**(5), 373–384 (2011)

6. Fawns, T.: An entangled pedagogy: looking beyond the pedagogy—technology dichotomy. Postdigital Sci. Educ. 1–18 (2022)
7. Jasanoff, S.: Dreamscapes of modernity: Sociotechnical Imaginaries and the Fabrication of Power. The University of Chicago Press, Chicago (2015)
8. Fawns, T.: Postdigital education in design and practice. Postdigital Sci. Educ. **1**(1), 132–145 (2019)
9. Knox, J.: Postdigital Research. In P. Jandrić (ed.), Encyclopedia of Postdigital Science and Education. Springer (2023)
10. Selwyn, N., et al.: What's next for Ed-Tech? critical hopes and concerns for the 2020s. Learn. Media Technol. **45**, 1–6 (2020)
11. Bozkurt, A., et al.: The manifesto for teaching and learning in a time of generative AI: a critical collective stance to better navigate the future. Open Praxis **16**(4), 487–513 (2024)
12. Giannakos, M., et al.: The promise and challenges of generative AI in education. Behav. Inf. Technol. 1–27 (2024)
13. Peláez-Sánchez, I.C., Velarde-Camaqui, D., Glasserman-Morales, L.D.: The impact of large language models on higher education: exploring the connection between AI and Education 4.0. Front. Educ. **9** (2024)
14. Ross, J.: Digital futures for learning: speculative methods and pedagogies. Routledge New (2023)
15. Rahm, L.: Educational imaginaries: governance at the intersection of technology and education. J. Educ. Policy **38**(1), 46–68 (2023)
16. Mann, S., et al.: Educational design fictions: imagining learning futures. In: Industry Practices, Processes and Techniques Adopted in Education: Supporting Innovative Teaching and Learning Practice, pp. 303–326 (2022)
17. Hasse, C.: Workplace Learning for Changing Social and Economic Circumstances. Routledge (2023)
18. Ernst, C., Schröter, J.: Media Futures: Theory and Aesthetics. Springer (2021). (2024)
19. Kukulska-Hulme, A., et al.: Innovating Pedagogy 2024: Open University Innovation Report 12. The Open University, Milton Keynes (2024)
20. Garcia, A., Mirra, N.: Speculative Pedagogies. Designing Equitable Educational Futures. Banks ed., Teachers' College Press, New York (2023)
21. Cooper, A., Reimann, R., Cronin, D., Noessel, C.: About face: the essentials of interaction design. Wiley (2014)
22. Rahm, L.: Help!? My students created an evil AI: on the irony of speculative methods and design fiction. Learn. Media Technol. 1–15 (2024)
23. Rheinfrank, J., Evenson, S.: Design Languages. Addison-Wesley, Boston (1996)
24. Carroll, J. M.: Making Use: Scenario-Based Design of Human-Computer Interactions. The MIT Press, Cambridge MA (2000). (2024)
25. Pratschke, B.M.: Generative AI and education: digital pedagogies, teaching innovation and learning design. Springer (2024)
26. Sandford, R.: Thinking with heritage: past and present in lived futures. Futures **111**, 71–80 (2019). (2024)
27. Noroozi, O., Soleimani, S., Farrokhnia, M., & Banihashem, S.K.: Generative AI in education: Pedagogical, theoretical, and methodological perspectives. Int. J. Tech. Educ. (IJTE) **7**(3), 373–385 (2024)
28. Powell, A.: Producing community and technology. Inf. Commun. Soc. **11**(8), 1068–1088 (2018). (2024)
29. Houlden, S., Veletsianos, G.: Impossible dreaming: on speculative education fiction and hopeful learning futures. Postdigital Sci. Educ. **5**(3), 605–622, (2023). (2024)
30. Salkind, N.J.: Narrative research. Handbook of research design and social measurement, 143–196 (2002). (2024)

31. Saldaña, J.: The Coding Manual for Qualitative Researchers. Sage (2015). (2024)
32. Clandinin, D.J., Connelly, F.M.: Narrative inquiry: Experience and story in qualitative research. Wiley, San Francisco, CA (2004). (2024)
33. Samala, A.D., Rawas, S., Wang, T.: Unveiling the landscape of generative artificial intelligence in education: a comprehensive taxonomy of applications, challenges, and future prospects. Educ. Inf. Technol. (2024)
34. Zhang, X., et al.: A systematic literature review of empirical research on applying generative artificial intelligence in education. Front. Digit. Educ. **1**, 223–245 (2024)

Children and Ozobots - The First Contact Reminiscence

Lenka Kaščáková(✉), Eva Severini, and Dušan Kostrub

Faculty of Education, Comenius University Bratislava, Račianska 59, 81334 Bratislava, Slovakia
{kascakova,severini,kostrub}@fedu.uniba.sk

Abstract. The study is aimed at investigating the critical thinking and action of pre-primary and primary education children in situations of interpreting and justifying the meaning of the functionality of ozobots. We present a research probe that was conducted in the environment of the UK Science Park - FabLab as well as in the environment of the schools that the children and pupils attend. The research tools and methods are group discussion, observation, indirect observation (through video recordings) and individual interviews. We analysed children's and students' actions and thinking in relation to manipulative activities, conceptual activity and evaluation related to ozobots. We were interested in the capacity to retain, reproduce experiences and transfer meanings. The results we present consider the developmental levels, direct experience, and types of judgments that children and students possess. In doing so, we point out that this type of teaching should rightly be discussed during undergraduate studies in teacher education and educational sciences.

Keywords: Child · Ozobot · Exploration · Thinking · Competence · Initial Experience

1 Introduction

The current era offers and brings a variety of educational opportunities related to the goal of making the teaching and learning process more effective and experiential. One of the possibilities is the implementation of robotics - ozobots in the teaching process from pre-primary education, thus enhancing the acquisition of the basics of robotics based on interaction with robots in a playful way. These robotic toys represent the most sophisticated individual and group learning opportunities of a playful nature, although it is difficult to ascribe to them the role of a toy or entertainment device and the term toy in this context takes on a different meaning. We are convinced that the use of robotics from pre-primary education onwards is promising, motivating, attractive and develops all children's competences.

2 Ozobots - Robotic Toy

Ozobot is one of the smallest programmable robots in the world with a diameter and height of 2.54 cm. It is an intelligent robot with a powerful brain that is programmable using visual codes. It can trace lines, recognize colours, or move freely on a surface.

Ł. Tomczyk (Ed.): NMP 2024, CCIS 2537, pp. 95–109, 2025.
https://doi.org/10.1007/978-3-031-95627-0_7

All ozobots work on a similar principle, using downward pointing cameras to detect the colour of a line underneath, about 5mm wide. Initially, it is a black line on which, with the help of sensors, it retrieves all the commands that are programmed. In addition to the black colour, the robot can also detect blue, green or red colours. These colours occur in different combinations, in the exact order they produce commands in succession. An important function of the ozobot is to read the rapidly alternating colours that are used to load a program into memory to perform a specific and intended movement. Ozobot decodes the lines by moving back and forth. When it reaches an intersection, it will head in a randomly selected direction. Ozobot robots come in several models on the market. For example, the Bits model has only wheels and a sensor, while the more advanced Evo model has Bluetooth connectivity and programming capability. Using different coloured markers, the user can draw paths on the paper surface for the robot to decode, thus giving commands such as slow down, speed up or stop, etc. It is a useful tool for teaching the basics of programming in a fun and interactive way for children from about 6 years old. Children learn about robotics, mathematics, programming, etc. in a practical and playful way. By simply drawing even more complex labyrinths, paths, intersections and creating more complete worlds to explore different constructions, fast paths, they will get to know the functions of a new-generation educational robot that is full of functional possibilities [1]. The authors of this study see this as an opportunity to prepare the current generation to take up future professional activities.

3 Proleptic Teaching

The teacher's speech in teaching is not water running over Teflon, and the words (verbalized thoughts) of the pupil cannot disappear like water in the desert.

Teaching is proleptic in nature, which means that it refers to the representation and assumption of the realization of future actions and development as if they already existed in the present or were in the process of being realized. It is teaching in which aspects of the future that come later are revealed and anticipated. Such teaching has a futuristically conceived contemporary meaning. Conscious anticipation based on retrospective and prospective assessment with acceptance of the phenomenon of dynamics of development and change is a prerequisite for learning and teaching to be meaningful, deliberate, organized, controlled, productive and effective processes. The concentrated effort of the learner, supported by the teacher, is oriented towards the near future. Several of the following activities are already happening in the present, making the future become the present. Capturing early changes (initially manifested in cues) in action draws attention to the goal (conclusion, end, result) that the teacher has in mind (intending to enable the learner to achieve it) and to the performance of specific actions that are linked to the desired goal (the goal as the conclusion, end, result of deliberate action). Conclusion, end, result as a proleptic goal acquires a causal meaning because, among other things, it stands at the centre of didactic contexts and links to the diagnosed current level of development, the established history, the concrete manifestations of action, the zone of potential development and translates into the zone of proximal development (action). The analysis of the dynamics of action and communication in the zone of proximal development is considered potentially useful in the design and implementation of specific didactic interventions. The conclusion, the end, the outcome as a future state (proleptic goal) assumes the role of an essential causal factor that significantly intervenes in the formation of the outcome through the active agency of the learner in the present. At the same time, it becomes a didactic phenomenon because it is consciously and deliberately operated in terms of didactic reality. The proleptic (containing aspects of individualization and differentiation) goal must be significant, it must invoke the potential identities of actionable self-acting and communicating pupils; it can be said to be personalized. When the composition (ordering) of action between the starting point (to be referred to) and the outcome (to be focused on) is accomplished by the active learner, we can speak of a proleptic conclusion, an ending. In concrete manifestations of the action, the elements of the intended goal are tentatively revealed ("mirrored" in them by the conclusion, the end, the result), but a certain stimulus (time) period filled with activities that activate potentials for inner growth, development, change still passes, only after which these manifestations of action and communication take on other, different forms/likenesses. Pedagogical diagnosis is decisive. In other words; the conclusion, the end, the result is the first in intention, but the last in action, in the performance of actions. It is a future state that can be spoken of as a present/actual right to emphasize its proximity and apparent certainty. In this way, the teacher can interweave present and future situations in the teaching with the pupils, which allows penetration into positions of understanding of what is done, why and how it is done, performed (these are cultural practices and discursive practices) in the adult world. Cultural practices and discursive practices are related to situations in which future events happen and are described as a present/living reality, thus emphasizing the certainty of performing actions. It is a representation of the development of learning and teaching as well as the conscious development of the learner. Approaching the future happens through transformative processes of applying past models to situations that are gradually moving away from the past (abandoned as ineffective, no longer usable, inappropriate, etc.). The essential role of the teacher is therefore to enable pupils to think critically and to offer them a pedagogically conditioned space for change if it is more functional, more applicable for the new generation. In this way, the main goal of education, which is transformation, is fulfilled. Cultural practices and discursive practices are the link between personal historical past, anamnesis, diagnosis and prognosis related to learning and preparation for new learning or life situations (bringing awareness of the logical implications of what will follow and what life will bring). Pupil/student and teacher attention is concentrated in the conception of cultural practices and discursive practices. Concepts such as instructional scaffolding and zones of development originating from Vygotsky [2] assist the teacher in this. The concept of prudent scaffolding (in the form of guided discourse) is defined as considering the teacher's support for the learner indirect, solely in the form of providing the dynamics of space, time and conditions for (self)reflection. The role of diagnosis is paramount and irreplaceable. Thanks to diagnosing, the teacher gets a picture of the actual state of the pupil's level of development, which has an actual form. Diagnosis is used to ascertain whether the pupils have already internalised the useful tools (and which ones) necessary for the activities that will follow. What the pupil possesses is a demonstrable fact. It is not verbalised but factual evidence. The acquisition of factual evidence is done by the teacher by penetrating the facts but considering the whole context.

The goal category has a guiding, dynamizing and integrating function in the teaching process. Other functions of the goal are the stage-setting, orienting, regulating and normative functions. Changes in the goal affect changes in the relationships of the structural elements of the teaching process. They also affect the means of goal realization. The formulation of a goal (as well as a system of goals) is a necessity; without goals, as landmarks, as clues in action, planned human activity is not possible. The aim of proleptic teaching is to utilize and process the maximum possibilities of the individual developmental levels for the benefit of the qualities of the pupil being developed; therefore, pupil-oriented goals consider the developmental dimensions. A set of goals defined in terms of pupil development thus constitutes an important guide in the teacher's decision-making process, which in perspective directs the achievement of the goals themselves and at the same time enables the transition from one developmental level to another. The individualized and differentiated approach is centred on the construction of the goal(s).

The role of history taking as a more detailed inquiry (set) of the necessary data to explain knowledge is essential. Thanks to the discovery of connections (critical moments, turning points) with the use of pedagogical diagnostics, the teacher obtains a preview of future events, processes to be related to the goals. The teacher also takes the certainty of his didactic decisions from the understanding of the connections he finds. Thus, the teacher can contextualize future events and thus emphasize the certainty of the execution of these events and the resulting actions. Prolepsis comes from anamnesis.

What does pedagogical logic give us? Pedagogical logic gives the position that the teacher is the key factor in teaching. Pedagogical logic focuses the teacher's thinking and action on didactic support for learning that moves away from the past by approaching the future and focusing fully on the present. Such thinking and acting requires a pedagogy of possibility. Possibility pedagogy provides support for dealing with learning situations, for stabilizing optimal conditions, in optimal conditions for eliminating pupil inactivity, for the need to take measures to increase attention, for transformative action, for a conscious attitude, for not ignoring the discrepancy between what the pupil can do and what he or she cannot yet do. Then the teacher is in tune with the pupil/pupils.

Behind the development (the emergence of fundamental changes), there is usually not a single factor, but a very complex set of influences that can at least be divided into two groups: the underlying causes and the triggering causes, namely: a) susceptibility/sensitivity (sensitization), b) the presence of critical moments, and c) the specific environment. Learning and teaching others happen as a combination of multiple phenomena that occur simultaneously (these are multidimensional and multifactorial factors). Proleptic teaching facilitates the development of strategic action related to learning processes. Proleptic teaching implies a diversity of development, by which is meant the strength and flexibility of the corresponding conditions in favour of development. The role of the teacher in proleptic teaching is crucial; the teacher should focus primarily on the pupils' goals - not on his or her own - to didactically support the learning processes by recognizing the pupils' past, present and future.

Long-term memory is episodic memory (personal events and temporal relationships are stored according to temporal sequence; these are episodic memories associated with direct and indirect experience, autobiographical information) and semantic memory (concepts, meanings, contexts/relationships, conceptual information are stored; this is semantic information associated with creating schemas, creating one's own concepts and conceptualizations, and adopting ready-made concepts and conceptualizations). It contains both concrete and abstract concepts, their storage is done through verbal encoding. Our study focuses on the pedagogical investigation of semantic memory. From a pedagogical point of view, we talk about the above levels of semantic memory. It is an organized knowledge of the world. Procedural memory is related to the performance of an act (it is an autonomous system). Memory is affected by retelling. Operative memory, selective attention, and inhibitory capacity are among the executive functions [3]. The process of receiving, processing, internalizing, and storing information as follows [4] (see Fig. 1):

1. Basic postulate: processing meaningful information causes more permanent retention of information compared to shallow information. Deep level processing is mainly influenced by meaning, meaningfulness (other associations, experiences, images). For didactic purposes, it is necessary that children and pupils are contacted with information coming from reference subjects who have direct, immediate and daily contact with the source, the originator of the information. Such bodies will provide meaningful and contextualised information.

   Attention as the focus and concentration of the mind on something specific (an action, object, process, etc.), the mental state of wakefulness. In other words, attention is the ability to create, manage and maintain an adequate state of activation, readiness for proper information processing. Mindfulness is also a process by which we can direct our mental resources to certain aspects of the environment that are most relevant and/or to the performance of certain activities that we deem most appropriate among the possible ones. With attention, one can focus on certain stimuli and ignore the other less important ones.
2. The basic postulate: the ability to direct attention and focus on something without other stimuli, whether external or internal, interrupting the activity being performed depends not only on other cognitive functions, but also on the structuring of stimuli in the didactic field (reality). For didactic purposes, it is necessary that the stimuli are optimised (using didactic principles) embedded in the structured context of the didactic field (reality). The attractiveness of the stimuli, the novelty of the stimuli, the reframing of the interest in the stimulus, the change of the point of view on familiar stimuli, the complexity of the stimulus are important conditions.

   Visual and auditory discrimination as visual and auditory discrimination is one predictor of the selective acquisition of specific information to be subsequently processed by the mind with an adequate response. The goal is to achieve an adaptive response, i.e. a deliberate, goal-directed response to sensory information/data. Visual and auditory discrimination is a highly active process of extracting sensory stimuli, assessing them, interpreting them, and retrospectively organizing the sensory stimulus.
3. The basic postulate: the process of extracting sensory stimuli, assessing them, interpreting them, and retrospectively organizing the sensory stimulus must be deliberate, consistent, specific, controlled, and directed toward hypothesizing them. Sensory data is thus just clusters of physical stimuli, and the human brain tries to interpret them in a meaningful and as probable way as possible. Data has a past and a future; it

changes, and each affects the other. They have hidden aspects that emerge under the influence of various conditions [5]. The sensory organs supply only vague and raw material that must be grasped by higher cognitive functions. For didactic purposes, the accompanying word, the pointing out of essential, important elements (as opposed to irrelevant or apparent ones), stimulating learning materials and relevant subject-object, multimodal learning resources need to be registered in the didactic field of attention.

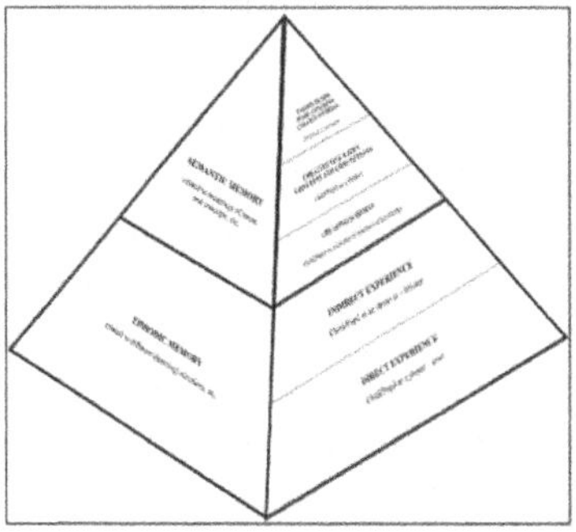

Fig. 1. Process of Receiving, Processing, Internalising and Storing Information. Source: Hernández [4].

The above ideas indicate reflections on the roles, goals of the teacher-researcher:

- Analyze the internal dynamics of the process of constructing knowledge.
- To clarify how this dynamic is affected through incorporation or adjustment in relation to new information and pre-existing representations in the minds of students.
- Investigate the conditions of instructional influence under which the "cognitive encounter" between new information and learner representations can orient the internal dynamics of revision, modification, reorganization, or differentiation of representations in a desirable direction. The mind, and with it the representations it stores and the psychological processes that take place within it, is an exceptional property of the learner [6].
- To change (conceptually), explore (methodologically) and adapt (methodologically) teaching for the benefit of learners.

Recommendation for teachers:

Focus on such key skills as goal setting, organization, cognitive flexibility, memory, and self-monitoring.

4 Qualitative Research

4.1 Research Problem

The object of our investigation was to explore the critical thinking and action of pre-primary children and primary pupils in situations of interpreting and justifying the meaning of the functionality of ozobots. Considering the fact, that children of pre-primary and primary education pupils forming our research sample are without direct experience with didactic aid - robotic toy, we consider it didactically beneficial and justified to know how children, pupils deal with them. Due to the initial contact, a change in the original knowledge will arise.

Subsequent paragraphs, however, are indented. Main scientific research focus - What happens when... (this is didactic hypothesizing as a prerequisite for initiating experimentation):

- Children and pupils will encounter Ozobot for the first time and have the space to manipulate it in activities?
- Will they complete the activities with accompanying words from engineers explaining the basic functions?
- After completing the activities, they will no longer be contacted by Ozobot, engaged in conversations about Ozobot, asked what Ozobot is, or asked to recall a specific event?
- But after three weeks, they will be invited to reflect, recap and report on an Ozobot-related event.

Considering also the rapid technical advances in education nowadays, we focused on investigating the initial experience of children and pupils (who have acquired only the framework information about ozobots) manifested in manipulative activities with a didactic aid - a robotic toy. Manipulation activities along with reasoning evoked the emergence of changes in original knowledge, which were demonstrated in the interpretations in the group discussion. A qualitative research methodology corresponding to the phenomenological genre was preferred for the treatment of the issue. Qualitative research suited us because it emphasizes individual and group understanding of the world. Qualitative research has the advantage of using the views of a small group of subjects where everyone can voice their opinion. To investigate the problem, we used a focus group to explore the subjective and socially conditioned views of children and pupils related to Ozobots. In our investigation, we focused on those manifestations of the subjects that were related to their awareness, reflection and interpretation in relation to the use of ozobots. We did not judge the opinions of our subjects; we analysed them and assigned meanings to them, which we also obtained from the subjects.

4.2 Research Aim and Research Questions

The aim of the research is to explicate the critical thinking and action of children and pupils in learning situations in interpreting the meaning of the functionality of ozobots. We set the following research questions:

- How do children and pupils formulate their interpretations related to the primary use of ozobots.
- How children and pupils process the initial information about ozobots.
- What are the content dimensions of children's and pupils' interpretations.

4.3 Research Tools and Methods

The research instruments and methods are group discussion, observation, indirect observation (through video recordings) and individual interviews. Group discussions can provide insight into processes that are otherwise hidden and difficult to penetrate externally [7]. During discussion groups, meaning is collectively given, meanings are negotiated, and identities develop through processes of social interaction between people (see Fig. 2).

Fig. 2. Implementation of Focus Group in Kindergarten and in Primary School. Source: authors' archive.

In the implemented focus groups, we played the role of moderator, active participant and actively participated in the exchange of ideas. We also assumed the role of "reporter", closely monitoring and summarizing what was said by whom, what position was taken. If someone did not express (communicate) their thoughts clearly enough, we asked for clarification, asking thought-provoking questions. After the two focus groups were over, we interpreted the meaning of the discussion itself. At the beginning of each focus group, the subjects were invited to present their thoughts (opinions) in the form of statements to the questions posed: 1. What is it that you encountered in FabLab? 2. How does it work/what can be done about it? 3. How can it be used in kindergarten/primary school?

Observation is seen as a mental perspective (the taking of it), an attitude, a process, a content, an indispensable operational tool (diagnosing, evaluating) of those who operate in the complex and ramified context of education and teaching; it is essential for the observation practitioner. It is necessary to go beyond the spontaneous attitude (and arbitrary action) and develop a specific methodology that is deliberately used to disc(s)know, understand, process the variety of verbal and non-implicit as well as explicit information and dynamics that simultaneously affect the life of the individual, or the relationship of the individual and the group. Therefore, it is important that the observation is embedded in the hypothesis of the chosen procedure. Observation is not an activity, but it is a systematic, deliberate, conscious, cognitively conditioned (rigorously conceived and critical) process in which all poles interact. Sustained focused gaze as a configured tool of observation is no longer a unilateral action but becomes a reciprocal action [8]. The observation took place in FabLab. Children and pupils were observed and subsequently participated in facilitated focus group discussions. The aim of the unstructured observation (without a pre-prepared schema) was to observe the initial contact with the Ozobots and the manifestations of the actions of the subjects.

4.4 Research Sample

The sample consisted of 15 children of compulsory pre-primary education, 9 boys and 6 girls, as well as 22 pupils of the last year of primary education, 11 boys and 11 girls. This is a convenience sample and a sample of homogeneous cases [9]. The convening sample consisted of children of pre-primary education and pupils of primary education, who in the process of the research formed a sample worthy of consideration, precisely because of their zero experience with the didactic aid - a robotic toy. Based on the primary information and subsequent practical experience, the sample carried out manipulative activities in real time, which also had a creative dimension. The subjects of our research sample were in the role of actors - doers and were gaining direct experience. Simultaneously, they were gaining indirect experience because they were in the role of observers - listeners. The activities performed by the subject were associated with an episodic situation. The sample of homogeneous cases consisted of the already mentioned subject. The subjects of our research were exposed to a group interview in which a topic related to the concept of ozobots was discussed. The group interview allowed the research subjects to voice an opinion derived from their practical experience with the thematic core of the object of study.

4.5 Research Design

Research implementation - the conceptual framework of the research design in our investigation (Fig. 3):

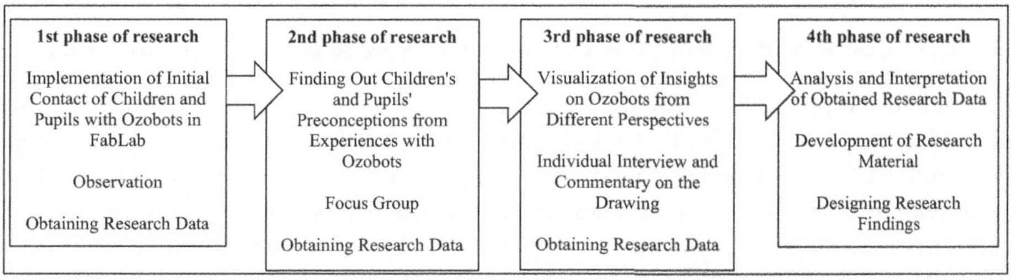

Fig. 3. Conceptual Framework for Research Design. Source: authors' archive.

4.6 Elaboration of the Research Material

A large amount of research material was elaborated using constant comparisons, which monitored the saturation of the identified categories. This involved comparing the events used for a particular category, integrating the categories and their properties, delineating the supporting elements of the theory, and conceiving the theory. The theory conceived is the result of examining the identified concepts and comparing whether they are part of the everyday life of children/pupils or not. Methodological principles of triangulation were also used; what was discovered in the appropriate context was determined. In particular, the aim of triangulation theory in the research described here was to understand and reconstruct meaning. We, as teacher-researchers, used a flexible way of understanding information based on inductive and participatory ways of information retrieval. We analysed the actions and thinking of children and students in relation to manipulative activities, conceptual activity and evaluation related to ozobots (see Figs. 4 and 5). We were interested in the capacity to retain, reproduce lived experiences and transfer meanings.

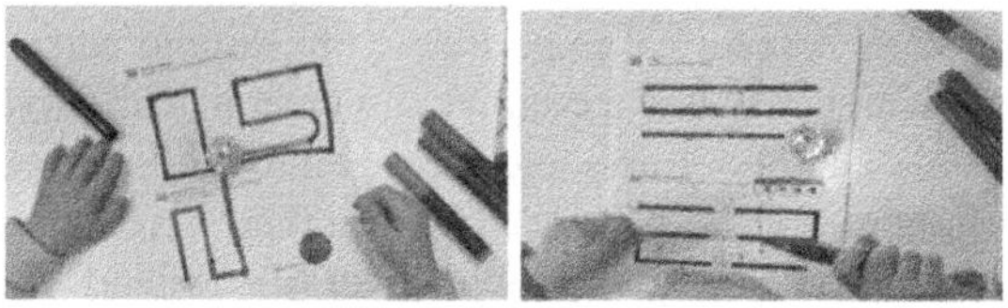

Fig. 4. Child and Ozobot 1. & Child and Ozobot 2. Source: authors' archive.

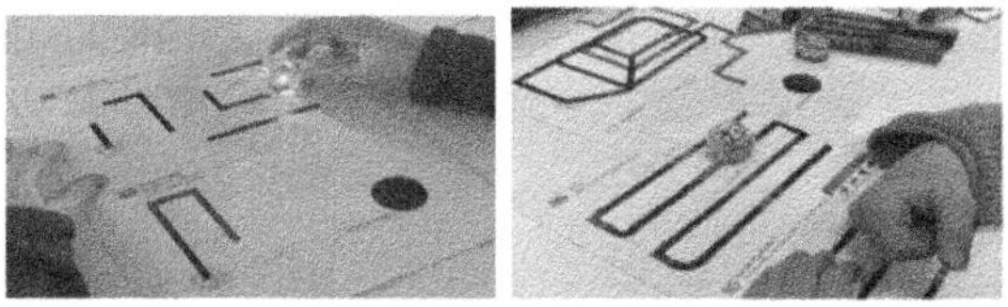

Fig. 5. Pupil and Ozobot 1. & Pupil and Ozobot 2. Source: authors' archive.

4.7 Research Results 1 from the Thematic Drawing and Their Interpretation

We applied the projective drawing technique to analyse the knowledge gained, which allowed us to work with children's and pupils' interpretations. It was about transferring the acquired and elaborated knowledge into graphic visualisation. A thematic drawing is an individual representation of a theme and through it is possible to indirectly "project" a certain mental content. Specific thematic drawings - representations have themselves indicated to us which categories we are to engage with. These categories are: low-statement and high-statement categories (see Figs. 6, 7, 8 and 9). The low-statement representations are saturated with the simplest and most basic elements of the reality depicted. They do not point to mutual and wider contexts.

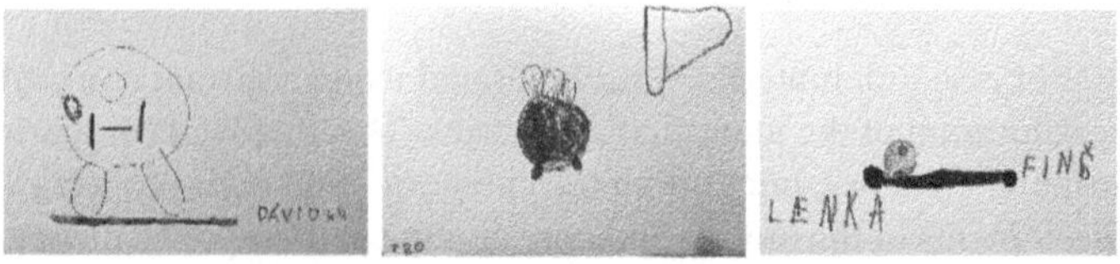

Fig. 6. Low-resolution Representations of Ozobots from Different Perspectives of Children in Kindergarten. Source: authors' archive.

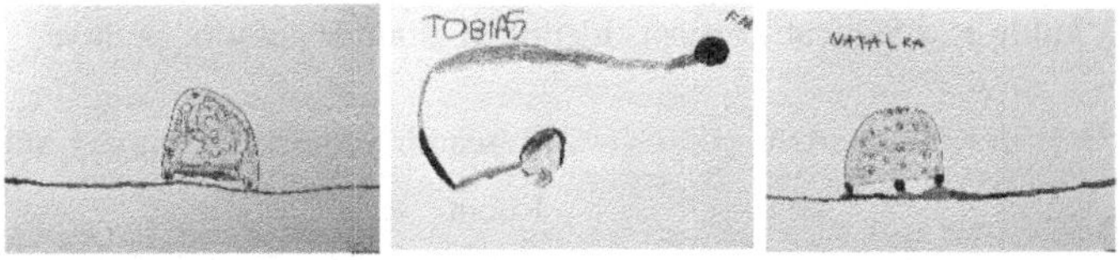

Fig. 7. Highly Informative Representations of Ozobots from Different Perspectives of Children in Kindergarten. Source: authors' archive.

Fig. 8. Low-resolution Representations of Ozobots from Different Perspectives of Pupils in Primary School. Source: authors' archive.

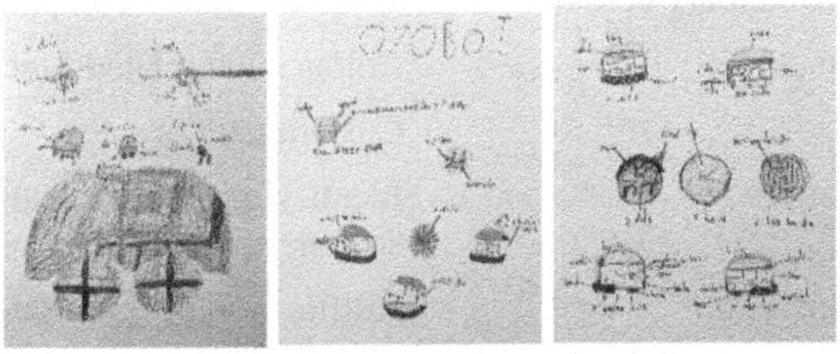

Fig. 9. Highly Informative Representations of Ozobots from Different Perspectives of Pupils in Primary School. Source: authors' archive.

4.8 Research 2 Results from the Focus Group and Their Interpretation

In analysing the data, we applied the open coding method [10] and based on this, we opened the text of the research material and using mental abstraction, we extracted the following categories and subcategories: features, components (related to question 1), functions, conditions of functioning (related to question 2), suggestions for use, and purposefulness (related to question 3). The groups actualize a communicative context in which their symbols, their language, their metaphors, the typical images of their world are revealed. Passages of group exchange have a highly interactive and metaphorical density, they are key in the work of documentary interpretation, which can explain worldviews and collective patterns of action. These passages, with their indications of the context or social environment of the interviewees, contain the modus operandi that guides the practical actions of individuals. Discussion groups allow us to access the typical meanings that are created by connecting spaces of shared experience. We have conducted focus groups in both preschool and elementary schools to uncover aspects of experience and perspectives that would be unattainable outside of group interaction. From our research perspective, the process of participants sharing and comparing ideas and experiences provides a rare opportunity to gain direct evidence of how children and pupils themselves understand commonalities and differences in themes (see Table 1).

Table 1. Identical Concepts Identified. Source: authors' archive.

Research Subjects in Kindergarten	Research Subjects in Primary School
Robotic toy	Robot
Robots	Robots
Ozobots	Ozobots
Luminous balls	
Circles	
Programming	Programming
Programming, but describes the calibration process	Precisely defined calibration with description
Footprint width	Footprint width
Child-dependent programming	Pupil-dependent programming
Movement of the ozobot on the footprint	Movement of the ozobot on the footprint
Base colour and complementary colours	Base colour and complementary colours
Colours and related functions	Colours and related functions
Custom path designs	Custom path designs
Identifying with the pattern	Identifying with the pattern and with a more specific specification
Justification of footprint width	Justification of footprint width
Marking footprints as line/lines	Marking footprints as line/lines
Sound source identification	
Sound coming from the speakers	
The child verbally imitates the sounds of the ozobot	
Special markers	
Source of entertainment	
Special toy	
Use of the ozobots as a special toy in activities	Suggestions for specific uses of the ozobots in teaching

4.9 Research Findings

We believe that the presence of the child learners in the FabLab science centre was a strong motivation issue that presented a significant intellectual challenge. The manipulative activities in conjunction with the understanding of logical situations represented a critical moment of elaboration of the curriculum for the children, pupils, the practical side of which had a smooth progression. The children, pupils received from the presenting subject in a concretized but uncontained form. The attractiveness of the learning environment and learning resources played a large role. The structured nature of the learning environment enabled children, pupils to penetrate a thematically unified concept. The children and pupils were exposed to the educational content in a graded way, in terms of didactic principles. We identified that the children, the pupils, presented their initial experiences with the Ozobots at a level of understanding/comprehension. Some children, pupils interpreted their presentations of experiences at a critical thinking level as they reasoned about the interrelationships between the elements. They also pointed out the reasoning behind the influencing factors. When assessing the cognitive level of processing, a significant finding is that children, pupils are at the level of understanding/comprehension and partly critical thinking. Children, pupils asked questions of the presenter, which made us realize that children, pupils engage an adaptive system of coping with the deficiencies of incompleteness or inaccuracy of information, its deliberate inquiry, searching, searching, but also creating. The actions of children, pupils in didactic situations referred to reasonable reasons for action. Reasonable reasons for action result in the reality of thoughts and actions of their interconnectedness. The acquisition of new knowledge is based on the change - continuous modification of concepts (notions) and conceptions (theories) which the child, pupil possesses. Pre-primary children choose to interpret using gestures, verbal and non-verbal communication. They do not verbalize some concepts but substitute this communication. Unlike primary school pupils, they do not use the concept of calibration. On the question of procurement of ozobots, we obtained affirmative responses from both groups of subjects. Lower-level self-concepts and concepts and their interpretation by description (how). Pre-primary children interpreted their experience of using ozobots at both the level of understanding/comprehension and at the level of concrete operations. The highest level of semantic memory is taking ready-made concepts and conceptions and communicating them (what). Communicating (what) the children have achieved. Primary pupils used critical thinking skills when justifying Ozobot programming - they are at the level of formal operations. Primary pupils verbalise their interpretations, using adequate concepts. They verbalized suggestions for specific uses of ozobots in the instruction. Detection of ozobot movement of patterns was demonstrated by both subjects. The interpretations of the children, pupils ranged from simple to full meaning.

The interesting aspect is that [11]:

- The primary school pupils expressed the view that the kindergarten children were unlikely to be technically proficient in the accuracy of the lines.
- Kindergarten children recreated the rotations and movement of an ozobot by demonstrating body movement.
- Kindergarten and primary school children interpreted the success of mastering a given problem situation.
- Kindergarten children and primary school pupils described the concept of the problem situation in detail.

Note that both groups of subjects had and followed the same conditions, but the graphical recording of the trace was technically more challenging for the kindergarten children. We agree with the research results, among which the autonomous and collaborative subject, who actively discovers and processes the learning through using of ozobots in collaboration with other subjects, has the upper hand. We consider as a valuable result those formed opinions of children and pupils that are anchored in socially acceptable explanations of the use of ozobots. Considering the fact, that the initiation of teaching in support of the use of ozobots is unprecedented in our conditions, it is necessary to talk about the emerging discourse in this area. How this discourse develops will depend on concrete experiences that allow for the mental abstraction of the contents of speech acts and thus create penetration into the interactions of the senses of other subjects. A positive aspect is the teacher-researchers' identification with the possibilities that the use of ozobots in teaching brings.

5 Instead of Conclusion

Children, pupils will encounter an Ozobot for the first time and will they have space to manipulate it in activities? Will they complete the activities with accompanying words from engineers explaining the basic functions? After completing the activities, will they no longer be contacted with the ozobot, engaged in conversations about it, asked about what an Ozobot is, or asked to recall a specific event? But after three weeks, they will be asked to reflect, recapitulate and report on the Ozobot event. This was didactic hypothesizing, which we understand as a prerequisite for pedagogical experimentation of a qualitative type. This hypothesizing of ours allowed us to reveal some causal relations, because this type of experimentation refers us to the motives from which it is possible to identify that something comes from something, that causes something. We conducted the verification processes through the processes of review and reassurance through retrospection. Revision followed action and reflection. By showing professional concern, we also show accountability. The information we gathered was supported by multiple methods, contrasting techniques and forms of evidence such as direct experience, direct and indirect observation, using different research subjects and the use of artefacts. At the same time, the results we present consider the developmental levels, direct experience, and types of judgments that children and students possess. Based on this, we believe that [12, 13]: (1) Teacher-researchers should focus on developing child/pupil-produced generalizations derived from the speech acts of the subjects. (2) Teacher-researchers are to focus on exploring group interactions in the use of ozobots, various materials and other didactic resources, with an emphasis on increasing autonomy in the actions and reasoning of children/pupils in collaboration with their classmates. Attention is also to be focused on the processes of coordinating multiple perspectives of learners in real and potential areas of their action. (3) Teacher-researchers are to focus on the processes of children's/pupils' emerging competences, including a focus on their professional competencies.

This is to point out that this type of teaching should rightly be discussed during undergraduate studies in teaching and educational sciences. We think that practice should also be enriched by this type of teaching. Building on this research, research will be conducted to explore critical thinking and action with undergraduate students using Ozobots specifically. We will of course continue to do further research with children and pupils.

Acknowledgment. The study was supported by KEGA grant 026UK-4/2022 The Concept of Constructionism and Augmented Reality in STEM Education.

References

1. Czakóova, K., Takáč, O., Végh, L.: Program code simulation by using Ozobot. Int. J. Adv. Nat. Sci. Eng. Res. **7**(10), 441–444 (2023)
2. Vygotskij, L.S.: Psychologie myšlení a reči. Portál, Praha (2004)
3. Meltzer, L.: Executive Function in Education. From Theory to Practice. 2nd edn. The Guilford Press, New York (2018)
4. Rodrigo, M.J., Arnay, J.: La construcción del conocimiento escolar. Paidós, Barcelona (1997)
5. Gregory, R.L.: Eye and Brain. The Psychology of Seeing. 5th edn. Oxford University Press, Oxford (1997)
6. Coll, C., Palacios, J., Marchesi, Á.: Desarrollo psicológico y educación. 2. Psicología de la educación escolar. Psicología y Educación. 2.ª edición. Alianza Editorial S. A., Madrid (2014)
7. Barbour, R.: Los grupos de discusión en Investigación Cualitativa. 2.ª edición. Ediciones Morata, Madrid (2019)
8. Rogora P.: L'osservazione: uno strumento operativo per "conoscere" e per costruire relazioni in contesti educativi e formativi. Università degli Studi di Torino, Facoltà di Scienze della Formazione, Corso di Laurea in Scienze dell'educazione (a.a. 2000–2001). Dispensa per il corso di pedagogia sperimentale (prof. Roberto Trinchero). https://www.far.unito.it/trinchero/psd/rogora.htm
9. Quintana Peña, A.: Metodología de Investigación Científi ca Cualitativa. In: Quintana Peña, A., Montgomery, W. (eds.) Psicología: Tópicos de actualidad. UNMSM, Lima, pp. 47–84 (2006)
10. Strauss, A., Corbinová, J.: Základy kvalitativního výzkumu. Albert, Boskovice (1999)
11. Kostrub, D.: Dieťa/žiak/študent – učivo – učiteľ, didaktický alebo bermudský tro-juholník? Rokus, Prešov (2008)
12. Kostrub, D.: Učiteľ výskumník - Profesia založená na výskume. Dizajny výskumu a premeny výučby. 1. vyd. Univerzita Komenského v Bratislave, Bratislava (2022)
13. Kostrub, D.: Základy kvalitatívnej metodológie. Keď interpretované významy znamenajú viac ako vysoké čísla. 1. vyd. Univerzita Komenského v Bratislave, Bratislava (2016)

Developing 21st Century Skills Through Micro:bits in Inclusive Education

Ján Gunčaga, Jana Lopúchová, and Martina Ambrušová(✉)

Faculty of Education, Comenius University Bratislava, Račianska 59, 813 34 Bratislava, Slovakia
{guncaga,lopuchova,ambrusova3}@fedu.uniba.sk

Abstract. The BBC micro:bit is a programmable mini-computer that serves as an excellent tool for developing digital skills, not only for students in mainstream schools but also for students with disabilities in their education. The application of micro:bits in education is becoming increasingly common, and their benefits are particularly evident in STEM subjects. This scientific study focuses on describing the use of micro:bits in inclusive education, emphasizing their role in supporting the development of digital skills and other competencies essential for the 21st century, such as critical thinking, creativity, flexibility, cooperation, communication, cultural awareness, civic, technical, and information literacy. The study addresses the advantages and challenges of working with micro:bits in an inclusive school environment and highlights the necessity of implementing new technologies and approaches in the education of all students. For the purposes of the study, interviews were conducted with seven computer science teachers in Slovakia who use the BBC micro:bit in their teaching and work with students with special needs. The thematic analysis method was used to process the interviews. The study's findings reveal that the BBC micro:bit supports the development of 21st-century skills among students in inclusive education at primary schools in Slovakia. At the same time, the study identifies the most significant benefits of the BBC micro:bit for teachers, as well as obstacles such as insufficient technical, financial, and material resources and the need for more time-consuming preparation by teachers to integrate this digital tool into the teaching process.

Keywords: Micro:bit · 21st-century Skills · Inclusive Education · Digital Technologies and Skills · Multidisciplinary Thinking

1 Introduction to the Issue

In the context of modern education, digital competencies and technical skills play an increasingly important role in ensuring essential and successful functioning in the 21st century. Critical thinking, creativity, flexibility, cooperation, communication, and well-developed technical and informational skills are key competencies required for students to become proficient and competitive in the digital world. At the same time, it is crucial that these competencies are developed not only within the teaching processes of mainstream schools but also in inclusive education, which provides access to these skills for

Ł. Tomczyk (Ed.): NMP 2024, CCIS 2537, pp. 110–128, 2025.
https://doi.org/10.1007/978-3-031-95627-0_8

students with disabilities. Just as students learn a language in school and must understand its various components (such as syntax, grammar, literary works, genres, etc.), they must similarly learn a programming language and discover their ability to think digitally. Understanding computational technologies, programming, and programming concepts has become a key skill for students in modern society—just as reading, writing, and basic arithmetic are fundamental educational skills for life [16].

One of the effective tools that has proven to be exceptionally beneficial in this field is the **BBC micro:bit**—a small, programmable mini-computer originally developed to support the teaching of computer science and programming for younger students. Scientists at the BBC (British Broadcasting Corporation), in collaboration with other industry partners, designed and developed this educational tool to encourage students to learn basic algorithmic skills [3]. The micro:bit is designed to be accessible and usable not only for tech-savvy individuals but also for beginners, including children with special educational needs. This tool enables students to learn interactively about the principles of programming, algorithmic problem-solving, and digital technologies through practical and creative activities. The micro:bit is a powerful educational tool that can enhance student learning outcomes and create a dynamic educational environment. It can be used across various technology, computing, and science-related subjects, as well as in integrated lessons or extracurricular activities.

Using the micro:bit not only increases students' interest in the subject but also helps develop computational thinking, problem-solving skills, creativity, numerical competencies, critical thinking, and other skills [11]. While there are no official curricula established for working with the micro:bit, it is easily accessible and provides flexibility for teachers to design and personalize individual tasks [9].

The **BBC micro:bit** is a device measuring 4.3 × 5.2 cm with a processor, accelerometer, and magnetometer sensors, Bluetooth and USB connectivity, a 25-LED display, two programmable buttons, and power options through USB or an external battery. The device's inputs and outputs are managed via five circular connectors that are part of a larger 25-pin edge connector. These allow for the attachment of numerous accessories, ensuring versatile use of the micro:bit [4] (Fig. 1).

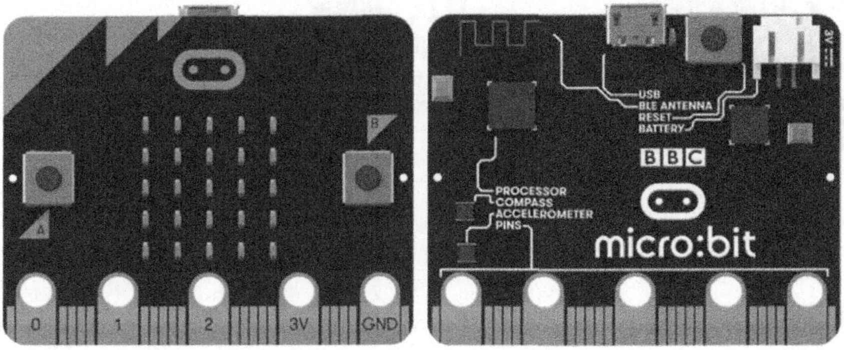

Fig. 1. BBC micro:bit – Front and Back Side (Source: University of Brighton).

Programs supported by the BBC micro:bit are coded in web-based programming environments and languages that do not require installation, such as MakeCode, Javascript integrated into MakeCode, Scratch, AppInventor, and Python. The program can be written in several ways: using an offline editor or the official online environment [4]. This online environment is an advantage as it helps teachers manage students' code even during remote learning.

The versatility of the BBC micro:bit is also supported by its use, which is not limited to in-person teaching in schools. It is equally well utilized in remote learning. We will demonstrate two web platforms that are most commonly used in school environments: **Microsoft MakeCode** (Fig. 2) and **Micro:bit Classroom** (Fig. 3).

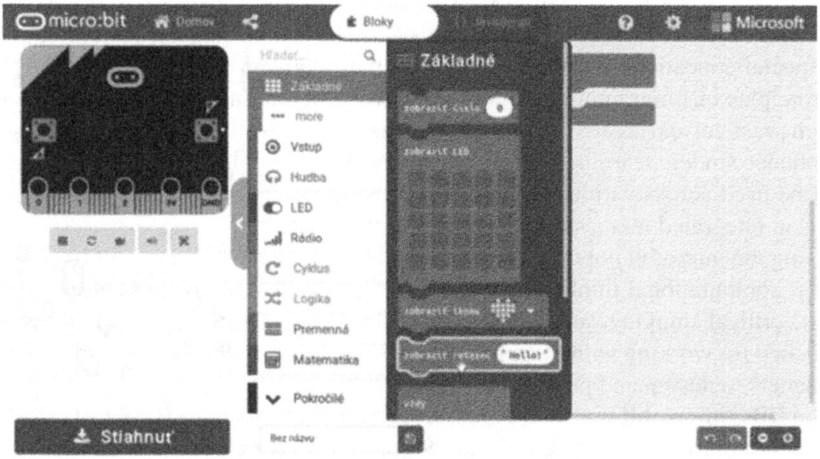

Fig. 2. MakeCode – Program Sample (Source: Učíme s hardvérom, https://www.ucimeshardverom.sk/materialy/microbit_makecode/digitalna_menovka/)

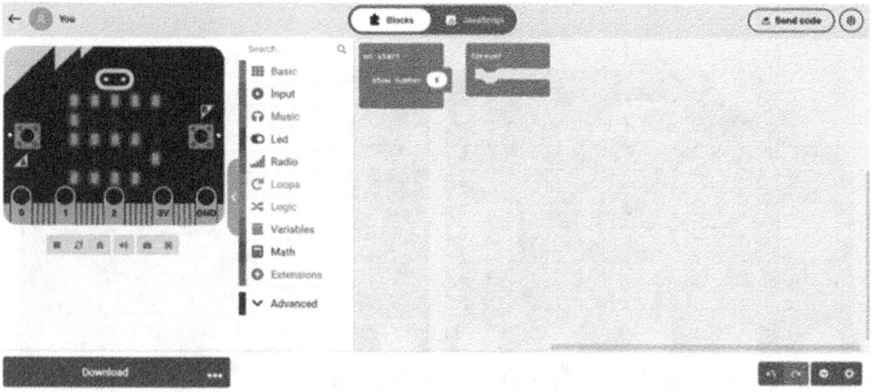

Fig. 3. Micro:bit classroom – Program Sample (Source: https://classroom.microbit.org/).

A teacher can conduct lessons through online teaching but can also assign tasks for independent work directly in MakeCode using comments. The teacher can prepare various types of tasks for students and let them solve them [8]. Due to its compactness and built-in sensors, which are a significant advantage compared to other microcontrollers, many technical processes can be simulated directly in the classroom. The use of expansion components, such as electrically conductive thread, LEDs, and a power board, provides an opportunity to understand how things work in our everyday lives. Additionally, these components enable simple experimental learning and help explain basic physical phenomena. There is a wide range of STEAM (Science, Technology, Engineering, Arts, and Mathematics) projects that can be realized through the BBC micro:bit, such as: games, security and safety, solving real-world problems, smart agriculture, creating art (e.g., paper-cutting lamps), or even designing a smart home [2, 17].

1.1 BBC Micro:Bit in Inclusive Education

The **BBC micro:bit** can be an effective tool in inclusive education due to its simplicity and ease of programmability. It is visual and concrete, providing immediate feedback, which are important parameters for its adaptability in an inclusive environment. Inclusive education is an approach that enables the full inclusion of students with disabilities into the regular educational process, thus supporting their active participation in teaching and the development of their personal and professional competencies. According to teachers, the BBC micro:bit proves to be an ideal tool for supporting the development of not only technical skills but also other areas needed for students' personal growth, such as the development of communication, cooperation, cultural awareness, and other key competencies for the 21st century. Given the rapid technological progress and the growing demand for digital competence, it is essential for educational systems to effectively respond to these changes and enable students to develop the skills required not only for their personal and academic development but also for their professional lives in an increasingly digitalized society. It can even be assumed that students with diagnoses such as autism or ADHD may have exceptional digital thinking abilities, making this teaching method particularly suitable for them [1].

The **BBC micro:bit**, as one of many tools, plays a key role in the development of practical digital skills needed for the 21st century. Working with micro:bits supports many areas of student development, such as critical thinking and creative problem-solving through hands-on projects that encourage collaboration and an innovative approach to designing practical solutions. It allows students to learn the basics of programming in a logical sequence, utilizing algorithmic thinking, which is essential in today's digital age. Using micro:bits, not only in education but also in extracurricular activities, fosters creativity and students' ability to implement innovative procedures, for example, in creating their own applications or building various electronic devices. It strengthens teamwork, develops critical thinking, analytical skills, and communication skills, all of which are essential for effective inclusive education for both mainstream students and students with special educational needs.

Inclusive education is currently a priority in many countries worldwide. An inclusive culture and the achievement of inclusive goals while adhering to the principles of inclusive education can be reached through various means. One of the less typical tools for developing students and digital skills for the 21st century is undoubtedly the **micro:bit**. Micro:bits in inclusive education allow for experimentation with multiple concepts, which significantly contributes to acquiring and improving technical skills and understanding STEM subjects. The lessons spent with micro:bits help develop adaptability and flexibility, enabling students to adjust to the ever-changing conditions of digital technologies and respond flexibly to new digital challenges. Here, we can clearly draw a parallel between the disability itself and working with micro:bits, particularly in the step-by-step process (coping with disability versus a step-by-step approach in working with the micro:bit), as well as overcoming obstacles and barriers and the effort required to do so.

Collaboration and teamwork are essential elements of many processes in the lives of all people. Without collaboration, the results of many activities would not be exceptional, which essentially demonstrates that when multiple individuals come together, both those who are able-bodied and those with disabilities in an inclusive environment, the results of their collaboration are of high creative quality with pragmatic effects. Working with micro:bits motivates students to solve problems and innovate together. Students can share their ideas and participate in completing tasks according to their abilities, which inherently strengthens their communication, cooperation, responsibility, and the ability to give and receive feedback. Ultimately, this contributes to building strong social bonds and social skills necessary for joint inclusive education. Students learn to clearly articulate their thoughts and opinions and present their ideas to others, strengthening their public speaking and argumentation skills. Teamwork in creating or solving projects leads to constructive discussions, where students learn to actively listen and respond to others' ideas.

Working with micro:bits promotes students' critical thinking by enabling them to solve real-world problems through programming. Students must analyze situations, identify problems, search for logical solutions, and try multiple ways to solve the problem. Micro:bits allow students to transfer theoretical knowledge into practice through hands-on learning and experimentation, and to optimize their proposed solutions. Finally, the visualization of results and the interactive features of micro:bits increase student engagement and motivation when solving problems. The use of micro:bits in inclusive education is highly flexible. Students can customize them according to their interests and needs, utilize additional additive technologies, and experiment with different approaches, which enhances their adaptability to new challenges. Just as additive technologies are utilized, the transfer of micro:bits can also be applied to various environments or fields. One such area is, for example, culture and traditions, where students can create applications or devices that preserve or promote different folk customs, languages, or historical aspects of culture. This fosters understanding and respect for different cultures and an open approach to diversity.

Information literacy is currently one of the key competencies, especially for students with disabilities. There are many ways and methods to acquire information literacy. Micro:bits can be a highly innovative and motivating tool for acquiring information (or modifying the ways of obtaining it), as well as practical skills. While working with micro:bits, students learn the ethical aspects of using digital tools (including AI) to acquire necessary information.

In addition to the aforementioned areas of student development, micro:bits can be a tool for enhancing technological and civic literacy and addressing various societal issues, such as ecology, health, etc.

Working with micro:bits contributes to the development of social responsibility in students and reinforces values such as trust and mutual support. Through projects focused on solving real-world problems, such as ecological issues or helping the community, students become aware of the importance of the ethical aspects of technology. In this way, students learn to consider the impact of their actions. Thanks to micro:bits, students have the opportunity to engage in activities that support community development and increase their sense of responsibility toward others.

To summarize, working with micro:bits offers significant benefits for students with disabilities in several areas:

Development of technical skills - Helps students learn the basics of programming, electronics, and technology, which can spark their interest in technical fields.

Development of creativity and self-realization - Allows students to create their own applications or devices, promoting their creativity and innovative thinking. Ultimately, even students with disabilities who may have deficits in certain developmental or functional areas, self-realization is a significant element in their sense of success and worth.

Development of social skills - Teamwork strengthens interpersonal skills and creates space for social interactions between healthy and disabled students.

Development of problem-solving thinking and logical reasoning - Programming and working with micro:bits teach students how to proceed step-by-step and break down problems into smaller parts. Simultaneously, synthesis is applied, where multiple solved sub-tasks together form a comprehensive solution to a problem.

Development of motor skills and sensory modalities - For students with physical disabilities, micro:bits can simulate interaction with the world and develop specific motor skills. Sensors and various devices allow students to experiment, learn about their environment, and interact with it.

Personalization and individualization - Micro:bits tailored to students' needs (personalization) can enable differentiated teaching, allowing each student to work at a level that suits their abilities and interests (individualization).

Self-esteem and motivation - Successfully solving tasks with micro:bits can significantly boost students' self-esteem and motivate them to continue learning and personal development.

However, it is important to consider several critical areas to ensure effective inclusive education with the use of micro:bits. These include: **Accessibility** (of materials, buildings, educational tools, and technologies); **Development of motor skills** (due to potential movement restrictions in students with disabilities); **Support for communication** (especially for students with verbal communication difficulties, the use of AAC, alternative communication methods, etc.); **Engagement of various sensory modalities** (hearing, touch, vision, smell, etc.); **Differentiation of teaching** (adapting tasks to various levels of skills and abilities of students with disabilities); **Support for collaboration** (e.g., creating environments that promote cooperation); **Emotional support** (through empathy, patience, attention, and understanding students' needs); **Evaluation of student progress**, which should be flexible and take into account individual achievements and development of each student.

The BBC micro:bit brings several benefits to teachers, making their lesson preparation more efficient, easing student motivation, and helping make lessons more engaging. For many educators, micro:bits have become an effective tool to engage students who are harder to motivate or those who face challenges in STEM subjects due to disabilities. In the study *Creating cool stuff*, 15 teachers expressed that micro:bit offers four main advantages in teaching: tangibility, creativity development, openness (ease of use), and programming skill development. Teachers receive support through various organizations that offer free online training. These organizations also provide numerous guides that simplify the process of teaching with BBC micro:bits, even in inclusive education settings. By sharing experiences from other educators, these organizations can serve as inspiration and examples for teaching with BBC micro:bit.

Moreover, programming with micro:bit is so simple and intuitive that teachers can confidently teach their subject without being experts in micro:bits. Teachers' experiences highlight how fun it can be to learn alongside students. Completing training courses and education can also enrich a teacher's portfolio of ideas and tasks, expanding their knowledge on this subject.

1.2 Teaching Programming in Slovakia

In the Slovak education system, programming basics begin to be taught in approximately the 7th grade of elementary school and continue into the 1st year of secondary school. The exact timing and content may vary depending on the specific school and its curriculum. According to the State Educational Program for the second stage of elementary schools (ISCED 2) in Slovakia, students are introduced to fundamental concepts in informatics, such as data, information, algorithms, and programs. The goal is to develop the ability to algorithmically approach a given problem and to build programming skills. At a higher level of education (ISCED 3), the goal of teaching informatics is to teach students basic concepts, procedures, and tools in informatics, including the development of programming skills, and to provide deeper understanding of algorithms, data structures, and programming applications in practice.

The State Educational Program allows the inclusion of basic programming fundamentals and the application of online programming environments such as MakeCode in lower grades and Python, Pascal, C, and Java at higher levels of education. For schools educating students with autism or other pervasive developmental disorders, the State Educational Program allows for work with a child-friendly programming language in the 8th and 9th grades of elementary school as part of the informatics subject, teaching elementary commands, and working with robotic kits. Students can follow instructions and search for algorithmic procedures and solutions in a child-friendly programming environment.

2 Context and Methodology of the Research

The issue of using micro:bits in education is relatively new, and for this reason, we raised many questions, such as how the use of BBC micro:bits contributes to the development of key competencies in students; how it influences students' critical thinking, creativity, or digital literacy? What are the strengths and weaknesses of using BBC micro:bits in education? How does working with micro:bits contribute to the development of students' digital competencies? Are there examples of good practices in the educational environment? We sought answers to these and many other questions in our research.

The research, the results of which are presented in this paper, was conducted in 2024 through interviews with seven informatics teachers who use BBC micro:bit devices in their classes to teach basic programming. The goal of the research was to determine how teachers perceive micro:bits in education, what significance they attribute to them, and to identify the positives, negatives, and challenges associated with the implementation of micro:bits in education. Each participant had experience using micro:bits ranging from 3 to 10 years. Given the teachers' positions in schools across Slovakia, the interviews were conducted in two formats: in person and online via the Microsoft Teams platform. The research sample consisted of teachers from various types of schools, with experience working with both regular students and students with special educational needs.

3 Results and Discussion

The data was processed using a thematic analysis of the interviews. We first read through the data multiple times and analyzed it in detail. We eliminated so-called empty statements and marked significant excerpts. Then, we identified common thematic units within the responses, capturing the opinions and experiences, as well as the individual perspectives of the teachers. These procedures allowed us to gain a detailed understanding of the use of micro:bits in the educational process and to describe them. In the following text, we will discuss each area in more detail.

The Importance Of BBC Micro:bits in Education. Although micro:bits are relatively new in education, there are schools and educators where they have already been used for several years. Educators, together with students, have had the opportunity to not only familiarize themselves with them but also work with them periodically and discover their capabilities. *"Micro:bit has finally brought something practical into the classroom. The lesson is interesting. Students have something tangible in their hands and receive immediate feedback. It's not just about the monitor and the screen, but also about students programming something and actually seeing changes on the micro:bit display."* Teachers particularly appreciate the practicality of micro:bits, and according to them, their significance is mainly motivational. *"The significance of micro:bits is very large. I teach at the primary level and have been using micro:bits in education since the third grade. The children love it, they are drawn into the lesson. All the possibilities, and the fact that they can use the computer and still have a physical board that creates all these effects."*

Many students today have trouble maintaining focus. While micro:bits are a significant motivational element in education, not all children enjoy working with them, and after a certain period, they lose interest. *"In general, micro:bits open up completely new possibilities in education. However, our students have poor concentration. After a while, it stops being interesting to them, they simply hit the limits of their thinking capacities. This is true even for those students who initially find micro:bits interesting."*

Another participant appreciated the playful approach to working with micro:bits: *"The significance is very large. Students learn new things in a playful way and thus gain the basics of programming."*

One of the teachers took a more multidimensional view and expressed the following: *"Micro:bit can be used not only for robotics but also for teaching computer science, environmental measurements, or even humanities subjects such as music education and so on. My experience with micro:bit is very positive."*

Ultimately, the economic aspect of micro:bits is also not negligible. *"It's affordable, and you can cover the entire curriculum with it. That's a big advantage. What I like most about micro:bits is their versatility, as they can be easily combined with things like 3D printing or Raspberry Pi, and so on. Moreover, there are many resources available that allow you to teach various subjects."*

Advantages of Micro:bits in Education. Participants consider micro:bits interesting and attractive, especially for students with autism, as they appreciate stable and structured environments. MakeCode provides this for them. Another advantage, particularly for students with special educational needs (SEN), is the minimal text included in the blocks. Another benefit is the colorful design of the blocks and their easy manipulation: *"They don't need to write anything, memorize complicated things; everything is prepared, and they just drag the block where they need it."* Another participant stated that another advantage of micro:bits is the immediate feedback, as students can immediately see what they programmed and whether they programmed it correctly.

Micro:bits bring joy to education: *"The joy of achieving something, creating something themselves, and coming up with something. Even just a simply drawn picture, a smiley face, or a heart... So it was incredible for them to see for the first time that they created something on the computer and the effect it had on the micro:bit."*

One participant compared the micro:bit to technology that connects students to the digital world: *"When students get a micro:bit in their hands, they can work with it. While in their home environment, many of them don't have access to anything similar. Of course, schools have different possibilities. What more can we give them than a stimulating environment? They have the opportunity to test their skills, compare themselves with others, achieve something, learn new things, and discover their abilities."*

The statement also included SEN students: *"They see the world through completely different eyes. But of course, we all see it through different eyes. After all, every student is different. And some may go further in their future lives if they have opportunities."*

Teachers also consider it an advantage that students can immediately verify whether what they programmed works or not. The student gets immediate feedback. *"Its strength is, first of all, that it is interesting, small, programmable, and there are many possibilities for children to try out. Of course, advanced functions require significant support from the teacher or more lessons to learn how it works, but students manage the basic blocks and simple projects."*

An interesting feature of micro:bits is that they contribute to the systematic development of students and logical step-by-step thinking: *"For those who enjoy it, you can clearly see progress in systematic work and algorithmization. And then also in the fact that they try to discover something new on their own."*

The fact is that the micro:bit is a multifunctional tool that can be beautifully connected with many subjects: *"Students can program a simple musical instrument, work with experiments, and thus connect the micro:bit with physics or natural sciences. So the micro:bit definitely has many advantages. Especially for older students."*

According to teachers, students progress very quickly and practically live with the micro:bit. They can operate it independently, prepare their projects, and be creative. They advance in simple programming, learning through play. *"They actually want the micro:bit to do something, perform a function, so they program. And they don't even realize it."*

Participants also highlighted the development of logical thinking through micro:bits: *"Children are exposed to programming basics at an early age, which can be an advantage for their further growth. They learn through play, which is fantastic. Even Comenius talked about it. They don't even realize they're programming. Learning is fun for them."*

Another feature that helps teachers is the versatility of the micro:bit, whether in terms of its connection to various components, add-on modules, or compatibility: *"Its compatibility is excellent. Even though it's the same board, when they make new versions, it's still compatible with many accessories and improvements. Robotic toys often don't have such backward compatibility, but the micro:bit always maintains it. This means that when I buy 10 micro:bits for one project, then buy 10 more micro:bits and add to their number over several years, everything is mutually compatible."*

Teachers further described micro:bits as relatively cheap and thus affordable for schools and students. *"LEGO and other electronic kits are quite expensive, and their prices keep rising. The micro:bit is very intuitive, provides a clear and formal environment, and does not require a lot of motor or mental skills from the student."*

From a practical standpoint, one of the advantages of micro:bits is their tangibility. This means that computer science does not "only happen" on the computer screen; students can physically hold the product, manipulate it, and see the real result. It is more concrete for them, and even for students with special educational needs, it can provide great satisfaction in their efforts. This implies that for students with any health-related disabilities, it is very important for the learning material to be something they can physically grasp. If students have physical disabilities, they can use various mechanisms to control the micro:bit, such as an adapted joystick. "We work a lot with 3D printing, where we can print aids or specific products of their work for these students. Also, adapting aids to control the computer. Thanks to this, they can use MakeCode. For students with intellectual disabilities, the platform is very simple and intuitive. They can follow colors, which makes it very easy for them. So the children are able to assemble codes just by color, and they can independently program a block that performs a function. Educators can adapt tasks and the environment on individual computers to suit the individual needs of students, considering their abilities and limits." If a programming task provides a practical and meaningful product or project, the outcome, including the experiences gained from solving it, is motivating. Such connections are supported by the tangible nature of the BBC micro:bit. Similar positive results regarding the use of the BBC micro:bit in teaching have been reported in research within Slovakia [7].

Disadvantages of Micro:bits in Education. Teachers consider the small screen on the micro:bit to be a disadvantage. Another disadvantage identified in the teachers' statements is that some schools do not have enough financial resources for educational aids and cannot secure additional devices for the micro:bits. *"If schools received such sets or had the option to buy a large set with more micro:bits, sensors, and accessories that they could use, I think that would really help."*

Financial limitations in securing projects are also often encountered in other studies. A research study from Boston University describes that one of the constraints currently preventing full and widespread implementation of the micro:bit project is financial resources. Teachers with limited budgets may realize that the costs of a fully functional and equipped project with all the devices and accessories could be prohibitive. One possible adjustment to reduce costs is using the free simulation tool on makecode.microbit.org, which allows for simulating what the micro:bit can do [12]. Another issue is the connection via the micro USB connector. *"These days, there are USB connectors that are more durable, and I definitely think the micro:bits could be connected with a different connector. But I don't see the 'C' connector as the best solution."* Another weak point could be the need for a larger number of teachers and the requirement for more time, which is also a disadvantage because it causes students to lose attention and motivation.

Introducing the micro:bit as a new element in teaching offers many opportunities for engaging and effective education, but it requires teachers to prepare by learning the basics of programming and getting familiar with the micro:bit environment. Some key recommendations for initiatives involving the introduction of the micro:bit into teaching are as follows:

- Teachers need time to prepare so they can integrate the BBC micro:bit into the curriculum, as well as time for training, planning, and curriculum development.
- Consultation with "experts" among teachers is needed to develop teaching materials using strong pedagogical approaches.
- Attention should be given to providing resources that cover several weeks, include supporting evaluation activities, and are connected to the current curriculum. This is more effective than providing many short and unconnected activities.
- Teachers should be offered opportunities for professional development in programming. In addition to subject knowledge and familiarity with the technology, it would be useful for teachers (whether future or active) to understand the pedagogical approaches applicable to programming. This can be achieved through professional development [15].

Teachers also commented on the more complex preparation for teaching. *"...but only at the beginning, until the teacher learns the instructions, what command is needed for what, and what its function is. It took me a while at first to prepare my lessons. It just needed more time. And the kids helped a lot because they tried many things on their own, even without us going through it, and they just wanted to click and see what would happen. It was so interesting that we learned from each other. Then they worked independently. I just had to give them the task."*

Teachers often ask themselves how to engage students and motivate them to work. Today's students and youth are part of the digital generation, who are not satisfied with printed books, paper, and pens. They want to explore, create, and be busy with something. If the school only has basic equipment, students lose interest fairly quickly. And then, when everything needs to be packed away, storage space becomes crucial, which is not always sufficient in classrooms. *"We faced the issue that when we want to tidy up the entire kit, we need larger transparent boxes where the whole set can fit. If you have more kits, there are many small components, and I see the problem in keeping it organized and completing each set because you also use elements from another kit during work, then it gets mixed up, and restoring it to its original state can be a problem."*

Development of Key Competencies for the 21st Century. Skills for the 21st century are crucial for success in a dynamic and rapidly changing environment, including in education. These include critical thinking, problem-solving, creativity and innovation, collaboration and communication, as well as digital literacy, among others. Critical thinking is especially essential for effectively analyzing information. Creativity and innovation are key for generating new ideas and approaches, which are vital in today's competitive environment. Collaboration and communication at all levels of educational institutions are also important. Finally, digital literacy is an absolute necessity, as digital and smart technologies have permeated almost all areas of life. Together, these skills form the foundation for a successful future career and personal development in the 21st century. STEM subjects (science, technology, engineering, and mathematics) play a critical role in shaping competency-based knowledge and developing 21st-century skills. These expected skills can also be supported by teaching the basics of programming. Therefore, integrating programming and robotics into education from an early age worldwide is key [13]. We were also interested in whether it is possible to develop these competencies through micro:bits in relation to the issue at hand.

Teachers expressed mostly positive opinions. Although not all of them mentioned every competency, they primarily see the significance of micro:bits in developing analytical thinking (in mathematics, one can reach a result through multiple paths, and a similar concept applies to micro:bit), in the development of communication skills (students need to communicate with each other, especially when checking their procedures), and in supporting interdisciplinary connections.

Another important competency, especially in today's information-saturated world, is critical thinking: *"The student sees that something was not done correctly and must change it. They have to think about how to change it, and possibly agree with the group and communicate it, defend their procedures, and eliminate undesirable obstacles."*

According to teachers, micro:bits also develop teamwork since students collaboratively prepare a project. They need to agree, work together, finish it, and present it. Analytical skills are developed as students decide which blocks to use when breaking down different parts of the project, realizing what needs to be prepared, and understanding the sequence of steps required to achieve the desired effect. They must consider what response each change they program will evoke. And they must account for the fact that not everything will go as planned and required. This also leads to the identification of another area in the research—team collaboration.

Key competencies also include social responsibility (mutual support, helping the community) and ethics of behavior, or adherence to moral values. According to the content of education outlined in the national curriculum, teachers guide students to help each other and create products/outcomes that will benefit broader communities. *"Well, if someone is struggling, they can ask me for help. But I teach them to turn to classmates who have already finished their work during the lesson. They go to them, ask, or call them to come and sit next to them. It's great—they know how to support and help each other."*

"Competencies are also developed when they engage in a project that helps and is useful. Projects with micro:bits can be focused on helping the community, such as sensors for seniors that alert them to danger. Students learn empathy and responsibility."

Teamwork. According to teachers, micro:bits can significantly impact communication in the classroom, student collaboration, and even support peer learning to a large extent. *"In any case, when I give students a task in which they need to do something together, they have to think about it. They must decide who will do what."*

In effective teamwork, it is crucial to delegate tasks and responsibilities for individual steps and actions. *"When I want to create something with students, I think about what I need to prepare and what command to give to ensure it goes through the display or produces a sound, or even closes a circuit. When the students understand the essence of each step and the display lights up or it starts beeping, chirping, or playing a melody, they realize that it is the result of their collective effort."*

However, not all students show interest in working with micro:bits. Therefore, teachers believe it is important for the group to honestly discuss the negative aspects of the process, admit mistakes, or acknowledge that some students have participated less or not at all. It is then up to the teacher to explain that not everyone knows everything, but everyone knows something, and each person has different abilities. *"Not everyone knows everything, so it's good when we're in a group, and each person can express themselves, then someone needs to present it. So, the students look for someone who is communicative and knows how to explain it."* However, in every group, there is usually a leader who becomes the main focal point of attention: *"I had a very clever student who missed a lot because of extracurricular activities, but when he came to school, he quickly caught up. When he was at school, he pointed out to others, especially those who were slacking off and didn't want to work. He was a leader-type and found his place in coordinating his peers. He could independently manage the group, learned how to take over my role, and collaborated with the other students."*

When working with micro:bits, students can inspire each other. *"Many kids are fascinated by sounds and creating songs. This is excellent, really. Kids try to compose songs, jingles."*

Creativity in Working with Micro:bits. Like any new element introduced into education, working with micro:bits requires a certain degree of creativity and flexibility from both teachers and students. From our perspective, micro:bits are essential in supporting creativity, as the output products are a reflection of how a student thinks, connects information, solves problems, and ultimately processes something meaningful and significant. *"This is especially evident when searching for different solutions. One task has* *multiple ways to accomplish it, and students explore these options to achieve the goal. They must use their creativity. In practice, we focused on finding as many solutions as possible, and students were rewarded for their efforts."*

Another teacher expressed a similar view, highlighting how creativity is fostered in programming with micro:bits: *"...because when I showed them the basic blocks and what could be done with them, I left the rest to them, allowing them to experiment. So, their success made them happy. If something didn't work out, they could either ask how to solve it or help each other, which also reflects that teamwork is functioning."*

As shown in the teachers' testimonies, mutual support and enjoyable, non-coercive learning are essential in working with micro:bits. One participant shared an excellent example: *"I taught at a small school with combined grades of third and fourth graders. The fourth graders had computer science, and the third graders had reading. I worked with the fourth graders on a project, while the third graders read. One student finished early and, in his free time, created a project. He took a micro:bit and programmed pictograms linked to the reading text from the textbook, using buttons A, B, and shake. Through these pictograms, icons, and symbols, he essentially retold the content of the article. He read or told the text, and when he reached a certain part, he pressed a button, and an icon appeared to complement the text. Later, I invited this student to my next art class with first and second graders. He stood in front of the class and used the micro:bit to tell the story to the younger students. It was a beautiful example of peer learning. He was 8 years old. It was a great experience for me and the students. So, his creativity was excellent."*

When working with micro:bits, students may not always get the program to work on the first try, leading to initial failure. However, it is the teacher's role to provide support and correctly guide the student: *"Creativity is especially evident when students try their own projects, using available accessories and experimenting with effects. They invent new uses and functions. The micro:bit forces students to search for the right processes and solutions because when it doesn't do what they need, they must return to the steps and figure out where the mistake is. They learn to deal with their own failures and correct them."*

Some research suggests a significant impact of digital educational tools, such as the BBC micro:bit, on the development of creativity. However, these studies are often limited by the short duration of the research [14] and other constraints that micro:bits may cause in teaching.

Development of Logical and Critical Thinking. Both logical and critical thinking are essential components of a student's competence profile. Teachers should support students in solving problems on their own and looking for available solutions, using all their knowledge and information. However, this information needs to be rationally assessed and filtered according to its importance and truthfulness (critical thinking) and used in the creation of products through their intellectual or practical activities (logical thinking).

One educator mentioned that working with micro:bits enriches their teaching, as students see that what they program is useful and practical. Another teacher emphasized the importance of scaffolding and positively motivating students towards independence.

The development of logical and critical thinking puts a significant burden on the teacher, requiring careful preparation of lessons and the logical sequencing of steps. *"I had to prepare for the lessons and allocate time to break down the material and prepare tasks for students. I'm not sure if there's a manual for micro:bit tasks for each grade, probably not. I created tasks tailored to my class."*

For working with micro:bits, a good level of perception from the student is important. If a student sees the individual steps of programming the micro:bit and subsequently sees or hears the programmed output, they are more likely to remember it. One participant expressed: "*...Micro:bit mainly allowed me to create an interesting lesson, and I felt good knowing I was delivering something engaging that captured the students' attention right from the start. And especially, that we could start programming in a playful way."*

Working with micro:bits fundamentally develops logical thinking in teachers as well. *"I really enjoyed it, even after completing the introductory training with 'Teaching with Hardware.' I tried to figure out how I could do things differently and looked for other solutions. Sometimes, I paused instructional videos to finish the task on my own first, then reviewed the solution process. It was clear that there were multiple solutions—at least two or three. So, this search for alternative ways to do things was confirmed. I believe I had logical thinking before, but micro:bits deepened it. I'm the type of person who would rather spend half an hour thinking about how to simplify my work and find an easier solution. I want to use what I know and what skills I have to find further solutions."*

Another participant mentioned that the micro:bit offered new, much more enjoyable ways of learning. Lessons with micro:bits, according to her, engage students and serve as excellent motivation. She particularly values the "big" projects that are visually impressive, such as smart cities, remote-controlled cars, and traffic lights. *"I enjoy it too. I'm not sure if it helped me with planning for practice, but it definitely expanded my horizons on how to help children get to the basics of programming, how to motivate them, and teach them these things."*

Regarding logical thinking, programming with the micro:bit requires planning and thought. Students must understand how to work with the micro:bit and grasp the individual requirements, among other things. Critical thinking is also evident through experimentation, and interaction is involved as students test different things with the micro:bit and find solutions through trial and error: *"Students must try various approaches to progress from a simpler problem to a more complex one, solve it, design it, and find a solution."*

Participants also recognize the presence of a creative approach to problem-solving in critical thinking. Since the micro:bit is a very versatile tool, various models and sensors can be connected to it, which encourages creativity in finding both conventional and unusual solutions. Furthermore, in these activities, they recognize that collaboration is vital, such as when sharing ideas, understanding algorithms, etc. *"Critical thinking is exactly about this: when a student creates a program that doesn't work, they must look for the mistake. They simply have to think and reuse what they've learned from a task."*

Micro:bits and the Development of Digital Literacy. In general, the research findings indicate that teachers consider micro:bits to be a suitable tool for acquiring and developing digital literacy. In today's modern world, where technological progress is advancing rapidly and computers and artificial intelligence are used for everything, it is challenging to choose what is appropriate for education and simultaneously think about why things work the way they do. As mentioned earlier, micro:bits motivate students to program, creating a "wow" effect and introducing an entertaining and engaging element into the classroom. These small chips are present in almost all digital devices, and students can learn about them in an age-appropriate manner and experience them in action. *"Students know many digital technologies, they can work with them, but micro:bit helps them create new and practical things very easily."* Another teacher added, *"Micro:bit is a great starting point for developing digital and analytical thinking. Students suddenly have m-blocks, LEGO digital toys, various displays, and boards at home. They engage in programming and constantly think analytically and creatively. They can apply this in the future!"*.

Here are a few participant statements regarding their personal experience with using micro:bits in teaching: *"I use micro:bits in technical and computer science subjects, and I have been working with them for a long time with good results. I use them in group lessons. The biggest challenge is how to engage students in technical subjects. I combine lessons so that we can work continuously. One lesson is too short, you just unpack the micro:bits, plug them in."*

"Programming isn't a problem for students, but when creating larger projects, especially when it was necessary to make something out of cardboard for the micro:bit, students with intellectual disabilities lacked fine motor skills. They didn't know how to use scissors properly and kept breaking them. I wanted to use a knife, but that's dangerous. Therefore, I see the importance of combining micro:bits with other activities where students can practice and develop their fine motor skills."

"We carried out a project, and the boys were very engaged. They created remote-controlled cars using micro:bit. It took them up to two hours to assemble the parts and attach the wheels, and they had a lot of fun with that. Then they programmed it in no time and used teamwork a lot."

"We worked with micro:bits, which were used to measure battery voltage. We also had a piano made from micro:bit and a small robot. A colleague made a calculator. We prepared a flower-watering demonstration using the micro:bit for school staff and other students."

"The students are very skilled. They independently work through projects, try things, and experiment. Their curiosity is a huge asset to their learning. They come to class thinking they are just going to program and don't even realize what they are actually programming. So when they find out that the hardware performs what they programmed, they are thrilled."

The Perspective of Micro:bits in Education. Many teachers consider the micro:bit to be an easily portable "pocket computer," a small device into which, when something is programmed, it actually works. Students receive immediate feedback. It is also promising in the sense that it works without being connected to a computer. However, it is not the only digital tool available. There are many others, but the micro:bit is significant for learning and developing programming logic. For younger students, the virtual environment Scratch can be used, which is very similar, but its disadvantage is that it is only virtual, through a PC monitor. However, the micro:bit is tangible, and students "feel" what they have programmed.

Thanks to the micro:bit, students have more opportunities to become familiar with programming. With the help of micro:bits, students can develop a better understanding of new technologies and gain a forward-looking perspective on the extent of their digital knowledge and skills. One advantage of the micro:bit is that it is relatively inexpensive, accessible, and useful. Not every student has computational thinking, and not everyone understands algorithmic processes and the digital component. Programming is a language like any other. So, when someone is not inclined toward it, it doesn't come easily. It is suitable for technically skilled students, as well as beginners, including children with special educational needs. This tool allows students to learn interactively about programming principles, algorithmic solutions, and digital technologies through practical and creative activities.

4 Conclusion

We consider the BBC micro:bit to be an exceptional educational tool for the development of school and personal skills in students with special needs. Teachers agree that the BBC micro:bit is a useful educational tool that helps students in inclusive education develop skills necessary for the 21st century. The greatest benefit of the BBC micro:bit in inclusive education is its ability to make lessons more engaging and interesting for students. It motivates them to perform at their best and encourages them to work. It brings the advantages of an environment that is original and adaptable to the individual needs of each student. In addition to developing algorithmic and digital competencies and 21st-century skills, it also offers the opportunity to experience success, which is an essential parameter in the individual and holistic development of students with special educational needs. The visual concept of the BBC micro:bit helps students in inclusive education verify correct solutions to tasks and provides immediate feedback. Block programming in the pre-configured Microsoft MakeCode environment supports the ability to break down tasks, plan sequences, and logically arrange smaller blocks into a whole. In acquiring new knowledge, the BBC micro:bit allows students to engage multiple senses simultaneously. It is an exceptional tool for the development of students with autism or ADHD, as it provides a stable, programmable, and predictable environment. Thanks to the Microsoft MakeCode block environment and downloading the programmed code to the micro:bit itself, working with the BBC micro:bit is engaging and creative. Students in inclusive education have the opportunity to learn more complex digital and algorithmic skills in a playful way. At the same time, they develop personal qualities that are part of soft skills, such as the ability to collaborate and communicate, as well as team-based and collaborative learning, all essential for the 21st century. Last but not least, the BBC micro:bit provides support to teachers in their role as educators, helping them create a creative and motivating environment for teaching STEM subjects.

Acknowledgments. The presented scientific study is a partial output of the project KEGA no. 055UK-4/2023 Prevention and Elimination of Socio-Pathological Phenomena in the Internet Environment for Individuals with Health Disabilities – Digital Safety for Inclusive Education.

Disclosure of Interests. This contribution serves exclusively to present partial research results. The activities carried out to obtain the partial results presented in this contribution were not funded by the aforementioned grant scheme.

References

1. British Council About the project. https://www.britishcouncil.me/en/programmes/education/21st-century-schools/about-the-project. Accessed 28 Dec 2024
2. Youth Code Jam Homepage, Neurodiversity in tech. https://www.youthcodejam.org/neurodiversity-in-tech. Accessed 28 Dec 2024
3. Lancaster University Homepage, Lancaster computer scientists help children of the world embrace coding: Making the BBC micro:bit. https://www.lancaster.ac.uk/sci-tech/research/impact/making-the-bbc-microbit/. Accessed 15 May 2024
4. Kvaššayová, N., Cápay, M., Petrík, Š., Bellayová, M., Klimeková, E.: Experience with using BBC Micro:Bit and perceived professional efficacy of informatics teachers. Electronics **11**(23), 3963 (2022). https://www.mdpi.com/1976636
5. Vladová, K., Šedibová, A., Tekelová, M., Ledneczká, G., Streickem, K., Uchnárová, A.: Štátny pedagogický ústav. Obsah vzdelávania pre 8. a 9. ročník detí a žiakov s autizmom alebo ďalšími pervazívnymi vývinovými poruchami. https://www.statpedu.sk/files/sk/svp/statny-vzdelavaci-program/vp-deti-ziakov-so-zdravotnym-znevyhodnenim/vp-deti-ziakov-autizmom-alebo-dalsimi-pervazivnymi-vyvinovymi-poruchami/obsah-vzdelavania-8-a-9-rocnik-au-mp-2012-web.pdf. Accessed 30 Dec 2024
6. Štátny pedagogický ústav: Informatika – inovovaný štátny vzdelávací program. Štátny pedagogický ústav. https://www.statpedu.sk/files/articles/dokumenty/inovovany-statny-vzdelavaci-program/informatika_nsv_2014.pdf. Accessed 30 Dec 2024
7. Cápay, M., Klimová, N.: Engage your students via physical computing! In: IEEE Global Engineering Education Conference, pp. 1216–1223. IEEE, UAE (2019)
8. Mansell, M., Klimová, N.: MakeCode simulátor - Dištančne s micro:bitmi diel 1. Enter study. https://enter.study/wp-content/uploads/2021/03/enter.study-distancne-s-microbitmi-makecode-simulator-diel-1.pdf. Accessed 15 June 2021
9. Sentance, S., Waite, J., Hodges, S., MacLeod, E., Yeomans, L.E.: "Creating cool stuff" - pupils' experience of the BBC micro:bit. In: Proceedings of the 48th ACM Technical Symposium on Computer Science Education (SIGCSE 2017), pp. 1–13. https://doi.org/10.1145/3017680.3017749. Accessed 14 Jan 2025
10. Using micro:bits in science as a cross-curricular tool. https://microbit.org/impact/case-studies/teachers-using-microbits-in-science/. Accessed 14 Jan 2025
11. Kiều, Q., Van Bien, N.: Micro:bit in science education: a systematic review. Jurnal Penelitian dan Pembelajaran IPA **9**(1), 1–14 (2023) https://doi.org/10.30870/jppi.v9i1.19491. Accessed 14 Jan 2025
12. Cheng, Y., Jackson, D.: From "in a sleep" to "stayed every day", engaging students and teachers with micro:bit smart-greenhouses. In: 14th International Conference on Computer-Supported Collaborative Learning (CSCL), pp. 295–296 (2021). https://example-link.org/conference-paper. Accessed 14 Jan 2025
13. Kanbul, S., Uzunboylu, H.: The importance of education in coding and robotic applications for acquiring 21st-century skills in Northern Cyprus. Int. J. Emerg. Technol. Learn. (iJET) **12**(01), 130–140 (2017). https://doi.org/10.3991/ijet.v12i01.6097. Accessed 12 Dec 2024
14. Lu, S.Y., Lo, C.C., Syu, J.Y.: Project-based learning oriented STEAM: the case of micro–bit paper-cutting lamp. J. Technol. Des. Educ. **32**, 2553–2575 (2021)

15. Sentance, S., Waite, J., Yeomans, L., et al.: Teaching with physical computing devices: the BBC micro:bit initiative. In: 12th Workshop in Primary and Secondary Computing Education (WIPSCE 2017), pp. 87–96 (2017). https://doi.org/10.1145/3137065.3137083. Accessed 14 Jan 2025
16. Schmidt, A.: Increasing computer literacy with the BBC micro:bit. IEEE Pervasive Comput. **15**(2), 5–7 (2016)
17. Voštinár, P., Knežník, J.: Using BBC micro:bit in primary and secondary schools for creating simple smart home. In: 43rd International Convention on Information, Communication and Electronic Technology (MIPRO), pp. 1–2 (2022). https://ieeexplore.ieee.org/document/9245314. Accessed 14 Jan 2025

The Cyberbullying Perception of Lower Secondary School Pupils

Milan Kubiatko[1(✉)] and Kristyna Balatova[2]

[1] J.E. Purkyne University, Pasteurova 1, 40096 Usti and Labem, Czech Republic
mkubiatko@gmail.com
[2] Mendel University, Zemedelska 1655, 61300 Brno, Czech Republic

Abstract. Cyberbullying is defined as aggressive behavior or actions of a group or individual using electronic means. The main aim was to find out the perception of cyberbullying among lower secondary school pupils. The partial aims were to identify the effect of variables as perception of social sites, gender, residence, time on social sites and others. The research was focused on lower secondary school pupils and a total of 506 pupils took part. The research consists of 19 Likert-type items regarding to cyberbullying and other items were focused on demographic variables. The Cronbach's alpha coefficient was used to determine reliability. The values of alpha for every part of tool were adequate (more than 0.70). To determine the relationship between the perception of cyberbullying and social networks the Pearson correlation coefficient was used. To detect statistically significant differences between groups based on independent variables, analysis of variance (ANOVA) was used, where the independent variables were demographic questions. Data from the attitude part were determined as the dependent variable. After processing the results of the questionnaire survey, it was found that there is not a relationship between the perception of cyberbullying and social sites (like Facebook, Instagram, etc,..). The results turned out to be statistically significant in the case of the distribution of pupils according to gender (higher score achieved girls), residence (town pupils achieved higher score), grades (inconsistent results) and victim knowing (higher core achieved pupils, who already know victim).

Keywords: Cyberbullying · Lower Secondary School Pupils · Quantitative Approach

1 Introduction

The study is focused on one of the current topics of our time, namely cyberbullying. Cyberbullying can be described as one of the forms of bullying. However, unlike traditional bullying, cyberbullying is dependent on information and communication technologies, including the Internet and mobile phones. These technologies are now commonly available and most of us cannot imagine life without them. In recent years, it has been noticed that increasingly younger children are using these technologies. Modern technologies bring many positive things to our lives and make our lives much easier. Unfortunately, the advantages provided by modern technologies are often accompanied

Ł. Tomczyk (Ed.): NMP 2024, CCIS 2537, pp. 129–145, 2025.
https://doi.org/10.1007/978-3-031-95627-0_9

by negative phenomena, and one of them is cyberbullying. Cyberbullying has many forms and uses many means to spread. The study is focused mainly on cyberbullying via social networks. Social networks can be considered a phenomenon of our time. Today, elementary school pupils commonly have access to the Internet, create profiles on social networks and use other services that the Internet environment offers. However, they do not always realize that there are some risks associated with using the Internet. Not only children, but also many adults, unfortunately, often do not realize that the information or photos they publish on social networks can be easily misused, and what is published on social networks or anywhere else on the Internet cannot be taken back. These materials then live a life of their own on the Internet, they can be easily copied or downloaded, and you never know when and in what form they may reappear.

2 Theoretical Framework

2.1 Cyberbullying as Main Concept

The term "cyberbullying" is used broadly, both in colloquial and formal use. First coined in 1999, there is no general consensus on a definition, although different versions usually include the use of digital technology to inflict harm repeatedly or to bully [1–3]. Most definitions of cyberbullying have modeled themselves on the more widely agreed-upon definition of traditional bullying, and it seems clear that there is some overlap between bullying and cyberbullying [4]. Bullying and cyberbullying are reliably correlated [5]. Yet, it has been argued that cyberbullying requires its own, separate scrutiny; several studies suggest it can cause harm above and beyond traditional bullying. Behaviors that are likely to be related to cyberbullying, such as online harassment and online sexual harassment, appear to be harmful and deserving of study [6].

Cyberbullying is characterized by several main features [7–9]:

1. Anonymity – The perpetrator can remain anonymous, and the victim may never know who bullied them. On the Internet, we encounter pseudonymity much more often than complete anonymity, which is one of the variants of partially limited anonymity, where some kind of intermediary identity is used, but without a link to the real identity [10]. The essential difference between pseudonymity and anonymity is that we are able to attribute various activities to a single originator. We can therefore contact them in the long term. A pseudonym can create social networks of contacts and build a reputation [11].
2. Transformation of the aggressor – The aggressor does not have to be a physically and socially strong individual, as is the case with traditional bullying. The aggressor here becomes an individual who is proficient in information technology. Therefore, it can apply to practically anyone.
3. Becoming a victim – Anyone can become a victim, just like an aggressor. Children who are addicted to mobile phones and the internet are at higher risk of cyberbullying.
4. There is no escape from cyberbullying – Traditional bullying is based on a physical encounter between the aggressor and the victim, which can be partly predicted and sometimes avoided. However, with cyberbullying, the aggressor can stalk the victim anytime, anywhere.

5. Absence of physical violence – Cyberbullying does not involve direct signs of bullying, such as torn clothing or loss of items that adults might notice. This makes it difficult for parents or schools to detect cyberbullying.
6. Repeated Hurting – In the case of even long-term physical bullying, each individual action is always a one-time thing, and therefore a closed matter in its own way. But in cyberbullying, when the victim receives an offensive email or text message, they can read it over and over again. Such attacks are something unfinished, acting permanently. The victim then lives with a feeling of constant pressure and never-ending or recurring attack. Written words often have a much greater impact than spoken words, precisely because they can read them repeatedly, whereas with spoken words they do not have to remember everything.
7. Wider audience – Cyberbullying through websites allows access to literally anyone with an Internet connection. Anyone in the world can become a spectator of cyberbullying. Moreover, cyberbullying does not have to happen repeatedly. It is enough for the aggressor to post humiliating photos of the victim on the Internet once. Anyone can then copy and distribute this photo.

Cyberbullying can also be divided into "direct attacks" or "proxy cyberbullying." In the case of "direct attacks," the aggressor sends messages directly to the victims. Examples include sending harassing, threatening, or cruel messages via SMS or email, stealing passwords and then using the adopted account, online voting (e.g., "who is cool and who is not"), impersonating someone else, sending malicious codes, and more [12].

2.2 Factors Affecting Cyberbullying

Cyberbullying, unlike bullying, is a relatively new phenomenon, but in the last few years, many authors have addressed this issue, and a wide range of different research has been conducted.

Slonje & Smith (2008) [13] sought to determine the nature of cyberbullying and its prevalence in schools in Sweden. The research was conducted in the form of a questionnaire and involved 360 respondents aged 12 to 20. The result was that 10% of respondents had experienced any form of bullying, while 5.3% of pupils had encountered cyberbullying. The research also showed that primary school pupils encountered bullying significantly more often (15.2% of respondents) than secondary school pupils (2.7% of respondents). The research also compared the frequency of cyberbullying in and out of school. It turned out that cyberbullying occurs more often outside of school than in school. This may be due to restrictions on the use of mobile phones and personal computers at school. Authors Smith et al. (2008) [3] found that cyberbullying is less frequent than traditional bullying and is reported more outside of schools. Mobile phone calls and text messages were the most common form of cyberbullying. The authors Vandebosch & Cleemput (2009) [14] analyzed how pupils between the ages of 10 and 18 understand the concept of cyberbullying. They pointed out that young people often interpret "cyberbullying" as "internet bullying" and associate this phenomenon with a wide range of practices. In order for cyberbullying to be considered true bullying, it should meet certain criteria: it should be intended to harm (the aggressor) and be perceived as harmful (to the victim), it must be repeated and carried out with a power imbalance between the aggressor and the victim. Ho et al. (2017) [15] examined the moderating effect of age on the relationship between parental mediation and cyberbullying perpetration. Multi-stage cluster sampling was used, in which lower secondary school children and secondary school adolescents participated in our survey. The results revealed that attitude, subjective norms, and the two parental mediations – active and restrictive mediation – were negatively associated with cyberbullying perpetration on social media. Age was a significant moderator of both parental mediation strategies and cyberbullying perpetration. Another study was carried out with 747 secondary school pupils studying in the 5th and 6th grades of public schools. "Cyberbullying Scale" and "Sensitivity towards Cyberbullying Scale" were used for data collection. As a result of the study, it was determined that the pupils' levels of engagement in cyberbullying behaviour were "low", whereas their sensitivity levels towards cyberbullying were "high". The gender and grade variables, and the difference between their cyberbullying sensitivity levels and mother education level, father education level, computer ownership, tablet ownership variables, were found to be significant. It was found out that there was a negative and moderate relationship between their cyberbullying behavior and their sensitivity towards cyberbullying [16]. According to Evangelio et al. (2022) [17] pupils experiencing cyberbullying at an early school age reported negative feelings, such as depression or anxiety. They are often linked to bullying scenarios and even to the same role (cyberbully, cybervictim or cyberwitness). Different programs have been shown to positively influence cyberbullying from a young age, important to prevent it, when children begin to use mobile phones and social media. Cabrera et al. (2024) [18] analyzed the difference of bullying (traditional bullying and cyberbullying) in rural and urban contexts. The results showed a similar proportion of intervention in all bullying roles and in polybullying in urban and rural context schools. The victimization and physical bullying perpetration is more frequent in schools in urban areas. In rural schools, aggression is normally aimed at schoolmates. The results in the next step showed the link between context and perpetration role. Victims in rural settings expressed greater distress than victims in schools in urban areas. Swastika (2025) [19] focused on mapping the incidence of bullying in elementary schools in Indonesia. In doing so, it analysed various forms, namely physical, verbal, relational and cyberbullying. The sample included a total of 1068 students. Cyberbullying is the least represented among students in this research. That is, 5.15% have encountered cyberbullying, but it is found that its impacts can have a longer-term character and more significant psychological impacts on victims. Cyberbullying most often involved threats via mobile phone (29%), offensive comments in the online environment (26%) and the dissemination of inappropriate content (17%). As for prevention, it is recommended to focus on school policy, especially on school prevention programs and on education about safe behavior in the online environment. A study by Ma et al. (2024) [20] investigated the prevalence of cyberbullying among adolescents and the factors contributing to their victimization. The aim was to identify risk factors associated with cyberbullying and to provide a scientific basis for targeted preventive measures to protect the mental health of adolescents. The sample included a total of 12,770 individuals from secondary and primary schools. Regarding the prevalence of bullying, it was found that 12.2% had ever been a victim of it, 0.9% had been an aggressor, and 2.9% admitted to being both a victim and an aggressor at the same time. Boys were more likely to be aggressors and girls were more likely to be victims. Other findings include that family conflicts, parental absence, punitive upbringing, or failure to thrive at school are risk factors for cyberbullying, as is the frequent presence of adolescents in an online environment or playing online games.

Sun et al. (2016) [21] reported cyberbullying behaviors from both male and female respondents, were meta-analyzed to examine if gender difference existed in cyberbullying perpetration. A statistically significant gender difference emerged, indicating that more males were involved in cyberbullying perpetration behaviors than females. Similarly, Zsila et al. (2019) [22] indicated that males were more likely than females to engage in cyberbullying when they had been previously bullied online. Furthermore, high anger rumination elevated the risk of perpetration among male cyberbullying victims, while repeated victimization in traditional bullying increased the risk of cyberbullying perpetration among females. Similar results were possible to find out in the study of Saladino et al. (2020) [23]. There was possible to find other studies with similar results [24–26].

Wang et al. (2019) [27] found out young adults (18–25 years) experienced the highest levels of cyberbullying during both time frames (lifetime and past month), the prevalence of cyberbullying was lower among older age cohorts. Another empirical study was carried out with a large sample of children and adolescents where 10–17-year-olds were presented with The European Bullying Intervention Project Questionnaire and European Cyberbullying Intervention Project Questionnaire. The clear age differences in bullying behaviors also suggest the appropriateness of tailoring anti-bullying programs to target specific age groups. The older respondents had higher experiences with cyberbullying [28]. Similar results, that younger pupils are often target of cyberbullying were possible to find out in other studies [24, 29, 30].

The number of studies, where the perception and experiences with cyberbullying and use of and attitudes toward social sites is limited. For example, Craig et al. (2020) [31] explored negative consequences of social sites using for adolescent health could include exposures to online forms of aggression. Vannucci et al. (2020) [32] provided results from random effects models indicated that there were positive, small-to-medium correlations between social media use and engagement in risky behaviors generally. Here were an insufficient number of independent samples available to conduct a random effect model for violence-related behaviors. Touloupis (2024) [33] investigated the use of Facebook and involvement in cyberbullying among students with learning disabilities in primary schools. The study involved 211 students (119 boys and 92 girls) from 6 classes in primary schools in Thessaloniki, Greece. The results showed that students with learning disabilities spend more time on Facebook and perceive it as an important part of their lives. Furthermore, these students are at higher risk of engaging in cyberbullying, either as victims or as aggressors. These students experience low self-esteem and loneliness, which increases the likelihood of cyberbullying (but only if intensive Facebook use was present). An interesting finding was that girls with learning disabilities were more likely to engage in cyberbullying than boys, which is not a common trend compared to other research. Regarding the prevention of cyberbullying, it is recommended to implement school media literacy programs, support the self-esteem and well-being of students with learning disabilities, and finally support parents in a mutual dialogue between the school and students with learning disabilities regarding safety in the online environment.

Similar results, which explored the significant relationship between social media use and cyberbullying were possible to find in other studies [34–36].

3 Research Aims

The aim of the research is to find out the cyberbullying perception among lower secondary school pupils.

The additional aims were:

1. To set whether there is a relationship between the perception of cyberbullying and social sites among lower secondary school pupils.
2. To determine whether the perception of cyberbullying differs between boys and girls.
3. To find out whether there is a difference in the perception of cyberbullying between individual grades of lower secondary school.
4. To determine whether the perception of cyberbullying differs between pupils from cities and villages.
5. To indicate whether there is a difference in the perception of cyberbullying between those who know a victim of cyberbullying and those who do not know any.

4 Methods

4.1 Respondents

A total of 506 pupils from lower secondary school were respondents, of which 265 were girls and 241 were boys. The pupils were from 6 elementary schools from different areas of Czech Republic. The largest number of pupils was in the eighth grade, with a total of 139 participating in the survey. The fewest were pupils from the sixth grade, with 112 participating. A total of 7% ($n = 33$) of pupils have encountered a victim of cyberbullying, of which 64% ($n = 21$) are girls and 36% ($n = 12$) are boys. All these pupils have a profile on one of the social networks. The representation of pupils from cities and villages is almost equal. 45% of pupils are from rural areas ($n = 228$), 55% from cities ($n = 278$). Most often, pupils encountered swearing, threats, mockery and ridicule, but also the publication of offensive or humiliating photos.

4.2 Research Tool

The questionnaire used for research purposes consisted of demographic variables, which were presented at the beginning of the research tool. The main part of the research consisted of three questionnaires. The first one from the author Quing Li (2008) [37], who investigated attitudes toward cyberbullying. In our research tool were used 6 items. The second questionnaire focuses on the evaluation of cyberbullying forms, it includes 13 items. The original author is Willard (2012) [38]. The third questionnaire is from author El Gazzar (2011) [39], whose research focused on the use of social networks, especially Facebook. The questionnaire included 25 items. All items were Likert type. All items were adapted for the age of respondents. The first questionnaire included scale from strongly disagree to strongly agree. The second questionnaire included a scale from the most harmful form to the least harmful form. And the perception of social sites questionnaire included scale from strongly disagree to strongly agree.

4.3 Data Analysis

The data obtained from the questionnaire survey was processed in Microsoft Office Excel and Statistica. The first step was to recode data from the responses in research tools to numerical form. All Likert type items were in positive meaning, except of two from the questionnaire regarding to attitudes toward cyberbullying, so the most negative item had got value 1 and the most positive item had got value 5. Next were determined basic statistical methods like mean score and standard error. In the next step the reliability of all three questionnaires was calculated. The Cronbach's alpha coefficient was used for the determination of reliability. The alpha values are presented in Table 1.

Table 1. Values of Cronbach's alpha for questionnaires.

Questionnaire	Values of alpha
Attitudes to Cyberbullying	.72
Evaluation of Cyberbullying forms	.71
Perception of Social Sites	.87

Some statistical methods and coefficients were also used during the processing. Cronbach's alpha was used to determine the reliability of the research tool. Pearson's correlation coefficient was used to determine the relationship between the perception of cyberbullying and social networks. Analysis of variance (ANOVA) was used to determine statistically significant differences between groups of independent variables, where the role of the independent variable was fulfilled by demographic questions, but also by two other questions, one of which determined whether the pupil knew a victim of cyberbullying Data from the attitude part were determined as the dependent variable.

This study adhered to ethical guidelines for research involving human subjects, ensuring that all participants were treated with respect and dignity throughout the research process. Prior to participation, informed consent was obtained from all respondents. Participants were provided with detailed information about the study's purpose, procedures, potential risks, and benefits, allowing them to make an informed decision regarding their involvement.

5 Results

The overall score for perception of cyberbullying was ($x = 2.56$), which indicated a medium level. However, the perception of cyberbullying was measured by two questionnaires, one on the attitudes and the second on the evaluation of cyberbullying forms. Based on this fact, the data obtained from questionnaires were evaluated separately. Figure 1 showed the distribution of score for every questionnaire. The attitudes toward cyberbullying were neutral, it means that some expressions of cyberbullying are important for the lower secondary school pupils, and some are not so important for them. The evaluation of cyberbullying forms by lower secondary school pupils achieved lower score, it means that pupils nearly every for of cyberbullying for harmful. The more detailed evaluation of items is presented below.

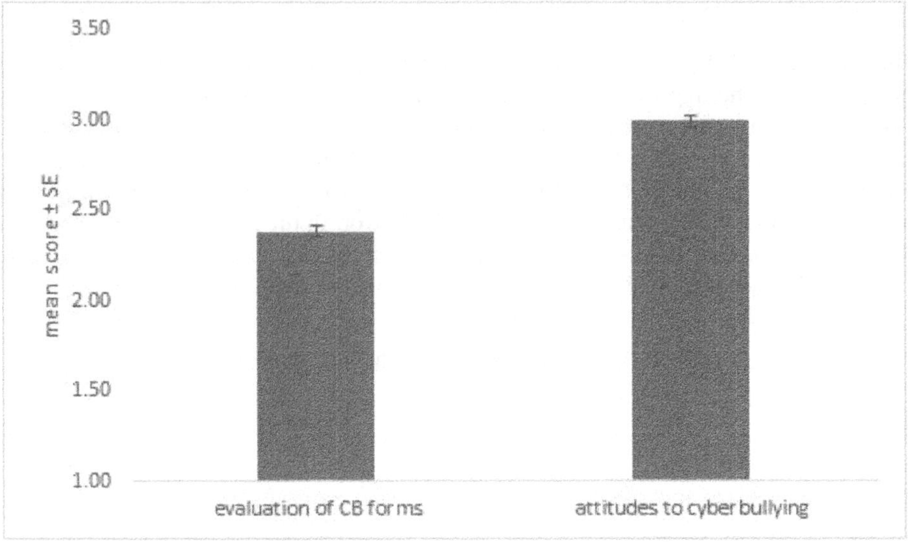

Fig. 1. Distribution of score for cyberbullying questionnaires.

The relationship between cyberbullying parts and perception of social sites was neutral. The relationship between attitudes to cyberbullying and perception of social sites was ($r = .03$; $p = .46$) and the relationship between evaluation of cyberbullying forms and perception of social sites was nearly totally neutral ($r = .001$; $p = .99$). So it means that perception of cyberbullying and perception of social sites are independent variables without any influence among them.

The effect of gender was significant at both questionnaires. Girls achieved higher scores in the attitudes to cyberbullying ($F = 12.53$; $p < .001$). It means that girls can recognize cyberbullying at schools and have got higher sensitivity to recognize the manifestations of cyberbullying. Boys achieved higher scores in the evaluation of cyberbullying forms ($F = 7.56$; $p < .01$). It means that girls consider cyberbullying harmful in comparison with boys. The distribution of score is in Fig. 2.

The next variable was grade. The effect of this variable was significant in the one case – evaluation of cyberbullying forms ($F = 4.98$; $p < .01$) Post-hoc test (Tukey?) showed that The youngest pupils achieved significant lower score in comparison with 8th and 9th grade pupils ($p < .05$ respectively $p < .01$). The mean score is presented in Table 2. The effect of grade on the attitudes to cyberbullying was insignificant ($F = 1.45$; $p = .23$).

The effect of respondents' residence was significant at one questionnaire. Respondents from town achieved higher scores in the attitudes to cyberbullying ($F = 14.41$; $p < .001$). It means that respondents from town are able to recognize cyberbullying at schools and have got the higher sensitivity to recognize the manifestations of cyberbullying. The residence of respondents had not got a significant effect in the evaluation of cyberbullying forms ($F = .23$; $p = .63$). The distribution of score is in Fig. 3.

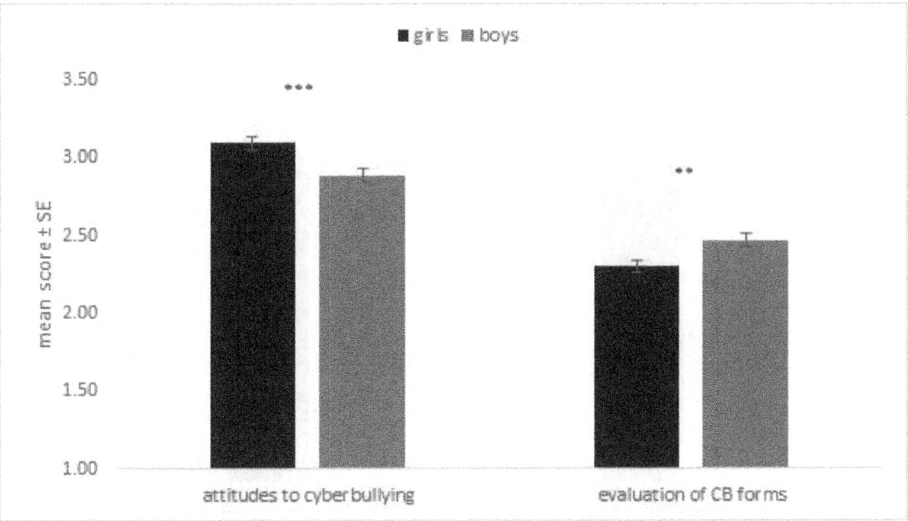

Fig. 2. Distribution of score for perception of cyberbullying with respect to gender.

Table 2. Distribution of score for perception of cyberbullying with respect to grade.

	Attitudes to CB (x)	Evaluation of CB forms (x)	Attitudes to CB (SE)	Evaluation of CB forms (SE)
6th grade	2.89	2.21	.06	.06
7th grade	3.07	2.33	.06	.06
8th grade	2.98	2.44	.06	.06
9th grade	3.02	2.52	.06	.06

x – symbol for mean score.
SE – symbol for standard error.

The last examined variable was knowing of cyberbullying victims. This variable had a significant effect in one of the questionnaires Respondents, who know any cyberbullying victim achieved higher score in the attitudes to cyberbullying ($F = 7.00$; $p < .01$). It means that respondents, who know any victim of cyberbullying, can recognize cyberbullying at schools and have got the higher sensitivity to recognize the manifestations of cyberbullying. The knowing of cyberbullying victims had not got a significant effect in the evaluation of cyberbullying forms ($F = 1.10$; $p = .29$). The distribution of score is in Fig. 4.

Table 3 includes the mean score for every item of questionnaires regarding cyberbullying.

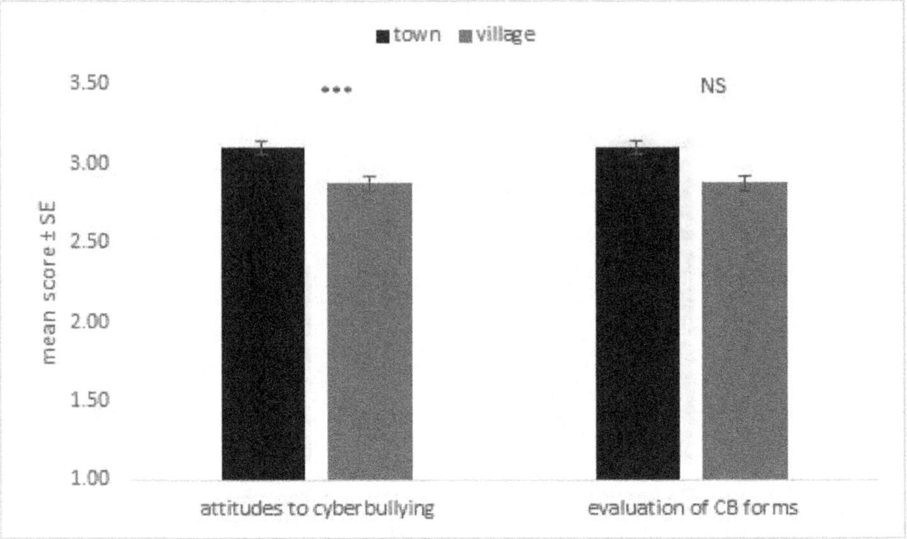

Fig. 3. Distribution of score for perception of cyberbullying with respect to residence.

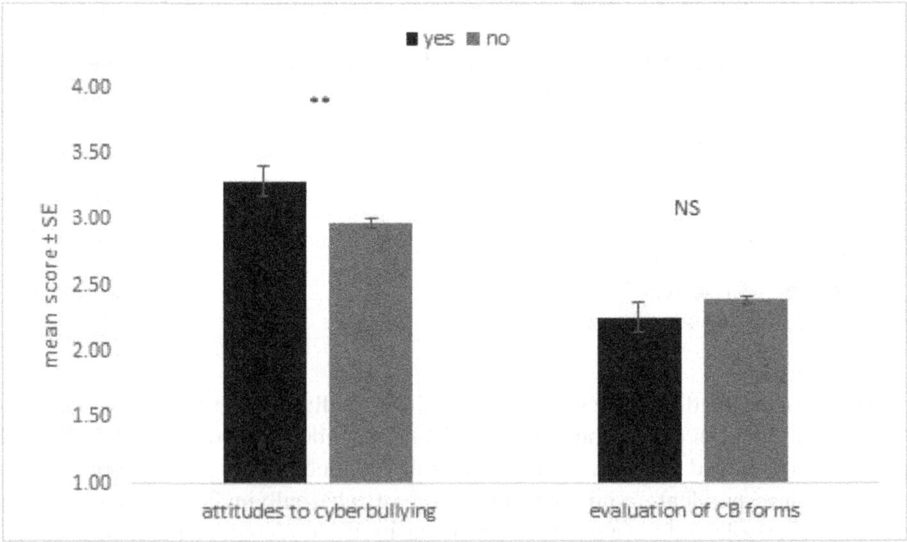

Fig. 4. Distribution of score for perception of cyberbullying with respect to knowing of cyberbullying victims.

6 Discussion

The research is focused on the problem of cyberbullying. The level of cyberbullying in the lower secondary schools was neutral, mainly the attitudes toward cyberbullying. On the other hand, cyberbullying forms were evaluated as harmful. Based on this fact,

Table 3. Mean score for every item of cyberbullying questionnaires.

Items	Mean score
I. Attitudes to cyberbullying	
1. I think that cyberbullying is also a problem at the school I attend	2.43
2. I think that cyberbullying should be talked about more in school	3.27
3. I am worried about cyberbullying	2.70
4. I can recognize cyberbullying	3.34
5. If I were to encounter cyberbullying, I know what to do	3.19
6. I want to learn more information about cyberbullying	3.04
II. Evaluation of cyberbullying forms	
1. Taking sound recordings, videos or photos and their follow-up publication with the purpose of harming the captured person	2.18
2. Insulting, mocking or other embarrassment via email, SMS or chat	2.79
3. Creation of websites, blogs or profiles, which with their content they humiliate and ridicule a specific person	2.09
4. Hacking someone else's profile on a social network or email and editing it to the detriment of the victim	2.02
5. Attacking users in discussion forums	3.06
6. Sending information about another person that is false or that person they harm other people	2.33
7. Excluding a person from an online group in a cruel way	3.06
8. Posting and sending material about another person that contains sensitive, private or embarrassing information. It also includes the transmission of private messages or images	1.89
9. Pretending to be another person and sending or posting materials, which harm this person	2.28
10. Sending harmful, false or cruel statements about another person to other people or posting such.materials on the Internet	2.20
11. Online harassment that involves a threat of harm or is significant intimidating	2.14
12. Repeatedly sending offensive messages via email or using others text messages to another person	2.63
13. Sending threatening, rude and vulgar messages about another person to an online group on the Internet or directly to that particular person via email or other text messages	2.28

it is possible to say that cyberbullying is the topic also among lower secondary school pupils and they are aware before different forms, which can create cyberbullied behavior. Similar results were also found by [40], who, using a similar research approach (quantitative, using a questionnaire with scaled items), detected a low level of cyberbullying in their chosen research sample. Edwards et al. (2016) [41] focused on cyberbullying of Hispanic, Asian and black youth, where they found that these races encounter cyberbullying less than white youth. If they encounter cyberbullying behavior, they have suicidal thoughts to the same extent as white youth. The reason was that ethnicities other than white had a lower level of socio-economic status, which was reflected in the absence of personal electronic devices [42]. Similarly [43] monitored the frequency of exposure to cyberbullying among children in Serbia and its relationship to physical and mental health and risky behavior. The most common types of cyberbullying were insults, harassment and slander on social networks. According to the author, this means that every tenth student in Serbia has encountered cyberbullying. Cyberbullying is also associated with significant psychological and physical health problems in children. When it comes to victims of bullying, they are also at higher risk of engaging in risky behavior, such as cigarette smoking, excessive alcohol consumption, etc. Low physical activity, obesity and overall poor health also contribute to a higher risk of cyberbullying.

Even though the distribution of pupils by gender turned out to be statistically insignificant, there are noticeable differences between girls and boys. Although girls encountered the term cyberbullying more often than boys, unlike boys, they would like to receive more information about cyberbullying and also think that this phenomenon should be talked about more in school. On the contrary, boys more often state that they can recognize cyberbullying and that they know what to do in such a case. Boys are also more likely to think that cyberbullying does not occur at their school. The fact that girls may encounter cyberbullying more often is confirmed by the research conducted by Smith et al. (2008) [3]. In their study, they stated that girls are more likely to encounter cyberbullying than boys, especially in the case of text messages and phone calls. Similar results were also brought by Serbian authors Popović-Ćitić et al. (2011) [44] who reported significant differences between boys and girls. Boys showed higher cyberbullying scores and were also victims of cyberbullying to a higher extent than girls. The study by [45] indicates that cyberbullying mainly affects boys and at the same time boys are more often victims of this negative phenomenon.

In the case of comparing data between individual grades, it is not possible to say unequivocally that differences in the perception of cyberbullying arise with the age of the pupils. For most questions, the results were mostly comparable, but there was almost always a significant percentage difference in only one of the grades. The largest number of pupils who have never encountered the term cyberbullying before are among the pupils of the sixth grade. This could also be because these pupils also spend the least amount of time on social networks compared to other pupils, and they also have the highest number of those who do not use social networks. The fact that cyberbullying occurs at the school they attend is most often reported by ninth-grade pupils. In particular, seventh-grade pupils would like to learn more about cyberbullying, and eighth-grade pupils would like to see cyberbullying discussed more at school. Pupils in the seventh and ninth grades can most often recognize cyberbullying. Seventh-grade pupils also most often stated that they would deal with cyberbullying, on the contrary, ninth-grade pupils reported this possibility the least. Pupils of the ninth and sixth grades most often encountered a victim of cyberbullying, the number of pupils in the other grades was significantly lower. This result differs from the results of the study published by Haferkamp et al. (2012) [46].

In their study, these authors state that 40% of older pupils (14–15 years old) and 35% of younger pupils (12–13 years old) were affected by cyberbullying. This difference could be due to the fact that older pupils are already more proficient in information technologies than younger pupils, they also spend more time on the Internet, and their parents do not monitor their activity on the Internet as much.

7% of the pupils met a victim of cyberbullying, of which 27% stated that they themselves were victims of cyberbullying. In the research carried out by Tarapdar et al. (2013) [47], it was shown that up to 38% of pupils encountered cyberbullying. The values from the research conducted by Slonje & Smith (2008) [13] differ less from the results found here. These authors state that 5.3% of pupils encountered cyberbullying. There are noticeable differences in opinions about cyberbullying among pupils who know or do not know a victim of cyberbullying. Pupils who know a victim of cyberbullying more often think that cyberbullying does not occur at their school. These pupils also more often state that they do not need more information about cyberbullying, but unlike those pupils who do not know any victims of cyberbullying, they state more often that this phenomenon should be discussed at school. They are also more concerned about cyberbullying, but more often they can recognize it and know what to do in this situation.

91% of lower secondary school pupils use social networks, and most of them spend two to three hours a day on social networks. These pupils also most often state that they would like to receive more information about cyberbullying. Sixth-grade pupils spend the least time on them, and ninth-grade pupils spend the most time on them. The more time pupils spend on social networks, the more often they encounter the term cyberbullying. It also turned out that pupils who spend less than one hour on social networks have the greatest fear of cyberbullying. Pupils who spend more time on social networks can recognize cyberbullying more often and more often know what to do in such a case.

7 Conclusion

This cyberbullying phenomenon is gaining strength and is becoming an integral part of the educational process with an impact on the private lives of the actors of this process. Based on the above, it is possible to suggest several implications for pedagogical practice that can be an inspiration for teachers in the performance of their mission. Teachers should be introduced to cyberbullying as a harmful phenomenon already during their studies, when they are preparing for the teaching profession. In addition to the usual subjects focusing on the content of the training of future teachers, the curriculum of higher education institutions preparing teachers should also include subjects related to manifestations of harmful behavior in schools. Within the framework of the above subjects, teachers would be direct participants in events during lessons in which cyberbullying behavior occurs. Future teachers should detect this form of behavior, identify aggressors and victims, detect how this type of harmful behavior occurs and, last but not least, propose solutions to manage these critical situations with the greatest possible elimination of damage.

The performance of the teaching profession is not only related to the transfer of the content of the subjects taught, but also to the educational impact on pupils, so that they become full-fledged members of society in the future without harmful manifestations that can affect their entire future private and professional life. Therefore, teachers should try to recognize unusual manifestations of pupil behavior in the classes in which they implement the teaching process. They should notice both manifestations of a dominant and submissive nature in pupils and draw their attention to them at least to the class teacher or educational counsellor.

Class teachers should be best informed about the composition of the pupil body within their competence. Based on this, they should be able to select pupils who stand at opposite poles of the arrangement of relationships within the class collective. This means identifying dominant individuals who may try to prove their position by cyberbullying or other forms of disrespectful behavior towards others, especially towards peers standing at the opposite pole, who are often referred to as outsiders. The class teacher should pay increased attention to both groups of pupils, conduct e.g. conversations with them on the topic of the above-mentioned harmful behavior, to prevent as much as possible the occurrence of damage that can have an irreversible impact on the mental health of submissive individuals.

The educational counsellor has an irreplaceable role in diagnosing and subsequently eliminating any manifestation of behavior that has a negative impact on both the educational process and the activities of pupils in the school and extracurricular environment. The educational counsellor should regularly conduct lectures and seminars, where he would draw attention to the negative impact, in our case, of cyberbullying behavior on pupils and their immediate environment. He could present real-life examples of how not only victims but also aggressors cope with cyberbullying in the future. It may happen that pupils who cause cyberbullying in their later life begin to feel guilty about their previous behaviour and this may affect their further work with unfavourable speech. The school management should, in cooperation with all elements operating in the educational facility, interpellated to eliminate any negative and harmful speech on the part of aggressors. These speeches should be punished with adequate punishment so that potential victims feel that they are no longer threatened by any attack in the future and that competent people will stand up for them. There is possible to include parents in the discussion about cyberbullying. According to many studies parents in many cases are not able to accept a fact, that child could play a role in the cyberbullying process (in the both case victim or aggressor). They can accept this fact in the communication with other parents, the communication with experts (like psychologists) is not acceptable for them. The guidelines for parents, how to behave in the process of cyberbullying is possible to find in many studies, for example Young and Tully (2019) [48].

Acknowledgement. The Operational Program Research, Development and Education of the Czech Republic for financing the project Smart City-Smart Region-Smart Community (Grant No. CZ.02.1.01/0.0/0.0/17_048/0007435) supported the present chapter.

References

1. Englander, E., Donnerstein, E., Kowalski, R., Lin, C.A., Parti, K.: Defining cyberbullying. Pediatrics **140**(Supplement 2), 148–151 (2017)

2. Patchin, J.W., Hinduja, S.: Bullies move beyond the schoolyard: a preliminary look at cyberbullying. Youth Violence Juvenile Justice **4**(2), 148–169 (2006)
3. Smith, P.K., Mahdavi, J., Carvalho, M., Fisher, S., Russell, S., Tippett, N.: Cyberbullying: its nature and impact in secondary school pupils. J. Child Psychol. Psychiatry **49**(4), 376–385 (2008)
4. Ybarra, M.L., Espelage, D.L., Mitchell, K.J.: Differentiating youth who are bullied from other victims of peer-aggression: the importance of differential power and repetition. J. Adolesc. Health. **55**(2), 293–300 (2014)
5. Kowalski, R.M., Giumetti, G.W., Schroeder, A.N., Lattanner, M.R.: Bullying in the digital age: a critical review and meta-analysis of cyberbullying research among youth. Psychol. Bull. **140**(4), 1073 (2014)
6. Cross, D., Lester, L., Barnes, A.: A longitudinal study of the social and emotional predictors and consequences of cyber and traditional bullying victimisation. Int. J. Public Health **60**, 207–217 (2015)
7. Peter, I.K., Petermann, F.: Cyberbullying: a concept analysis of defining attributes and additional influencing factors. Comput. Hum. Behav. **86**, 350–366 (2018)
8. Rosa, H., et al.: Automatic cyberbullying detection: a systematic review. Comput. Hum. Behav. **93**, 333–345 (2019). https://doi.org/10.1016/j.chb.2018.12.021
9. Zhang, W., Huang, S., Lam, L., Evans, R., Zhu, C.: Cyberbullying definitions and measurements in children and adolescents: summarizing 20 years of global efforts. Front. Public Health **10**, 1000504 (2022)
10. Moore, A., Fredheim, R., Wyss, D., Beste, S.: Deliberation and identity rules: the effect of anonymity, pseudonyms and real-name requirements on the cognitive complexity of online news comments. Polit. Stud. **69**(1), 45–65 (2021)
11. Jain, A.K., Sahoo, S.R., Kaubiyal, J.: Online social networks security and privacy: comprehensive review and analysis. Complex Intell. Syst. **7**(5), 2157–2177 (2021)
12. Von Marées, N., Petermann, F.: Cyberbullying: an increasing challenge for schools. Sch. Psychol. Int. **33**(5), 467–476 (2012)
13. Slonje, R., Smith, P.K.: Cyberbullying: another main type of bullying? Scand. J. Psychol. **49**(2), 147–154 (2008)
14. Vandebosch, H., Van Cleemput, K.: Cyberbullying among youngsters: profiles of bullies and victims. New Media Soc. **11**(8), 1349–1371 (2009)
15. Ho, S.S., Chen, L., Ng, A.P.: Comparing cyberbullying perpetration on social media between primary and secondary school students. Comput. Educ. **109**, 74–84 (2017)
16. Gündüz, Ş, Akgün, F., Özgür, H.: Determination of secondary school students' levels of sensitivity towards cyberbullying and cyberbullying behaviour. Participatory Educ. Res. **8**(1), 70–89 (2021)
17. Evangelio, C., Rodríguez-González, P., Fernández-Río, J., Gonzalez-Villora, S.: Cyberbullying in elementary and middle school students: a systematic review. Comput. Educ. **176**, 104356 (2022)
18. Cabrera, M.C., Larrañaga, E., Yubero, S.: Bullying/cyberbullying in secondary education: a comparison between secondary schools in rural and urban contexts. Child Adolesc. Soc. Work J. **41**(4), 617–631 (2024)
19. Swastika, J.U.: A survey on elementary school bullying. Int. J. Teach. **2**(1) (2025)
20. Ma, J., et al.: Analysis of prevalence and related factors of cyberbullying-victimization among adolescents. Children **11**, 1193 (2024)
21. Sun, S., Fan, X., Du, J.: Cyberbullying perpetration: a meta-analysis of gender differences. Int. J. Internet Sci. **11**(1), 61–81 (2016)
22. Zsila, Á., Urbán, R., Griffiths, M.D., Demetrovics, Z.: Gender differences in the association between cyberbullying victimization and perpetration: the role of anger rumination and traditional bullying experiences. Int. J. Ment. Heal. Addict. **17**, 1252–1267 (2019)

23. Saladino, V., Eleuteri, S., Verrastro, V., Petruccelli, F.: Perception of cyberbullying in adolescence: a brief evaluation among Italian students. Front. Psychol. **11**, 607225 (2020)
24. Chen, L.M., Cheng, Y.Y.: Perceived severity of cyberbullying behaviour: differences between genders, grades and participant roles. Educ. Psychol. **37**(5), 599–610 (2017)
25. Wang, P., Wang, X., Lei, L.: Gender differences between student–student relationship and cyberbullying perpetration: an evolutionary perspective. J. Interpers. Violence **36**(19–20), 9187–9207 (2021)
26. Schell-Busey, N., Connell, N.M., Walding, S.: Examining gender differences in a social norms prevention program for cyberbullying. Int. J. Bullying Prev. 1–15 (2023)
27. Wang, M.J., Yogeeswaran, K., Andrews, N.P., Hawi, D.R., Sibley, C.G.: How common is cyberbullying among adults? Exploring gender, ethnic, and age differences in the prevalence of cyberbullying. Cyberpsychol. Behav. Soc. Netw. **22**(11), 736–741 (2019)
28. Pichel, R., Foody, M., O'Higgins Norman, J., Feijóo, S., Varela, J., Rial, A.: Bullying, cyberbullying and the overlap: what does age have to do with it? Sustainability **13**(15), 8527 (2021)
29. Sevcikova, A., Smahel, D.: Online harassment and cyberbullying in the Czech Republic: comparison across age groups. Zeitschrift für Psychologie/J. Psychol. **217**(4), 227–229 (2009)
30. Betts, L.R., Metwally, S.H., Gardner, S.E.: We are safe but you are not: exploring comparative optimism and cyber bullying. J. Technol. Behav. Sci. **4**, 227–233 (2019)
31. Craig, W., et al.: Social media use and cyber-bullying: a cross-national analysis of young people in 42 countries. J. Adolescent Health **66**(6), S100–S108 (2020)
32. Vannucci, A., Simpson, E.G., Gagnon, S., Ohannessian, C.M.: Social media use and risky behaviors in adolescents: a meta-analysis. J. Adolesc. **79**, 258–274 (2020)
33. Touloupis, T.: Facebook use and cyberbullying by students with learning disabilities: the role of self-esteem and loneliness. Psychol. Rep. **127**(3), 1237–1270 (2024)
34. Viner, R.M., et al.: Roles of cyberbullying, sleep, and physical activity in mediating the effects of social media use on mental health and wellbeing among young people in England: a secondary analysis of longitudinal data. Lancet Child Adolescent Health **3**(10), 685–696 (2019)
35. Sampasa-Kanyinga, H., Hamilton, H.A.: Use of social networking sites and risk of cyberbullying victimization: a population-level study of adolescents. Cyberpsychol. Behav. Soc. Netw. **18**(12), 704–710 (2015)
36. Parris, L., Lannin, D.G., Hynes, K., Yazedjian, A.: Exploring social media rumination: associations with bullying, cyberbullying, and distress. J. Interpersonal Violence **37**(5–6), NP3041-NP3061 (2022)
37. Li, Q.: Cyberbullying in schools: an examination of preservice teachers' perception. Can. J. Learn. Technol. **34**(2), 1–13 (2009)
38. Willard, N.: Cyber Savvy: Embracing Digital Safety and Civility. Corwin Press (2012)
39. El Gazzar, N.: Adolescents' perception and attitudes towards social media network in Egypt: a survey. Sci. J. Radio TV Res. **5**, 1–26 (2011)
40. MacDonald, C., Roberts-Pittman, B.: Cyberbullying among college students: Prevalence and demographic differences. Procedia Soc. Behav. Sci. **9**(2010), 2003–2009 (2010)
41. Edwards, L., Kontostathis, A.E., Fisher, C.: Cyberbullying, race/ethnicity and mental health uutcomes: a review of the literature. Media Commun. **4**(3), 71–78 (2016)
42. Iceland, J., Wilkes, R.: Does socioeconomic status matter? Race, class, and residential segregation. Soc. Probl. **53**(2), 248–273 (2006)
43. Kangrga, M., et al.: Recognizing the frequency of exposure to cyberbullying in children: the results of the national HBSC study in Serbia. Children **11**(2), 172 (2024)
44. Popović-Ćitić, B., Djurić, S., Cvetković, V.: The prevalence of cyberbullying among adolescents: a case study of middle schools in Serbia. Sch. Psychol. Int. **32**(4), 412–424 (2011)

45. Wong, D.S.W., Chan, H., Cheng, C.: Cyberbullying perpetration and victimization among adolescents in Hong Kong. Child Youth Serv. Rev. **36**(1), 133–140 (2014)
46. Haferkamp, N., Eimler, S.C., Papadakis, A.M., Kruck, J.V.: Men are from Mars, women are from Venus? Examining gender differences in self-presentation on social networking sites. Cyberpsychol. Behav. Soc. Netw. **15**(2), 91–98 (2012)
47. Tarapdar, S., Kellett, M.: Cyberbullying: insights and age-comparison indicators from a youth-led study in England. Child Indicators Res. **6**(3), 461–477 (2013). https://doi.org/10.1007/s12187-012-9177-z
48. Young, R., Tully, M.: 'Nobody wants the parents involved': social norms in parent and adolescent responses to cyberbullying. J. Youth Stud. **22**(6), 856–872 (2019)

Di.Co.EACH. - Digital Competence in Early Childhood: Educating Parents and Teachers in Conscious, Critical and Creative Uses of Digital Media

Francesca Russo(✉), Renata Metastasio, and Fabio Presaghi

Department of Psychology of Developmental and Social Processes, Sapienza University of Rome, 00185 Rome, Italy
francesca.russo@uniroma1.it

Abstract. This study is part of a national and multidisciplinary project [Code PRIN 2022XFX3EN] aimed at investigating the children's interaction with social media in family (with parents) and school contexts (with teachers) to assess their understanding of and attitudes toward digital devices, digital practices, and abilities. This contribution focused on how significant adults, i.e., parents and educators, can cooperate to sustain young children's use of digital media for educational purposes.

The research in its entirety also involved parents of children aged 0–6, but here we introduce the data relating to educators and teachers. An Italian sample of 501 teachers in the 0–6 school system were enrolled in this study via an online survey. Participants answered many questions, including opinions and attitudes towards digital devices, the leading digital devices available, etc.

Interesting results emerged regarding which, for how long, and for which activities the digital devices are most used in the school context. Furthermore, meaningful opinions emerge about the ideal context and age group in which it is preferable to use digital tools.

Digital devices pose risks but also give children, their parents, and teachers opportunities to promote approaches preparatory to acquiring digital skills, starting from considering parents' and teachers' characteristics and interactions.

Keywords: Media education · Social and Professional topics · Digital skills

1 Introduction

Nowadays, children are part of a technology-saturated society, where digital media are increasingly incorporated within the family environment in the Global North [1]. A Common Sense Census found that 98% of American families with children aged 0–8 hold at least a mobile device that accounts for a third of children's screen time [2]. EU Kids Online data further show that children grow up in media-saturated environments [3]. Recent findings from a representative panel of Italian parents show that all the families

Ł. Tomczyk (Ed.): NMP 2024, CCIS 2537, pp. 146–159, 2025.
https://doi.org/10.1007/978-3-031-95627-0_10

surveyed hold at least a smartphone and 84% at least a tablet [4]. Despite this increase, children's media use is not something new. Starting from the emergence of editorial publishing in the 18th century up until the spread of modern smartphones and tablets in the 21st century, media have long been in relation to the domestic environment and its members [5]. Such a relationship has always spurred many controversies, especially concerning whether and how children should interact with media, following two main discourses focused on opponents' pessimistic stances or supporters' enthusiastic views [6]. In this view, parents are seen as the main accountable actors for governing children's relationship with the media, particularly regarding screen time in early childhood [7]. Starting from the late '90s, with the rise of content targeted at infants, the American Academy of Pediatrics [8] argued that children under two should not be allowed in front of a screen, and children 2 to 5 for no more than two hours a day. While this warning was held in place for a while, it rarely matched the reality of many families, leading the AAP [9] to update its guidelines, recognizing that rigid screen time rules are no longer possible in today's media-saturated ecology and that high-quality educational contents may promote children's learning and development with caregivers' guidance. Scholars have questioned the screen time debate, for it sets unrealistic expectations that overemphasize parents' responsibilities [10] and fails to conceive a systemic outlook on the phenomenon, such as the one provided by the "3Cs" Child-Content-Context framework, focused on children's individual characteristics, the quality of the contents they interact with, and the broader physical and relational contexts where this interaction takes place [11]. The physical and relational context is relevant here, encompassing the places and actors children experience digital media with. In this regard, the family and the school are the two leading educational milieus children have experience [12], with parents and educators scaffolding these experiences as "more knowledgeable others" [13]. This claim also holds true for young children's digital media use [14].

Based on the above evidence, in the present study, we investigate children's experience in the Italian integrated 0–6 school system with digital media and their educational opportunities by focusing on how significant adults can cooperate to sustain young children's oriented use of digital media for educational purposes. The importance for families and educators to cooperate has long been documented as favorable for children's development [15]: investing in good cooperation between families and educational services to foster constructive and positive uses of digital media starting from early childhood, in turn, may prove significant. Previous research indicates how the age of first use of ICTs positively predicts children's digital skills acquisition [16]. Studies on the use of tablets at home and preschool also found that when well-coordinated, they can promote emergent writing and letter knowledge, foster children's acquaintance of letters, symbols, and words on the screen (in integration with non-digital approaches), and stimulate the acquisition of technical skills [14]. Taken together, these studies support that when it comes to children and digital media, "the main driver of development is not the technological tool at hand but the unique configurations of activities, material resources, relationships, culturally grounded practices, and the interactions that emerge from them within and across settings" [17].

Concerning this hitherto little-explored theme, this project intends to promote interdisciplinary research (combining medical, pedagogical, psychological, and sociological perspectives) to enrich the literature and promote greater awareness among parents, educators, and teachers about the risks and opportunities posed by the presence of electronic devices in children's lives, promoting approaches preparatory to the acquisition of digital skills as they develop and grow up. We wanted to focus attention on an early age group (0–6), by detecting and comparing adults' attitudes regarding the use of Digital Devices (DD) by children.

As previously mentioned, it's easy to understand the importance of considering how the actors with whom children experience digital media have confidence in their ability to deal with and best use digital devices. Investigating how teachers and educators recognize technology's benefits and feel confident using it is crucial. Benefits, reflections and actions related to Media Education and digital competence are usually promoted from school age, particularly primary school [18]. In the present study, we will focus on the crucial contextual components of the educational services' use of educational digital media and contents – such as whether these are present and used or not within a service and to what degree, whether and how they are incorporated within the pedagogical planning and philosophy of the service, etc. – as well as educators' own attitudes towards digital media as educational tools in early childhood education, digital skills, experiences of digital media training, and mediation practices adopted.

Specifically, we were interested in understanding in which context (home or school) and in which age group (0–3 or 3–6 age group) teachers believe it is preferable to use DD.

Consequently, the two main hypotheses of this research are:

1. *Teachers/Educators are more in favor of the use of DD by older children*
2. *Teachers are more in favor of using DD in the school context rather than at home*

2 Materials and Methods

2.1 Sample

501 Italian nursery (n = 360, 71.86%) and pre-school (n = 141, 28.14%) teachers completed 100% of the questionnaire battery. Considering only the sample of participants who completed the entire battery of questionnaires, the average age was approximately M = 43 (SD = 11; Men n = 7; Men M = 41.43; SD age = 10.69; Women n = 479; Women M = 43.4; SD = 10.81).

2.2 Measures

All teachers and educators completed the following sections of the questionnaire:

- INFORMATION ABOUT THE EDUCATIONAL STRUCTURE: This section concerns collecting information on the type of structure where you work (nursery; preschool), the number of educators present in the educational structure, and the Municipality and province where the educational structure where he/she works is located.
- INFORMATIONS ABOUT EDUCATORS AND TEACHERS: This section concerns the information collection on the gender and age of the educator/teacher, the years working in the educational facility, and the contractual position (fixed or permanent).

- ATTITUDE TOWARDS THE USE OF DD IN SCHOOL: We asked teachers the extent to which they believe nursery school teachers should rely on the use of DD by children aged 0–6. Is made up of 6 items (e.g., "How much do you think that children's use of DD is: irreplaceable") assessed on a response scale of 5 steps (1 = not at all; 5 = completely). The reliability of the measurement was good (McDonald $\omega = 0.92$).
- ATTITUDE TOWARDS THE USE OF DD FOR TEACHING: We asked teachers to rate how much they believe educators should rely on the use of DD for educational purposes in nursery or preschool. We used a list of 8 items (e.g., "A passing fad which, in the majority of cases, does not change the way of educating/teaching.") were used with a rating scale rated on a 5-step scale (1 = for disagree; 5 = completely agree). The reliability of the measurement was also good (McDonald $\omega = 0.91$).
- DD IN USE IN THE EDUCATIONAL STRUCTURE: Teachers were asked to indicate which DD of a list was available in their educational structure.
- FREQUENCY OF USE OF DD IN EDUCATIONAL CONTEXTS: We asked teachers to rate (with a 5-step response scale ranging from 1 = never; to 5 = at least once a day) the frequency of use they DD for educational activities in their educational structures.
- ACTIVITIES WITH DD: We asked teachers to rate the frequency with which they carry out a series of educational activities using DD.
- DD PRESENT AT HOME: We asked teachers to indicate which DD are present in their home.
- FREQUENCY OF USE OF DD AT HOME: We asked teachers to rate the frequency with which they carry out a series of activities with DD for personal purposes.
- PROFESSIONAL ACTIVITIES WITH DD AT HOME: We asked teachers to rate the frequency with which they carry out a series of activities with DD for their educational group at home.
- DEGREE OF APPROVAL FOR THE USE OF DD for educational purposes with children 0–3: We asked teachers to rate the degree to which they approve (rated on a 5-step rating scale with 1 = for not at all favorable; and 5 = completely favorable) the use of DD at home and at school by children in the 0–3 age group.
- DEGREE OF APPROVAL FOR THE USE OF DD with children 3–6: We asked teachers to rate the degree (5-step rating scale ranging from 1 = for not at all favorable; to 5 = completely favorable) to which they approve the use of DD at home and school by children in the 3–6 age group.

2.3 Procedure

All respondents completed an online survey using the Qualtrics platform between April 2024 and October 2024. Participants agreed to participate in the study and signed an informed consent form following the Declaration of Helsinki. The Sapienza University of Rome Ethics Committee approved the study. Participants involved in the study were recruited from associations, schools, pediatricians, and cooperatives.

2.4 Statistical Analysis

The main focus of the study is to explore the teachers' habits in the use of DD at school and home contexts, and how these habits differ between nursery and pre-school teachers.

To this aim, for the measures for which it was possible to calculate the average, we computed t-tests to compare the averages reported by the nursery school teachers with those of the preschool teachers. For reliability of measures, we computed McDonald's omega index. For variables available in form of frequencies, we calculated the chi-square testcomputed to verify whether one of the response categories is over-represented (or under-represented) and its association with the Nursery/Preschool teachers. Missing values were simply casewise exluded from the analysis.

3 Results

The average age of our sample was approximately M = 43, with nursery teachers slightly younger than pre-school teachers (Table 1). The average number of years of experience in educational contexts is approximately M = 17 (SD = 10), while considering the years of experience as a function of the permanent contractual position, the average is M = 7.92 (SD = 9.05) and for those with temporary contracts is M = 18.2 (SD = 9.46).

Table 1. Descriptive statistics (M, SD) of age and length of service (in years) according to educational structure

	Nursery		Preschool		t.test	df	p
	M	SD	M	SD			
Age	41.20	10.60	48.93	9.16	−8.05	290.18	<.001
Years of service in educational facilities	14.90	9.49	21.11	10.17	−6.18	238.23	<.001

Approximately, of 501 respondents, 360 are employed in a nursery (n = 360, 71.86%) and 141 in pre-school (n = 141, 28.14%) Approximately 45.85% declare they have a contractual position as an Educator/Teacher with a permanent contract, while approximately 7.96% have a fixed-term contract.

As shown in Table 2, the digital devices most present in educational structures are pc, the printer, the digital camera and the tablet.

Table 3 shows how the activities most carried out with digital devices, both in nurseries and in preschools, are Use educational games, Listen to/See stories and See videos of experiences carried out in educational contexts.

Comparing the activities carried out with DDs in nursery schools and preschools (Table 3), it emerged that in preschool there is a tendency to use DD for listening of music, watching films or cartoons, videos made in educational contexts and processing images or videos, compared to nursery schools. On the other hand, nursery school has a greater tendency to create immersive/virtual environments.

Overall, a very limited use of digital devices emerges in the educational context, with the highest peak of use occurring once a month (Use educational games, Listen to/See stories).

Table 2. List of Digital devices available in the educational structure

	Frequency		Chi-square	df	p
	Nursery	Preschool			
Smart TV	9	11	0.20	1	0.655
Digital camera	152	46	56.75	1	<.001
Scanner	123	56	25.08	1	<.001
PC	262	96	76.97	1	<.001
Tablet	147	42	58.33	1	<.001
Printer	180	75	43.24	1	<.001
Multimedia stations	11	7	0.89	1	0.346
Programmable robots	5	22	10.70	1	0.001
E-book reader	3	0	3.00	1	0.083
Smart speakers	13	3	6.25	1	0.012

Table 4 shows the diffusion and habits of DDs present in the homes of nursery school and preschool teachers.

In educators and teachers homes', digital cameras, tablets, smart TVs and programmable robots are the most common digital devices (Table 4).

Table 5 shows that for personal use, Use email, Access social networks (e.g. FB, Whatsapp, etc.) Listen to music, Download and use applications and Read news in newspapers/web TV/other, are the activities most carried out by those surveyed in the study. These activities are carried out quite frequently, given that the respondents declare that they carry them out "sometimes/often".

Comparing nursery and pre-school teachers, emerges the tendency to carry out the same activities with the DDs available in their homes, with the exception of the use of DDs for videoconferences, that preschool teachers use more frequently than the to nursery school teachers. On the contrary, nursery teachers reported higher tendency to buy on digital platforms than preschool teachers.

Table 5 shows that for personal use, Use e-mail, Access social networks (e.g. FB, Whatsapp, etc.) Listen to music, Download and use applications and Read news in newspapers/web TV/other, are the activities most carried out by those surveyed in the study. These activities are carried out quite frequently, given that the respondents declare that they carry them out "sometimes/often".

From the comparison it emerged that educators and teachers tend to carry out the same activities with the DDs available in their homes, with the exception of the use of DDs for videoconferences, which the preschool teachers carry out more frequently than the to nursery school teachers, and of purchases on digital platforms where instead educators report frequencies significantly higher than those of preschool teachers.

For professional use (Table 6), both groups use the DD approximately once a month to do researches, exchange material with colleagues and prepare material for educational and teaching activities. The differences between the averages of the two groups on these

Table 3. Activities carried out with Digital Devices in educational facilities

	Nursery		Preschool			df	p
	M	SD	M	SD	t test		
Listen to music	1.20	0.77	1.41	0.95	−2.06	162.29	0.041
Listen to/See stories	3.18	1.73	2.91	1.58	1.51	210.12	0.133
Watch cartoons	1.99	1.25	2.43	1.31	−3.01	185.43	0.003
Use educational games	3.79	1.37	3.88	1.29	−0.62	203.05	0.538
Create immersive/virtual environments	2.62	1.83	2.04	1.44	3.30	243.45	0.001
See videos of experiences carried out in educational contexts	2.87	1.53	3.52	1.46	−3.89	201.57	<.001
Search for further information/materials	1.15	0.61	1.24	0.75	−1.16	163.48	0.247
Process images/photos	1.03	0.26	1.46	0.98	−4.41	111.82	<.001
Connect with children from other schools/nurseries	1.04	0.29	1.10	0.45	−1.25	141.34	0.212
Carry out educational experiences with digital tools	1.24	0.84	1.23	0.86	0.02	188.00	0.985

Note: 5-step response scale (1 = Never; 2 = At least once a year; 3 = At least once a month; 4 = At least once a week; 5 = At least once a day)

three activities are significant, the preschool teachers use DD more often than their nursery colleagues for the three activities above.

Basing on data showed in Table 6, preschool teachers report a greater frequency of use of DD at home for their educational group of children compared to nursery school teachers.

For professional use, both groups use the DD approximately once a month to do researches, exchange material with colleagues and prepare material for educational and teaching activities. The differences between the averages of the two groups on these three activities are significant, the preschool teachers use DD more often than their nursery colleagues for the three activities above.

From the comparison it emerges that, in general, preschool teachers report a greater frequency of activities carried out at home with DDs for their educational group compared to nursery school teachers.

Considering attitudes and opinions, from the comparison it emerges that overall the attitude of nursery school teachers and pre-school teachers quite agree that in the context in which they work the use of digital devices by an educator/teacher is *useful and necessary* (Table 7).

Table 4. Diffusion of Digital Devices in the homes of educators and teachers

	Frequency		Chi-square	df	p
	Educators	Preschool Teachers			
Smart TV	232	86	67.03	1	<.001
Digital camera	258	97	73.02	1	<.001
Scanner	98	47	17.94	1	<.001
PC	155	78	25.45	1	<.001
Tablet	245	101	59.93	1	<.001
Printer	101	37	29.68	1	<.001
Multimedia stations	55	26	10.38	1	0.001
Programmable robots	196	87	41.98	1	<.001
E-book reader	14	5	4.26	1	0.039
Smart speakers	63	18	25.00	1	<.001

Asking the attitude towards the use of DD by children aged 0–3 years at home and in the educational structure, it emerges that educators are more favorable to the use of DD in nursery school than preschool teachers. Additionally, they are more favorable to the use of DD in the educational context rather than at home (Table 8).

Lastly, compared to the age group 3–6 years, the respondents appear more favorable to the inclusion of digital devices, once again underlining the preference for their use in the educational context rather than at home (Table 9).

4 Discussion

Overall, in this research, there was a clear greater involvement of nursery (71.86%) compared to preschool teachers (28.14%). According to the educational structure, the descriptive statistics of age and length of service show that nursery school teachers are younger and have fewer years of service than preschool teachers. Respondents, on average, are not very young but still have a long career path ahead of them. This result stimulates suggestions, including the possibility of organizing various training meetings on the correct use of digital devices during a career that has not yet ended. In support of this, in fact, we also underline the discrepancy between teachers' generally favorable attitude towards the use of DDs and the limited frequency of their use. This gap could be filled by integrating continuous professional training/school policies to support digital education.

According to our results, the educational structures where educators and teachers who participated in the survey work, are provided with various digital devices. Specifically, the digital devices most present in educational structures are pc, the printers, digital cameras, and tablets. These are tools (especially the first two) usually used for documenting family activities. In contrast, tablets in nurseries have been widely used

Table 5. List of activities carried out with DDs for personal use and frequency of use of DDs at home by educators and school teachers

	Educators		Preschool Teachers		t test	df	p
	M	SD	M	SD			
Listen to music	3.93	0.98	3.81	1.02	1.06	184.92	0.29
Download and use applications	3.67	0.97	3.51	1.02	1.42	183.44	0.16
Read books/ebooks	2.12	1.38	2.20	1.35	−0.49	196.12	0.62
Upload videos, images, etc	3.49	1.08	3.66	0.99	−1.47	206.18	0.14
Play online	1.76	1.14	1.97	1.18	−1.60	185.31	0.11
Read news in newspapers/web TV/other	3.69	1.02	3.62	1.17	0.53	170.55	0.60
Watch videos on websites (e.g. Youtube)	3.53	1.07	3.51	0.95	0.21	214.31	0.83
Use email	4.52	0.71	4.51	0.68	0.16	198.85	0.87
Participate in a video conference (e.g. Skype/FaceTime)	3.10	0.93	3.42	0.91	−3.09	194.34	0.00
Access social networks (e.g. FB, Whatsapp, etc.)	4.39	0.83	4.24	0.88	1.55	181.32	0.12
Write on blogs/participate in forums	1.67	0.92	1.67	0.96	−0.04	184.31	0.97
Shopping/selling on the internet (e.g. Ebay)	3.16	1.11	2.82	1.19	2.53	180.88	0.01

Note: 5-step response scale (1 = Never; 2 = A little; 3 = Sometimes; 4 = Often; 5 = Always)

for managing communication with families (attendance tracking, uploading documentation). Also interesting is the presence, even with minimal frequency (27), of robots that suggest coding courses and multimedia stations which suggest investments in the organization of "technological" spaces designed for children.

Regarding the activities with digital devices in educational settings, data highlight that educators and teachers use digital devices to diversify the activities. These vary according to the children's age groups: In both settings, they use DD for educational games and listen to stories. But, specifically, in preschool, there is a tendency to listen to more music, watch films or cartoons, watch videos made in educational contexts, and process images or videos, if compared to nursery schools. On the other hand, there is a greater tendency to create immersive/virtual environments at nursery school. The

Table 6. List of activities (with relative frequencies) carried out with digital devices at home for the children of the educational group

	Educators		Preschool Teachers		t test	df	p
	M	SD	M	SD			
Search for music tracks	2.67	1.27	3.36	1.16	−5.04	208.76	<.001
Download and use applications	1.82	1.11	2.21	1.15	−2.94	184.70	0.004
Consult forum	2.09	1.19	2.18	1.24	−0.62	184.80	0.535
Watch videos	2.68	1.29	3.24	1.07	−4.32	229.34	<.001
Do researches	3.28	1.19	3.82	1.05	−4.36	215.81	<.001
Exchange materials with colleagues	3.11	1.21	3.47	1.16	−2.72	200.37	0.007
Prepare material for educational and teaching activities	2.91	1.25	3.76	0.99	−6.99	239.65	<.001
Have online meetings with parents	1.65	0.83	2.01	0.88	−3.66	182.02	<.001

Note: 5-step response scale (1 = Never; 2 = At least once a year; 3 = At least once a month; 4 = At least once a week; 5 = At least once a day).

Table 7. Attitudes of Educators and Preschool Teachers towards the use of devices in educational contexts

	Educators		Preschool Teachers		t value	df	p
	M	SD	M	SD			
Irreplaceable	2.61	1.31	2.33	1.07	2.14	234.29	0.03
Counterproductive	2.25	1.19	2.14	1.04	0.92	218.04	0.36
Useful	3.73	1.01	3.74	0.88	−0.06	218.90	0.95
Limiting with respect to learning	2.56	1.15	2.36	1.10	1.55	201.15	0.12
Necessary	3.05	1.22	2.93	1.17	0.93	200.73	0.35

Note: Response scale from 1 (Not at all agree) to 5 (Completely agree).

correspondence between the child's developmental level and adapted activities should probably explain these data.

Overall, very limited use of digital devices emerges in the educational context, with the highest peak of use occurring once a month, above all for educational games and listening to/seeing stories. On the contrary, from the data, it emerges that connecting

Table 8. Attitudes of Educators and Preschool Teachers towards the use of devices in educational contexts and at home by children aged 0–3

	Educators		Preschool Teachers		t.test	df	p
	M	SD	M	SD			
In favor of the use of DD in the nursery	2.19	1.26	1.89	0.98	2.45	242.78	0.01
In favor of the use of DD at home	2.06	1.07	1.89	0.93	1.55	216.80	0.12

Note: 5-step response scale (1 = Not at all favorable; 2 = Not very favorable; 3 = Neither much nor a little; 4 = Fairly favorable; 5 = Completely favorable).

Table 9. Attitudes of Educators and Preschool Teachers towards the use of devices in educational contexts and at home by children aged 3–6

	Educators		Preschool Teachers		t.test	df	p
	M	DS	M	DS			
In favor of the use of DD in the Preschool	2.68	1.23	2.90	1.13	−1.63	207.18	0.10
In favor of the use of DD at home	2.51	1.04	2.45	0.99	0.57	198.84	0.57

Note: 5-step response scale (1 = Not at all favorable; 2 = Not very favorable; 3 = Neither much nor a little; 4 = Fairly favorable; 5 = Completely favorable).

with children from other institutions is very rare. Data obtained from our sample show a widespread presence of digital devices in Italian educational facilities but, at the same time, still limited use of DD in educational activities, despite educators and teachers appearing overall favorable to their use. Possible hypotheses could be not feeling sufficiently capable of using digital devices most suitably for the optimal development of the child, the preference for educational activities that do not involve digital devices, or, more simply, an aspect of social desirability that must be taken into account in quantitative research.

Moving into a more private dimension of the participants, i.e., the domestic context, in educators and teachers' homes, digital cameras, tablets, smart TVs, and programmable robots are the most common digital devices. In this regard, it is necessary to distinguish between activities carried out with digital devices for private or professional use. Data show that teachers and educators use mostly digital devices for e-mail, access social networks (e.g. FB, WhatsApp, etc.), listen to music, downloading and use applications, and read news in newspapers/web TV. In this case, contrary to the data relating to the school context, a higher frequency of use emerges. Indeed, these activities are carried out quite frequently, given that the respondents declare that they carry them out "sometimes/often". In a comparison between educators and teachers, data show that they tend to carry out the same activities with the DDs available in their homes, except the use of DDs for videoconferences, which the preschool teachers carry out more frequently than the nursery school teachers, and of purchases on digital platforms where instead educators report frequencies significantly higher than those of preschool teachers.

For professional use, both groups use DD to do research, exchange material with colleagues, and prepare material for educational and teaching activities. It is important to highlight the differences between the averages of the two groups on these three activities because they are significant: the preschool teachers use DD *more often* than their nursery colleagues for the three activities above, probably working with an age group that lends itself to a more significant number of activities. Again, as the use of DD in the educational context, the frequency of professional use is low: approximately once a month.

In conclusion, exploring the participants' opinions about using DDs in the educational context, their attitudes are overall positive. Both educators and teachers believe that integrating DD into teaching is *necessary* and *useful*. These data are further confirmed later when they express to be quite in favor of using them, satisfying the two initial hypotheses of this study. However, some differentiations must be made. When asked about the attitude towards the use of DD by children aged 0–3 years at home and in the educational structure, it emerges that educators are more favorable to using DD in nursery school than preschool teachers. Additionally, they are more favorable to using dd in the educational context than at home. Lastly, regarding the age group 3–6 years, the respondents appear more favorable to including digital devices, once again underlining the preference for their use in the educational context rather than at home. This result stimulates the consideration of possible concrete solutions to streamline the dialogue between home and school in the correct, aligned use of digital devices.

5 Limits and Conclusion

A significant limitation of the research is using self-report questionnaires as the main data collection tool. Educators and teachers may have responded in a not completely truthful way due to social desirability, reporting what others expect of their behavior instead of what they do. This can lead to bias in the data collected, affecting the validity of the results. To reduce our concerns about social desirability bias, it could also be useful to integrate qualitative research.

The sample represents an additional limitation. Although the research sample is large, it is not statistically representative of the entire population considered about the geographic area of membership, gender, age of birth, and length of service.

Moreover, the study did not consider important contextual variables such as the existence of school policies. These may influence how educational practices integrate technology and support for preschool and kindergarten teachers who work with children ages 0–3 and 3–6. For example, some schools and kindergartens may have policies that actively encourage the use of technology by providing appropriate digital devices and resources. In contrast, others may have severe restrictions or lack the necessary infrastructure. School policies also influence the training of teachers/educators in the use of technology: institutions that invest in continuing education and technical assistance make the use of technology in educational activities effective and creative. Without this, teachers and educators may feel less prepared and less confident in integrating technology into their daily practices.

However, the results can guide the development of the research presented and the identification of new research questions. The first result is that we are dealing with teachers who are familiar with digital resources, which they use daily in their personal lives. However, teachers at school prefer using technologies without network resources, with traditional ways of use; therefore, the learning potential for children related to using DDs is not placed in the classroom context.

The tendency of teachers to be more supportive of the use of DDs in educational contexts rather than in family contexts suggests further investigation into larger samples because one might foreshadow the presence of a typical paradox in the relationship between the in and out-of-school with the boundary, represented, precisely by digital technology and access to the Internet. This aspect can also directly reflect how digital devices can create a distance, a generational gap, and between contexts, precisely, between school and family.

The greater favorability of using digital devices in educational settings rather than at home and with older children may be motivated by teachers' justified fear that children may engage in unsafe browsing and enact unmanaged and unsupervised ways of using devices when read from an educational perspective raises the issue of the difficult balance between children's right to carry out first-hand explorations of digital resources and the necessary safety - of parents and educators - in accompanying such explorations.

Finally, an interesting finding is teachers' use of the technological resources available in their schools. The physical presence of artifacts is not enough to perceive their usability: it is necessary to activate the process of appropriation, which is a culturally connoted process.

The set of results presented prefigures an investment at the educational level in the perspective of media education; Training should be designed appropriately to meet the specific needs of teachers and educators working with preschoolers; this could influence teachers' and educators' attitudes and involvement in adopting technology-based practices or new educational methodologies.

References

1. Livingstone, S., Blum-Ross, A.: Parenting for a Digital Future. Oxford University Press, Oxford (2020)
2. Rideout, V.: The Common Sense Census: Media Use by Kids Age Zero to Eight. Common Sense Media, San Francisco (2017)
3. Smahel, D., et al.: EU Kids Online 2020. EU Kids Online (2020)
4. Zaffaroni, L.G., Amadori, G., Mascheroni, G.: DataChildFutures 2021: Survey results. DataChildFutures (2022)
5. Wartella, E.: Smartph\ones and tablets and kids. In: Donohue, C. (ed.) Exploring Key Issues in Early Childhood and Technology, pp. 27–31. Routledge, London (2019)
6. Wartella, E., Jennings, N.: New members of the family: the digital revolution in the home. J. Fam. Commun. **1**(1), 59–69 (2001)
7. Wartella, E., Robb, M.: Historical and recurring concerns about children's use of the mass media. In: Calvert, S.L., Wilson, B.J. (eds.) The Handbook of Children, Media, and Development, pp. 7–26. Blackwell Publishing, Hoboken (2008)
8. AAP.: Committee on Public Education. Media education. Pediatrics **104**, 341–343 (1999)
9. AAP.: Growing up digital: Media research symposium. Washington, DC (2015)

10. Cino, D., Mascheroni, G., Wartella, E.: "The kids hate it, but we love it!": parents' reviews of circle. Media Commun. **8**(4), 208–217 (2020)
11. Lauricella, A., Blackwell, C.K., Wartella, E.: The "new" technology environment: the role of content and context on learning and development from mobile media. In: Barr, R., Linebarger, D.N. (eds.) Media Exposure During Infancy and Early Childhood, pp. 1–23. Springer, Cham (2017)
12. Bronfenbrenner, U.: The Ecology of Human Development: Experiments by Nature and Design. Harvard University Press, Cambridge (1979)
13. Vygotsky, L.S.: Mind in Society. Harvard University Press (1980)
14. Neumann, M.M., Neumann, D.L.: The use of touch-screen tablets at home and pre-school to foster emergent literacy. J. Early Child. Lit. **17**(2), 203–220 (2017)
15. Epstein, J.L., Salinas, K.C.: Partnering with families and communities. Educ. Leadersh. **61**(8), 12–19 (2004). European Commission (2019). Open Science. https://ec.europa.eu/info/sites/default/files/research_and_innovation/knowledge_publications_tools_and_data/documents/ec_rtd_factsheet-open-science_2019.pdf
16. Haddon, L., Cino, D., Doyle, M.A., Livingstone, S., Mascheroni, G., Stoilova, M.: Children's and young people's digital skills: a systematic evidence review. KU Leuven, Leuven: ySKILLS (2020)
17. Barron, B., Levinson, A.M.: Media as a catalyst for children's engagement in learning at home and across settings. In: Gee, E., Takeuchi, L., Wartella, E. (eds.) Children and Families in the Digital Age, pp. 13–36. Routledge, New York (2018)
18. Calvani, A., Fini, A., Ranieri, M.: Valutare la competenza digitale. Erickson, Trento (2011)

Parents' and Preschool Educators' Perspectives on Digital Devices in Early Childhood. Preliminary Findings from the Research Project PRIN "Di.Co.Each"

Federica Ranzani[1](✉), Claudio D'Antonio[2], Cosimo Di Bari[2], and Silvia Demozzi[1]

[1] Department of Education Studies, University of Bologna, Via Filippo Re 6, 40126 Bologna, Italy
federica.ranzani2@unibo.it

[2] Department of Education, Interculture, Literature and Psychology, University of Florence, Via Laura 48, Florence, Italy

Abstract. This article presents some preliminary findings from the Italian research project PRIN "Di.Co.Each." It reports on the qualitative analysis of a corpus of 23 focus groups collected to explore the perspectives, beliefs, and experiences of significant adults regarding the relationship between digital devices (DDs) and early childhood (0–6 years). The study involved 87 parents, 116 preschool educators working in the 0–6 Italian integrated education systems, and 36 pediatricians, recruited via convenience sampling. The data were analyzed using thematic analysis with a predominantly inductive approach. Focusing on *children's uses* and *adults' needs* as voiced by the parents and the 0–6 educational staff, results shed light on the relevance of training caregivers in conscious, critical, and creative uses for fostering awareness of both opportunities and limitations set up by children's use of DDs in the domestic and formal education environments.

Keywords: Digital Competence · Early Childhood · Parental Education · Educational Services 0–6 · Focus Group

1 Introduction

Over the last decades, the presence of digital devices (hereafter, DDs) in children's everyday lives has grown exponentially in the Global North [1, 2]. The relationship between childhood and DDs has historically spurred heated public debate, often polarized around two opposing positions, namely "discourses of concern" (also referred to as "media panic" [3]) and "discourses of celebration" ([4] p. 361; see also [5, 6]). When it comes to early childhood (0–6 years), this polarization is particularly evident and is strictly intertwined with contemporary social discourses on parental responsibilities, according to which parents are the main accountable subjects for managing young children's screen exposure, especially in terms of regulating times and contents [7]. Since the

Ł. Tomczyk (Ed.): NMP 2024, CCIS 2537, pp. 160–170, 2025.
https://doi.org/10.1007/978-3-031-95627-0_11

late '90s, attempts to govern children's interactions with DDs have been at the forefront of the agenda of many institutions. Most notably, the American Academy of Pediatrics in 1999 [8] issued influential guidelines recommending that children under 2 should not be exposed to screens at all, and children aged 2 to 5 should be limited to no more than two hours of screen time per day. However, given the increased pervasiveness of digital media in today's everyday life, in 2015 the AAP [9] revised these guidelines for them not being suitable for contemporary media-saturated family environments. Stressing the importance of high-quality educational content and adult supervision, the AAP updated guidelines resonate with research questioning the time-centered debate and emphasizing instead the crucial role of contents and contextual features in which child-media interaction occurs (see, among others, [10, 11]). More recently, the World Health Organization (2019 [12]) along with pediatric societies, including the Italian Pediatric Society (2018 [13]), released guidelines recommending that children younger than 2 years old should avoid screen time altogether, and that children aged 2 to 5 should be limited to 1 h of screen time per day, thereby shifting the focus back to the screen time debate.

While parents' mediating role has long been discussed, even for the socially shared set of unrealistic expectations overemphasizing parental responsibility [14], educational staff working in 0–6 educational services also play a critical role in shaping young children's relationship with DDs. As a matter of fact, the home and preschool settings constitute the primary educational environments wherein children can experience DDs and develop digital competence [15, 16]. In order to enhance the educational opportunities set up by DDs in these environments and foster children's agency and critical fruition since early childhood, research as well as policymakers have underscored the importance of a collaborative relationship between families and educators. Indeed, the family-(pre)school educational alliance is widely regarded as the cornerstone for granting children a safe and healthy development [17–19]. However, occurrences of misalignments [20] and a sense of disconnection between parents and educators regarding children's use of DDs have also been documented [21]. From this standpoint, it becomes crucial to investigate the experience of young children in both the domestic sphere and the 0–6 educational services, focusing on how significant adults, i.e., parents and educators, perceive the use of DDs in early childhood and collaborate (or not) to scaffold children's use of DDs. The research project PRIN "Di.Co.Each" aims to address this pedagogically relevant issue, as the next section illustrates.

2 The Research Project PRIN "Di.Co.Each": Promoting Digital Competence in Early Childhood

Building on the premises outlined above, the Italian research project PRIN "*Di.Co.Each. Digital competence in Early Childhood: educating parents and teachers in conscious, critical and creative uses of digital media*" aims to investigate the experience of children aged 0–6 with digital devices in the Italian context. The project is funded by the Next Generation Europe and the Italian Ministry of the University and Research. It involves the University of Florence (PI), the University of Bologna, and the University of Rome "La Sapienza".

The overarching objective is to promote digital competencies in early childhood as a prerequisite for the development of responsible and conscious digital citizenship. To achieve this goal, the project involves significant actors mediating the relationship between DDs and early childhood, above all families, educators, and healthcare practitioners. Ultimately, the project aims to promote greater awareness among parents and practitioners about the risks and opportunities posed by the presence of DDs in early childhood.

In order to enrich scientific literature on digital competence in early childhood and empirically investigate the experience of children in the Italian integrated 0–6 system and in the household, the following research actions have been carried out:

1) A systematized literature review on the construct of digital competence in early childhood;
2) Focus groups with parents, educators/teachers, and pediatricians aimed at understanding their perspective on children's uses of DDs within the family environment and educational and healthcare services;
3) Two surveys addressed to parents and educators/teachers aimed at collecting data on the presence, habits, attitudes, and uses of DDs by young children in domestic and 0–6 educational settings.

Results from the literature review, focus groups, and surveys will be triangulated, constituting the basis for the following step of the project: action research. During this final phase, the staff of different educational services will be involved in co-designing with researchers a media education path aimed at promoting conscious, critical, and creative uses of DDs within educational services. Once implemented, families will be encouraged to access services so as to engage in media education activities with their children. The proposed experiences are intended to provide an opportunity to understand the active role that children can play in DDs-based activities when mediated by adults.

For the purpose of this article, we outline the preliminary results of the focus groups conducted with parents and the educators and teachers of 0–6 educational services.

3 Data and Methodology

The article reports on data from a corpus of 23 focus groups conducted with significant adults, namely parents (N = 9), educational staff working in 0–6 educational services (N = 9), and family pediatricians (N = 5). Specifically, the study involved a total of 239 participants: 87 parents, 116 preschool teachers, and 36 pediatricians. Data were collected between January and May 2024 in Florence, Bologna, and surrounding municipalities. Participants were recruited by the authors through convenience sampling, with the support of different institutions and associations. Written informed consent was obtained by all participants in compliance with Italian law n. 196/2003 and EU Regulation n. 2016/679 (GDPR, 2016/679) before data collection.

3.1 Analytical Procedures

The focus groups have been conducted with the aim of gathering information on the perspectives, perceptions, beliefs, and experiences of significant adults regarding the use of DDs in early childhood (0–6 years). In order to bring to light and analyze the main issues of concern emerging from the participants' point of view, data were analyzed through thematic analysis [22]. A mainly inductive approach was used to grasp themes treated as relevant by participants and not assumed aprioristically by the researchers [23].

All focus group sessions were audio and video-recorded and independently transcribed by two researchers. Each focus group was given an ID and transcribed verbatim, with paraverbal and non-verbal behavior omitted. The emerging themes and sub-themes were developed after repeated reading of the transcripts and iteratively adjusted to reach discursive intercoder agreement through the convergence of different perspectives [24]. Data were coded and analyzed using the software NVIVO12.

4 Results

The final coding scheme provisionally consists of the following macro themes, listed in alphabetical order: adults' uses, children's uses, concerns, covid19, grandparenting, media education, needs, and parenting.

For the purposes of this article, we report a synthesized overview of the major preliminary findings separated for each group category. In particular, for space reasons, we focus on *children's uses* and *adults' needs* as voiced by the parents and the 0–6 educational staff.

4.1 Children's Uses of Digital Devices

The Voice of Parents

Types of Devices. A widespread presence of DDs in young children's everyday family lives has been depicted by parents. Smart TVs/TVs and parents' smartphones are referred to as the devices most frequently used by children in the domestic environment. TVs are mainly used to watch cartoons but also listen to background music when children are engaged in other non-digital activities. Smartphones are reported to be mainly used for video calls with long-distance relatives, watching and/or creating pictures, and listening to music. Other devices used by young children are digital cameras, Virtual Assistants like Amazon Alexa or Apple Siri, and above all parents' tablets, which are mainly used for watching videos or using recreational apps.

Motivations. Children's use of DDs is often motivated by the need to entertain the child when parents are engaged in household activities, especially if they are at home alone and do not have any third-party support. In particular, parents' and children's tiredness are frequently reported as significant reasons for children's use. In other words, if they are particularly tired or alone and perceive that the child needs to be entertained or calmed down, they are more likely to let the child use DDs (echoing the commonsensical notions of DDs as "digital babysitter" and "digital pacifier"). Other specific situations in which DDs are typically used to entertain or relax the child (also by those few parents who declare that they completely forbid the use of DDs at home) are the care of the ill child (e.g., during nebulizer treatments), the management of long trips (e.g., in the train), or for specific events like "cinema nights". Communication with long-distance relatives is another common reason for children's use of DDs. Interestingly, parents also report that the unavoidability of children's exposure to DDs in contemporary society is for them a motor for introducing children to DDs in the safe space of the domestic environment.

Rules. Parents place particular emphasis on establishing rules for their children's use of DDs at home, with time and content restrictions being the most frequently reported strategies. Time restrictions often involve setting specific time limits (e.g., "just 15 min" or "only between 8:00 and 8:30 pm"), sometimes supported by the use of timers. Alternatively, acceptable usage boundaries are tied to the completion of a specific activity (e.g., "she can watch just two episodes"). As for the contents, they are overall selected by the parents themselves but also negotiated with the children (according to the age-specific competencies). Parents maintain that the older the child is, the more they adopt permissive strategies by promoting children's self-selection of content (still under specific circumstances and parental supervision). The parents involved in the study expressed divergent views on the use of DDs during mealtimes: while some parents declare using them at home and in public settings (e.g., at the restaurant) to guarantee a smooth and easy unfolding of the meal, others explicitly say to forbid it to favor communication and enhance quality family time.

Beliefs. Parents perceive children's relationship with DDs as characterized by confidence, competence, immediacy, and intuitiveness. The representation of young children as extremely fast learners with a sort of "inner disposition" toward the use of DDs is common: if, on the one hand, parents are intrigued by the potential for their children to develop digital competencies from an early age, on the other hand, this immediacy and confidence raise concerns. Additionally, parents consistently stress the importance of alternating digital and non-digital activities for promoting children's well-being. This variation in experiences is strictly related to parental mediation, which is often reported as a necessary condition for children's engagement with DDs. In this regard, only a small number of parents indicated that they allow their children to use DDs autonomously without parental supervision.

Concerns. Parents expressed numerous concerns regarding young children's use of DDs, spanning psycho-physical and socio-relational risks. Chief among these are fears of developmental delays, particularly in the neuro-cognitive domain, as well as eyesight disorders, disruptions to circadian rhythms, difficulties in distinguishing the "real" and digital worlds, reduced focus and attention, risk of alienation, diminished interest in face-to-face interactions, loss of empathy, and the potential for addiction. Parents also voiced concerns about the risks associated with DDs use during later developmental stages, particularly in pre-adolescence and adolescence, when maintaining control over time and content becomes, according to them, more challenging. Specific worries during these stages include social isolation, conformity to peer pressures, and exposure to cyberbullying. At the same time, parents expressed apprehension about the risk of social exclusion if their children are not exposed to digital devices, reflecting a tension between the potential harms of use and the consequences of non-use.

The Voice of Preschool Educators

Types of Devices. Interesting insights also emerge from focus groups conducted with educators and teachers working within 0–6 educational services. When available, the most used devices include tablets, projectors, overhead projectors, Bluetooth speakers, digital cameras, and digital microscopes. Educators reported a range of educational activities supported by digital technologies, including the creation of immersive environments, capturing photos and videos, listening to stories or music, and exploring the surrounding environment and nature.

Motivations. The educators consider the widespread presence of technology in society and at home a reason for the unavoidable introduction of DDs in preschool settings: since young children are constantly exposed in their everyday lives, educators argue that expert guidance in safe environments, such as educational services, is essential to foster digital competence and mitigate risks associated with unsupervised use. Furthermore, the teachers and educators involved see the potential of DDs in promoting creativity, imagination, and emotional skills as well as enhancing children's enthusiastic participation in peer activities. Another reason for using DDs is the possibility offered by tablets and smartphones to capture and revisit educational experiences through video recordings and pictures, thereby fostering self-recognition and autobiographical memory.

Rules. When it comes to establishing rules, educators report that no digital-specific restrictions are implemented. Instead, they apply general time and space constraints that are valid for both digital and non-digital experiences.

Beliefs. Like parents, educators and teachers perceive children as confident and competent users of DDs. Such intuitive use is generally negatively connotated as it is attributed to excessive screen exposure at home and, more broadly, in society. In this regard, parents' or grandparents' use of DDs during home-school transition moments is treated as highly problematic by the educational staff. Furthermore, according to the educators involved, integrating digital and non-digital activities is the *conditio sine qua non* for using DDs in 0–6 educational services, together with the realization of a defined pedagogical project with specific educational objectives. The mediating role of educators is also considered the key ingredient for promoting creative and agentive uses of DDs by young children. Overall, geographical and age differences seem to play a role in educators' beliefs concerning digital competence in early childhood[1]. Educators working in more densely populated urban contexts seem more likely to have at their disposal and use DDs within educational services, and they also appear to acknowledge their educational value. This is also true for younger educators, who seem to use DDs more often and with more awareness of their educational uses with children. In contrast, older educators and those working in less populated rural areas seem to use DDs less often (when available in their services) and tend to express limited proficiency with technology. A factor that may make a difference in teachers' practices and beliefs is their participation (or not) in Media Education training. Educators who have attended ad hoc training typically display more awareness of the risks and are more attuned to the creative and critical potential of using DDs within educational services. Finally, explicit aversion to the use of DDs by

[1] Further analysis is needed to corroborate this data.

children is more commonly reported for the 0–3 age range, reflecting greater concern for developmental risks in this early stage.

Concerns. Educators and teachers highlight several major concerns regarding children's use of DDs. These include the potential loss of relational skills, risks of alienation, diminished interest in the "real" world, and difficulties in managing boredom and moments of waiting. Additional concerns involve challenges in developing autonomy, as well as fears about negative impacts on motor development, attention, creativity, and imagination. Educators also raise issues related to privacy and cybersecurity, emphasizing the importance of safeguarding children's personal information. Unlike parents, however, educators rarely reference pre-adolescence and adolescence in their discussions, focusing primarily on the early childhood years.

4.2 Adults' Reported Needs

The Voice of Parents

Media Education. Parents have frequently expressed the need for specific media education training that provides unambiguous, clear, expert-based guidelines on how to manage the relationship between their children and DDs. In particular, they seek to gain a deeper understanding of the risks and potential effects of DDs on children's development and to be educated in conscious and creative uses. Education on web-related risks is another common need. Furthermore, parents specifically ask for media education training to be implemented within the educational services attended by their children.

Peer Support. In addition to media education, parents highlight the need to enhance opportunities to engage in peer support, where they can share experiences and practices with other parents in a collaborative atmosphere.

Judgment Suspension. Finally, a sense of social judgment concerning the management of their children's use of DDs has been voiced by many parents. They fear being labeled as "bad parents", whether they allow their children to use DDs or not. The following sentence is particularly emblematic in this regard: "everything you do is wrong". From this standpoint, the parents involved in the study communicate the need to suspend social judgment on their parenting choices and practices as well as the need to be heard. This reflects a broader need for support in their caregiving practices during the early years of children's lives.

The Voice of Preschool Educators

Media Education. Educators and teachers consistently reported the need for a media education path in the 0–6 educational services wherein they work[2]. First, they request ad hoc training on the effects of DDs on children's health and development; second, they ask for expert-based, unambiguous, updated guidelines; third, they communicate the need to become competent in creative uses of DDs in their working practices and to

[2] This is true also for those educators and teachers who have already attended in the past media education programs.

be more knowledgeable about age-targeted contents; fourth, they highlight the need to be confident in handling privacy-related issues. Interestingly, they also mention the need to be specifically trained in how to communicate with families regarding children's use of DDs so as not to convey a judgmental stance. Furthermore, they believe that families need to receive ad hoc training in parental mediation and digital competences.

Adequate Tools. Another common need relates to the acquisition of adequate technological tools for educational services. Educators and teachers frequently complain about the lack of modern, functioning devices, whose costs are often too elevated for the budget of the services. Strictly related is the request for adequate spaces wherein implementing structured digital-based activities.

5 Discussion

The article reported on some preliminary results of the thematic analysis of 23 focus groups conducted as part of the research project PRIN "Di.Co.Each. Digital competence in early childhood: educating parents and teachers in conscious, critical and creative uses of digital media". Focusing on the voices of parents and educators working in the Italian 0–6 integrated system, the analysis unveiled their perspectives, beliefs, and representations regarding the relationship between DDs and early childhood.

Examining parents' and educators' views on *children's use*, they report a pervasive presence of DDs in the daily lives of young children, confirming a trend broadly documented in previous literature [1, 2, 25]. Among the parents, references to letting their children use DDs for managing household activities and the emphasis on time and content rules seem to index, on the one side, the challenges contemporary families (especially mothers) face in conciliating personal, family, and work time, while on the other, awareness of their educational role in mediating child-DDs interaction. These themes resonate with social discourses on parental responsibility [14] and culturally informed models of performing good parenting [26, 27]: the parents involved in the study explicitly acknowledge the cruciality of accompanying children in safe and creative uses of DDs, but at the same time, struggle with balancing this mediating role with their emotional and physical exhaustion and limited support systems in childcare. When it comes to rules and motivations, educators and teachers of the corpus depict quite a different scenario. The absence of digital-specific rules within the educational services may be due to the relatively limited and time-restricted digital experiences implemented thus far. As for the motivations, they emphasize the development of children's digital competence in a safe and supervised space as well as the educational potentials of DDs in promoting, among other things, creativity, imagination, self-recognition, and memory development. The pervasive presence of DDs in society is seen by both parents and educators as a compelling reason to introduce children to these technologies at an early age, fostering familiarity and competence from the outset. Common perspectives between parents and preschool educators can also be traced with respect to the beliefs and representations of children as confident, intuitive, and competent DD users, with a sort of "inner disposition". Although this belief has been widely questioned by scholars [28, 29], its presence attests to enduring influence in social discourses of the commonsensically spread notion of young people as "digital natives" [30]. Furthermore, both parents and educators underscore the importance of alternating digital and non-digital experiences for children's well-being and healthy development, displaying awareness of recent guidelines [9, 12, 13]. While recognizing the educational opportunities offered by DDs, they also give voice to manifold concerns about potential risks, including impacts on cognitive, emotional, and physical development, social isolation, privacy issues, and medical problems. This data reflects caregivers' nuanced awareness of both the opportunities and risks associated with DD use in young children's lives. Additionally, it corroborates the tension in their mediating role as they seek to minimize risks related to inappropriate, passive use while maximizing the educational opportunities [31]. However, conflicting visions are also at stake: when it comes to attributing responsibility for children perceived over-exposure to DDs, educators tend to blame parents and their "incompetent" caregiving practices. This blame discourse deserves critical attention and further investigation as it may indicate a lack of alignment or collaboration between significant caregivers [20].

Finally, when considering *adults' needs*, media education is unanimously recognized by participants as unavoidable for contemporary caregiving roles. As the family and the school are the two main educational milieus children have experience of [32], parents and educators seem to align with the need of scaffolding children's digital experiences as "more knowledgeable others" [33]. Furthermore, while parents' references to the need for peer support and judgment suspension echo the complex and multifaceted difficulties of contemporary families (see, among others, [34]), educators' reported need for adequate digital tools and spaces seems to mirror the limited material resources experienced by many Italian social and educational services.

6 Concluding Remarks

While media education research and actions are typically promoted from primary school [35], the Italian research project "Di.Co.Each" explores digital competence in preschool-aged children. The preliminary results attest to the pedagogical significance of upholding theoretical reflection and empirical investigation on DDs in early childhood. The qualitative thematic analysis of focus groups with significant adults has illuminated the main representations, perspectives, and issues of concern of parents and educators working in the Italian 0–6 integrated education system. Although these findings are not generalizable, they emphasize the importance of training significant adults in conscious, critical, and creative uses, fostering awareness of both opportunities and limitations set up by children's use of DDs in the domestic and formal education environments. Moving beyond polarized visions that either demonize or idealize DDs in early childhood, further analysis is needed to gain an in-depth understanding of all themes emerging from significant adults' voices, including pediatricians.

Acknowledgments. We would like to thank the families and professionals who participated in the study. We are also grateful to the municipality of Florence, the municipality of Russi, the municipality of Savona, the Cooperative ARCA (Florence and Livorno), the Cooperative Abbaino (Florence), the Cooperative CADIAI (Bologna), the "Associazione Culturale Pediatri" (ACP), and the "Associazione Media Educazione Comunità" (MEC).

Fundings. The research project PRIN "Di.Co.Each" has been funded by the European Union – Next Generation Union (Cod. PRIN 2022XFX3EN; CUP B53D2301972 0006).

References

1. Rideout, V.: The Common sense census: media use by kids age zero to eight. Common Sense Media, San Francisco (2017)
2. Rideout, V., Robb, M.B.: The common sense census: media use by kids age zero to eight, 2020. Common Sense Media, San Francisco (2020)
3. Drotner, K.: Dangerous media? Panic discourses and dilemmas of modernity. Paedagog. Hist. **35**(3), 593–619 (1999)
4. Drotner, K.: Children and digital media: online, on site, on the go. In: Qvortrup, J., Corsaro, W., Honig, M.S. (eds.) The Palgrave Handbook of Childhood Studies, pp. 360–375. Palgrave Macmillan, Hampshire (2009)
5. Eco, U.: Apocalittici e integrati. Comunicazioni di massa e teorie della cultura di massa. Bompiani, Milano (1964)
6. Wartella, E., Jennings, N.: New members of the family: the digital revolution in the home. J. Fam. Commun. **1**(1), 59–69 (2001)
7. Wartella, E., Robb, M.: Historical and recurring concerns about children's use of the mass media. In: Calvert, S.L., Wilson, B.J. (eds.) The handbook of children, media, and development, pp. 7–26. Blackwell Publishing, Hoboken (2008)
8. AAP Committee on Public Education. Media education. Pediatrics **104**, 341–343 (1999)
9. AAP Committee on Public Education. Growing up digital: Media research symposium. Washington, DC (2015)
10. Blum-Ross, A., Livingstone, S.: The trouble with "screen time" rules. In: Mascheroni, G., Jorge, A., Ponte, C. (eds.) Digital Parenting: The Challenges for Families in the Digital Age, pp. 179–187. International Clearinghouse on Children, Youth, and the Media (2018)
11. Lauricella, A., Blackwell, C.K., Wartella, E.: The, "new" technology environment: the role of content and context on learning and development from mobile media. In: Barr, R., Linebarger, D.N. (eds.) Media Exposure During Infancy and Early Childhood, pp. 1–23. Springer, Cham (2017)
12. World Health Organization. Guidelines on physical activity, sedentary behaviour and sleep for children under 5 years of age. World Health Organization (2019)
13. Bozzola, E., et al.: Media devices in pre-school children: the recommendations of the Italian pediatric society. Ital. J. Pediatr. **44**(69), 1–5 (2018)
14. Cino, D., Mascheroni, G., Wartella, E.: "The kids hate it, but we love it!": parents' reviews of circle. Media Commun. **8**(4), 208–217 (2020)
15. Lindeman, S., Svensson, M., Enochsson, A.B.: Digitalisation in early childhood education: a domestication theoretical perspective on teachers' experiences. Educ. Inf. Technol. **26**(4), 4879–4903 (2021)
16. Neumann, M.M., Neumann, D.L.: The use of touch-screen tablets at home and pre-school to foster emergent literacy. J. Early Child. Lit. **17**(2), 203–220 (2017)
17. Epstein, J.L., Salinas, K.C.: Partnering with families and communities. Educ. Leadersh. **61**(8), 12–19 (2004)
18. Gigli, A.: L'alleanza con le famiglie: una potente risorsa educativa. Edizioni Junior-Bambini (2021)
19. Bove, C.: Scuola-famiglia: un'alleanza necessaria. In: De Vogli, S. (ed.) Dialoghi sull'educare, pp. 19–26. Erickson, Trento (2019)
20. Contini, M. Dis-alleanze nei contesti educativi. Carocci, Roma (2012)

21. Livingstone, S., Blum-Ross, A.: Parenting for a Digital Future. Oxford University Press, Oxford (2020)
22. Braun, V., Clarke, V.: Using thematic analysis in psychology. Qual. Res. Psychol. **3**(2), 77–101 (2006)
23. Corbin, J.M., Strauss, A.: Grounded theory research: procedures, canons, and evaluative criteria. Qual. Sociol. **13**(1), 3–21 (1990)
24. Cornish, F., Gillespie, A., Zittoun, T.: Collaborative analysis of qualitative data. In: Flick, U. (ed.) The SAGE Handbook of Qualitative Data Analysis, pp. 79–93. Sage, Thousand Oaks (2013)
25. Zaffaroni, L.G., Amadori, G., Mascheroni, G.: DataChildFutures. Rapporto sui risultati dell'indagine 2020. Zenodo (2022)
26. Demozzi, S., Gigli, A., Cino, D.: I media digitali come strumenti per "esercitare e performare" la genitorialità (parte 1): literature review e presentazione della ricerca. Rivista Italiana Educazione Familiare **15**(2), 79–92 (2019)
27. Demozzi, S., Gigli, A., Cino, D.: I media digitali come strumenti per "esercitare e performare" la genitorialità (parte 2): analisi e discussione dei risultati. Rivista Italiana Educazione Familiare **15**(2), 93–111 (2019)
28. Di Bari, C.: I nativi digitali non esistono. Educare a un uso consapevole, creativo e responsabile dei media digitali. Uedizioni (2023)
29. Ranieri, M.: Le insidie dell'ovvio. Tecnologie educative e critica della retorica tecnocentrica. ETS (2011)
30. Prensky, M.: Digital natives, digital immigrants part 2: do they really think differently? On the Horizon **9**, 1–6 (2001)
31. Livingstone, S., Ólafsson, K., Helsper, E.J., Lupiáñez-Villanueva, F., Veltri, G.A., Folkvord, F.: Maximizing opportunities and minimizing risks for children online: the role of digital skills in emerging strategies of parental mediation. J. Commun. **67**(1), 82–105 (2017)
32. Bronfenbrenner, U.: The Ecology of Human Development: Experiments by Nature and Design. Harvard University Press, Cambridge (1979)
33. Vygotsky, L.S.: Mind in Society. Harvard University Press (1980)
34. Milani, P.: Educazione e famiglie. Ricerche e nuove pratiche per la genitorialità. Carocci, Roma (2018)
35. Calvani, A., Fini, A., Ranieri, M.: Valutare la competenza digitale. Erickson, Trento (2011)

AI in Education

AI in Education - Mapping Theoretical Frameworks for Digital Literacy: DigComp 2.2, AI Literacy Competency Framework, AI Literacy TPACK, the Machine Learning Education Framework, the UNESCO AI Competency Framework for and Teachers and Other Innovative Approaches

Łukasz Tomczyk(✉)

Institute of Education, Jagiellonian University, Cracow, Poland
lukasz.tomczyk@uj.edu.pl

Abstract. The aim of this article is to highlight the theoretical underpinnings in the formation of media and digital competence in the use of AI. This topic is one that needs addressing due to the intensive development of AI technology, which is making an increasingly visible incursion into both private and professional life. There is no doubt that AI has also entered the education sector, becoming something of a game-changer in teaching and educational processes. This situation has therefore necessitated a change in the theoretical framework for digital and media literacy (DL&ML), which has been undergoing constant transformation in recent years due to the intensive development of AI-based software. This article reviews the most popular theoretical frameworks relating to the formation of skills and knowledge in the use of AI. Based on a comparison of DigComp 2.2, AI Literacy Competency Framework, AI literacy TPACK, The Machine Learning Education Framework, The UNESCO AI Competency Framework, it was noted that: 1) there is currently a lack of consensus on a clear definition of DL&ML areas and indicators in AI; 2) the vast majority of theoretical frameworks do not have their own research tools and rely on a high degree of flexibility to diagnose this DL&ML area depending on contextual considerations; 3) the current theoretical frameworks related to AI allow the measurement of DL&ML using qualitative approaches; 4) the theoretical frameworks defining DL&ML are changing with the development of AI; 5) the lack of explicitness in defining DL&ML makes it difficult to conduct longitudinal and comparative research; and 6) each of the theoretical frameworks analysed emphasises a different area of AI use and the anticipation of the consequences associated with it.

Keywords: digital literacy · digital skills · theoretical framework · AI · generative artificial intelligence · digital education · formal education · non-formal education

Ł. Tomczyk (Ed.): NMP 2024, CCIS 2537, pp. 173–191, 2025.
https://doi.org/10.1007/978-3-031-95627-0_12

1 Introduction

Digital and media literacy is a key competence in the modern world. Being proficient in the use of information and communication technologies (ICT) is as natural for most people as speaking their mother tongue, doing calculations, and being able to interact with others [1]. ICT proficiency is not only a marker of being modern, but has become one of the elementary skills that determine quality of life [2, 3]. ICTs dominate almost every industry and continue to transform manufacturing, management, processing, logistics, commerce, and many other processes. The transformation of lifestyles through new media is also evident in the education sector, which takes advantage of ICT through electronic communication, access to MOOC-type platforms, e-learning, and OER, among others [4, 5]. Effective use of ICT, defined as digital and media literacy (DL&ML), is one foundation in effective learning and teaching [6]. However, knowing how to use basic e-services and software alone is not sufficient. The dynamically changing world of cyberspace brings new opportunities in the form of new software, new e-services, and new hardware. This is how DL&ML indicators are changing. The increase in opportunities offered by cyberspace is changing - broadening the indicators for measuring the effectiveness of ICT use. Basic indicators are now being systematically supplemented by new areas, such as those related to the exponential growth of software based on generative artificial intelligence (AI).

This article focuses on analysing the new and updated theoretical framework related to the definition and consequent measurement of DL&ML in the field of AI. Addressing this topic is justified not only by reference to the above-described processes, but also by the need to create new didactic solutions in both formal and non-formal education to reinforce knowledge and skills relating to the use of the most popular AI-based software, including ChatGPT (OpenAI), Gemini, Claude, Midjourney, DALL-E, Microsoft Co-Pilot, Jasper AI, Notion AI, Synthesia, Canva AI, DeepL, Grammarly, Copy.ai, ZeroGPT, Scribbr, and others. The emergence of new websites means that the domain of AI is growing in popularity, though this brings challenges in terms of defining and measuring the knowledge, skills, and attitudes that allow full, effective, and intentional, as well as legally and ethically compliant, use of AI. Technological novelties are therefore an accelerator of change for the theoretical framework that defines DL&ML.

Using the UNESCO report 'International Forum on AI and the Futures of Education under the theme of Developing Competencies for the AI Era', in this paper digital and media competences narrowed to the area of generative AI use will be understood and defined as the ability to use AI and understand AI-generated data. Digital competence in this area will also include patterns of AI use with ethical behaviour. In accordance with this UNESCO report [7], today's users of new technologies should also have an awareness of the extent to which AI can be useful in their professional and private lives, what is it unrealistic to expect AI to do, and when this type of software can cause harm [7]. This area of digital competence is distinguished from the other DL&ML components by, among other things, knowledge, skills, and ethical behaviour in relation to software that is highly dynamic and able to generate digital content that has a visible impact on people's lives. This means that, against the background of the other DL&ML components, the area relating to AI is much more dynamic than that of the underlying digital competences (e.g.

those related to using an operating system, electronic communication, or e-commerce platforms).

This paper looks to review the current and most popular literature that defines D&ML in the field of AI. The study fills a gap in terms of comparative theoretical frameworks that form the basis for educational activities aimed at creating real social change through modernising educational systems, enhancing the effectiveness of learning and teaching, and drawing attention to the challenges and risks that AI brings. Based on a literature search covering the most influential journals in the field of media pedagogy (e.g. Computers and Education, Information and Education Technologies, and the British Journal of Educational Technology), as well as the use of academic databases such as Google Scholar and Scopus, it was noted that the following theoretical frameworks are most commonly used to create pedagogical and andragogical innovations: DigComp 2.2, AI Literacy Competency Framework, AI literacy TPACK, The Machine Learning Education Framework, and The UNESCO AI Competency Framework for Teachers. Therefore, taking into account the increasing number of diagnostic studies that measure the level of DL&ML in the use of AI, the lively discussion on didactic models using AI for different educational levels, and the wealth of definitional and theoretical approaches, it was decided in this paper to seek to illustrate the current state of theoretical development underlying the update of the theoretical framework delineating DL&ML.

2 Overview of the Theoretical Framework

2.1 DigComp 2.2

DigComp 2.2 The Digital Competence Framework for Citizens is a framework document prepared with the European Commission that sets the direction for the development of media and digital competences. DigComp 2.2 defines knowledge, skills, and attitudes in five main areas: information and data, collaboration and communication, digital content creation, security, and problem solving. Each of these areas has specific competency categories that round off the core set. DigComp 2.2 has eight levels of digital and media competences, ranging from basic to highly specialised. These levels characterise knowledge and skills in detail [8]. In the latest version of DigComp 2.2, there are many references to digital competences related to AI.

The AI-related areas of INFORMATION AND DATA LITERACY included in DigComp 2.2 show the breadth of AI application. In this area, attention is drawn to the conscious use of AI, highlighting how many systems collect information on user activity in search engines, social media, and popular applications. The second issue that arises in this area is the adaptation of generated content to specific users. The digital competence indicators presented also show the need to weigh benefits against risks, e.g. when using applications that collect information about the activities undertaken. An important part of digital and media competence in this dimension is the ability to recognise content that leads to manipulation and the creation of information bubbles. These components of digital and media competences, due to the universality of DigComp 2.2, can be easily transposed into both formal and non-formal education programmes [8].

For the area of COMMUNICATION AND COLLABORATION, an interesting set of indicators emerges that define DL&ML, which are primarily concerned with the ability to grasp the differences between communicating with a human being and with an AI-based system that mimics a human being. Coaching the software by creating a recommender system is also an important skill. The skills indicated should create a sense in modern users that the data they provide to AI systems can be used to improve those systems. The area under review emphasises that the modern ICT user must have a concrete awareness of the vast range of AI applications, in sectors that at first glance do not match. It is also an important skill to configure software and hardware to intentionally limit data collection by AI-based systems. Each of the dimensions analysed draws attention to the balance between enthusiasm for AI and caution against its potential negative effects.

The next category, DIGITAL CONTENT CREATION, clearly emphasises the importance of having knowledge not only of AI's collection of information about users (as found in the previous categories), but also of using the data provided to AI to generate content that is difficult to distinguish from human-generated content. The area of AI-related content creation also raises questions about the integration of such content into one's own work (e.g. artistic, educational, expert). Having an awareness of the proper labelling of AI-generated creations becomes an issue that raises other questions, e.g. about copyright and intellectual property rights. In the dimension analysed, another important component of digital and media competence is the ability to verify the veracity of materials that can now readily be generated by AI. Ethical aspects are an equally important component of such knowledge and skills, which is linked to human agency in the fair and non-divisive implementation of AI in private and professional life.

The category of digital security is an indispensable component when using any kind of e-services or IT equipment. In the context of AI, it acquires particular importance as highlighted in the 'safe' area of DigComp 2.2. Analysing the opportunities and threats identified in the previous sections of the theoretical framework, the issue of security is complemented by indicators of proficiency in the use of ICT relating to the knowledge of legal acts related to data protection, and the ability to assess the opportunities and threats of sharing one's own data in AI-based software. The security aspect also draws attention to environmental issues, as well as social issues (affecting almost everyone) relating to what could be termed the 'algorithmisation' and 'platformisation' of human life. The AI-related aspects of security listed in this section go beyond the typical perception of the risks arising from widespread AI implementation and compel action beyond individual digital security concerns.

The last of the DigComp 2.2 components where AI-related knowledge and skills can be found concerns SOLVING TECHNICAL PROBLEMS. This area highlights an extremely important assumption, namely that AI is not an independent entity, but a technology created and improved by humans. Having this awareness results in shedding the myths associated with AI. Among the competences related to problem solving through AI, it was pointed out that the modern ICT user should have an awareness related to identifying the applications of these systems in the recognition of complex data (e.g. medical), favouring decision-making in unusual situations. The area related to problem-solving overlaps with the earlier section on communication; however, in this aspect, the necessity of including a competence related to being aware of AI's continued lack of perfection, e.g. in machine translation, is emphasized.

The latest DigComp 2.2 Digital Competency Framework provides an expert, up-to-date basis for the design and implementation of learning activities using the latest advances in digital literacy. DigComp 2.2 is a set of very detailed guidelines that build a theoretical framework for assessing proficiency in the relatively new field of AI. The inclusion of AI-related items in the latest version of DigComp forces a redefinition of existing digital and media literacy catalogues, providing a global stimulus to the discussion on the social mechanisms of AI. DigComp focuses much of its attention on the informed and therefore safe use of AI in everyday and professional life. DigComp 2.2, due to its relatively precise description, becomes the starting point for building training programmes for both formal and non-formal education. The framework does not demonise AI, but draws attention to critical points of consideration with the technology.

2.2 AI Literacy Competency Framework

An interesting approach to shaping AI digital literacy is presented by Long & Magerko [9]. Based on an analysis of the available material on AI proficiency, they have identified seventeen components that make up the AI Literacy Competency Framework. The framework for using AI includes: '1) Recognising AI - distinguishing technological artefacts that use AI from those that do not; 2) Understanding AI - critically analysing and discussing the characteristics that make an entity 'intelligent'. Discussing the differences between human, animal, and machine intelligence; 3) Interdisciplinarity - identifying different ways of thinking about and developing 'intelligent' machines. Identifying technologies that use AI, including those in cognitive systems, robotics and machine learning; 4) General vs. narrow AI - distinguishing between general AI and narrow AI; 5) AI strengths and weaknesses - identifying the types of problems AI does or does not handle well. Identifying when AI should be used and when it is better to use human skills; 6) Imagining future AI - imagining future applications of AI and considering how they will affect the world; 7) Representations - understanding what a knowledge representation is and describing examples of such representations; 8) Decision making - identifying and describing examples of how computers reason and make decisions; 9) Steps in machine learning - understanding the steps involved in machine learning and the challenges that each step presents; 10) The role of humans in AI - recognising that humans play an important role in programming, model selection and tuning AI systems; 11) Data literacy - understanding the basic concepts involved in data literacy; 12) Learning from data - recognising that computers often learn from data (including personal data); 13) Critical interpretation of data - understanding that data requires interpretation. Describing how training examples in a data set can affect the results of an algorithm. 14) Action and reaction - understanding that some AI systems have the ability to physically act in the world; 15) Sensors - understanding what sensors are and how computers perceive the world through them. Identifying the types of data received by different sensors and recognising how different sensors support different types of representation and reasoning; 16) Ethics - identifying and describing different perspectives on ethical issues in AI: privacy, employment, misinformation, 'singularity', decision-making, diversity, bias, transparency and accountability; and 17) Programmability - understanding that agents are programmable' [9].

The AI Literacy Competency Framework is offers the possibility for the user to concoct their own measurement items. The conceptual proposal of Long & Magerko's [9] places a strong emphasis on understanding AI and locating this technology in different life contexts as well as in different theoretical contexts. The issue of data collection, e.g. through sensors, or understanding a tool's strengths and weaknesses is evident in both the AI Literacy Competency Framework and the DigComp 2.2 model. However, it is important to be aware that the proposal [9] is very flexible, which is evident, among other things, in the multiplicity of practical approaches based on the concept [10–13], which extract selected elements from the 17 components of digital competence for their interventions.

The transposition of the framework proposed by Long & Magerko [9] allows for a flexible definition of the component competences and is linked to the time of emergence of this theoretical basis, or, in other words, the time of the Covid-19 pandemic, but also a time that some may consider ancient history in the rapid development of AI. ICT has always been a rapidly developing field, but that is as nothing compared to the dramatic rise in AI, both in terms of capability and popular use. In other words, the set of knowledge and skills related to the use of AI may be much more extensive now than five or more years ago due to the increase in the efficiency of data generation by the systems analysed, as well as the growth in application areas or the availability of an increasing wealth of AI-based applications for less IT-savvy users. Therefore, when analysing a framework of a few years ago, it is important to be aware that the dynamic development of AI is conditioning changes in the theoretical and methodological foundations related to media pedagogy.

2.3 AI Literacy TPACK Framework

An interesting theoretical framework based on the popular TPACK model [14] was presented by a team of researchers from Hong-Kong [15]. The researchers considered the ways in which digital competence related to the use of AI can be defined, as well as how this relatively new skill can be measured. Based on an analysis of 30 articles based on a variety of methodological approaches (quantitative research, qualitative research, blending, theoretical analysis), the researchers identified four main components of the AI literacy framework [15]:

1. Know & understand AI - 'Know the basic functions of AI and how to use AI applications'.
2. Use & apply AI - 'Applying AI knowledge, concepts, and applications in different scenarios'.
3. Evaluate & create AI - 'Higher-order thinking skills (e.g., evaluate, appraise, predict, design) with AI applications'.
4. AI ethics - 'Human-centred considerations (e.g., fairness, accountability, transparency, ethics, safety)'.

The general theory of the AI literacy Framework was subsequently extended by the researchers cited earlier [15] with analyses related to the TPACK Framework in areas relating to: technological knowledge (e.g. on software and hardware, AI-related agents), pedagogical knowledge (e.g. experiential learning, collaborative learning, constructivism), and content knowledge (e.g. related to technological awareness, ethics of AI use, five big ideas related to AI). The approach proposed by Ng [15] was complemented by exemplary measurement methods, such as quantitative methods ('Use knowledge tests to assess students' AI cognitive gain and abilities'), qualitative methods ('Use videos, documents, pictures, presentations, students' interactions with AI agents and projects to examine students' AI cognitive and non-cognitive abilities'). The overview of methods for diagnosing the level of proficiency in using AI took the form of 32 completely different measurement methods using knowledge and skills tests and self-evaluation (including taking into account the dimensions of attitude towards AI and motivation to use AI). Among the soft methods related to the evaluation of proficiency in AI use, measures such as the analysis of portfolios created within PBL and in-depth interviews about the process of AI use [15], which are not commonly employed, also emerged.

The analysis of the AI literacy concept of the TPACK Framework shares many characteristics with the theory on which it is based, namely TPACK [16] (Tomczyk & Fedeli, 2021). This is one of the most widely used approaches in media pedagogy allowing us to emphasise the naturally complementary areas of technology, pedagogy (methodology), and digital content. These areas interlock to form a harmonious whole. Gaps in any one area create a burden for another area. For example, a lack of methodological skills (pedagogical skills related to specific didactics) can lead to ineffective use of AI to achieve teaching goals. In addition, poor quality digital content generated by AI or a lack of knowledge of AI-based pedagogical software also becomes a factor resulting in the failure to achieve teaching goals. In other words, having digital literacy stands in close relationship to pedagogy and technology. The AI literacy TPACK Framework therefore does not go beyond its underlying TPACK theory and, at the same time, is characterised by a high degree of voluntariness in the measurement of digital competence (including teacher digital competence). Furthermore, the availability of a diverse and rich palette of methods for diagnosing digital competences (more than 30 types) makes it difficult to carry out longitudinal studies that allow for generalisation, but at the same time offers the chance to select a diagnostic tool that is appropriate to the context of the educational activity. It should also be emphasised that the four dimensions underpinning digital competence, namely [15]: 1) Know & understand AI, 2) Use & apply AI, 3) Evaluate & create AI, 4) AI ethics - are the pillars that make it possible to create customised tools adapted to the educational stage, the type of education (formal, informal), to the educational form (online, blended, stationary) and, above all, the educational goals. In summary, the AI literacy TPACK Framework is characterised by a high degree of recognisability due to the underlying theory from which it is derived, as well as being a theoretical basis that offers great potential for adaptation to different didactic considerations, but at the same time it is characterised by a lower focus in terms of measurement indicators, for example, compared to DigComp 2.2.

2.4 The Machine Learning Education Framework

Another example of a theoretical framework guiding the shaping of digital competences in AI is the concept developed by Natalie Lao [16] in the development of her doctoral dissertation defended at the Massachusetts Institute of Technology (USA). Lao poses a very legitimate question related to the transformation of the style of use of AI, which should not only be based on the passive consumption of content produced by AI, but should also, as part of the educational process, lead to an active 'co-creative' use of AI. In the conceptualisation of The Machine Learning Education Framework, the emphasis is on moving away from the role of consumer to becoming - maturing into - a 'do-it-yourself' AI expert. The following diagram illustrates the basic areas that make up the framework, which were implemented and validated in the experiment (Fig. 1).

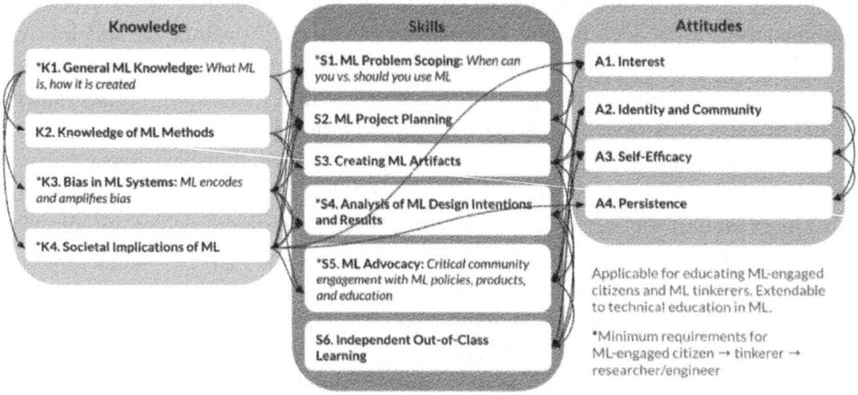

Fig. 1. The Machine Learning Education Framework. Source: Thesis Ph. D., Massachusetts Institute of Technology, Department of Electrical Engineering and Computer Science (Lao, 2020).

The Machine Learning Education Framework (MLEF) is also directed towards average users, i.e. without extensive knowledge of the programming or mathematics underlying AI. The MLEF has been tested in practice among high school and university students enabling them, among other things, to create their own AI systems that classify images and sound. The research was carried out using proprietary tools including the analysis of digital artefacts [16].

The matrix defining competences according to the MLEF is divided into three co-occurring main categories. The first is machine learning knowledge, including issues of social impact on machine learning. The second component is skills, such as analysis, planning, creation, advocacy, and individual action (using the concept of PBL). The final component of the MLEF is attitudes, i.e. the key elements leading to constructive and ethical use of AI (interest, building a sense of efficacy, and persistence in experimenting with AI). Knowledge thus forms the basis for skill-building, while attitudes reflect the qualities that should develop among users during the constructive co-creation of new AI-based solutions. Skills, on the other hand, are not only practical activities, but define specific diagnostic indicators achieved in the course of practice activities (in the computer lab under the guidance of an instructor-trainer) as well as in the course of self-learning (e.g. in training AI-based models). Lao's [16] concept proposed is characterised in detail in Table 1.

Table 1. The Machine Learning Education Framework with learning outcomes and definitions.

Knowledge	
1. General ML knowledge	Know what machine learning is (and is not). Understand the entire pipeline of the creation of ML systems
2. Knowledge of ML methods	Identify when to use a range of ML methods across the breadth of the field (e.g. k-nearest neighbours, CARTs or decision trees, neural networks, ensemble methods). Understand how different methods work
3. Bias in ML systems	Understand that systems can be biased, and the different levels and ways in which bias can be introduced
4. Societal implications of AI*	Understand that ML systems can have widespread positive and negative impacts. Consider the ethical, cultural and social implications of what they do
Skills	
1. ML problem scoping	Determine which problems can and should be solved by ML
2. ML project planning	Plan a solution which is sensitive to both technical and contextual considerations
3. Creating ML artefacts	Use tools to create appropriate artefacts
4. Analysis of ML design interactions and results*	Describe the explicit and implicit design intentions of an ML system. Critically analyse the intentions against how the system can and should be used
5. ML advocacy*	Critically discuss ML policies, products and education
6. Independent out-of-class learning	Students seek learning experiences outside the classroom
Attitudes	
1. Interest	Students are engaged and motivated to study the topic
2. Identity and community	Students contribute to and learn from a community of peers and/or broader online communities who are interested in ML
3. Self-efficacy	Students are empowered to build new, meaningful things
4. Persistence	Students continue and expand their engagement with ML

Source: [16]

Against the background of the other theoretical frameworks, this one is concerned with the very extensive digital competences in AI. The MLEF proposal is based on a pedagogical experiment implemented in practice that seeks to redress the stereotypes about the use of AI. The shift from the role of consumer of content to active creation places The Machine Learning Education Framework in the group of theoretical frameworks that seem to be aimed at advanced digital users. However, this is only a stereotypical view, as this type of framework can be implemented both within formal education (e.g. secondary technical schools with a computer science or related profile) and higher education, as well as within non-formal education (e.g. specialised courses). The MLEF also shows how the levels of passive and advanced use of AI vary, as demonstrated, among other things, with the use of four levels of proficiency assessment for creating one's own AI-based solutions (Appendix A Curriculum Rubric - ML Education Framework). The proposal prepared by Lao [16] represents an elaborate complement to the advanced level of frameworks such as DIGCOMP and can be used in a variety of mandatory projects to prepare engineering students in the field of computer science.

2.5 The UNESCO AI Competency Framework for Students

A recent report prepared by UNESCO [17] makes it clear that the digital competences for using AI for students are significantly different from the competences proposed in, for example, the DigComp 2.2 model. Miao & Shiohira highlight in the introduction to the report that in 2022 only 15 countries had learning objectives related to using AI included in their official curricula. The main axes of the competency model proposed by UNESCO are similar to those proposed by Ng [14] and cover 1) Understanding, 2) Using and 3) Creating. The issue of ethics in this model is incorporated into the three components in a slightly different way than in the proposal of Ng [14]. Nevertheless, as can be seen in Table 2, the ethics of AI use, despite taking a different content layout than that proposed by Ng [14], is actually the fourth main pillar of the competency model. Table 2 below briefly presents the assumptions of each model.

Table 2. The UNESCO AI Competency Framework for students.

Competency aspects	Progression levels		
	Understand	Apply	Create
Human-centred mindset	Human agency	Human accountability	Citizenship in the era of AI
Ethics of AI	Embodied ethics	Safe and responsible use	Ethics by design
AI techniques and applications	AI foundations	Application skills	Creating AI tools
AI system design	Problem scoping	Architecture design	Iteration and feedback loops

Source: (Miao & Shiohira, 2024)

The AI competence model aimed at students is divided into three elementary areas. The first level stands for comprehension, which provides the basis for familiarisation with AI capabilities. In this area, students learn about the basic concepts, the assumptions underlying AI, methods of data acquisition and processing, and content. Understanding builds the foundation for using the entire range of AI-based software. The second level proposed by UNESCO is application, which is linked to the formation of the ability to transfer theoretical knowledge to solving tasks, including the critical-constructive evaluation of individual AI-based tools. As the authors of the report point out, in many cases this level may be the final stage in the student's education on AI. The last pillar proposed by Miao & Shiohira [17] is the creation level, which by implication is the most advanced level and is directed at students who are interested in co-creating new solutions based on AI. In the third pillar, activities involving designing and testing one's own tools are evident, alongside developing critical appraisal skills and the social impact of AI, as well as knowledge of the legalities of AI. At this stage, the need to integrate knowledge and advanced skills intertwined with the ethical and responsible design of systems using AI is discernible. Within each of the pillars that make up the composite student AI competency model, other 'soft' skills are developed, such as those of analysis, evaluation, anticipation, communication, and responsibility [17].

The UNESCO model [17] contains highly detailed indicators for each level. The characteristics of the model include clearly defined components of the competences that should be achieved. For the components making up the model in a given area, there are assigned CURRICULAR GOALS, which should be included in official education programmes, as well as SUGGESTED PEDAGOGICAL METHODS (a layer covering specific methodologies), and finally recommendations relating to LEARNING ENVIRONMENTS, which are guidelines conducive to achieving the specific goals that have been set. The UNESCO model is an elaborate and well-thought-out matrix in the field of AI education, which can be used, for example, by governmental institutions that do not have official solutions in this area. Developed by a team of researchers affiliated to UNESCO, the document also includes a proposal for assessing progress for each of the dimensions: understanding, applying, and creating. The document offers very precise proposals [17] for assessing progress towards the stated learning goals. The theoretical framework discussed is universal in the context of the application of subject teaching and allows for the integration of AI in the teaching of a variety of subjects, not only those directly related to computer science. In conclusion, the UNESCO AI Competency Framework for students is a milestone in the development of a digital competence framework for AI that can be used in an unlimited way, providing an opportunity for the creation of national formal education programmes in computer science or cross-curricular pathways that include AI. At the same time, it is important to bear in mind that this model has not been fully tested for global effectiveness and is an a priori assumption, e.g. in contrast to at least the Machine Learning Education Framework [16].

2.6 The UNESCO AI Competency Framework for Teachers

From the data cited by UNESCO in 2022, only seven countries had a theoretical framework defining the formation of digital competences in teachers for the use of AI. Given the increasing popularity of AI among students and the growing interest of stakeholders around school institutions to modernise learning and teaching with edtech, UNESCO felt it was reasonable to prepare a global theoretical framework that can be used both in the lifelong learning process and in the education of future generations of teachers. The framework developed in the theoretical perspective is intended to facilitate the understanding of the scopes of application of AI in the teaching process, while in the practical dimension it is aimed at supporting teachers in the safe, useful, and ethical use of generative artificial intelligence [18].

Technological changes over the last years have necessitated an update to the UNESCO ICT competency Framework for Teachers. Miao & Cukurova [18] added areas related to the use of AI in education to the base document. UNESCO's latest proposal is an updated theoretical framework covering 15 new digital competences falling under five core areas: Human-centred mindset, Ethics of AI, AI foundations and applications, AI pedagogy, and AI for professional learning. The theoretical framework proposed by Miao & Cukurova [18] is based on several important assumptions that are consistent with the general assumptions of the modern school. The framework emphasises the importance of humanistic and social foundations in the implementation and use of AI in education, while also highlighting the potential of the technology in supporting the development of students and teachers, and drawing special attention to the risks posed by the technology. Among the foundations underlying the UNESCO ICT Competency Framework for Teachers, the ethical and legitimate use of AI and the promotion of inclusivity are strongly emphasised.

The concept of the AI Competency Framework for Teachers (AI CFT) is presented in the form of a two-dimensional matrix, consisting of five aspects of AI competences that develop at three levels of sophistication, making a total of fifteen competency blocks. The first dimension encompasses five key components that are essential for teachers to operate in order to use AI effectively and ethically as a teaching resource, as well as being a source for creating teaching materials. The first dimension includes: 1) Human-centred mindset, i.e. values and attitudes focusing on interactions between humans and AI, which educators should understand and implement in educational work 2) Ethics of AI in which the principles, legal norms according to which AI should be implemented in educational and didactic processes are important; 3) AI foundations and applications constituting conceptual knowledge and skills for the selection of AI for educational content; 4) AI pedagogy being intentional activities related to the effective selection of AI in both the preparation and implementation phases of the didactic process, as well as the evaluation of educational outcomes. These are the competences that enable the intentional and effective combination of pedagogy and AI to support preparation for teaching, education, and assessment; and 5) AI for professional development, which represents the knowledge and skills needed to use AI to support teachers' professional development. These five areas mutually intersect and support the implementation of AI in the school ecosystem in a coherent manner. The UNESCO AI Competency Framework for teachers also includes a second dimension, which is a three-stage pathway for the development of digital competences in the area under review. The first level (acquire) are the core competences that all teachers should possess. The second level (deepen) concerns the competences needed to design and implement effective strategies to combine AI and pedagogical concepts. The final level (create covers the advanced competences related to configuring AI for innovative use in education. The five component competences of AI intersect with these three levels of sophistication [18]. The entire concept is presented in Table 3.

Table 3. The UNESCO AI Competency Framework for teachers.

Aspects	Progression		
	Acquire	Deepen	Create
1. Human-centred mindset	Human agency	Human accountability	Social responsibility
2. Ethics of AI	Ethical principles	Safe and responsible use	Co-creating ethical rules
3. AI foundations and applications	Basic AI techniques and applications	Application skills	Creating with AI
4. AI pedagogy	AI-assisted teaching	AI–pedagogy integration	AI-enhanced pedagogical transformation
5. AI for professional development	AI enabling lifelong professional learning	AI to enhance organizational learning	AI to support professional transformation

Source: [18]

As with The UNESCO AI Competency Framework for students, this theoretical framework aimed at teachers contains a highly precise delineation of each area. The UNESCO AI Competency Framework for students covers teachers' digital competences for using AI and operationalises the objectives for the learning base for each of the 15 areas. In addition, each area includes examples of core activities to achieve the objectives [18]. A sample knowledge test is also included, which can be a source of inspiration for local implementations. In summary, the UNESCO framework is characterised by a high level of complexity, which consists of different levels of sophistication, from a more passive use of AI to a more constructive and creative approach. Both frameworks, intended for teachers and students, are a precise description of the requirements and evaluation approaches, allowing the selection of AI-based software according to the situational context, the educational stage, or the financial conditions. The proposed approach can be used both in the lifelong learning process and as a basis for building teacher preparation courses.

3 Discussion

The literature currently offers many theoretical approaches for understanding and using AI. Knowledge and skills relating to the proficient use of AI have many components, depending on the author's perspective (more technical or somewhat pedagogically oriented, e.g. student education or teacher education). Knowledge is seen primarily as an understanding of the designations of AI-related concepts, perception of AI, reflection on the application of AI, understanding the impact of AI, linking technical and social layers, or ethically interpreting the use of AI and the implications that AI processing may bring [19]. The wealth of theoretical frameworks demonstrates the importance of this technology in both professional (school) and private life. The use of AI is becoming increasingly normalised in many professional and social groups, just as the use of search engines did some time ago, for example. The dynamic development of technology is forcing an update of the theoretical framework. The transformation, associated above all with new possibilities of processing and generating data, forces the inclusion of new knowledge, skills, and attitudes into the theoretical framework related to DL&ML. This is a natural process and typical of the emergence of new technologies in society.

Referring to the empirical part, an oscillation between an opportunity paradigm and a risk paradigm is evident in each of the assumptions presented [6]. Thus, the theoretical framework relating to the use of AI noticeably draws attention to the risks of a new technology that is much more dynamic and versatile than the earlier e-services that are now part of the framework that defines DL&ML. Concerns and previous human experiences are therefore translated into theoretical frameworks that guide formal and non-formal education for a variety of pedagogical and andragogical interventions.

The six theoretical frameworks presented are characterised by different approaches to defining their components. There are frameworks that are similar in their approach to defining level of proficiency, as well as frameworks that do not have indicators defining level of proficiency in ICT use. The most precise and extensive scale is found in the DigComp 2.2 concept. All the frameworks analysed have been developed over the last five years, the period in which AI has most grown in popularity. Each of the analysed frameworks has a different set of indicators (items) that define competences in the use of AI. Also evident in this variation is the area of AI use. The vast majority of the theoretical frameworks do not have their own measurement tools, which, on the one hand, is a limitation for conducting relevant, reliable, and longitudinal research, while, on the other hand, it allows a high level of adaptability of the theoretical concepts to the teaching conditions in the individual interventions. All frameworks are also characterised by a high degree of adaptability of the general learning objectives to their own, specific learning objectives determined by the nature of the group. A detailed comparison is presented in Table 4.

Table 4. Comparison of the theoretical framework.

	DigComp 2.2	AI Literacy Competency Framework	AI literacy TPACK framework	The Machine Learning Education Framework with learning outcomes and definitions	The UNESCO AI Competency Framework for students	The UNESCO AI Competency Framework for teachers
Levels of advancement	8	Lack of clearly defined	Lack of clearly defined	Advanced	3	3
Year of the framework	2022	2020	2021	2020	2024	2024
Number of digital and media competence areas related to AI	5	17	4	3	4	5
Number of items defining the DL	73	Lack of clearly defined	Lack of clearly defined	14	12	15
Available diagnostic tools	Ability to develop your own	Lack of clearly defined	32 ways to measure - adaptable	Proprietary tools - adaptable	Some sample proposals - adaptable	Some sample proposals - adaptable
Flexibility of the theoretical framework	Adaptable to the specific needs of the target group	Adaptable to the specific needs of the target group	Adaptability of the model for teacher education and future teachers	Possibility to transpose the model into training programmes requiring advanced knowledge and skills in the use of AI	Adaptability to national infromation education programmes	Can be used with both in-service teachers and pre-service teachers

Source: own source

When analysing the theoretical framework for shaping digital competences, it should be borne in mind that the data presented in the empirical section do not provide a complete picture. According to data from the UNESCO report [20], there are currently more than a dozen core curricula for formal education (primary, middle, high schools), which are profiled for the systems of individual countries. Countries with their own separate or integrated AI digital competence frameworks include: Armenia, Austria, Belgium China, India, Korea, Kuwait, Portugal, Qatar, Serbia, Germany, Bulgaria, Jordan, and

Saudi Arabia [20]. The emergence of local theoretical frameworks relating to AI at the level of formal education is an understandable phenomenon and stems from the principle of updating the content of education [21, 22], which, in the case of a relatively new field such as AI, requires the transposition of the possibilities arising from the technology into the objectives and content of education. It is understandable, therefore, that national equivalents of various official education programmes covering the use of AI are emerging. However, the official - most often ministerial - equivalents of education programmes largely include the theoretical frameworks presented in the overview section of this article, being derivatives of these adapted to their own system of verification of learning outcomes, and anchored to their own system of subject areas of education (e.g. computer science, technology, STEM cross-curricular pathways). The richness of theoretical frameworks in the case of formal education, however, creates difficulties in analysing secondary data within the comparative framework of digital competence levels. However, this is a universal challenge and is also typical for the measurement of basic digital and media competences [15, 23].

The theoretical frameworks presented are not exhaustive of all the ways of defining digital competence in AI. Currently, there is a visible trend related to the exponential growth of ways of defining the use of AI according to profession or age. In the literature, it can be seen that there are already first attempts to measure this skill among pre-school children (using the concept of the AI4KG curriculum) [24]. This approach is highly innovative in terms of research methodology for pre-school children, and also shows that the use of AI can occur before the formation of other key competences (e.g. reading and writing). Attempts to build proprietary theoretical frameworks in AI aimed at the youngest children, e.g. in the age range of 3 years and above, go beyond the standard age groups of AI users. Nonetheless, after looking at examples of 'AI for Kids'-type curriculum solutions, it is clear that they map to practical activities (e.g. the ludic sphere), which is one of the main activities in the age group [25, 26]. Attempts of this kind may also raise concerns for psychologists and media educators arising typically from developmental tasks (not directly related to AI), as well as the risk paradigm of media pedagogy.

In media pedagogy, on the other hand, there are increasing attempts to define catalogues of AI digital competences aimed at children of younger school age. Such efforts make use of, among other things, the six big ideas of the AI literacy intelligence-based curriculum for primary school students and are also based on measurements using mixed methods as well as arts-based approaches [27]. Given the richness of theoretical concepts, there are also emerging attempts to create research tools using cumulative expert knowledge (Delphi method), which aim to create age-appropriate diagnostic tools that are linked to the postulated level of digital competence for a given developmental period [28]. This type of research is crucial because of the need to build diagnostic tools that can be standardised and have wider application [29].

A group that has been of particular interest to researchers working on the topic of diagnosing style of AI use in recent months are teachers themselves. This is evident in the number of publications about the digitalisation of education and AI, as well as in studies aimed at building diagnostic solutions such as, for example, the AI readiness scale for teachers [30], and the implementation of tools enabling self-assessment of proficiency in using AI - Development and validation of teacher artificial intelligence (AI) competence self-efficacy (TAICS) scale [31]. The wealth of theories, approaches, implementations, and diagnostic tools related to teachers is reflected in systematic analyses of the literature, which confirm how many methodological possibilities and limitations the application of AI in this professional group brings [32].

The concept of AI literacy is not solely assigned to professional groups associated with the IT sector. Defined variously according to the needs and experiences of the group that defines it, AI literacy has several common components related to the understanding and application of this e-service. The unifying factor of knowledge, skills, and attitudes is the ability to construct commands for artificial intelligence. An activity referred to as prompt engineering [33] is the underlying skill. Although this activity forms the basis for the effective use of generative artificial intelligence it is not always included in the theoretical framework defining this part of digital competence [34].

The search for an optimal education model in its current form involves mapping a variety of definitional approaches to AI, consideration of the specifics of the target group, and the ways in which AI is used in a given collective [35]. Attempts to measure the proficiency of AI use are in close relation to the specificity of the group in which they are conducted [36]. The approach of the individual development of theoretical frameworks and the ways in which they are validated can also be seen through the lens of the AI tools that are used in a particular intervention - a pedagogical or andragogical innovation [37]. The richness of the various theoretical approaches is also evident in the ways in which learning outcomes are verified, with this taking the form of knowledge and skills tests [38] and analysis of project outcomes [39]. The issue of skills diagnosis is therefore an area as intensely developing as the foundations defining DL&ML indicators in the field of AI.

4 Conclusions

This literature review is part of a constructive-critical reflection on the theoretical frameworks guiding education in a rapidly changing socio-technical reality. The literature offers the first studies in this area [40] arguing for the need to develop coherent concepts for this important area. In recent years, a number of proposals for a general theoretical framework for digital and media competences have been developed; however, none of them creates an undisputed universal reference point for formal and non-formal education. The analysis carried out in this article confirms that the attempt to develop a single theoretical framework, applicable in every context, defining areas and performance indicators for the use of AI is an exercise doomed to failure at the current stage of development of this technology. The multiplicity of approaches determined by life needs, professional needs, and assumptions of general educational policies (or lack thereof) determines the freedom in defining general and specific educational goals, as well as their means of evaluation. This difficulty raises a number of new challenges in comparing proficiency in the use of AI both in a longitudinal perspective (changes in proficiency from year to year in given occupational and age groups) and for international comparative studies.

Acknowledgments. This article was written as part of the REMEDIS project, which is supported in Poland by the National Science Centre - NCN [2021/03/Y/HS6/00275] under the CHANSE

ERA-NET Co-fund, awarded funding from the European Union's Horizon 2020 Research and Innovation Programme [contract number 101004509].

References

1. Koppel, I., Langer, S.: Basic digital literacy-requirements and elements. Rev. Práxis Educ. **16**(42), 326–347 (2020)
2. Radovanović, D., et al.: Digital literacy key performance indicators for sustainable development. Soc. Inclus. **8**(2), 151–167 (2020)
3. Choudhary, H., Bansal, N.: Addressing digital divide through digital literacy training programs: a systematic literature review. Digit. Educ. Rev. **41**, 224–248 (2022)
4. Canbek, N.G., Hargis, J.: Educational innovation in e-learning: MOOCs and OER movements in Turkey. Glokalde **1**(1), 19–32 (2015)
5. Song, Z.X., Cheung, M.F., Prud'Homme, S.: Theoretical frameworks and research methods in the study of MOOC/e-learning behaviors: a theoretical and empirical review. In: New Ecology for Education—Communication X Learning: Selected Papers from the HKAECT-AECT 2017 Summer International Research Symposium, pp. 47–65. Springer, Singapore (2017)
6. Tomczyk, Ł.: Digital competence among pre-service teachers: a global perspective on curriculum change as viewed by experts from 33 countries. Eval. Program Plann. **105**, 102449 (2024). https://doi.org/10.1016/j.evalprogplan.2024.102449
7. Miao, F., Holmes, W.: International forum on AI and the futures of education, developing competencies for the AI era: synthesis report. UNESCO, Paris (2020)
8. Vuorikari, R., Kluzer, S., Punie, Y.: DigComp 2.2: the digital competence framework for citizens, EUR 31006 EN. Publications Office of the European Union, Luxembourg (2022)
9. Seo, K., Tang, J., Roll, I., Fels, S., Yoon, D.: The impact of artificial intelligence on learner–instructor interaction in online learning. Int. J. Educ. Technol. High. Educ. **18**, 1–23 (2021)
10. Southworth, J., et al.: Developing a model for AI across the curriculum: transforming the higher education landscape via innovation in AI literacy. Comput. Educ.: Artif. Intell. **4**, 100127 (2023)
11. Lee, I., Perret, B.: Preparing high school teachers to integrate AI methods into STEM classrooms. In: Proceedings of the AAAI Conference on Artificial Intelligence, vol. 36, no. 11, pp. 12783–12791 (2022)
12. Alam, A.: A digital game based learning approach for effective curriculum transaction for teaching-learning of artificial intelligence and machine learning. In: 2022 International Conference on Sustainable Computing and Data Communication Systems (ICSCDS), pp. 69–74. IEEE (2022)
13. Koehler, M., Mishra, P.: What is technological pedagogical content knowledge (TPACK)? Contemp. Issues Technol. Teach. Educ. **9**(1), 60–70 (2009)
14. Ng, D.T.K., Leung, J.K.L., Chu, S.K.W., Qiao, M.S.: Conceptualizing AI literacy: an exploratory review. Comput. Educ.: Artif. Intell. **2**, 100041 (2021)
15. Tomczyk, Ł., Fedeli, L.: Digital literacy among teachers–mapping theoretical frameworks: TPACK, DigCompEdu, UNESCO, NETS-T, DigiLit leicester. In: Proceedings of the 38th International Business Information Management Association (IBIMA), pp. 244–252. International Business Information Management Association (2021)
16. Lao, N.: Reorienting machine learning education towards tinkerers and ML-engaged citizens. Massachusetts Institute of Technology, Department of Electrical Engineering and Computer Science (2020)

17. Miao, F., Shiohira, K.: AI competency framework for students. United Nations Educational, Scientific and Cultural Organization, Paris (2024)
18. Miao, F., Cukurova, M.: AI competency framework for teachers. United Nations Educational, Scientific and Cultural Organization, Paris (2024)
19. Chiu, T.K.F.: A holistic approach to the design of artificial intelligence (AI) education for K-12 schools. TechTrends **65**(5), 796–807 (2021)
20. UNESCO: K-12 AI curricula—a mapping of government-endorsed AI curricula. United Nations Educational, Scientific and Cultural Organization, Paris (2022)
21. Villanueva, R.G.A., Martínez, N.M., Reducindo, I.R.: Continuous curriculum updating: an alternative approach to periodical reformulation in university. Currere Praxis **1**(1), 60–74 (2024)
22. Chiu, T.K., Chai, C.S.: Sustainable curriculum planning for artificial intelligence education: a self-determination theory perspective. Sustainability **12**(14), 5568 (2020)
23. Vissenberg, J., et al.: Report on the results of a systematic review of the individual and social differentiating factors and outcomes of media literacy and digital skills. KU Leuven: REMEDIS (2023)
24. Su, J.: Development and validation of an artificial intelligence literacy assessment for kindergarten children. Educ. Inf. Technol. (2024)
25. Yang, W.: Artificial Intelligence education for young children: why, what, and how in curriculum design and implementation. Comput. Educ.: Artif. Intell. **3**, 100061 (2022)
26. Su, J., Zhong, Y.: Artificial intelligence (AI) in early childhood education: curriculum design and future directions. Comput. Educ.: Artif. Intell. **3**, 100072 (2022)
27. Yim, I.H.Y.: Artificial intelligence literacy in primary education: an arts-based approach to overcoming age and gender barriers. Comput. Educ.: Artif. Intell. **7**, 100321 (2024)
28. Chung, K., Kim, S., Jang, Y., Choi, S., Kim, H.: Developing an AI literacy diagnostic tool for elementary school students. Educ. Inf. Technol. (2024)
29. Kim, K., Kwon, K.: Exploring the AI competencies of elementary school teachers in South Korea. Comput. Educ.: Artif. Intell. **4**, 100137 (2023)
30. Ramazanoglu, M., Akın, T.: AI readiness scale for teachers: development and validation. Educ. Inf. Technol. (2024)
31. Chiu, T.K.F., Ahmad, Z., Çoban, M.: Development and validation of teacher artificial intelligence (AI) competence self-efficacy (TAICS) scale. Educ. Inf. Technol. (2024)
32. Rizvi, S., Waite, J., Sentance, S.: Artificial Intelligence teaching and learning in K-12 from 2019 to 2022: a systematic literature review. Comput. Educ.: Artif. Intell. **4**, 100145 (2023)
33. Knoth, N., Tolzin, A., Janson, A., Leimeister, J.M.: AI literacy and its implications for prompt engineering strategies. Comput. Educ.: Artif. Intell. **6**, 100225 (2024)
34. Laupichler, M.C., Aster, A., Raupach, T.: Delphi study for the development and preliminary validation of an item set for the assessment of non-experts' AI literacy. Comput. Educ.: Artif. Intell. **4**, 100126 (2023)
35. Laupichler, M.C., Aster, A., Schirch, J., Raupach, T.: Artificial intelligence literacy in higher and adult education: a scoping literature review. Comput. Educ.: Artif. Intell. **3**, 100101 (2022)
36. Wang, B., Rau, P.-L.P., Yuan, T.: Measuring user competence in using artificial intelligence: validity and reliability of artificial intelligence literacy scale. Behav. Inf. Technol. **42**(9), 1324–1337 (2022)
37. Carolus, A., Augustin, Y., Markus, A., Wienrich, C.: Digital interaction literacy model – conceptualizing competencies for literate interactions with voice-based AI systems. Comput. Educ.: Artif. Intell. **4**, 100114 (2023)
38. Chiu, T.K.F., et al.: Developing and validating measures for AI literacy tests: from self-reported to objective measures. Comput. Educ.: Artif. Intell. **7**, 100282 (2024)

39. Kong, S.-C., Cheung, M.-Y.W., Tsang, O.: Developing an artificial intelligence literacy framework: evaluation of a literacy course for senior secondary students using a project-based learning approach. Comput. Educ.: Artif. Intell. **6**, 100214 (2024)
40. Yue Yim, I.H.: A critical review of teaching and learning artificial intelligence (AI) literacy: developing an intelligence-based AI literacy framework for primary school education. Comput. Educ.: Artif. Intell. **7**, 100319 (2024)

Challenges for Education Based on Empirical Model of GAI in Schools – What Are the Concerns of Polish Primary School Teachers?

Jacek Pyżalski(✉)

Faculty of Educational Studies, Adam Mickiewicz University in Poznan, Poznań, Poland
pyzalski@amu.edu.pl

Abstract. The article is based on empirical study and explores concerns of Polish primary school teachers (grades 4–8) (N = 995) concerning the integration of generative artificial intelligence (GAI) in schools. The article uses data from a representative survey in the representative national sample and the teachers filled in the questionnaire presenting 25 predefined threats and assessed the likelihood of their occurring.

The main results of the conducted survey display significant fears concerning student addiction to GAI systems (81% of teachers think this as likely), ethical issues such as academic fraud, and potential negative learning effects like reduced critical thinking in students. Teachers also presented concerns about negative social impact - predominantly important interpersonal relations at school, such as weakening peer relationships and reducing of boundaries between virtual and real-world interactions. Digital inequalities in access to technology and ethical risks, including misuse of AI-generated content, were among serious concerns of teachers.

The study results show the necessity of well-designed interventions, including teacher training on AI technologies, the development of dedicated digital literacy programs for students, and ethical and organizational guidelines for GAI use at school level. A proposed educational model identifies GAI's multifaceted roles in schools, from assisting teachers and students to addressing systemic challenges. These findings contribute to the present discussion on integrating GAI into educational systems.

Keywords: Generative Artificial Intelligence (GenAI) · Primary teachers · Concerns · risks

1 Introduction

This article presents empirical data on Polish teachers' concerns regarding the implementation of generative artificial intelligence (GAI) in school environment. The study is based on a representative sample of Polish primary school teachers (N = 995) and

Ł. Tomczyk (Ed.): NMP 2024, CCIS 2537, pp. 192–204, 2025.
https://doi.org/10.1007/978-3-031-95627-0_13

examines their perceptions of the likelihood of specific risks associated with the integration of GAI in schools. The introduction provides a brief overview of the important characteristics of GAI, its potential positive impact on education (as well as challenges that it brings), and a new proposed educational model [1, 2] for implementing this technology in schools. This framework is partly a proposed foundation for interpreting the results.

1.1 Main Features of GAI and Its Development

Generative Artificial Intelligence (GAI) has appeared as a modern technology in the digital era. It influences both societal dynamics and people's behaviors, particularly in highly developed countries where technology is widely used [3–5]. Discussions surrounding GAI often ambiguous (showing radical advantages or disadvantages that may potentially occur). It means this technology has dual potential to impact many professional fields and enhance social structures. Education here seems to be one of its most significant areas of impact and profound changes [6–10].

Basic Characteristics of Generative AI

GAI poses three core characteristics that make it unique and at the same time a powerful force that can influence education:

1. **Advanced Machine Learning:** Differently than traditional algorithms, GAI systems use machine learning models are able to process and synthesise different data types, such as text, images, audio, and numerical data. By analysing vast datasets, often named as big data, these tools produce new outputs that were not possible in the past [1, 2, 11]
2. **Creative Outputs:** GAI main ability is content creation [generation]. It can produce diverse kinds of content in different forms. The examples are essays, literature texts, visuals, math analyses, and multimedia (films, photos). The quality of the results may be close human-generated content or above. Beyond creativity, GAI systems may analyse an modify different kind of materials and to some extent undertake decisions or solve problems [1, 2, 11].
3. **Human-Machine Interaction:** Perhaps the most groundbreaking aspect of GAI is its ability to understand and respond to natural language prompts created by users so the communication resembles communication among humans.
4. **The conversational interface,** facilitated by advanced language models, has made access to AI technologies very easy and intuitive [1, 2, 11, 12]. This changed the situation completely making GAI a collaborative partner for a user (mostly due to the natural language communication) [2].

Those features make technology a "game changer" in education at different levels but at the same time bring a lot of challenges that are mirrored by the attitudes of education professionals. This article goes deeper into exploring the perception threats connected to implementation of GAI in education expressed by concerns of Polish primary school teachers.

1.2 The Impact of GAI on Education

The advent (and widespread use) of GAI represents a visible shift in educational world. It offers both transformative opportunities and serious challenges. GAI, typified by products like ChatGPT and other large language models is represented in numerous other commercial and open- source tools. Such tools impact students, teachers and everything that takes place within the school context. At the same time, its integration into educational settings raises ethical issues and problems concerning academic integrity, and the occupational training of educators [1, 2, 6, 13, 14].

GAI's potential lies in its flexibility. It offers applications across a broad spectrum of educational activities, from adaptive learning platforms that tailor content to individual student needs to tools that help teachers with grading, lesson planning, and curriculum preparation. Studies show also its potential to build inclusiveness by targeting barriers connected for instance to cognition problems (individualization of education). That is particularly valid in multicultural settings where GAI tools support communication between students and teachers from many sociocultural backgrounds and with diverse needs [1, 2, 10]. Additionally, by providing targeted feedback, GAI provides opportunities for self-directed learning, empowering students to explore knowledge themselves [6, 15].

The implementation of GAI in education brings also serious problems. Ethical concerns, including the risk of plagiarism, uncritical reliance on AI-generated content, violent use of GAI (cyberbullying) and biases in outputs seem to be very serious and may have profound negative consequences[1, 15]. Teachers and students must address these issues and preserve traditional pedagogical practices and educational values.

The Role of GAI as Potential Education Paradigm-Shift Tool

One of the most significant contributions of GAI is its ability to change the focus of education from output to processes in learning. Traditionally, we were focused on outputs, such as essays or exams and the cognitive and creative processes seemed to be less important provided the results are present. With GAI's ability to generate required outputs, educators are now encouraged to design assessments that are focused on critical thinking, problem-solving, and cognitive skills. Otherwise, traditional assessment methodology may easily be subject to unethical conduct such as plagiarism since GAI may be easily used for producing outputs that are not connected to students' real abilities [1, 16].

Moreover, the use of GAI raises questions about the new roles of teachers and students. Teachers, who traditionally serve as main sources of knowledge, are now facilitators guiding students in their interactions with AI tools. This shift shows the importance of AI literacy, which includes understanding how GAI systems work, their limitations, and the ethical considerations connected to their use. For students GAI potentially offers opportunities to develop digital competences and critical evaluation skills (including skills connected to information analysis) [9]. It is worth underlying that a central role of those information navigation digital skills have been also underlined with regard to other information and communication technologies [17].

Ethical Considerations and Challenges in GAI Integration

The integration of GAI into education also requires close examination of ethical issues.

Concerns about academic dishonesty have been often discussed before but now they are more important, since students can use GAI to generate output without learning anything. Numerous scholars advocate for developing proper policies and frameworks (also legal) to address those risks.

Additionally, the possibility of GAI to produce biased or clearly inaccurate content calls for media literacy training programs that equip users with the skills that enable critically evaluation of AI-generated outputs [1, 2, 9, 16].

In a school context, teacher training plays a vital role in addressing these challenges. Research indicates that many educators feel not prepared to implement Gen AI tools into their daily work. The cause may be both a lack of technical knowledge and understanding of AI tools [9, 15]. Teacher training programs should focus not only on the technical aspects of GAI but also on its pedagogical implications, ensuring that teachers can use AI to enhance, rather than disintegrate, the learning process [1, 2].

GAI's Broader Implications for Education Policy and Research

At a very general level, the rise of GAI calls for more radical change in educational policies and methodologies. Langran et al. [15] suggest that institutions must adopt a proactive approach, integrating GAI into teacher education programs and developing curricula that reflect the realities of an AI-driven world. This includes necessary interdisciplinary collaborations between philosophers, educators, digital engineers, and policymakers to ensure that AI integration is in line with broader societal values and needs.

Furthermore, empirical research is needed to explore the long-term impacts of GAI on young people in educational context. Studies should examine not only the effectiveness of AI-enhanced teaching and learning strategies but also the social and psychological effects of GAI on students and teachers. We should focus on understanding how students interact with those tools and what the school can do to improve this impact and avoid risks [1, 2].

1.3 The Model of GAI Use in Schools

As already stated above Generative Artificial Intelligence has transformative potential for education, offering applications that may be used for numerous purposes from enhancing administrative efficiency to redefining pedagogical practices implemented in a classroom. A structured framework is essential to understand its potential, ensuring that educators, students, and administrators perceive its diverse capabilities also in their own context. For this article the model presents also areas that may be connected to the teachers concerns that are explored empirically. The proposed model (Fig. 1), developed by the author of this article, categorizes GAI's roles into five interconnected functions, each tailored to address specific educational areas [1, 2].

In the first role, GAI acts as an educator's assistant - referred to as "The Squire."in the proposed model. This role of GAI widens teachers' instructional capabilities by possibility of generating and customizing educational resources and bringing new understanding concerning occupational activities. Educators, as the users of GAI in this context, can shift many of their tasks to GAI tools. For instance, they may create and adapt teaching materials, ensuring they are accessible to learners with particular needs. GAI also aids

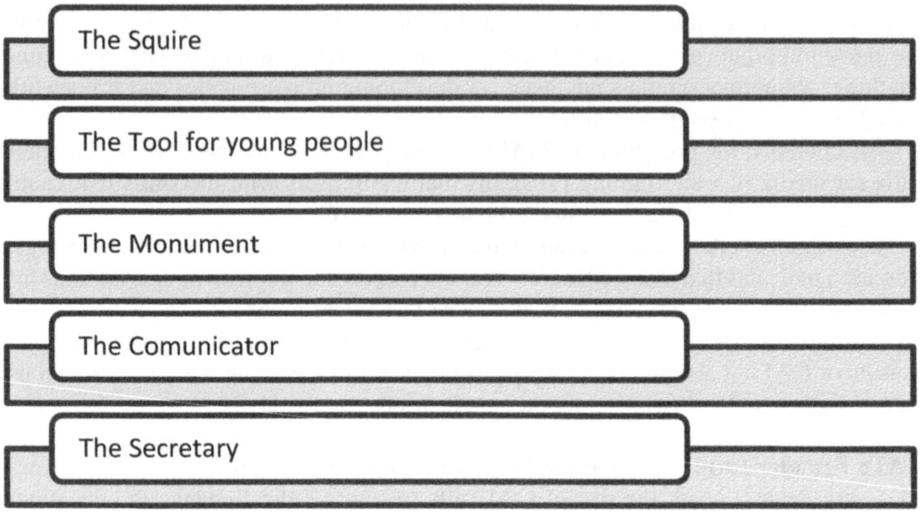

Fig. 1. The model of GAI in schools by Pyżalski [1, 2]

in lesson planning, offering structured plans and well-organized curricula. This can save time and allow teachers to focus on another professional tasks they normally have not enough time for (e.g. relations with students). GAI ability to translate materials into different languages promotes inclusivity and knowledge exchange, while tools that may simplify texts make complex content accessible to those with lower skills. Furthermore, GAI facilitates the creation of assessments tailored to learning objectives. In this context such tools offer teachers a support for evaluating student progress. To fully use this role, educators must develop competences in identifying areas where GAI adds value, creating precise prompts to create valuable outputs. The key teacher skill seems to by able to critically evaluate the quality and relevance of the content GAI generates - that confirms that educational professional knowledge is still crucial in the era of GAI in education [1, 2].

GAI's second role, "The Tool for Students" defines GAI as a resource for learners, with teachers only providing guidance. In this role, students gain access to GAI tools that support self-directed learning and helps to revise and understand learning material. For example, language learners can create conversational partners or personalized exercises targeting their specific needs or ask GAI to assess their performance. This approach, when properly organized, develops digital literacy and adaptability. Those are essential skills for life in an AI-driven world that is already there. By empowering students with skills needed for GAI usage, teachers can create an environment that promotes student autonomy and lifelong learning [1, 2].

In the third role, "The Monument," GAI becomes a subject of study rather than a tool for practical use by teachers or students. By fulfilling this role educators design lessons/materials that present the development of AI, its societal implications, also its ethical (and sometimes even legal) aspects. This role emphasizes the importance of AI ethical literacy. This helps students to understand potential risks associated with AI, such as biases in generated content, misinformation and privacy concerns. It also fosters awareness in students concerning potential negative impact of GAI on them or others (e.g. cyberbullying). They should understand how AI influences industries, governance, and social interactions (also in terms of politics). By examining those broader implications, students develop a better understanding of AI's transformative power but also are more resilient to potential threats.

GAI also functions as "The Communicator", facilitating interaction among various people in the educational environment (teachers, students, parents). Its linguistic capabilities make it an efficient tool for generating communicates that may be used in various interactions in schools. It is crucial to remember though these tools may improve efficiency, it is crucial to be authentic in human interaction particularly in the fields of education. In this context usage of GAI may bring numerous problems. Therefore, the responsible decision may mean not involving those GAI tools in human interactions.

Finally, GAI may be used as "The Secretary," managing time-consuming administrative tasks that divert educators from their main responsibilities. In this capacity, GAI may conduct report generation, proces data for decision-making, and edit documents. By handling such tasks, GAI enables educators and administrators to focus on strategic priorities, improving the work of schools as institutions.

The proposed model shows that implementing GAI in education may actually mean different things. Those different fields of implementation bring different potential advantages and disadvantages that with this clear understanding may be fully understood.

In this article we are mostly focused of potential challenges that may be heard in concerns of teachers and my be connected to the GAI role represented in all modules of the above proposed model.

2 Methodology

The aim of the study presented in this article was to investigate the use of generative artificial intelligence (AI) among teachers of grades 4–8 in primary schools across Poland with the special focus on teachers concerns connected to GAI implementation. Participants were selected using stratified random sampling to ensure proportional representation across Poland's provinces and the geographic distribution of schools in urban, rural, and mixed urban-rural municipalities. Of the 995 teachers, 82% were women, 17% were men, and 1% identified as "other". The age distribution showed that 41% were aged 46–55, 28% were 36–45, 18% were over 55, and 11% were under 35. Regarding residence, 34% lived in rural areas, 29% in towns with populations between 20,000 and 100,000, and 21% in smaller towns with fewer than 20,000 residents. A total of 995 teachers participated, of whom 25% reported using generative AI at least once in their professional teaching practice.

Specifically, the research focused on exploring teachers attitudes towards those technologies as well as identifying the activities undertaken by teachers who actively use generative AI and analysing the contextual factors influencing its application. In this article we explore the small proportion of the results namely teachers concern about possible future impact of GAI on education (mostly through impact on students and teachers). Quantitative data were collected via an online survey conducted in December 2023.

This research was conducted under the auspices of the NASK (Research and Academic Computer Network – National Research Institute) project titled *Nationwide Quantitative and Qualitative Research on the Educational Use of Generative Artificial Intelligence by Teachers of Grades 4–8 in Primary Schools* [1].

This article examines the frequency of concerns regarding the future impact of information and communication technologies (ICT) as reported by teachers across the entire sample, including both those who have used generative artificial intelligence (GAI) technologies in their classrooms and those who have not (N = 995). Participants were presented with a list of 25 potential concerns, developed based on prior qualitative interviews with teachers actively used GAI (N = 20) and a comprehensive literature review. Using a four-point scale ("definitely likely", "rather likely", "rather unlikely", and "definitely unlikely"), teachers assessed the perceived probability of each concern occurring in the future.

3 Results

The Table 1 presents teachers assessments concerning the perceived probability of each concern of GAI in education materializing in the future.

Table 1. Polish teachers concern about future impact of GAI on students and teaching staff

Possible negative impact	Definitely likely (%)	Rather likely (%)	Don't know/Hard to say (%)	Rather unlikely (%)	Definitely unlikely (%)
Young people will become addicted to using GAI systems	41	40	10	8	2
Young people, using GAI systems, will commonly deceive teachers	34	42	11	11	2
Young people will be manipulated by various entities	33	38	15	11	2
Boundary between the real and virtual world will blur	32	42	11	12	2
GAI systems will think for young people - they will stop doing it independently	32	43	8	14	2
Using GAI systems will weaken mutual relationships among young people	31	39	11	17	2

(*continued*)

Table 1. (*continued*)

Possible negative impact	Definitely likely (%)	Rather likely (%)	Don't know/Hard to say (%)	Rather unlikely (%)	Definitely unlikely (%)
Young people will believe unverified/unreliable information	30	46	11	11	2
Young people will not acquire practical skills	29	38	10	19	4
The knowledge of young people will be very shallow	29	39	13	15	4
Young people will build relationships with GAI systems rather than real people	27	39	13	18	4
Deepening the educational gap between communities with more/less tech access	24	41	17	15	2
Students with problems will not seek help from mental health professionals	20	39	15	21	5
Increased concerns about GAI systems taking control over people	20	35	17	23	5
Young people will not learn how to use GAI systems properly - limited usage	19	39	20	18	4
Increasing educational inequalities among young people	17	38	20	27	1
Rising concerns about finding jobs in the future	17	36	17	27	4
GAI systems will have limitations - suitable for some subjects but not others	15	30	30	21	4
Promoting unethical behaviour patterns among young people	14	33	23	26	4

(*continued*)

Table 1. (*continued*)

Possible negative impact	Definitely likely (%)	Rather likely (%)	Don't know/Hard to say (%)	Rather unlikely (%)	Definitely unlikely (%)
Weakening relationships between teachers and young people	13	32	29	26	5
Widening the gap between English and non-English-speaking countries	13	27	29	26	4
Lowering teachers' creativity	12	32	15	34	8
Teachers will not be needed as young people will teach themselves	10	23	14	38	14
The teaching profession will become redundant - GAI systems will take over tasks	9	18	12	44	16

As already stated in the Introduction the integration of GAI into educational contexts has gathered a lot of attention, raising both enthusiasm for its huge potential and awareness concerning risks and challenges. This analysis as defined above highlights the perceptions of educators regarding the potential of negative impacts of AI on young people and teachers.

Teachers' Main Concerns

The survey results show a few key areas that teachers perceive as future problems connected to GAI usage. One of the most prevalent is the fear that young people will become addicted to using AI tools. 41% of respondents identify this negative effect as "definitely likely" and another 40% think it is "rather likely." This worry appears to be similar to fears connected to other digital technologies, such as social media and gaming, where problematic use has been well-documented in many young people populations [18]. The immersive and interactive nature of AI-driven tools may cause this risk to increase. This may be mostly due to imitating/copying human-like communication as well as the potential temptation to shift numerous tasks to GAI tools (that may cause in long term inability to perform those tasks by humans).

Another vital concern is the potential for manipulation that can affect students or that GAI may be used by the students to cheat or manipulate others (also teachers). A total of 76% of respondents predict it is likely that young people will use AI to deceive teachers, mostly by generating assignments without genuine understanding and true capabilities. In parallel 71% of educators worry that students may be manipulated by external actors through GAI systems. This aligns with broader societal concerns about the misuse of GAI for disinformation or instrumental use of GAI by system providers. These fears underline the need for new digital literacy programs that empower students to critically evaluate information and use AI tools in ethical way. This underlines the role of the second component of AI implementation model presented above in this article (the Tool in hands of students).

Fears Related to Cognitive and Social Development

Teachers also express fears about the potentially negative impact of GAI on cognitive and social development. Three fourths of respondents suggest that GAI systems will "think for young people", potentially lowering their ability to engage in critical thinking. Similarly, 7 in 10 teachers fear that the usage of GAI will weaken peer relationships. These concerns seem to be justified, but the participants may overestimate the deterministic role of AI and not the importance of the way it is used. Research seems to show that when properly implemented, GAI tools can potentially improve, rather than replace, critical thinking and interpersonal skills [14].

Another significant fear involves potential lack of boundaries between the offline and online worlds (as perceived by young people). Almost three fourths of respondents predict this as a likely outcome of GAI impact. This concern is similar to the discussion on influence of digital immersion on identity formation and world perception in adolescents. This was in the past mostly discussed in the context of virtual reality and social media. Currently, evidence specific to GAI-driven educational tools and their developmental impact is needed. This gap underlines again the importance of further research to explore the ways in which GAI might influence students' sense of self and their interactions with the world. This will lead also to the need of teaching not only through GAI but also about GAI that was underline as the Monument component of the model presented in this article.

Inequalities and Ethical Concerns

The fact that usage of GAI may deepen existing inequalities is the important area of concern among teachers who took part in the research. About 65% of respondents worry about potential educational gaps between communities and individuals with different levels of technological access and digital skills. This fear is justified, as differences in infrastructure, training, and resources could increase the divide between privileged users and the rest of populations. Policymakers (in different sectors) should try to smooth these inequalities by ensuring equal access to GAI tools. These measures mean also providing opportunities for training for all educators and students also those from vulnerable populations. Those problems are also well documented in former studies conducted in numerous countries and environments [19, 20].

Additionally, 47% of respondents fear that GAI might promote different forms of unethical behaviour among young people, such as academic dishonesty or reliance on AI-generated content. These fears call for preparation of professionally clear guidelines and ethical frameworks to regulate the use of AI in education. Teachers should know proper strategies to foster responsible AI use and mitigate unintended adverse consequences.

Conclusions

While many of the fears outlined in the survey are understandable, they may not all be equally rational or evidence based. Additionally, the concerns may reflect what is presented on popular media about those topics. For instance, concerns about addiction and manipulation, though also present as connected to other digital technologies, are still not explored in GAI context. We still lack proper evidence specific to GAI systems in educational settings, meaning more well-designed research projects in this area are more than needed.

Similarly, fears about the inflation of critical thinking or weakening of relationships may reflect a broader resistance to technological changes in education. However, it surely is the ground for developing sound educational methodologies for GAI implementation in schools that support learning processes.

At the same time, some concerns, such as the potential for deepening inequalities, are supported by robust evidence from other domains and the technologies implemented before occurrence of GAI [21, 22]. The digital gaps remain a persistent challenge that may be only magnified by GAI technologies. With lack of proactive interventions, GAI could increase existing disparities. Similarly, ethical concerns about the unethical use of GAI are clearly justified, as evidenced by instances of producing deepfake cyberbullying content. Addressing these challenges requires a collaborative work that involve educators, policymakers, technological companies, and researchers representing different disciplines.

Practical Implications

Analysis of the presented results leads to some ideas that should be implemented in practice to make the implementation of GAI in school more efficient and at the same time pedagogically wise. Some of them were already signalised above in the section presenting results of the study.

Firstly, enhanced teacher training seems to be necessary. Educators need adjusted training programmes, that will help them to understand GAI's benefits and drawbacks. This should enable them to integrate GAI tools effectively in their daily work and address potential risks that may affect students and the learning processes itself. Those training activities should consider teachers' concerns since their emotions and attitudes may negatively impact their involvement in training activities and engagement in GAI wise implementation at schools [1, 2]. It should be reminded there that some threats may materialize only if GAI is not implemented properly – they are not inevitable.

To achieve wise GAI implementation in education this ethical guidelines should be elaborated and implemented. Clear policies must be developed within education field to regulate the ethical use of AI, including mechanisms to detect and deter misuse of different kind (at many levels including school levels).

Students must be prepared for GAI through dedicated digital literacy programs. The schools may provide opportunities to learn critical evaluation of GAI-generated outputs and usage of GAI tools responsibly (also in a social context). The programs should also focus on strong, and weak features of GAI tools (GAI as Monument in our model).

Additionally, inequalities should be addressed. Policymakers must provide investments in infrastructure and resources. This should have the effect that all students and teachers, no matter what their socioeconomic background is, could benefit from GAI technologies. This mean not only focussing on material side (hardware and software) but also dedicated and adjusted media education programs for vulnerable groups.

All these activities should be based not on assumptions but reliable data. Therefore, we need more empirical research in the field. We need studies that explore the long-term influence of AI on cognitive and social development, as well as its potential to cause inequalities. Particularly experimental and longitudinal studies may be beneficial in this respect. In this context the most valuable should be experimental studies exploring different kinds of GAI implementation (methodologies) that seem crucial when it comes to actual influence and good or bad outputs.

References

1. Pyżalski, J. (ed.): Generative Artificial Intelligence in Polish Schools – Paving the Way: Quantitative and Qualitative Research Among Teachers of Grades 4–8 in Primary Schools. NASK, Warszawa (2025, in press)
2. Pyżalski, J.: Generative artificial intelligence: verification of educational applications model. In: Forum Pedagogiczne (2025, in press)
3. Makridakis, S.: The forthcoming Artificial Intelligence (AI) revolution: its impact on society and firms. Futures **90**, 46–60 (2017)
4. Sabherwal, R., Grover, V.: The societal impacts of generative artificial intelligence: a balanced perspective. J. Assoc. Inf. Syst. **25**(1), 13–22 (2024)
5. Torczyńska, M.: Sztuczna inteligencja i jej społeczno-kulturowe implikacje w codziennym życiu. Kultura Hist. **36**(2), 106–126 (2019)
6. Cao, L., Dede, C.: Navigating a world of generative AI: suggestions for educators. Harvard Graduate School of Education (2023)
7. Fatyga, B.: Przepełniony dysk: kompetencje poznawcze i cyfrowe współczesnej młodzieży. In: Pyżalski, J., Łuczyńska, A. (eds.) Sztuczna inteligencja. Prawdziwe zmiany w edukacji, pp. 99–110. Fundacja Szkoła z Klasą, Warszawa (2024)
8. Maziarz, M.: Edukacja medialna X.0 – kształtowanie myślącego człowieka. In: Pyżalski, J., Łuczyńska, A. (eds.) Sztuczna inteligencja. Prawdziwe zmiany w edukacji, pp. 45–58. Fundacja Szkoła z Klasą, Warszawa (2024)
9. Isidori, M.V., Muccini, H., Evangelista, C.: Teachers and the challenges of generative artificial intelligence (AI): a survey in primary and secondary schools. Ital. J. Spec. Educ. Inclus. **XII**(1), 197–202 (2024). https://doi.org/10.7346/sipes-01-2024-18
10. Plichta, P.: Sztuczna inteligencja, edukacja specjalna i nierówności (nie tylko cyfrowe). In: Pyżalski, J., Łuczyńska, A. (eds.) Sztuczna inteligencja. Prawdziwe zmiany w edukacji, pp. 126–140. Fundacja Szkoła z Klasą, Warszawa (2024)
11. Fazlagić, J., et al.: Sztuczna inteligencja (AI) jako megatrend kształtujący edukację: jak przygotowywać się na szanse i wyzwania społeczno-gospodarcze związane ze sztuczną inteligencją?. Instytut Badan Edukacyjnych, Warszawa (2022)
12. Barreto, F., Moharkar, L., Shirodkar, M., Sarode, V., Gonsalves, S., Johns, A.: Generative artificial intelligence: opportunities and challenges of large language models. In: International Conference on Intelligent Computing and Networking, pp. 545–553. Springer, Singapore (2023)
13. Chen, X., Xie, H., Zou, D., Hwang, G.J.: Application and theory gaps during the rise of artificial intelligence in education. Comput. Educ.: Artif. Intell. **1**, 100002 (2020)
14. Wu, R., Yu, Z.: Do AI chatbots improve students learning outcomes? Evidence from a meta-analysis. Br. J. Edu. Technol. **55**(1), 10–33 (2024)
15. Langran, E., Searson, M., Trumble, J.: Exploring new horizons: generative artificial intelligence and teacher education. Association for the Advancement of Computing in Education (AACE) (2024)
16. Mateus, J.C., Cappello, G., Lugo, N., Guerrero-Pico, M.: Communication educators facing the arrival of generative artificial intelligence: exploration in Mexico, Peru, and Spain. Digit. Educ. Rev. **45**, 106–114 (2024)

17. Livingstone, S., Mascheroni, G., Stoilova, M.: The outcomes of gaining digital skills for young people's lives and wellbeing: a systematic evidence review. New Media Soc. (2021). https://doi.org/10.1177/14614448211043189
18. Pyżalski, J., Walter, N., Tomczyk, Ł: Problematic internet use: pre-pandemic scale of the phenomenon among adolescents in the three Visegrad countries (Czech Republic, Poland, Slovakia). N. Educ. Rev. **69**, 65–81 (2022)
19. Ventrella, F.M., Cotnam-Kappel, M.: Examining digital capital and digital inequalities in Canadian elementary schools: Insights from teachers. Telematics Inform. **86**, 102070 (2024)
20. Samuelsson, U., Olsson, T.: Digital inequality in primary and secondary education: findings from a systematic literature review. In: Media and Education in the Digital Age: Concepts, Assessments, Subversions, pp. 41–62 (2014)
21. Tawfik, A.A., Reeves, T.D., Stich, A.: Intended and unintended consequences of educational technology on social inequality. TechTrends **60**(6), 598–605 (2016). https://doi.org/10.1007/s11528-016-0109-5
22. Rafalow, M.H., Puckett, C.: Sorting machines: digital technology and categorical inequality in education. Educ. Res. **51**(4), 274–278 (2022). https://doi.org/10.3102/0013189X211070812

ChatGPT as a Learning Tool for Migrant Students with Disabilities in Upper Secondary Vocational Education: An Intersectional Study

Emmanouela V. Seiradakis[1,2](✉)

[1] Technical University of Crete, Chania, Greece
eseiradaki@tuc.gr
[2] Hellenic Open University, Patras, Greece

Abstract. Current research on generative AI use in education has predominantly focused on students with dominant middle-class identities in higher education (HE) settings. Vocational education and training (VET) remains an under-researched field, mirroring its lower social standing in Greece and elsewhere. Likewise, the potential of ChatGPT in fostering inclusive education for disabled migrant students has received little attention. Drawing on intersectionality, this study explores the ChatGPT learning experiences of six of these students, who are served yet unserved by the Greek upper secondary VET system. Emerging themes of in-depth interviews included: i) ChatGPT as an in-class participation facilitator, ii) ChatGPT as on-call support and, iii) Drawbacks. Findings explicate how intersections of cultural positioning, disability, class, age and gender shape marginalized students' learning experiences with ChatGPT in the context of contemporary neoliberal educational policies in Greece. Attention to how diverse social positionings shape ChatGPT-assisted learning can add depth to the current discourse on contextualizing generative AI assisted pedagogies tuned to diverse local contexts and students' needs.

Keywords: Generative AI · ChatGPT · vocational education and training · migrant students · disabilities · intersectionality

1 Introduction

Current generative AI educational research has overwhelmingly focused on students with nascent middle-class identities within higher education settings [1, 2]. These studies have sought to investigate how low-cost generative AI applications such as ChatGPT can facilitate students' learning processes in diverse fields. Findings from these works steadily show ChatGPT has now become an integral part of students' routines, offering instant, low-cost, and personalized support. Compared to higher education, vocational education and training (VET) still constitutes an under researched field which perhaps mirrors its low social positioning in Greece and elsewhere [3, 4]. Additionally, the few works on the potentials of ChatGPT in fostering inclusive education have focused on children with disabilities [5–7], which once again limits the discourse and reinforces the

Ł. Tomczyk (Ed.): NMP 2024, CCIS 2537, pp. 205–219, 2025.
https://doi.org/10.1007/978-3-031-95627-0_14

misconception that only one specific group of students faces exclusion. In reality, many student groups continue to be excluded, particularly those with intersecting identities such as adult migrant students with disabilities [8]. The current work aims to fill this intersectional gap within the generative AI educational literature and focus on students who are frequently overlooked, leaving them marginalized in classrooms, schools, and society. More specifically, the study uses Crenshaw's intersectionality concept [9], in order to investigate how these students use ChatGPT not just as a learning aid, but as a surviving tool to navigate and counter systemic barriers related to their disability, social class, linguistic and cultural identities which the Greek VET system tends to overlook. The research questions mirror both the theoretical standpoint and the investigative nature of the study:

How do migrant students with disabilities use ChatGPT in Greek VET upper secondary schools? How are their learning experiences with ChatGPT shaped by the intersections of disability, cultural, class, and gender identities within the Greek context of upper secondary VET education?

1.1 An Intersectional Approach to Understanding Marginalized Students' Use of ChatGPT

In this paper, I use intersectionality in order to gain an understanding of the diverse ChatGPT use experiences of students who are served but unserved by the Greek secondary education VET system. Intersectionality is founded on the acknowledgement that inequality does not emerge in isolation but results from the complex interplay of various social identities, power dynamics, and lived experiences. Law scholar and activist Kimberlie Crenshaw initially created the concept in order to expose the concealed multilevel discrimination lower-strata women of color encountered within the legal system in the US. Since then, intersectionality has been employed in diverse fields, such as healthcare, psychology, sociology and education mostly focusing on disparities of individuals with multiple marginalized identities [10]. In education, intersectionality has been used to investigate how students and teachers' simultaneous social positionings within specific sociocultural contexts generate inequality [11]. Central to the framework of intersectionality are multidimensionality and contextualization. Multidimensionality reflects how intersectionality recognizes that social identities such as race, ability, class, gender, sexuality, ethnicity, age or other factors such as geographical location, are not separate or independent. Instead, they intersect simultaneously and generate both overt and covert forms of advantage or disadvantage. Contextualization refers to how these intersecting identities are shaped by specific sociocultural and time conditions [10].

McCall [10] distinguishes three main types of intersectional research: the anticategorical which rejects fixed all social categories or identities, the intercategorical which compares inequalities between groups to explicate systemic inequality and mainly employs quantitative research designs, and the intracategorical which focuses on differences within a single category to highlight micro-level inequality [10]. In the current study I use intracategorical intersectionality in order to highlight how ability and migration as well as other social identities such as social class and gender limit migrant students' access to inclusive VET educational environments in Greece and how they use ChatGPT as a tool to learn and achieve their aspirations, within a neoliberal educational context. More specifically, I explore how the current neoliberal policies (macro-level) in contemporary Greece shapes these students' use of ChatGPT for learning purposes (micro-level) [10].

Neoliberalism currently is the leading ideology in K-12 and higher education in Greece [12, 13]. Despite differences across national and historical contexts, neoliberal policies share a common objective: promoting private capitalist profit. This pursuit of profit comes at the expense of all public services, including the provision of free education.

In Greece, the privatization of education emerged in the beginning of last century [12]. Following the decade-long financial crisis and the 2019 election of the current conservative Greek government, the neoliberal restructuring of the educational system has accelerated, as s series of legislative reforms further minimized the social character of public education [12, 13]. While "excellence," "meritocracy," and "inclusion" encapsulate the core rhetoric of the Greek government, the reality is that public education is free only on paper. In practice, Greece has the largest shadow education system in Europe, with the vast majority of parents being heavy consumers of costly private educational services [14]. Privatization of educational costs have decreased significantly expenditure for public education which suffers from multiple systemic barriers, including extreme teacher shortages especially in islands, rural and disadvantaged areas, poor infrastructure and overcrowded classrooms with a very high student-teacher ratio [12, 13].

Students with disabilities and/or with diverse linguistic and cultural backgrounds are even more underserved in the Greek education system. Although special education, is obligatory and constitutes a part of the unified public education, (Law 3699/2008), the quality of educational services students receive overwhelmingly depends on household's purchasing power. A gigantic private SEN sector with specialized educators and therapists caters to students with disabilities, while in public schools students are often deprived of basic support, with special educators arriving months late or not at all [15]. Intercultural education for migrant students also depends on familial capital, as the Greek migrant education system is built on integration policies driven by monolingual and monocultural ideologies across K-12 education, neglecting the diverse learning needs and social backgrounds of migrant students with and without disabilities. [16–20]. In fact, the European Commission's classification of educational support systems for migrant students in EU member states places Greece in the category of non-systematic support, highlighting the lack of a coherent policy to support them, particularly adults [20].

1.2 The Greek Secondary VET Context

VET is implemented differently across the globe. In countries, such as Sweden, Germany and Norway, VET is based on a knowledge-based approach, blending academic and vocational learning. In other countries such as the US, the UK, Canada and China, VET is founded on a narrower skills-based approach, mostly providing training in a set of definite skills deprived of a wider academic knowledge basis [22].

In Greece, VET is offered at the upper-secondary and post-secondary level. Upper secondary VET is provided by vocational upper secondary schools (EPAL), where students aged 16+ receive general academic education during the first year and subsequently choose a vocational field for two years. The fields available include Engineering, Tourism, Finance, Healthcare, Maritime Studies and Agriculture. Upon completion, students can sit the Panhellenic exams i.e. the national-level university entrance exams or continue with an extra optional year for apprenticeship. VET secondary schools are divided into morning and evening schools. Evening VET schools serve a diverse student population, including many migrants and Greeks from lower socioeconomic backgrounds [23, 24].

In Greek society, there is a cultural preference for general education over vocational education and training [25]. Although both the Greek mainstream media and the current government fiercely promote the numerous advantages of VET, such as the ability of the VET system to equip students with skills directly related to the labor market, vocational secondary schools still hold a low social standing among dominant middle-class Greek families who disapprove VET as it prepares students for artisan occupations with poor social status [23–25]. In contrast, general upper secondary schools (GEL) are seen as offering higher-quality education, social networking with the elite, easier access to higher education and subsequent entree to prestigious professions [4]. In fact, only 25% of Greek families choose VET schools, most of whom come from low socio-economic strata [23].

2 Method

2.1 Participants and Settings

I recruited participants through my social network, more specifically through personal contacts with evening VET school teachers at the island of Crete and subsequently visited each school in person. The sample consisted of six first-generation migrant students from Albania, Romania and Egypt aged between eighteen to forty-one who are pursuing vocational education while managing various intersecting challenges such as learning disabilities, chronic health conditions, and socio-economic constraints. Their time in Greece varied from four to eight years. All participants had a formal diagnosis of a disability and/or a chronic condition, provided by the Educational and Consulting Support Centre (KEDASY) or Centers for Certifying Disability (KEPA) or equivalent agencies in their home countries. To ensure a homogeneous sample, participants were selected based on the criterion that they were either current or former students of an evening secondary VET school and had been using ChatGPT for more than six months.

My participants' current occupations and future aspirations were directly related to current political and social pressures to connect vocational education with labor market outcomes, even more so for migrants. Both in Greece and elsewhere migrants' choices are frequently confined by systemic discrimination and stereotype essentialism [26]. Maria for example is a caregiver for the elderly, which is very common for Albanian migrant women in Greece [27]. She wants to obtain her certification in order to work as a nurse privately. Emad from Egypt, works in hotel maintenance and construction which are common fields for African and Asian male migrants [28]. He wants to finish high-school so that he can work as a certified electrician. Ardian, currently works as a car mechanic and wants to obtain formal certification in the field. Naira from Albania is a young single mother of a three-year old boy. She currently works as a waitress in a five-star hotel. Her goal is to graduate and move on to a more advanced position within the same hotel.

Panos from Albania and Anna from Romania were the only two participants who aspired to pursue higher education. Panos, currently working as a car mechanic, entered university through the Panhellenic exams and is now a first-year student in Marine Engineering. Anna, who works as a cleaner in Airbnbs, is in the 12th grade and preparing to sit for the Panhellenic exams in a few months. Despite being one of the top students at her school, Anna's dream of attending medical school feels "too big" for her, and she wrestles with self-doubt, shaped by the intersectional challenges of her migrant background and socio-economic status. Her second option is nursing school. Anna decided to pursue this goal after receiving encouragement from her teachers, despite receiving little support from her family and lacking the financial and emotional capital middle-class students have.

2.2 Interviews

All the interviews were conducted in person. They varied in length, ranging from forty minutes to two hours due to breaks. They had the form of an open discussion, but at the same time followed a specific structure to ensure consistent ChatGPT use topics were addressed by each participant [29]. These topics encompassed: (i) the participants' lived experiences related to ChatGPT use for learning purposes; (ii) the interconnection of their identities, such as being migrants and/or having a disability to their learning experiences with ChatGPT.

In the interviews, participants were invited to share their life stories, discuss the challenges they encountered while living in Greece, and reflect on their schooling experiences here. The last part of the interview specifically focused on their use of ChatGPT for school. The interviews were digitally recorded, and informed consent was obtained from all participants prior to their participation. The names of all participants were pseudonymized, and certain personal details were omitted to ensure the protection of their identities and maintain confidentiality.

2.3 Data Analysis

I implemented narrative analysis during which I went through each transcript and wrote annotations about each participant [29]. During this process, I noticed commonalities around participants' disability, cultural and linguistic identities, social class and their relation to ChatGPT use for learning purposes [30]. For example, several participants talked about the lack of multilingual teachers in their schools as an incentive for using ChatGPT in order to navigate the schooling process more smoothly. Subsequently, using a qualitative software, I carried out open coding. In the first cycle, I open coded data after I went through each sentence and created first-level descriptive codes. Using these first-level codes, I framed potential themes and created a codebook. I then proceeded to second-level coding [29]. Through this process, I explicated patterns about the interconnected systems of power and marginalization encountered by disabled migrant students' schooling experiences in Greece and their connection to ChatGPT use.

3 Findings and Discussion

3.1 ChatGPT as an In-Class Participation Facilitator

The intersections of participants' social identities as working-class migrants with disabilities generated a range of covert barriers to their active engagement in class. They all experienced feelings of embarrassment, self-doubt even fear, of seeming inferior to their teachers and peers. These negative emotions functioned as triggers for ChatGPT use during the actual lesson. Naira provides an example of the interaction of such multiple marginalities. In the extract below, she describes how her social identities as a dyslexic student and a migrant with low Greek language skills essentially discouraged her from participating in class and how ChatGPT helped her overcome some of these internalized barriers.

> *I felt embarrassed to talk, my Greek isn't good, I didn't want to hold the class back...Then one of my classmates installed ChatGPT on my phone and showed me how it works. It's totally different to google translate, I use it for instant explanations in class, not just translation...I get the point, then it is much easier for me to participate.* (Naira, 21, Albania, Dyslexia)

Other participants described how they have been using ChatGPT for translanguaging purposes to communicate and interact with their Greek-speaking, monolingual teachers. Some participants felt that migrant students with a low-level in Greek and English are frequently marked as outsiders in classroom interactions. They described how other students commonly interpret teachers' instructions or translate things for them, yet this process is not only time consuming but also creates a burden to their peers. Maria explained how she has been using ChatGPT for instant translation which in turn has reduced her need for help by other students:

> *I used to ask from other students to translate things for me, but it is tiring for them and the teachers and it is also embarrassing...Now I only ask someone to translate for me only when I don't have time, when the teacher says something, like instructions which I don't understand.* (Maria, 41, Albania, Dyslexia, Diabetes)

Panos recognized teachers in Greek VET schools encounter multiple obstacles in providing inclusive intercultural learning environments for all migrant students, even more so for migrant students with disabilities. Nevertheless, he also believed that the use of Greek-only instruction essentially marginalizes migrant students who are multilingual as they are prohibited from taping into their cultural and linguistic backgrounds and jeopardizes their training and work prospects. The extract below illustrates how he believes that Greek-only practices bear the message that other languages and identities are degraded and how ChatGPT used by the teachers as a f translanguaging strategy, promotes migrant students' feelings of belonging:

Albanian students for example, like me and others with even a lower level in Greek, are essentially blocked from participating, not because teachers are bad or racist, but simply because teachers are all Greek, they do not speak another language, they have tons of students from different levels, from different backgrounds, it is virtually impossible to explain everything to a student's language...With ChatGPT, both teachers and students use Greek, Albanian, Arabic, it is still difficult but the situation in class is much better than what it used to be. (Panos, 19, Albanian, Dyslexia)

Naira and Maria further reflected on how some of their Greek teachers use ChatGPT for experimenting with an offhand translanguaging, allowing students to use orally their mother tongues even though Greek is norm:

The English teacher uses it all the time in class to explain things in our language...She lets us use it as well so we can speak more comfortably and blend Greek with our native languages...The other day she also gave us a handout explaining English spelling and pronunciation rules in Albanian which was very helpful because I struggle due to my dyslexia. (Naira, 22, Albania, Dyslexia)

Our Math teacher uses ChatGPT and connects it on the projector and as he is teaching something he uses it for explaining things in different languages when we ask him which is extraordinary especially for me, I do not understand Math. (Maria, 41, Albania, Dyslexia, Diabetes)

Emad stated that his Greek language teacher now uses ChatGPT in order to create a tests and materials based on his individual needs:

She is such an amazing teacher. She understands my hearing problem, she knows my Greek language level is low and she does whatever she can...She gives me notes in Arabic, with dialogues or words I need for work and for everyday things, she creates tests for me that are simpler than the tests for the rest of the class. (Emad, 19, Egypt, Mild hearing loss)

This theme shows how ChatGPT was used by participants as tool to mitigate multiple forms of exclusion, including linguicism, ableism and sexism and participate more in the classroom. For these participants, linguistic anxiety and hesitation are not simply internalized personal struggles, but manifestations of wider power dynamics that position them as outsiders in the classroom. The preceding extracts however, indicate that ChatGPT has facilitated the creation of minor cracks within the Greek educational system and its rigid authoritative status of monolingual and monolithic curricula [18–21]. These seemingly negligible yet critical cracks are of great importance for creating inclusive learning from "the bottom-up," disputing the hegemonic discourse of Greek [20].Although participants indicated that their teachers are non-experts in translanguaging practices or special education, and tend to rely on traditional teaching methods, such as following the textbook, findings suggest that these educators-despite the systemic barriers of the Greek VET system [23] have begun incorporating ChatGPT into their teaching pedagogies to accommodate their students disabilities and embrace their cultural backgrounds.

3.2 ChatGPT as On-Call Support

Participants described using ChatGPT as a personal tutor at home, highlighting how structural and interpersonal factors intersect and encourage its use. Their narratives revealed discomfort in repeatedly asking questions, a reflection of both internalized stigma [31] and the exclusionary dynamics within the classroom. Emad, for example, expressed empathy for his overburdened teachers, who struggle to manage large classes, some with students exhibiting challenging behaviors. As a result, he prefers to remain silent and turn to ChatGPT at home for clarification. His statement below reflects internalized ableism [32] and the ways in which his identity as a disabled, non-native speaker of Greek shapes his educational experience and encourages ChatGPT use:

> *My hearing problem and my low level in Greek means it takes ages for me to ask something and for them (teachers) to understand what I am asking...I feel sorry for them really...I am not alone in there, they have to take care of the other students as well...It's like a routine for me now, I go home and ask whatever I don't catch in class. Then, if I still have questions I ask the teacher.* (Emad, 19, Egypt, Mild hearing loss)

Intersections of gender, age, and nationality also functioned as facilitators for ChatGPT use at home as revealed by Maria's account. Being an older Albanian woman in a classroom dominated by younger students fluent in Greek heightened her sense of exclusion [33]. Fear of being judged for asking "basic" questions encouraged her to disengage from classroom interactions and turn to ChatGPT as a learning tool at home:

> *I am afraid making stupid questions...They will see me as the old Albanian lady who doesn't know what she's talking about...Now, instead of asking something teachers to help me and feel sorry for me, I use ChatGPT at home, specific things related to my job as a caregiver or other things related to nursing so I can get my certification.* (Maria, 41, Albania, Dyslexia, Diabetes)

Ardian also explained how he uses ChatGPT for comprehending difficult concepts in his classes. His account below demonstrates how ChatGPT, essentially provided culturally-responsive scaffolding, tailor-made to his needs as a dyslexic student [34], which facilitated his transition from abstract to concrete understanding [35] of a difficult concept a few days ago:

> *The other day we were talking about fuels and viscosity, which is difficult to understand but it's very important for me as car mechanic, I couldn't understand it in class, not just because of Greek, it is difficult...I went home, asked ChatGPT multiple times in Albanian, told it to make it simple for me, then I understood it.* (Ardian, 21, Albania, Dyslexia, Dyscalculia, ADHD)

Participants' narratives further revealed ChatGPT is used for facilitating communication with teachers and other students. Naira's extract below highlights how intersecting factors such as disability and language barriers shape her use of ChatGPT as a tool for communication:

I use it for writing emails to teachers, for Viber groups with my classmates for projects, for social media...Not just for spelling, it helps with words and with content, structure it's perfect...I have been much more active because I don't feel stressed whether what I am writing in Greek is proper. (Naira, 21, Albania, Dyslexia)

Further in his interview, Ardian explained how he uses ChatGPT for a variety of school-related tasks, including writing assignments, emails and messages as it helps him manage some of the difficulties caused by his dyslexia and ADHD [36]. He described how the tool assists him in organizing his thoughts and producing clear, coherent writing. Additionally, Ardian stated that using ChatGPT reduces his stress and boosts his confidence in communication, as it ensures that his Greek writing is "proper" and helps him mitigate social and linguistic stigma [37]:

I cannot describe to you how much it has helped me with writing in Greek. Everything from essays to messages to my friends or emails to teachers or other students...In the past, I was always worried about being humiliated because of my Greek. (Ardian, 21, Albania, Dyslexia, Dyscalculia, ADHD)

From an intersectional perspective, this theme shows ChatGPT facilitates learning by offering a safe learning-space where participants develop their agency against overlapping systems that suppress them, including ableism, migrant precarity, gendered ageism and linguistic stigma. For Maria, ChatGPT helps bridge the knowledge gaps triggered by her low participation in class. Her identities as an "older" Albanian woman in Greece's undervalued care sector and her chronic conditions, keep her silent at school but at home she seems more empowered to learn at her own pace. Emad's reliance on ChatGPT emerges from the collision of his hearing difficulties and the internalized masculine expectations of male Muslim migrant manual workers in Greece [38] that render his requests for repetition in class as tiring or disruptive. His reluctance to participate in class and turn to ChatGPT at home is not simply a matter of personal "insecurity", it is socially constructed by gendered and racialized expectations of vulnerability. Unlike women who are readily portrayed as vulnerable, racialized migrant men like Emad, are often expected to be self-sufficient which reinforces his hesitation to ask for help. Similarly, Ardian and Naira use ChatGPT not only as a tool to enhance their academic performance but also as a strategy to survive overlapping linguicism and ableism which link writing difficulties to intellectual deficits and racialized markers of "otherness".

3.3 ChatGPT as a Key to HE

Two out of the six participants shared their experiences using ChatGPT in preparation for higher education. Panos, went through the mentally and physically draining Panhellenic exams last year. Contrary to the vast majority of middle-class students in Greece [38], his preparation relied mainly on ChatGPT and the guidance of a teacher who helped him navigate the tool effectively:

They all attend private schools, their parents get the best private tutors per subject, I don't blame them, if I could, I'd probably do the same. I only had ChatGPT and a teacher who taught me how to use it properly…For Greece, passing these exams with no private tutoring is unthinkable. (Panos, 19, Albanian, Dyslexia)

He then elaborated on how he relied on ChatGPT daily as a substitute for private education, highlighting how Greece's shadow education system disproportionately excludes migrant students with disabilities and those from lower socio-economic backgrounds from HE access [13, 14, 39]:

I used it extensively last year for Math, for Marine Engines, Maritime Law, Essay writing, generally for all the courses that I was tested in the Panhellenic exams and it worked…I am talking to you right now as Marine Engineering cadet…My family had no money for frontistiria and my dyslexia made everything harder and I still got in…Before going to this school and before ChatGPT I had never imagined I could do it. (Panos, 19, Albanian, Dyslexia)

Similarly, Anna, currently in the 12th grade preparing for the panhellenic exams, explains how ChatGPT is her strategy to counterbalance her lack of economic capital for private tutoring. As a migrant student with dyslexia from a disadvantaged background, Anna fluctuated amid feelings of pessimism and frustration, as she tirelessly studies, works and goes to school. Her account revealed how she essentially operationalized these negative emotions into a justification for using ChatGPT in order to achieve her dream and enter medical school, currently the most prestigious school in Greece [40]:

I want med school, if not, nursing…I know I am aiming high, maybe too high… There are a lot of barriers, not just my horrible Greek and my dyslexia and my anxiety…I use it daily, it creates mock tests for me, it creates case studies similar to the ones I am expected to work on in the exams, Math problems, MCQ tests just to make sure I have understood specific chapters and so on. (Anna, 19, Romania, Dyslexia, Anxiety disorder)

Anna further explained that at the time of the interview, there was no teacher for the Anatomy and Physiology courses which constitute two of the most demanding subjects for the Panhellenic exams, after the assigned teacher went on maternity leave. A substitute arrived one month later but soon resigned. This situation is not uncommon at Crete and other Greek touristic islands where persistent teacher shortages are driven by the surging living costs [41]. Meanwhile, students from lower socio-economic backgrounds like Anna are left to prepare for these high-stake exams on their own devices:

What can you do right? We are just waiting. It happens with teachers here all the time, but this year is really important for me…Teachers like everyone else cannot really survive here with one wage, they get peanuts as well…For now, ChatGPT is my only teacher for Anatomy and Physiology.

Anna's and Panos' narratives reveal the multiple marginalization encountered by VET students in Greece whose intersecting cultural, disability and social class identities collide with systemic barriers which in turn block their access to higher education. Anna is part of a VET system that not only fails to provide support tailored to her needs as a dyslexic migrant student with anxiety but also deprives her of critical support such as an Anatomy and Physiology teacher, whose absence clearly jeopardizes her preparation for the Panhellenic exams. For Panos and Anna, ChatGPT partially replaces the Greek shadow education system which they cannot afford, in order to cope with an exam-based system that clearly privileges middle-class native speakers of Greek. By emulating private tutoring, ChatGPT helps them disrupt internalized beliefs that low-income migrants like them, are not "fit" for higher education. Their reliance on generative AI, explicates the exclusion they are experiencing in the Greek VET system but at the same time it reframes "impossible" aspirations as battles worth fighting for.

3.4 Drawbacks

The first and most common drawback of ChatGPT mentioned by two out of six participants was cost. Anna's account was particularly intense. ChatGPT has evolved to her most "precious tool" for the Panhellenic exams. Her goal to enter medical school means she needs the newest version of ChatGPT-4:

> *I pay for GPT-4 because I need it for solving math or science problems and for my financial situation right now, yes it's expensive. There is inequality even in ChatGPT...Other students don't have to worry about this, they have tutors for every subject, they have the paid version but they don't pay for it, they don't work, they have time. For, me the twenty euros is half of a day's work, hard work they cannot even imagine.* (Anna, 17, Romania, Dyslexia & Anxiety Disorder)

Some participants acknowledged that ChatGPT has become a new dependency, which in some cases may hinder their learning and limit their ability to think independently [42]. For instance, Naira mentioned that she now uses ChatGPT as a tool to answer various questions about school subjects she dislikes, but she seemed to question the actual value of her learning gains: *If you use it all the time and you just copy paste things, I think you actually become dummer and you don't even realize it.* Maria, described how she constantly uses ChatGPT for assignments and exercises teachers assign for homework, especially in subjects she is not good at. She emphasized however, that she turns to ChatGPT not because she lacks interest, but because she wants to avoid appearing lazy to her teachers whom she respects deeply:

> *I use it for Math, because I don't understand Math and I am embarrassed to go to class with nothing, so I ask it to solve the problems...Our teacher is so nice and he really wants us to learn...I do not want to seem like a tourist, lazy you know?... In Albania we used to respect our teachers so much. Here, Greeks are more relaxed. They don't care. I care.* (Maria, 41, Albania, Dyslexia, Diabetes)

Covert misinformation [42] was another disadvantage of ChatGPT mentioned by two participants. Panos in particular, described how he reproduced false information last year when he sat the Panhellenic exams:

If you don't know what to ask the information is too general and superficial, especially in the free version and other times the information is false but it appears as correct and if you don't ask the teacher or if you don't cross-check it, you actually learn and false information...It happened to me in the Panhellenic exams in Maritime Law, thank god, it didn't cost me much. (Panos, 19, Albania, Dyslexia).

Maria, Emad and Naira further reported feelings of frustration or confusion when using ChatGPT, as it commonly fails to understand and respond appropriately to their questions [42]. Maria's extract below highlights a broader issue in human-ChatGPT interactions, where the technology often fails to meet our expectations, especially if we luck adequate generative AI competence and prompting skills [35]. It also explicates, that learning how to use ChatGPT demands time, a type of capital working-class Albanian women like Maria, rarely have [43]:

> *Sometimes really, I am actually shouting at if it really is an actual person. I have gotten better in asking it the right things but many times it just doesn't get what I am asking... But ok, it is polite, it says I'm sorry and gives you another answer...I don't have time to sit and learn how to write the correct prompts...Some teachers tell me how to do it, but I don't have time, I work ten hours a day, then I babysit the grandchildren, then I come here.*

4 Conclusion

The current study set off to explore ChatGPT use in Greek evening upper secondary VET schools among migrant students with disabilities, a subject that has not been previously investigated. Participants' narratives reflect how disabled migrant students cope with socioeconomic disparities both in and out of classroom walls within the Greek state education context. Overall, findings suggest that within Greek evening VET schools, the management of inclusion of students with diverse social identities is largely left to educators' own devices. Although teachers' efforts to create inclusive environments in VET schools are important and should be praised, they remain within the framework of individual initiative, which when not backed-up by macro-level policies is fractional and inadequate.

ChatGPT cannot replace the teachers still absent from participants' schools. It cannot provide Anna with the emotional support she needs for the Panhellenic exams, nor can it engage with her cognitively in the same way that would allow her to cope with these exams as equitably as her middle-class peers. It cannot counterbalance the absence of interculturally trained teachers and special education teachers for Emad and the other participants. It is however a low-cost, easily accessible tool that can potentially complement and support learning, especially for students who are marginalized by the system.

While this study provides valuable intersectional insights, it exhibits certain limitations. As a qualitative intracategorical intersectional study, it has focused on capturing the complexity of the lived experiences of specific marginalized students using ChatGPT, thus findings cannot be generalized. Conducted at a single VET school in Greece with a small number of participants from specific cultural backgrounds and with specific disabilities, these findings may not fully represent the broader reality of how migrant students with disabilities use ChatGPT. Additionally, since the analysis is based on participants' experiences, perceptions, and opinions as interpreted by the researcher, there is a possibility of subjective bias. Nevertheless, this study is the first intersectional exploration of how marginalized VET students engage with generative AI. Current findings can inspire future intersectional works to refine, expand, and deepen the understanding of generative AI's role in mitigating educational inequalities.

4.1 Implications

Current findings not only shed light to novel educational affordances of ChatGPT for students with multiple marginalized identities, they bear specific implications regarding the use of generative AI within the Greek VET context. First and foremost, there is a pressing need for Greek policymakers to provide comprehensive training to VET teachers on the pedagogical use of generative AI underpinned by contemporary inclusive intercultural teaching approaches. As educators, we must move beyond merely seeking answers from ChatGPT and implement culturally responsive and differentiated teaching approaches that embrace our students' multiple social identities. Secondly, as generative AI technologies like ChatGPT become more widespread in diverse educational settings, it is critical for the Greek Ministry of Education and for policymakers elsewhere to launch national-level solid ethical frameworks that will provide teachers and students with clean-cut guidance on their ethical use. This includes identifying potential risks related to data privacy issues, bias, and the potential for generative AI to exacerbate existing educational disparities, particularly for vulnerable populations.

Through this study, I have demonstrated how intersectionality can stretch our understanding of the unique facets of ChatGPT for educational use by students who deviate from the norm. Currently, the vast majority of education researchers, policymakers, and practitioners investigating the potentials of generative AI applications tend to downplay the interplay of students' multiple social identities and as a result ignore their intersecting struggles, and their unique learning experiences with ChatGPT. Intersectionality invites researchers in education to comprehend the particularities of students' lived experiences and can help them understand how generative AI can contribute to creating inclusive learning environments across educational contexts.

References

1. Deng, R., Jiang, M., Yu, X., Lu, Y., Liu, S.: Does ChatGPT enhance student learning? A systematic review and meta-analysis of experimental studies. Comput. Educ. **227**, 105224 (2024)
2. Heung, Y.M.E., Chiu, T.K.: How ChatGPT impacts student engagement from a systematic review and meta-analysis study. Comput. Educ. Artif. Intell. 100361 (2025)
3. Billett, S.: Perspectives on enhancing the standing of vocational education and the occupations it serves. J. Vocat. Educ. Train. **72**(2), 161–169 (2020)
4. Konidari, V.: Territoriality as an analytical lens for exploring educational disadvantage. A qualitative study of VET students in Italy, France, and Greece. Int. J. Qual. Stud. Educ. **37**(4), 1093–1110 (2024)
5. Rakap, S.: Chatting with GPT: enhancing individualized education program goal development for novice special education teachers. J. Spec. Educ. Technol. **39**(3), 339–348 (2024)
6. Rakap, S., Balikci, S.: Enhancing IEP goal development for preschoolers with autism: a preliminary study on ChatGPT integration. J. Autism Dev. Disorders 1–6 (2024)

7. Seiradakis, E.V.: Unpacking experts' opinions on ChatGPT potential assistive roles and risks in early childhood special education. In: Tomczyk, Ł. (eds.) New Media Pedagogy: Research Trends, Methodological Challenges, and Successful Implementations. NMP 2023. Communications in Computer and Information Science, vol. 2130. Springer, Cham
8. Brown, M., Gravani, M.N., Slade, B., Jõgi, L: Integrating migrants through adult language programmes: a comparative case study of four European countries. Integr. Migrants Labour Mark. Eur. **25**, 155–169 (2020)
9. Crenshaw, K.: Race, gender, and sexual harassment. Cal. l. Rev. **65**, 1467 (1991)
10. McCall, L.: The complexity of intersectionality. Signs: J. Women Cult. Soc. **30**(3), 1771–1800 (2005)
11. Tefera, A.A., Fischman, G.E.: Beyond good intentions in Special Education policy: engaging with critical disability intersectional research. Qual. Inq. **30**(1), 48–58 (2014)
12. Koutsoklenis, A., Karagianni, Y.: Neoliberal–neoconservative educational reforms and the inclusion in education of disabled students in Greece: the case of the institution of special assistant. Soc. Sci. Humanit. Open **9**, 100863 (2024)
13. Giavrimis, P.: Shadow education as a tool of "colonization" of public education. Int. J. Educ. Reform **34**(1), 71–87 (2025)
14. Bray, M.: Shadow education in Europe: growing prevalence, underlying forces, and policy implications. ECNU Rev. Educ. **4**(3), 442–475 (2021)
15. Koutsoklenis, A., Papadimitriou, V.: Special education provision in Greek mainstream classrooms: teachers' characteristics and recruitment procedures in parallel support. Int. J. Incl. Educ. **28**(5), 561–576 (2024)
16. Kostoulas, A.: Challenging normative influences in refugee and migrant education: reflections of a trainee teacher cohort. Teach. Teach. Educ. **139**, 104454 (2024)
17. Bosch, J., et al.: How do teachers view multilingualism in education? Evidence from Greece, Italy and The Netherlands. Lang. Educ. 1–20 (2024)
18. Giavrimis, P., Dimitriadou, S.: Interculturality in Greek education. J. Ethnic Cult. Stud. **10**(3), 72–88 (2023)
19. Giavrimis, P.: Disability, migration, and education. Greek primary teachers' conceptualisations. Intercult. Educ. **35**(4), 443–461 (2024)
20. Giavrimis, P.: Inclusionary policies for migrant and refugee students in Greek education. Int. J. Educ. Reform 10567879231191508 (2023)
21. Barkoglou, G., Gravani, M.N.: Exploring adult migrants' learning needs using an empowerment-critical approach: a biographical research. In: Chad, H., Hoggan-Kloubert, T. (eds.) Adult Learning in a Migration Society, pp. 67–79. Routledge (2021)
22. Rintala, H., Nokelainen, P.: Standing and attractiveness of vocational education and training in Finland: focus on learning environments. J. Vocat. Educ. Train. **72**(2), 250–269 (2020)
23. Giannakaki, M.S., Batziakas, G.: 'This is a beautiful school. This school is useless!!'Explaining disengagement in a Greek vocational school through the examination of teacher ideologies. Res. Post-compulsory Educ. **21**(4), 409–433 (2016)
24. Kotsifakos, D., Kiriakos, D., Kalovrektis, K., Psaromiligkos, Y., Douligeris, C.: Research and analysis in the cognitive principles of Vocational Education and Training in Greece at the beginning of the 21st Century. Appl. Syst. Innov. **7**(5), 98 (2024)
25. Sanz de Miguel, P., Barrientos, D., Markowitsch, J.: The role of social partners in experimenting with 'dual training'in statist skills regimes: a comparison of Greece, Portugal, and Spain. Journal of Vocational Education & Training 1–22 (2024)
26. Vehviläinen, S., Souto, A.M.: How does career guidance at schools encounter migrant young people? Interactional practices that hinder socially just guidance. Int. J. Educ. Vocat. Guid. 1–18 (2019)

27. Lazaridis, G.: Filipino and Albanian women migrant workers in Greece: multiple layers of oppression. In F. Anthias and G. Lazaridis (Eds.), Gender and migration in Southern Europe, pp.49–79. Routledge (2020)
28. Floros, K., Jørgensen, M.B.: Tracing the future of migrants' labour relations. Experiences of institutionalised migrant precarity in Denmark and Greece. Polit. Geogr. **77**, 102120, (2020)
29. Saldaña, J., Omasta, M.: Qualitative Research: Analyzing Life. Sage Publications, Hoboken (2016)
30. Collins, P.H., Bilge, S.: Intersectionality. John Wiley & Sons, Hoboken (2020)
31. Haft, S.L., Greiner de Magalhães, C., Hoeft, F.: A systematic review of the consequences of stigma and stereotype threat for individuals with specific learning disabilities. J. Learn. Disabil. **56**(3), 193–209 (2023)
32. Campbell, F.A.K.: Exploring internalized ableism using critical race theory. Disabil. Soc. **23**(2), 151–162 (2008)
33. Jule, A.: Gender, Participation and Silence in the Language Classroom. Palgrave Macmillan, London (2016)
34. Cummings, C.M., Gómez-Fuentes, N.I., Gonsalves, V.: Understanding dyslexia in multilingual environments. In: Villarreal, A. (Ed.), Hispanic Perspectives on Student Support and Community Empowerment, pp. 257–288 IGI Global Scientific Publishing (2025)
35. Garcia-Varela, F., Bekerman, Z., Nussbaum, M., Mendoza, M., Montero, J.: Reducing interpretative ambiguity in an educational environment with ChatGPT. Comput. Educ. **225**, 105182 (2025)
36. Cheng, S., Coghill, D., Zendarski, N.: A rapid systematic review of attention-deficit/hyperactivity disorder (ADHD) and high order writing: current findings and implications for intervention. Res. Dev. Disabil. **123**, 104180 (2022)
37. Brooks, M.D.: "She doesn't have the basic understanding of a language": using spelling research to challenge deficit conceptualizations of adolescent bilinguals. J. Lit. Res. **49**(3), 342–370 (2017)
38. Husain, M.: Youth Migrant Workers: Class and Intersectionality. In Masculinity and Mental Health of Muslim Men of Colour, pp. 95–113. Springer, Cham (2024)
39. Giannopoulou, I., Efstathiou, V., Korkoliakou, P., Triantafyllou, G., Smyrnis, N., Douzenis, A.: Mental health of adolescents amidst preparation for university entrance exams during the second pandemic-related lockdown in Greece. J. Affect. Disorders Rep. **8**, 100339 (2022)
40. Sianou-Kyrgiou, E., Tsiplakides, I.: Similar performance, but different choices: social class and higher education choice in Greece. Stud. High. Educ. **36**(1), 89–102 (2011)
41. Traianou, A.: Evaluation and its politics: trade unions and education reform in Greece. Educ. Inq. 1–20 (2023)
42. Hua, S., Jin, S., Jiang, S.: The limitations and ethical considerations of Chatgpt. Data intelligence **6**(1), 201–239 (2024)
43. Xhaho, A., Çaro, E., Bailey, A.: Empowerment or a double burden? Work, family, and agency among Albanian migrant women in Greece. Gend. Place Cult. **28**(10), 1431–1451 (2021)

Influence of Generative AI on Higher Education from a Business Students' Perspective: A Delphi Study

Ludvík Eger(✉)

University of West Bohemia, Univerzitní 8, 301 00 Pilsen, Czech Republic
leger@fek.zcu.cz

Abstract. Higher education has been profoundly impacted by the rapid development and growth of Generative AI technologies. Higher education institutions (HEIs) have responded in a diverse and fragmented way to these emerging opportunities in 2023/2024. The Delphi technique was used in this study as a valuable method to gain information about the perceptions of business students regarding the implementation of AI in the teaching and learning process. Among the main impacts of AI on higher education identified by students, the top positions were held by Automation which simplifies routine activities and enables rapid data analysis, Access to many up-to-date information resources, and New interactive forms and learning methods. Students do not believe that AI will replace teachers in their role in education. The findings of this study highlight the transformative potential of Generative AI technologies in higher education. The student experience of Generative AI applications will continue to evolve. HEIs must responsibly monitor the development of AI and need to be proactive in monitoring and governing the use of Generative AI tools, as they present both challenges and opportunities.

Keywords: Higher Education · Artificial Intelligence · Generative AI Applications · Delphi Study

1 Introduction

The rapid development and growth of Generative AI technologies are having a profound impact on higher education. Generative AI continues to evolve rapidly, in the next few years it will drive innovation and improvements in higher education too, but it will also create a myriad of new challenges not only in the education process [1–4].

Generative AI, demonstrated by Large Language models such as ChatGPT or Gemini, has reshaped how machines interact and produce text that closely resembles human writing. It operates by identifying patterns in extensive large datasets and using this insight to generate responses that are both coherent and contextually relevant. These AI models have surprised the world with their ability to understand complex and diverse human languages and produce rich and structured human responses. OpenAI [5] brought forward a new shift in this technology in April 2024 and we can expect further positive changes in this area to emerge now more in the order of months.

Ł. Tomczyk (Ed.): NMP 2024, CCIS 2537, pp. 220–227, 2025.
https://doi.org/10.1007/978-3-031-95627-0_15

Higher education institutions (HEIs) have responded in a diverse and fragmented way to these emerging opportunities in 2023/2024. Some HEIs have banned and limited the use of Generative AI, while others have started to implement it by publishing guidance for students on how to engage with this new phenomenon. At present, it seems evident that banning its use does not make sense, but the regulation and ethical dimensions of the use of Generative AI are important topics. It is possible to state that the most HEIs are currently in the process of reviewing their policies around the use of AI tools and their implications for academic integrity [3, 6, 7].

The application of AI in education is gaining popularity in practice. Given its relative newness and complexity, it´s not surprising that its role has not yet been adequately investigated in the teaching and learning process. Thus, the research gap is in understanding the role of Generative AI in the teaching and learning process, as its impact has not yet been adequately investigated.

This study highlights, in line with Choi [8], that the viewpoints of students are essential for making sense of the impact that Generative AI will have on HEIs in the future concerning learning, teaching, assessment, and administration. Thus, the purpose of this qualitative study is to investigate, from the point of view of students, how Generative AI impacts higher education. In the light of the current experience of the implementation of Generative AI in higher education, the following question is posed:

RQ: From the perspective of students, how does Generative AI influence and transform the teaching and learning process in higher education?

2 Generative AI and Higher Education

The release of ChatGPT and its implications for higher education have caused a lot of controversy, but there are clear opportunities to improve student learning and access [9]. The literature has also revealed a need for a student voice in the discussion about AI implementation so far and that there is potential for AI tools to enhance the effectiveness of the teaching and learning process [8–10].

The findings of research focused on transforming higher education with AI [11] suggest that future higher education should be transformed to train students to be future-ready for employment in a society powered by Generative AI.

HEIs and academics should be aware of the implementation of AI tools in the teaching and learning process. As a new resource, the tool Generative AI can also influence academic norms towards student cheating behaviour and public perceptions of higher education. This demonstrates a need for further research and discussion about the implications of AI tools in HEIs, including innovative teaching and learning practices, ensuring equitable access to educational opportunities, and ethical use of AI.

Generative AI tools bring a range of both challenges and opportunities. Lim et al. [3] argue that it is important for HEIs to remain vigilant and proactive in observing and governing the use of such tools. For example, Choi [8] focused the review on the four major educational domains – learning, teaching, assessment and administration. Similarly, Slimi [12] argues that AI has the potential to revolutionize education by personalizing teaching methods to suit individual student needs, providing prompt feedback, and automating administrative tasks. Karimi and Khawaja [13] summarised the benefits of AI for higher education as follows: revolutionising teaching and learning methods, personalised learning, intelligent tutoring, streamlining administrative tasks, data-driven decision making, enhanced accessibility and inclusivity, and enhancing student experiences.

This study was also inspired by the messages and study materials reported by universities in relation to opportunities and challenges for AI in education. Oxford University [14] mentioned that AI has already begun transforming various industries, from healthcare to transportation. The issues that will need to be addressed were personalized and adaptive learning, automating administrative tasks, improving accessibility, concerns over data privacy and ethics, teacher training for AI integration, and the digital divide and learning inequality. The University of Texas [15] underlines innovative pedagogical strategies that can be a major shift in teaching practice. Wilfrid Laurier University [16], regarding the topic of Generative AI in teaching and learning, considered the roles of AI in these areas: peer-led learning & collaboration, accessing resources, content streaming, and engaging with educational developers. The evolving AI landscape creates new resources to support the study process in higher education. HEIs [17] can also equip students with the necessary skills and competencies to succeed in AI-driven industries, thereby propelling their long-term opportunities.

The student/learner experience of generative AI is continuing to evolve [10]. The evolving AI landscape creates new resources to support the study process in higher education. HEIs can also equip students with the necessary skills and competencies to succeed in AI-driven industries, enhancing their long-term prospects.

3 Method

The Delphi method was used to address the research question. It is a formal consensus method and a systematic means for measuring and developing consensus among participants regarding a particular topic [18, 19]. This method or technique is accepted as a useful method for solving problems, as a planning tool for forecasting future trends, and for recruitment purposes [20, 21]. The Delphi technique may also be used to further clarify or validate findings from previous surveys and also in this research the method did not try to "predict" the future of implementation of AI at faculties, but rather attempted to reach an understanding on the selected topic.

The Delphi method uses a set of carefully designed questionnaires with summarised information and feedback of opinions derived from earlier responses of participants to gain new information about a particular topic [18]. It is conducted over several rounds, initial and subsequent [21]. Some authors suggest that the number of rounds for Delphi should be determined a priori; others, however, suggest that the process should stop when agreement has been reached [22].

Delphi may be characterized as a method for structuring a group communication process and can be useful in gathering the opinions of a large number of people in order to provide data for formulating or clarifying a selected topic and discovering areas of consensus. In this sense, the primary goal of Delphi is consistency of opinion from a group of experts (students) regarding an area of interest, here on the Implementation of AI in the teaching and learning process at university.

The conducted research used four key features which may be regarded as necessary for defining a procedure as a 'Delphi'. These are anonymity, iteration, controlled feedback and statistical aggregation of the group response.

The selection of the panel of participants (business university students) is a critical aspect of the Delphi method [23]. Participant panel selection in this research was based on the following criteria: the participant is a business student (master's program) and he or she has first-hand experience with the application of AI for solving learning tasks. The research using the Delphi technique used four separate groups. The number of participants in the groups was as follows, the first group contained 22, the second 17, the third 16, and the fourth 18 participants. It is important to mention that almost 50% of respondents already had at least part-time work. All students fell within Generation Z [24, 25] and had above-basic ICT skills [cf. 26]. At the beginning of the summer semester of 2024, the students were introduced to the implementation of AI in organizations and education in a lecture. Afterward, they completed several activities for business students. This was the beginning of the implementation of AI in the educational process at our faculty.

In the first round (initial stage), information about the subject matter was gathered and a list of items was created to formulate the questionnaire. The specifically designed and constructed online questionnaire for the present research contained 9 items intending to reflect the main impact of AI on higher education found in the literature reviewed in this research (see above). For the input of the data in questionnaire 1, the items were ordered alphabetically.

In the second round, the participants were asked to rate the items in the questionnaire using a predetermined 5-point Likert scale ranging from 'Not at all important' to 'Very important'. The Delphi moderator applied measures of central tendency to determine consensus from the second round.

The third round provided feedback from the previous round to reach a final consensus or indicate whether a consensus could be reached [18]. First, questionnaire 2 was constructed and launched. The participants were invited to rank the 9 main impacts of AI on higher education with the first being the most important and the 9th being the least important. To measure the degree of consensus in the ranking of the items across all participants within an expert panel, Kendall's coefficient of concordance (W) in Eq. (1) is applied in the third round. Kendall's W ranges from 0 (no agreement) to 1 (complete agreement).

$$\mathrm{W} = \frac{\sum x^2 - \frac{(\sum x)^2}{\mathrm{n}}}{\frac{1}{12}k^2 * (n^3 - \mathrm{n})} \tag{1}$$

Note. k = number of respondents (panellists), n = number of factors [27].

4 Results

Table 1 shows how selected students' groups of business study programs rank the main impact of AI on higher education recommended by selecting surveys in relative importance.

Table 1. List of the main impacts of AI on higher education according to group evaluation

	Groups		Overall place		
Impacts of AI	First	Second	Third	Fourth	
AI will impact personalized and effective student learning	3.36	3.29	3.16	3.65	5
AI will support the development of students' critical thinking and creativity	3.00	2.88	2.47	3.15	7
Automation and AI will simplify routine activities and enable rapid data analysis	4.56	4.82	4.84	4.45	1
AI will support access to many up-to-date information resources	4.16	4.12	4.42	4.15	2
AI will bring new interactive forms and methods of learning	4.20	3.59	4.00	4.35	3
AI contributes to more effective and fairer assessment of learning	2.20	2.47	2.32	2.60	8
AI using chatbots will bring 24/7 support for students	4.08	3.35	3.95	4.20	4
AI will impact the future careers of current HEI students	3.16	3.24	3.11	3.05	6
AI will significantly replace teachers in HEI	2.08	2.24	2.05	1.90	9

Source: Own

The Kendall W value obtained is 0.465 for the first group, 0.409 for the second group, 0.546 for the third group, and 0.429 for the fourth group of students, which indicates moderate agreement.

As can be seen from Table 1, the order of importance of selected competencies was very similar for all four groups. On the other hand, the obtained Kendall W values show that there are individual differences in participants' views on the main impacts of AI on higher education.

5 Discussion

The Delphi technique was used in this study as a valuable method to gain information about the perceptions of business students regarding the implementation of AI in the teaching and learning process. The main purpose was to find out how the target group of business university students perceives the main impacts of AI on higher education. The study provides an insight into the expectations of university students (Generations Z) when they think about AI.

Among the main impacts of AI on higher education identified by students, the top positions were held by Automation which simplifies routine activities and enables rapid data analysis, Access to many up-to-date information resources, and New interactive forms and learning methods. Then follows an impression that AI using chatbots will bring 24/7 support for students. On the other hand, students do not believe that AI will replace teachers in their role in education and that AI will effectively affect the evaluation process.

This study follows research by Sullivan et al. [9] with the focus on student learning and their assessment. The results are in line with a previously published paper by Karimi and Khawaja [13] on the mentioned benefits of AI in higher education. They see potential in transforming teaching and learning methods, further, in streamlining administrative tasks, and in improving the quality of student experiences. On the other hand, they underline that the successful incorporation of AI into the higher education system is connected with large investments in software, infrastructure, and staff training.

For example, Zhang and Aslan [28] highlighted the possibility to use AI applications as intelligent tutors or agents that provide customized, timely and appropriate materials, guidance and feedback to learners. Our findings show that the students see the first part of this assumption as optimistic but they expressed negative views about using AI applications for assessment. This finding differs from that supporting the use of AI for student assessment as well [e.g. 8, 12].

HEIs must responsibly monitor the development of AI and need to be proactive in monitoring and governing the use of Generative AI tools, as they present both challenges and opportunities. The acceleration of research in this area as a result of recent technological advances is highlighted [28]. Academics must harness the potential of AI to transform higher education and contribute to the development of new skills for graduates.

To evaluate the effects of AI in higher education [11], and to understand user experiences and perceptions [29], more interdisciplinary and transdisciplinary research [30] and evaluation are needed.

6 Conclusion

This study investigated how AI is currently being applied across higher education and its potential future evolution and impact on the teaching and learning process from the students' point of view. The findings of this study highlight the transformative potential of Generative AI technologies in higher education. The study presents key themes identified using the Delphi technique, including opportunities and barriers from business students' point of view. The findings presented here can serve as a research agenda for future research and the academic community to identify research priorities and gaps in this field.

The findings suggest that future higher education should use Generative AI as a tool that simplifies routine activities and enables rapid data analysis, offers many up-to-date information resources, and new interactive forms and learning methods, and brings students support 24/7. For HEIs, it is important to adapt and embrace the use of AI tools in a way that supports student learning and prepares them for the challenges of a dynamically developing digital world. The study also discussed the outcomes for academics and practitioners and proposed a future research agenda to examine the ongoing shift driven by rapid AI implementation in education.

Limitations

The findings presented here do not represent the views on all current and rapidly developed applications of Generative AI. Another limitation could be connected with the context of this study, the Czech Republic and April 2024. Lastly, the Delphi method represents a qualitative research approach, and its results cannot be generalized on a statistical basis.

Acknowledgments. This study is supported by Visegrad Fund project No. 22410227.

Disclosure of Interests. Author has no competing interests to declare that are relevant to the content of this article.

References

1. Bobula, M.: Generative Artificial Intelligence (AI) in higher education: a comprehensive review of challenges, opportunities, and implications. J. Learn. Dev. High. Educ. **30**, 1–27 (2024)
2. Djokic, I., Milićević, N., Djokic, N., Malcic, B., Kalas, B.: Students' perceptions of the use of artificial intelligence in educational services. Amfiteatru Economic **26**(65), 294–310 (2024)
3. Lim, W.M., Gunasekara, A., Pallant, J.L., Pallant, J.I., Pechenkina, E.: Generative AI and the future of education: Ragnarök or reformation? A paradoxical perspective from management educators. Int. J. Manag. Educ. **21**, 100790 (2023)
4. Michel-Villarreal, R., Vilalta-Perdomo, E., Salinas-Navarro, D.E., Thierry-Aguilera, R., Gerardou, F.S.: Challenges and opportunities of generative AI for higher education as explained by ChatGPT. Educ. Sci. **13**, 856 (2023)
5. OpenAI. https://openai.com/. Accessed 30 Aug 2024
6. Crawford, J., Cowling, M., Allen, K.: Leadership is needed for ethical ChatGPT: character, assessment, and learning using artificial intelligence (AI). J. Univ. Teach. Learn. Pract. **20**(3), 1–21 (2023)
7. European Commission (2024). Shaping Europe's digital future, AI Act. https://digital-strategy.ec.europa.eu/en/policies/regulatory-framework-ai. Accessed 30 Aug 2024
8. Choi, H.J., Hickman, E.K., Monaham, B.M., Schwarz, D.: ChatGPT goes to law school. J. Legal Educ. **387** (2022)
9. Sullivan, M., Kelly, A., McLaughlan, P.: ChatGPT in higher education: considerations for academic integrity and student learning. J. Appl. Learn. Teach. **6**(1), 31–40 (2023)

10. Jsic. Joint Information Systems Committee. Students perception of generative AI. https://www.jisc.ac.uk/reports/student-perceptions-of-generative-ai?utm_medium=social&utm_source=twitter&utm_campaign=ncai&utm_content=. Accessed 30 Aug 2024
11. Chiu, T.K.F.: Future research recommendations for transforming higher education with generative AI. Comput.d Educ. Artif. Intell. **6**, 100197 (2024)
12. Slimi, Z.: The impact of artificial intelligence on higher education: an empirical study. Eur. J. Educ. Sci. **10**(1), 17–33 (2023)
13. Karimi, H., Khawaja, S.: The impact of artificial intelligence on higher education in England. Creat. Educ. **14**, 2405–2415 (2023)
14. Oxford University: Generative AI: the potential of AI in education. What does Claude* say? https://www.it.ox.ac.uk/article/generative-ai-opportunities-and-challenges. Accessed 15 Sep 2024
15. The University of Texas at San Antonio: Generative AI, Teaching and Learning. https://provost.utsa.edu/academicinnovation/artificial-intelligence/. Accessed 15 Sep 2024
16. Wilfrid Laurier University: Teaching excellence and innovation. Generative AI in Teaching and Learning. https://researchcentres.wlu.ca/teaching-and-learning/building/generative-ai-in-teaching-and-learning.html. Accessed 15 Sep 2024
17. Complete College America: CCA's Resources for Generative AI and Student Success. https://completecollege.org/resource/cca-releases-new-resources-for-ai/. Accessed 31 May 2024
18. Green, A.R.: The Delphi technique in educational research. SAGE Open **4**(2), 1–8 (2014)
19. Linstone, H.A., Turoff, M.: The Delphi Method. Techniques and Applications. Addison-Wesley, Reading, MA (1975)
20. Nevo, D., Chan. D.Y.A.: Delphi study of knowledge management systems: scope and requirements. Inf. Manag. **44**(6), 583–597 (2007)
21. Geisser, F.M., Alschuler, N.K., Hutchinson, R.: A Delphi study to establish important aspects of ethic review. Dimensions REC Rev. **6**(1), 21–24 (2011)
22. Humphrey-Murto, S., de Wit, M.: The delphi method - more research please. J. Clin. Epidemiol. **106**, 136–139 (2019)
23. Pollard, C., Pollard, R.: Research priorities in educational technology: a Delphi study. J. Res. Technol. Educ. **37**(2), 145–160 (2005)
24. Cesco, S., Zara, V., De Toni, A.F., Lugli, P., Evans, A., Orzes, Q.: The future challenges of scientific and technical higher education. Tuning J. High. Educ. **8**(2), 85–117 (2021)
25. Egerová, D., Kutlák, J., Eger, L.: Millennial job seekers' expectations: how do companies respond? Econ. Sociol. **14**(1), 46–60 (2021)
26. Eurostat: Digital skills. ICT users. Individuals' level of digital skills (from 2021 onwards). https://ec.europa.eu/eurostat/databrowser/view/isoc_sk_dskl_i21/default/table?lang=en&category=isoc.isoc_sk.isoc_sku. Accessed 15 Dec 2023
27. Chráska, M.: Metody pedagogického výzkumu. [Methods in education research] Grada, Prague (2007)
28. López-Chila, R., Lierena-Izquierdo, J., Sumba-Nacipucha, N., Cueva-Estrada, J.: Artificial intelligence in higher education: an analysis of existing bibliometrics. Educ. Sci. **14**(1), 47 (2024)
29. Villarreal, M.N., Vilalt-Perdomo, E., Salimas-Navarro, D.E., Thiery-Aguilera, R., Gerardou, F.S.: Challenges and opportunities of generative AI for higher education as explained by ChatGPT. Educ. Sci. **13**, 856 (2023)
30. Zhang, K., Aslan, A.B.: AI technologies for education: recent research & future directions. Comput. Educ. Artif. Intell. **2**, 100025 (2021)

AI in Didactics in the Light of Applications, Students' Acceptance and Practical Recommendations

Katarzyna Potyrała[1(✉)] and John Oversby[2]

[1] Cracow University of Technology, Kraków, Poland
katarzyna.potyrala@pk.edu.pl
[2] Science Education Futures, London, UK

Abstract. The main aim of the research was to show the gap in previous research on the practical application of AI in science education and the acceptance by University students of AI-assisted learning in a world of growing application possibilities. The authors focused on a review of the reports, with particular emphasis on research conducted in 2021–2024 about the possibilities and effectiveness of the use of AI in subject education. The analyses carried out showed that researchers mostly consider the technical aspects of AI in education. The second group of articles discusses factors that enhance students' motivation to learn and their active participation in cognitive processes. However, most tools are not conducive to the development of students' metacognitive competences and reinforce the behaviorist model based on instructional teaching and reinforcement (most often positive). The reflection on students' learning experiences with AI-enhanced learning was supported by surveys conducted among 60 students of science and technical faculties. The results indicate a low level of acceptance of the use of AI in secondary and higher education by students of natural sciences.

Keywords: AI · science education · students' acceptance · literature review

1 Introduction

Artificial intelligence (AI) has dominated the discourse on the future of education. AI is concerned with computer-based technology that can reason, learn, and act in such a way that would normally require human intelligence. It is also constructed to analyze large data sets that would be difficult or even impossible for humans to analyze. Artificial intelligence inputs are vast sets of data, using algorithms to look for patterns and relationships that can be incorporated into future algorithms. At present, it seems that artificial intelligence operates in narrow areas, such as language, or pictures. Google Search is one form that is narrow. There are others such as autocorrect.

Teaching and learning are highly complex, and are at present, dominated by human-centered processes. The objects of teaching, often embodied in published syllabuses, and embedded in the types of questions set in examinations, are constructed by humans. Responses to questions in such examinations do follow patterns and could be interpreted

Ł. Tomczyk (Ed.): NMP 2024, CCIS 2537, pp. 228–247, 2025.
https://doi.org/10.1007/978-3-031-95627-0_16

using AI, and personal feedback given to learners using AI generated text. However, bypassing the human teacher would mean that their teaching would not benefit from seeing such feedback, and their relationship with the learner would not be enhanced by engaging with this feedback. This example indicates a limit to the undoubted benefits of AI here. As another example, a recently published piece of research by The Endowment Education Foundation (evaluation report by Roy, et al.) targeted at 11–12 year old science students claimed 'lesson and resource preparation time spent by the ChatGPT group was 69% of the time spent by the non-GenAI group'. The resources referred to were quizzes and tests. Further details are available in the extensive evaluators' report [29].

Many questions are asked about how to critically reflect on the possibilities of using AI tools to achieve better results without excessive fear for the future of the teaching profession and the future of humanity in general [16]. The researchers ask, among others the following questions: How do we make informed, intentional decisions about the role of AI in the classroom? How can students develop critical relationships with these tools? How can imaginative applications of AI technologies enhance learning? (https://aipedagogy.org/about/)

Zhai et al. prepared a review of artificial intelligence (AI) in Education from 2010 to 2020, focusing mainly on the issues of applications of selected AI tool capabilities in the organization of education, communication and evaluation of teaching and learning [37]. Some researchers reach further in these analyses, to the early 90s of the twentieth century. Fan, Zheng & Jiao reviewed research from 2011 to 2022, highlighting the integration of educational theories with AI-based online learning [11]. Later papers advocate future directions of research that seek to deepen our understanding of the dynamic relationships between AI and education [4]. All researchers emphasize the need for more empirical research to check the real effects of AI applications in education.

2 Examples of AI Opportunities for Practical Applications

General solutions and tips for teachers-beginners in AI tools, have been proposed by scientists from Harvard University as part of the "AI Pedagogy" project. According to them, the most important values in the work of an AI-assisted teacher are: critical (e.g., they do not assume that AI tools are necessarily a value-add or that they belong in all educational settings); ethical (they contextualize the use of these tools, considering their impact on representation, bias, the environment, etc.); evolving (they aim to keep this collection of resources up to date with the latest technological and pedagogical developments); and experimental (we are all learning). No one has all the answers, experimenting (they aim to continuously experiment, iterate, reassess, and revise), imaginative (they treat generative AI technologies as the potential to push our thinking and expand our communication in interesting ways, inclusive (they aim to spotlight a diversity of educators and forms of knowledge). The authors guide potential users through possible artificial intelligence applications and familiarize them with the basics of their use in a very general way.

This preliminary analysis of the research subject literature underlined that the most of the articles are about knowledge about AI and tools without examples of their concrete use in school or academic practice in relation to various subjects of education.

What we are interested in (subject didactics) is most often related to gamification and mobile learning (m-learning), especially in science education. For example, we can learn how game elements affect the motivation of students, and how the interaction between students and a mobile app for Science Education can promote students' scientific competences development and self-regulated learning. To achieve this, adaptive gamification as an alternative approach was used [38] and a learning approach was designed, Inquiry-Based Science Education and the BSCS 5E (teaching model for Science Education designed by the Biological Sciences Curriculum Study [34]. The main assumptions of these studies were based on confirmed opinions that: 1/ motivation is crucial in science education and acquiring scientific knowledge and skills [14] and connection between motivation to engage in science and academic performance [32]. Even though motivation towards science can impact the learning process [31], it is essential to note that various factors, like personal interests, personality traits, and cognitive style, can contribute to individual motivation [32]; 2/ a grounded, participatory, and user-centered approach will be the best way to develop competences in the field of natural sciences what was revealed through the teachers' conceptions about the potential impact of the conceptualized mobile app to provide a comprehensive and practical Science Education learning and to enhance students' scientific competences development and self-regulated learning [34].

Data analysis allowed inference about the expected adequacy of the proposed learning approach and its potential to promote a comprehensive and practical approach in Science Education, by allowing exploration of correlated digital educational resources, namely animations, games, simulations, quizzes and information areas. Furthermore, the teachers' answers also allowed inferences about the expected adequacy of the proposed learning approach to promote the student's scientific knowledge, skills and attitudes development [34].

The research focused on motivation [38] showcased the results of a quantitative semi-experimental investigation into the impact of adaptive gamification on learner motivation and perceptions in science education. The findings offer new perspectives and enhance the utilization of adaptive gamification. Authors discovered valuable insights into how to customize gamification, particularly by demonstrating that the program user typology is one of the most relevant approaches for identifying user preferences regarding game elements. However, in this implementation, the adaptation of game elements and learning strategies was not solely based on a single user type. They recognized that motivations can be fluid and may change during gameplay. Therefore, the foundation for adaptation was the learner's profile rather than a static adaptation that classifies individuals solely based on their user profiles after an initial selection, as proposed in the previous literature.

Remote learning platforms have a high motivational, participatory and self-regulatory potential, provided that they take into account various factors related to the learning process. An example of good practice in this area is implementing e-learning modules. The proposed (by the authors) AI-EELF method introduces multiple learning models to enhance teaching quality and predict the student learning style. The experimental results show that the proposed AI-EELF achieves high performance, prediction ratio in determining students' learning style and improves teaching quality compared to other existing methods educational platforms [12].

According to Sibel Erduran too little attention in science education concerns how AI is transforming the nature of science (NOS) itself and what such transformation implies for the education of young children [10]. For education, it is critical to ask what AI-informed NOS is, what skills it demands of learners, and how schools can aim to achieve them. The current reports on subject didactics in the field of science do not provide many examples of purposeful applications. We come across surveys on the potential of Artificial Intelligence (AI) Chatbots in enhancing digital dialogue for students [2] or study examined the factors influencing accounting students' acceptance of AI in learning [23].

Analyzed research mostly focuses on the technical aspects of the use of AI in education. The second group of articles concerns factors that strengthen students' motivation to learn and their active participation in their own cognitive processes. Most tools (including mobile applications) are not conducive to the development of students' metacognitive competences and consolidate the behavioral model based on instructional teaching and reinforcement (most often positive). There is a lack of research on actual learning (understanding, questioning, problem-solving, reasoning, experimenting) in relation to specific subject content in AI-aided science education.

3 AI-Aided Science Learning

Quick finding and creation of information by AI (artificial intelligence), visualization of the structure of various structures in AR (augmented reality), immersion in space achieved through the use of VR (virtual reality), launching gamification processes, independent creation of content and exchanging it with participants of social groups around the world – these are just some of the situations in which the reward system is activated, and From here, it is only a step to create permanent traces in memory, i.e. learning. However, it should be mentioned that such mechanisms are questioned for several reasons.

As physiologists write, tolerance to the rewarding effect develops over time and, consequently, in order to be able to achieve the same expected effect, the dose or amount of the "motivational" factor must be increased. Such disturbed, addictive behavior becomes a habit that can later take the form of addiction, for example to the Internet [35]. The results of the research confirm that the constantly stimulated reward system by uncontrolled contact with the Internet can lead to addictions, the mechanism of which is similar to addictions to food, drugs, shopping or gambling.

Learning means constantly weaving many connections between the student's thinking structure and information, which are not a simple relationship between stimuli and reaction. In the act of learning, the student needs the help of others to overcome the mechanisms of confrontation between the unknown and the new. It is a very complex process and the belief that a reward (positive reinforcement) received for a well-solved task means educational success (lasting and operative knowledge) is very illusory. André Giordan, like Edgar Morin in his "Introduction to Complex Thinking"[1], believes that the act of learning is understood as a whole that gives the individual the ability to "meet the

[1] This concept, the first formulation of which is found in the book *Science with Consciousness* (1982), expresses a form of thinking that accepts the interweaving of each field of thought and transdisciplinary. The term complexity is understood in the sense of its etymology "complexes", which means "that which is woven together" (source: Wikipedia).

challenge of the complexity of the world" and only when confronted with the reality of everyday life do we verify the value of the "rewards" received for certain tasks that exist outside the broader context [13]. Hence the unambiguous indication for problem-based and situational learning with the use of AI.

Learning is mental activity. Everything is "a matter of interaction," André Giordan tells us [13]. The student is a true master of the game, he must be the "inventor" of his learning, the reward for him can be overcoming his own limitations, facing a difficulty, getting out of his comfort zone and experiencing something new. In this process, the emotional dimension takes on great importance. The student must be "concerned about his confidence" and constantly verify it, but he must not feel threatened by the loss of a potential reward. True knowledge must be contextual and "biodegradable". These processes seem to be still beyond the reach of pedagogical research.

Research clearly indicates that metacognition has two dimensions: metacognitive knowledge, which indicates what learners know about learning in terms of their own cognitive abilities, specific tasks and knowledge of available and appropriate strategies, and metacognitive regulation, which indicates what learners do in terms of learning, in terms of monitoring and controlling their own cognitive processes. Pedagogical reflection focuses too little on these issues, especially in the field of natural sciences. There is a lack of indicators describing metacognitive competences, i.e. specific descriptions of skills and abilities that individuals use to monitor, control and reflect on their own learning and thinking processes in terms of specific educational content. By developing these indicators, individuals could become more aware of their own learning and thinking processes and improve their ability to regulate and control them, and the reward system would be more coupled with awareness of learning goals and outcomes.

4 Methodology of the Research

The main aim of the reflection was to show the gap in the research on the practical application of AI in education. The specific goals were focused around: analysis of AI in relation to secondary and higher school science education and the methodology of the research carried out in this area, specify the claims made for AI in secondary and academic education, analyze the experiences of natural and technical students in relation to the use of AI in teaching and learning practices and their acceptance of the use of AI in education.

Research main problems was following: What are the students' experiences of using AI in education in the light of pedagogical research? Detailed problems: 1/ What AI tools do students use at different educational stages to learn different subjects (with particular emphasis on science)? 2/To what extent do AI-based educational practices support the learner in the learning process? 3/What is the level of acceptance of students of technical and natural sciences faculties regarding the use of AI in formal and informal education?

The main hypothesis is as follows: The AI in education research is carried out in the same way in extremely limited areas with very limited topics that work linearly with older and brighter students. This is why there is so little evidence. It is also why there is unlikely to be more general evidence of effectiveness and students' knowledge of the possibilities of using these tools in learning.

Detailed hypotheses: 1/ Science and technology students do not use AI tools in both their learning and research work because teachers at the secondary school level have not equipped them with the right skills needed to approach AI creatively. 2/ Selected school and academic practices in the form of the use of games and learning on online platforms do not introduce students to critical thinking and multilateral learning with the use of AI. 3/ Students' level of knowledge and previous learning experiences in the use of AI in education are related to students' level of acceptance of AI.

In search of an answer to the research question, non-reactive research methods were used, focused mainly on the analysis of the content of various messages about the learning process with AI during subject education. As Earl Babbie [3] points out, the forms of communication can include books, websites, online platforms and the parts of which they are composed or collections composed of them. Possible units of analysis were scientific articles, educational computer games, e-learning platforms and bookmarks on websites. Content analysis as a way of observation required a thoughtful use of "what" is communicated. The analysis of data collected by this method, as in the case of other methods, addresses the questions of "why" and "with what result" [3]. It was assumed that the method used is quasi-analytical and concerns social products that enable the understanding of the main mechanisms of learning and communication of people in order to improve the educational process.

The authors focused on a review of the most quoted reports, with particular emphasis on research conducted in 2021–2022 and 2023–2024 about the possibilities and effectiveness of the use of AI in subject education.

In addition, in a group of 60 students (technic fields of study and science field of study), a diagnostic survey was carried out using the technique of a questionnaire (Likert scale) consisting of 30 statements, to which the student could respond by marking the answer on a 5-point scale (yes – rather yes – I don't know – rather no – no). Statements in the survey questionnaire are presented in the Table 1. This scale is an example of an ordinal scale, because the answers have order, but the distances between successive answers are not strictly measurable (e.g., the difference between "no" and "rather not" is not the same as the difference between "rather yes" and "yes"). The design of the research tool was inspired by the guidelines of Venkatesh, Morris, Davis & Davis [36] on the model of student acceptance testing of AI-assisted learning. Statements in the survey questionnaire are presented in the Table 1.

The questionnaire statements cover general applications of AI (e.g. health, education, industry), specific AI technologies (e.g. neural networks, ChatGPT), attitudes towards AI (e.g. ethical use of AI, its impact on education), and the experience of AI users in education.

Statements about general uses of AI (2, 3, 5, 6) focus on the global impact of AI on lives, including education, which fits with the general topic of the questionnaire.

Statements about education and AI technology (10, 11, 12, 13) focus on the use of AI in the context of teaching and personalization of the learning process, which is in line with the main theme of the study.

Statements about their experiences with AI in education (14, 15, 16, 17) explore respondents' attitudes towards the use of AI in education and their ability to critically evaluate the technology.

Table 1. Statements in the survey questionnaire

1/ In secondary school, a teacher explained the possibilities of using AI when learning a science subject.
2/ AI is dynamically changing many aspects of life, affecting, among other things, the professional sphere
3/ AI is dynamically changing many aspects of life, including supporting the process of learning natural sciences.
4/ Artificial intelligence (AI) encompasses a wide range of technologies and computer systems capable of performing tasks that typically require human intelligence, including reasoning, learning, and perception.
5/ In healthcare, AI improves diagnostics by automating the analysis of medical images, and in industry, it optimizes manufacturing processes and improves safety.
6/ In social services, AI increases operational efficiency, although systems that support rather than replace human interaction are preferred.
7/ In education, AI can be used to personalize learning, tailoring content to the individual needs of students, including students with disabilities.
8/ Neural networks are computational models inspired by the work of the human brain, designed to recognize patterns and solve problems through data-driven learning.
9/ In the era of the digital society and AI, it is important to learn critical thinking, as there is a risk of conflict between trust in the teacher and AI tools.
10/ ChatGPT as a tool to enrich the learning process can be used at any stage of education, both by teachers and students, regardless of their level of technological advancement.
11/ ChatGPT can be used to support teachers in the preparation of various teaching materials, such as lesson plans, outlines, and tasks for students.
12/ ChatGPT can support the creation of questions for quizzes, tests, and true-or-false tasks, help create creative projects, and act as a consultant in the organization of teamwork.
13/ To ensure equal access to AI development, tools similar to ChatGPT should be incorporated into the educational process, and teachers and students must internalize the principles of responsible and ethical use of these technologies.
14/ The experience I have gained in the field of learning with AI goes beyond the functions of a text translator and a tool that makes it easier to find answers to questions.
15/ I use ChatGPT to prepare written works and I usually don't check the sources of information.
16/ I assume that GPT can make mistakes or generate inaccurate answers.
17/ The use of ChatGPT can be considered plagiarism.
18/ One of the most important tools that have changed modern education is online collaboration platforms
19/ Apps like Kahoot! or Quizlet, allow teachers to create quizzes, games, and other forms of knowledge testing in an engaging way.
20/ Learning management systems such as Moodle or Google Classroom are becoming an indispensable part of modern education and are tailored to the individual needs of students.

(*continued*)

Table 1. (*continued*)

21/ LMS (Learning Management Systems) offer teachers the ability to create, store, and manage learning materials in one place. Students can access online lessons, assignments, and quizzes, enabling remote learning and self-retrieval.
22/ Systems based on advanced AI algorithms can adapt the educational material to the individual needs of the student, analyzing their progress and learning difficulties.
23/ Teachers in secondary school use selected applications and online platforms to individualize the learning process of students.
24/ Teachers in secondary school use selected applications and online platforms to visualize natural phenomena and processes.
25/ Teachers in secondary school use AI and select online applications and platforms to create realistic simulations of biological, chemical or physical processes, allowing students to experiment interactively.
26/ Apps often used by teachers, such as Google Earth and Explore.org, allow students to virtually travel to nature reserves and observe animals in their natural habitat. This allows students to better understand issues related to biodiversity and environmental protection.
27/ I know the possibilities of using BioDigital Human or Anatomy 3D from biology lessons at secondary school.
28/ I know the capabilities of AI tools in planning research work and the implementation of its stages.
29/ As a student, I participated in pedagogical experiments in which an AI-assisted experimental class achieved better results in a science subject than a control class learning in a traditional way.
30/ Individually, I try to get to know AI tools because they can help me learn science subjects.

Statements about specific AI applications and tools (8, 9, 20, 22, 25) address more specific technological aspects such as neural networks, learning management systems (LMS), and learning support tools.

The basis was 3 elements that make up the technology user acceptance model (according to Venkatesh, Morris, Davis & Davis [36]: 1/ individual reaction to using information technology, 2/ intention to use information technology, 3/ actual use of information technology. They correspond to the following statements of the questionnaire: 1/ 2,3,8,9,10,13,17,18,20; 2/ 4,5,6,7,11,12,19,21,22; 3/ 1,14,15, 16, 23, 24,25,26,27, 28,29,30.

5 Research Results

The analysis of source materials allows us to identify the best described practices in the use of AI in science education. These include, mainly:

a. Personalize educating with AI

AI-enhanced personalized learning for the natural sciences is used in some study examples. These research examined students' development in science courses including biology, chemistry, and physics using artificial intelligence algorithms. AI algorithms tailored learning resources to each student's unique requirements, accounting for both their areas of strength and growth. Teaching was more effective because students were specifically guided to instructional materials that corresponded with their skill level. Findings: The significance of individualized approaches in education is demonstrated by the higher science test scores and increased learning engagement of students utilizing personalized AI systems [17].

b. AI in biology and ecology education

Artificial intelligence is used in biology education, as demonstrated by the study's examples of AI-based simulations used to educate ecology. These research taught and learned ecology through computer simulations powered by artificial intelligence. Through the use of interactive technologies, the students were able to model natural systems like food chains, water circulation, and biogeochemical cycles. Results: The simulations enhanced student engagement, helped them grasp complex ecological ideas, and allowed them to put what they had learned into practice. AI made it possible to create dynamic, lifelike virtual settings that were not possible in a conventional classroom [28, 30, 1].

c. AI in chemistry education

Examples of the study use AI-powered virtual labs to teach chemistry. Through the creation of AI-powered virtual laboratories, these research have made it possible for students to conduct online chemical experiments. The AI system tracked the students' behavior while they conducted experiments, providing real-time corrections and recommendations. Results: Chemical experiments that would have been challenging or impossible to do in more conventional settings can now be carried out safely and interestingly thanks to artificial intelligence. The pupils' interest in and comprehension of chemical processes improved [33, 24, 9].

d. The use of AI in physics teaching and learning

AI-powered interactive physics learning systems are used in some of the experiments. These studies examined how AI-based learning systems can be used to study physics, specifically mechanics, thermodynamics, and optics. After evaluating the students' responses, the AI systems modified the questions' level of difficulty and gave them instant feedback. Findings: Through individualized instruction, students who utilized AI-assisted learning platforms demonstrated improved exam scores and a deeper comprehension of challenging physics concepts [26].

e. The use of AI in assessing and analyzing student achievements

Studies that use AI-based assessment systems for scientific teaching are given as examples. This type of study concentrated on assessing students' work in scientific courses using AI-based techniques. Students' responses to both closed-ended and open-ended questions were examined by the AI systems, which found mistakes that might point to a lack of knowledge of important ideas. Findings: AI technologies in result analysis made it possible to evaluate students' development more quickly and accurately, which let teachers better tailor the curriculum to each student's needs [19].

f. AI in creating interactive learning tasks

Examples of the studies applied AI-generated interactive questions for science subjects. In this kind of study, artificial intelligence was used to generate interactive questions and tasks for science students. AI could create questions tailored to the student's level, taking into account their previous answers and level of proficiency. Results: The AI system successfully adapted the tasks to the level of students, which increased their motivation to learn and improved their results in tests. By dynamically matching tasks, students were less stressed and more engaged [7].

g. AI in the creation of adaptive learning materials

Examples of the studies applied adaptive learning systems in science education using AI. The studies concerned the use of AI-based adaptive systems in environmental education. These systems analyzed the progress of the learners and, based on this, provided personalized learning materials that responded to their learning needs and difficulties. Results: Students using such systems achieved better results in science subjects and also showed higher levels of engagement in learning [8].

A total of 50 source texts on research on the use of AI in science education were analyzed. The number of studies devoted to the above issues (a-g) is presented in Fig. 1.

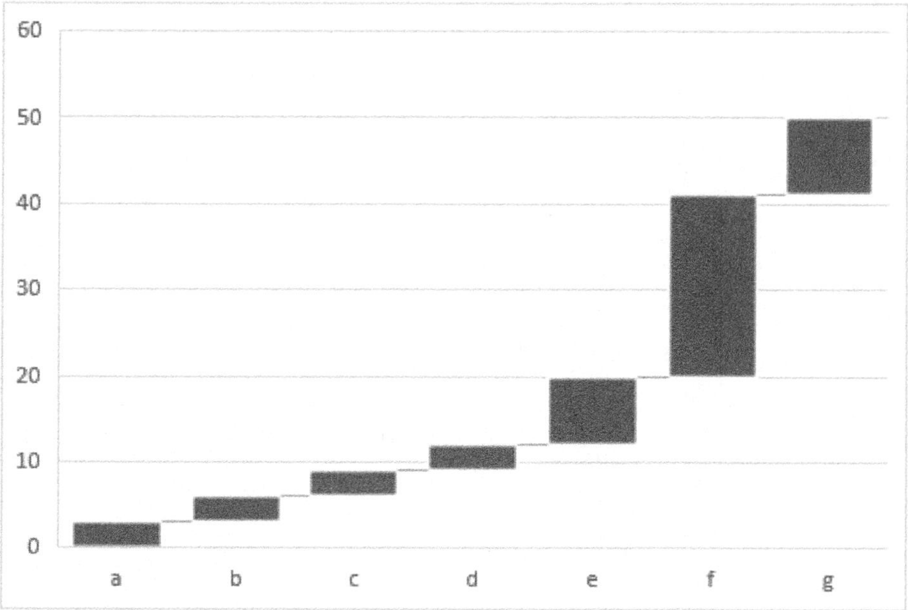

Fig. 1. Number of analyzed research carried out in 2023–2024 in seven thematic areas: a- Personalize educating with AI, b-AI in biology and ecology education, c-AI in chemistry education, d-The use of AI in physics teaching and learning, e-The use of AI in assessing and analyzing student achievements, f-AI in creating interactive learning tasks, g-AI in the creation of adaptive learning materials.

The figures are due to the availability of the research conducted in 2023–2024 in the given thematic scopes (a-g).

Most of the research conducted in 2023–2024 was related to interactive tasks for students created with the use of AI (Fig. 1). This applies to both tasks posted on online platforms and those that are elements of educational games.

The results of the survey are presented in Fig. 2 and Fig. 3.

A comparison of the results of the research (Fig. 2) allows us to conclude that students can see connections between the development of AI and their professional sphere (statement 2), but they do not associate the possibilities of AI with the process of learning science subjects (statement 3), perhaps because teachers in secondary school did not test such possibilities with them (statement 1).

Students have a general knowledge of AI (statement 4) and its impact on improving diagnostics, automating medical image analysis, and in industry optimizing production processes (statement 5), but it should be expected from their answers that this knowledge is acquired on their own, not in class (statements 29 and 30).

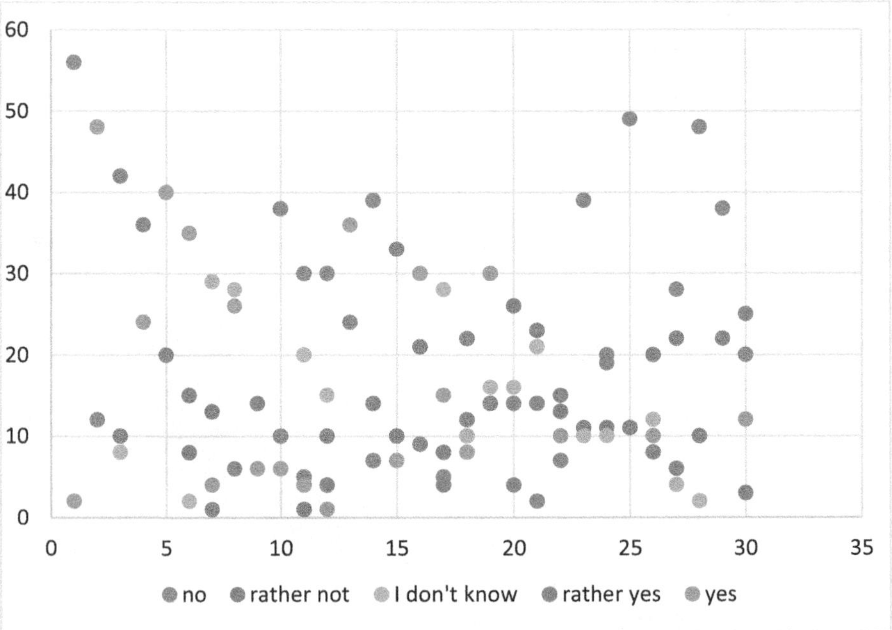

Fig. 2. Overall results of the survey

Interestingly, students participating in the research (students in the field of technical and natural sciences) do not know the capabilities of AI tools in planning research work and the implementation of its stages (statement 28, similar results were obtained in focus interviews). In addition, in the opinion of students, teachers in secondary school do not use AI tools and selected applications and online platforms to create realistic simulations of biological, chemical or physical processes, which would allow students to experiment interactively and deepen their understanding of natural processes (statements 25–27), students are also unconvinced about the use of online applications and platforms in the teaching process in the context of learning (statements 23–24). This is probably the reason for the strongly divided opinions of students about systems based on advanced AI and LMS algorithms, which can adapt educational material to the individual needs of the student, analyzing his or her progress and learning difficulties (statement 21–22).

We noted (statement 19) familiarity with applications such as Kahoot! or Quizlet, in the context of teachers creating quizzes, games and other forms of checking knowledge in a way that engages students (in focus interviews, students pointed out that these simple and ready-made applications are mainly used by primary school teachers), while most students are not convinced that this is conducive to the learning process on an individual basis (statement 20).

Over 60% of the surveyed students believe that online collaboration platforms have changed the educational landscape (statement 18), and during focus group interviews they expressed positive opinions mainly about those academic online platforms that engage students in role-playing games and are not only focused on lecture slides and evaluation tasks. The students emphasized that the platforms are not connected to AI tools.

The students' experience in learning with AI does not go beyond the functions of a text translator and a tool that facilitates searching for answers to questions (88% of responses regarding statement 14 and statements during the focus study).

More than half of the students participating in the research do not know that the use of ChatGPT can be considered plagiarism (statement 17), although they use ChatGPT to prepare written works, usually without checking the sources of information (statement 15). At the same time, most are aware that ChatGPT can make mistakes or generate inaccurate answers (statement 16). All students expressed the opinion that in order to ensure equal access to AI development, tools similar to ChatGPT should be incorporated into the educational process, and teachers and students must assimilate the principles of responsible and ethical use of these technologies (statement 13, answers rather yes:24, yes:36).

There were mostly negative responses or no opinions on the issue of statements 12 and 11, which means that students do not know whether ChatGPT can support the teacher in preparing various forms and tools to activate students and help create creative projects or act as a consultant in the organization of teamwork. Rather, they see the risk of a conflict between trust in the teacher and AI tools (statement 9), while not seeing a threat to interpersonal relationships (statement 6). On more general issues, students are more divided, but most believe, mainly on the basis of popular science reports (which was emphasized in focus interviews), that ChatGPT should be seen as a tool to enrich the learning process, which can be used at any stage of education, both by teachers and students, regardless of their level of technological advancement (statement 10). At the same time, the lack of good educational practices and knowledge about AI (statement 8) does not allow most students to take a positive attitude towards the statement that AI can be used in education to personalize learning, adapting content to the individual needs of students, including students with disabilities (statement 7).

The results of the study also allowed us to look at the level of acceptance of the use of AI tools in education by students of technical and natural sciences fields of study. The acceptance rate of AI applications in education by students of technical and natural sciences faculties was based on the ratio of the number of positive responses to the total number of responses.

An acceptance rate score of 55.22% for technical students suggests that just over half of respondents show a positive attitude toward AI, but it's not an overwhelming majority. Most respondents don't reject AI, but not everyone accepts it (Fig. 3).

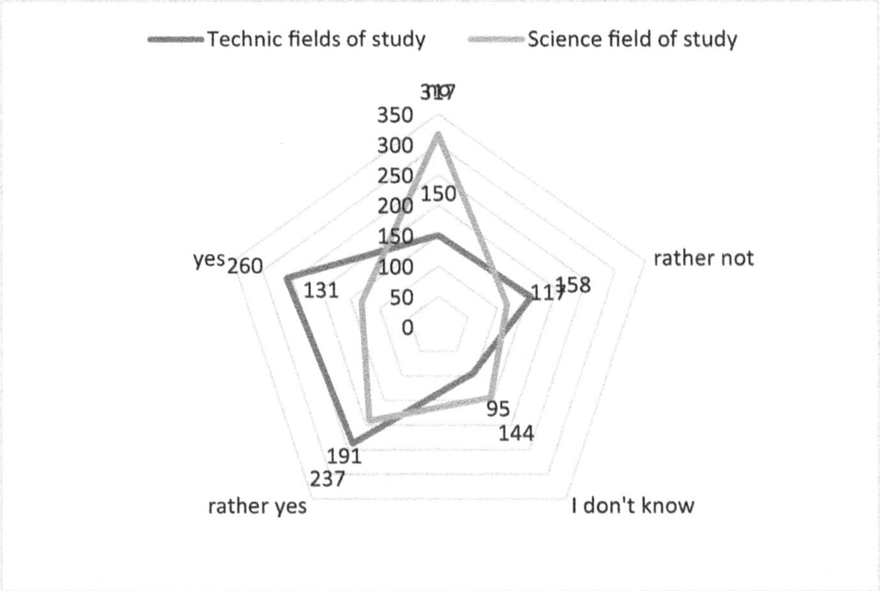

Fig. 3. The overall number of responses in the five categories in both study groups.

Positive answers ("yes" and "rather yes" answers combined) constitute 55.22% of the group of students of technical faculties. This means that just over half of respondents are willing to accept or have a positive attitude towards artificial intelligence. This may indicate that AI is viewed in a generally acceptable way, but there is no widespread enthusiastic consensus for full implementation. The answers "I don't know" and "rather not" suggest that a large proportion of people (in this case about 28%) do not yet have a clear opinion about AI or are unconvinced about its applications. This could be due to a lack of knowledge about AI, fears of implementing it, or the need to understand the technology better.

The answers ("no" + "rather not") indicate people who are clearly negative about AI. That's about 34% of respondents who may have concerns about its safety, impact on workplaces, privacy or ethics. The scale of acceptance of AI by technical students indicates that their acceptance of AI is still in development. 55.22% is a positive but not dominant proportion, suggesting that AI technology may be seen as promising but may require further education of students and developing confidence in its applications.

For science students, the AI acceptance rate in education in the broad sense is 35.78% (Fig. 3). This percentage of positive responses suggests that only slightly more than a third of respondents are positive about artificial intelligence. The vast majority of responses (64.22%) indicate a negative or neutral approach to AI, which may suggest concerns, distrust, or lack of knowledge about the technology. Therefore, it is worth conducting further analysis to understand what factors influence these results and to undertake appropriate educational or communication activities.

Although the general statements (e.g. 2, 5) deal with broad changes in society and technology, and the more specific statements (e.g. 8, 10, 14) deal with specific tools and experiences in education, which may be more related to the practical aspects of using AI, overall the statements proved to be consistent internally. The Cronbach coefficient alpha was calculated for the data obtained, which were treated as numbers that represent responses on a 5-point Likert scale, and then the internal consistency of these responses was checked. A score of $0.7 < \alpha < 0.8$ indicates average consistency between statements that measure the same construct which was confirmed by the analysis of correlations between the answers to individual statements (e.g. 14, 15, 16, 17 and 10, 11, 12, 13). The Pearson correlation coefficient between variables was used. A strong positive correlation ($r = 0.7$–0.9) was found between the variables in the statements 14 and 15, 10 and 11, 10 and 12, 11 and 12, and 13 and 17. A moderate positive correlation ($r = 0.4$–0.6) was recorded for statements 3 and 7, 25 and 26, 29 and 25, 25 and 26, 1 and 24, and 1 and 25.

Figure 4 has been used to interpretation and confirmation of the selected relationships described above. In particular, the analysis of correlations contributed to the verification of hypothesis number 3. The research has shown a significant correlation between students' level of knowledge and previous learning experiences in the use of AI in education to their level of acceptance of AI (e.g. the relationship between statements 7 and 14, 14 and 23).

It can be stated, that the respondents have the most negative perception of the actual use of AI tools in practice related to science learning (Fig. 5), which is related to their negative educational experiences in this area (or lack of any experience in this area). This further confirms hypothesis 1.

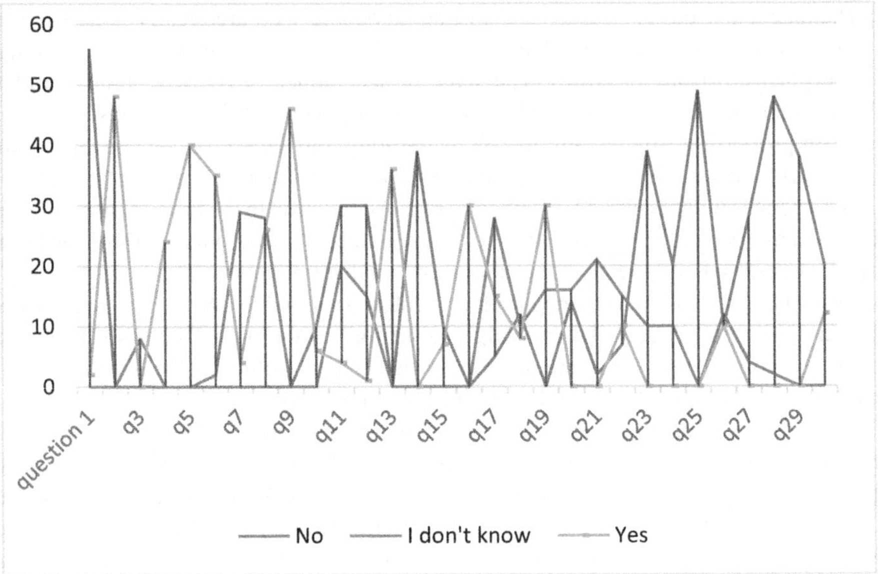

Fig. 4. Correlation ranges between statements (q1–30) in three groups of responses (No, I don't know, Yes). Number of respondents = 30.

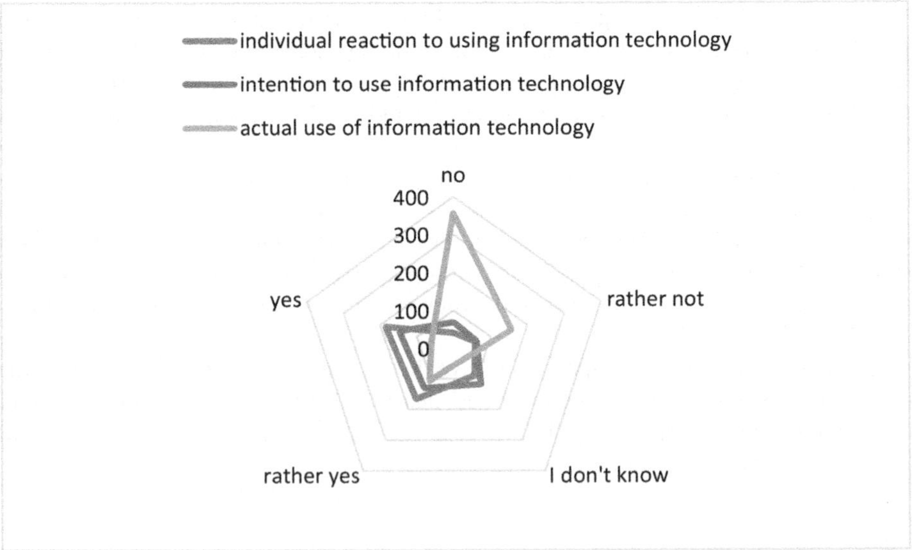

Fig. 5. Numerical indicators for statements assigned to the three elements of the acceptance model.

6 Discussion and the Conclusions

The research points to a diverse, but mostly limited, experience of students with the integration of AI in the teaching process and their diverse attitudes towards this technology, especially in the field of life sciences. On the one hand, many researchers emphasize the positive impact of AI on the learning process in science subjects. The use of intelligent learning systems that analyze student progress and tailor teaching materials to their individual needs can contribute to a more personalized approach to learning [20]. For example, AI-based applications can automatically deliver tasks of increasing difficulty depending on the student's progress, making learning more effective and pace-paced [6]. However, surveys show that students do not have such educational experiences either at the secondary or higher education level.

Students who have access to AI in the life sciences often indicate greater motivation to learn and a better understanding of difficult issues. Research shows that AI-based technologies help students visualize complex biological, chemical, or physical processes, which enables them to better absorb knowledge. An example is the use of computer simulations to learn chemical processes, which in a traditional way would be difficult to understand only on the basis of a textbook or lecture [15]. However, there is currently a lack of diverse educational practices in this area and accompanying scientific research.

On the other hand, there are also concerns among students about excessive trust in AI and its impact on the development of students' independence [27]. Pedagogical research indicates that some people, especially in secondary schools, may be too reliant on technology, making it difficult to develop critical thinking and self-solving skills. In the context of science subjects, which require both an analytical approach and an understanding of the principles governing nature, it is important that AI acts as a support rather than a substitute for the student's independent work. It seems that in recent years there has been a lack of research on the course of the teaching process in connection with the emergence of new educational tools and therefore there is a lack of purposeful and critical use of them.

Another important aspect is the issue of uncertainty and fear of too much automation of the educational process. Some students and teachers are concerned that AI may lead to a simplification of teaching, which will make them lose the chance to gain a deeper understanding of science subjects. Many people fear that AI will focus mainly on tests and tasks, not giving students enough space to develop research, experimental, or practical skills [21]. Despite these concerns, in our research we find the advantage of the use of interactive tasks and mobile applications focused on a specific result of students' activity and positive reinforcement, over the questioning and personalized use of learning tools.

The results indicate that the vast majority of people are not completely convinced of the advantages and possibilities of AI, which may be due to various factors confirmed by the literature on the subject of research.

1/ Lack of knowledge and understanding: Many people may not understand what artificial intelligence is and how it affects their lives. The answer "I don't know" in particular suggests that respondents may not have enough knowledge about AI to make an informed decision. They may find it difficult to assess its potential or risks, which is a common problem in the context of new technologies [5].

2/ Fears and distrust: Answers such as "no" and "rather no" may be due to concerns about AI. Often, people are afraid that technology may negatively affect their lives, e.g. by threatening their privacy, workplace or control over their own lives. Many people may also be wary of potential abuses related to the use of artificial intelligence [22].

3/ The importance of education about artificial intelligence [25]. The results show that there is a clear need for educational activities that can help increase the acceptance of AI in society. Here are some areas where education can play a key role:

a. Education on the basics of AI

To improve your understanding of AI, it is worth focusing on teaching the basic concepts and mechanisms that underpin AI. Many people don't know the definition of AI, its applications, or how it works. Educational programs can focus on: explaining what AI is, how it works and in what fields it can be used, especially from the point of view of shaping research and critical attitudes in the exact and natural sciences; making it easier to understand how AI differs from other technologies, such as automation or robotics, to avoid confusion and confusion between these concepts. This is especially important for students of non-technical faculties.

b. Counteracting the fear of the unknown

Fear and distrust of AI often stem from its perception as a "black box" – something unpredictable and uncontrollable. Educational programs should focus on: transparency of AI algorithms – how AI makes decisions, what data is used, and what mechanisms are built in to minimize the risk of errors; data security – increasing awareness of the principles of personal data protection in AI systems and methods of protection against abuse.

c. Showing the benefits of AI

Many people may find it difficult to see the practical benefits of AI in their daily lives. To increase acceptance, education should show how AI can support everyday life:

- applications in health – how AI helps diagnose diseases, analyze medical data, and create new therapies,
- applications in education – how AI supports teachers in personalizing learning and adapting educational materials to individual student needs and STEM educational standards [18],
- work applications – how AI can increase productivity and work efficiency, especially in routine tasks.

d. Inclusivity in AI education.

It is worth ensuring that AI education is available not only to specialists, but also to people (pupils, students) from different social backgrounds and different educational needs. An inclusive approach can involve: organizing workshops that will be available to students and teachers at all levels of education, creating educational materials in an accessible form, adapted to different levels of knowledge, popularizing learning and teaching using the possibilities of the latest technologies.

e. Social initiatives and communication

It is important to increase the presence of expert voices in the public debate that will be able to explain the benefits and potential risks of AI in the case of science education and allow teachers and students to express their concerns and questions, which can contribute to greater engagement and understanding of the topic. The result of 35.78% positive responses indicates that the acceptance of AI among the public is still at a relatively low level. To change this, it is crucial to invest in education that will help society better understand artificial intelligence, its potential, but also the challenges associated with its development. Focusing on transparency, benefits and safety, as well as spreading awareness across different groups in society, will help increase the acceptance of AI and its proper implementation in the future. In the context of the analysis of the results, 55.22% of positive responses are a good basis for further efforts to popularize and increase the acceptance of artificial intelligence in education.

7 Study Limitations and Recommendations for Future Research

In our research, we used the Research Rabbit tool to discover related articles, books, and other scholarly resources, based on pre-selected publications. This allowed the visualization of the network of links between different publications, authors and topics, which facilitated the management of large amounts of literature, as well as allowing for easier comparison of the results of different studies. However, we have encountered restrictions on access to full content, especially in the case of closed databases or paid publications. The article recommendations were accurate, but they did not always perfectly correspond to specific areas of research. Therefore, the choice of source material for analysis was dictated by the availability of English-language resources. In the end, we focused on only 50 thematically related articles.

The research sample (students of technical and natural sciences) was small due to the time limit of the research. That is why we recommend: a) repeating this investigation in other countries; b) collecting more data among younger adolescent learners; c) collecting data from teachers of adolescents and university to investigate what they know, especially about pedagogy.

Disclosure of Interests. The authors have no competing interests to declare that are relevant to the content of this article.

References

1. Alam, A.: Intelligence unleashed: an argument for AI-enabled learning ecologies with real world examples of today and a peek into the future. In: AIP Conference Proceedings, vol. 2717, no. 1. AIP Publishing, June 2023
2. Alwazzan, M.S.: Investigating the effectiveness of artificial intelligence chatbots in enhancing digital dialogue skills for students. Eur. J. Educ. Res. **13**(2), 573–584 (2024)
3. Babbie, E.: Podstawy badan społecznych. Wydawnictwo Naukowe PWN, Warszawa (2013)
4. Bandara, W., Senanayaka, S.: Use of artificial intelligence in education: a systematic review. In: International Research Conference on Smart Computing and Systems Engineering (SCSE), vol. 7, pp. 1–5 (2024)

5. Calo, R.: Artificial intelligence policy: a primer and roadmap. U. Bologna L. Rev. **3**, 180 (2018)
6. Chen, W., Lo, S.: The use of artificial intelligence in science education: a review of the literature. Educ. Tech. Res. Dev. **68**(4), 1771–1795 (2020)
7. Copur-Gencturk, Y., Li, J., Atabas, S.: Improving teaching at scale: can AI be incorporated into professional development to create interactive, personalized learning for teachers? Am. Educ. Res. J 00028312241248514 (2024)
8. Demartini, C.G., Sciascia, L., Bosso, A., Manuri, F.: Artificial intelligence bringing improvements to adaptive learning in education: a case study. Sustainability **16**(3), 1347 (2024)
9. Dutta, S., Ranjan, S., Mishra, S., Sharma, V., Hewage, P., Iwendi, C.: Enhancing educational adaptability: a review and analysis of AI-driven adaptive learning platforms. In: 4th International Conference on Innovative Practices in Technology and Management (ICIPTM), pp. 1–5, IEEE (2024, February)
10. Erduran S.: AI is transforming how science is done. Science education must reflect this change. Science **22**, 382 (2023). (6677):eadm9788. https://doi.org/10.1126/science.adm9788. Epub 2023 Dec 21. PMID: 38127735
11. Fan, O., Zheng, L., Jiao, P.: Artificial intelligence in online higher education: a systematic review of empirical research from 2011 to 2020. Educ. Inf. Technol. **27**, 7893–7925 (2022)
12. Fu, X., Lokesh Krishna, K., Sabitha, R.: Artificial intelligence applications with e-learning system for China's higher education platform. J. Interconnect. Netw. **22**(Supp02), 2143016 (2022)
13. Giordan, A.: Apprendre! Belin (1998)
14. Glynn, S.M., Brickman, P., Armstrong, N., Taasoobshirazi, G.: Science motivation questionnaire II: validation with science majors and nonscience majors. J. Res. Sci. Teach. **48**, 1159–1176 (2011)
15. Holmes, W., Bialik, M., Fadel, C.: Artificial Intelligence in Education: Promises and Implications for Teaching and Learning. Center for Curriculum Redesign, Boston (2019)
16. Karan, B., Angadi, G.R.: Potential risks of artificial intelligence integration into school education: a systematic review. Bull. Sci. Technol. Soc. **43**, 67–85 (2023)
17. Khan, R., Ghasempour, E.: A review of AI-enhanced personalized learning systems: implications for the learning sciences. In: Proceedings of the 18th International Conference of the Learning Sciences-ICLS 2024, pp. 1694–1697. International Society of the Learning Sciences (2024)
18. Kuźmińska-Sołśnia, B.: Competences of the modern teacher – the need for improvement in the era of artificial intelligence. Contin. Educ. Adults **125**(2), 155–172 (2024)
19. Liao, X., Zhang, X., Wang, Z., Luo, H.: Design and implementation of an AI-enabled visual report tool as formative assessment to promote learning achievement and self-regulated learning: an experimental study. Br. J. Edu. Technol. **55**(3), 1253–1276 (2024)
20. Luckin, R., Holmes, W., Griffiths, M., Forcier, L.B.: Intelligence Unbound: The Future of Uploaded and Machine Minds. MIT Press, Cambridge (2016)
21. McArthur, D., Lewis, A.: Leveraging artificial intelligence for education. J. Educ. Technol. Dev. Exchange **12**(3), 34–52 (2019)
22. Mularz, K.: Deepfake as a generator of fictitious content and real distrust. J. Media Stud. **25**(3), 45–67 (2024)
23. Musyaffi, A.M., Baxtishodovich, B.S., Afriadi, B., Hafeez, M., Adha, M.A., Wibowo, S.N.: New challenges of learning accounting with artificial intelligence: the role of innovation and trust in technology. Eur. J. Educ. Res. **13**(1), 183–195 (2024)
24. Nguyen, T., Sirichokcharoenkun, Y.: The limitations and potential of ChatGPT in chemistry education. J. Chem. Educ. **100**(12), 1234–1246 (2023)

25. Nowicka, E.: Artificial intelligence as a challenge for media education. Family Upbringing **31**(2/2024), 205–217 (2024). J.
26. Nurahman, A., et al.: Improving STEM literacy on the topic of organic solar cells through an ai-powered personalized learning platform: a case study of pre-physics teachers. In: Proceedings Series of Educational Studies, pp. 61–72 (2023)
27. Nye, B.D., Häfner, J.: Artificial intelligence in education: opportunities and challenges for schools and teachers. Int. J. Educ. Technol. High. Educ. **17**(1), 17–28 (2020)
28. Reyhani Haghighi, S., Pasandideh Saqalaksari, M., Johnson, S.N.: Artificial intelligence in ecology: a commentary on a chatbot's perspective. Bull. Ecol. Soc. Am. **104**(4), e2097 (2023)
29. Roy, P., Poet, H., Staunton, R., Aston, K., Thomas, D.: ChatGPT in Lesson Preparation: A Teacher Choices Trial National Foundation for Education Research. Slough, UK (2024)
30. Salimova, S.: Applications and inclusive aspects of robotic techniques and artificial intelligence in biology education: applications and inclusive aspects of robotic techniques and artificial intelligence in biology education. Buxoro davlat pedagogika instituti jurnali **4**(4), 45–58 (2024)
31. Schönfelder, M.L., Bogner, F.X.: Between science education and environmental education: how science motivation relates to environmental values. Sustainability **12**, 1968 (2020)
32. Schumm, M.F., Bogner, F.X.: The impact of science motivation on cognitive achievement within a 3-lesson unit about renewable energies. Stud. Educ. Eval. **50**, 14–21 (2016)
33. Tatenov, A., Sarsenbaeva, Z., Azimbaeva, G., Tugelbaeva, K., Zaurbekova, N.: Evaluating the effectiveness of a virtual laboratory for inorganic chemistry education. Res. Sci. Technol. Educ. 1–13 (2023)
34. Tavares, R., Marques Vieira, R., Pedro, L.: Mobile app for science education: designing the learning approach. Educ. Sci. **11**(2), 79 (2021)
35. Witek, B.: Uzależnienia – syndrom XXI wieku? Częstochowskie Wydawnictwo Archidiecezjalne REGINA POLONIAE, Częstochowa (2024)
36. Venkatesh, V., Morris, M.G., Davis, G.B., Davis, F.D.: User acceptance of information technology: toward a unified view. MIS q. 425–478 (2003)
37. Zhai, X., et al.: A Review of Artificial Intelligence (AI) in Education from 2010 to 2020. Complex 8812542:1–8812542: 18 (2021)
38. Zourmpakis, A.-I., Kalogiannakis, M., Papadakis, S.: Adaptive gamification in science education: an analysis of the impact of implementation and adapted game elements on students' motivation. Computers **12**(7), 143 (2023)

Acceptance of Artificial Intelligence in the Classroom: Transforming Pedagogical Approaches and Student Learning in Morocco

Abdelmounim Bouziane[1](✉) and Karima Bouziane[2,3]

[1] LIRO Labo, ENCG, Chouaib Doukkali University, Fès Street, 24000 El Jadida, Morocco
bouzianeabdelmounim@gmail.com

[2] ALCS Lab, FLSH, Chouaib Doukkali University, Jabran Khalil Jabran Avenue, 24000 El Jadida, Morocco

[3] CEOS.PP, ISCAP, Polytechnic of Porto, São Mamede de Infesta, Portugal

Abstract. The integration of artificial intelligence (AI) in educational settings has the potential to revolutionize pedagogical approaches and enhance student learning outcomes. This study examines the impact and acceptance of AI tools, particularly ChatGPT, on the learning experiences of 2,129 students from the Department of English Studies at the Faculty of Letters and Human Sciences in El Jadida, Morocco. Data were collected through a questionnaire administered to all students (1,900 answers were handed in) and through interviews conducted with 20 groups of 32 students each, representing 30% of the population. Quantitative data were analyzed using principal component analysis (PCA), while qualitative data from interviews were used to understand and comment the result of statistical analysis. The findings reveal a growing tendency among students to use AI tools, especially ChatGPT, to understand various language rules and improve their writing skills. However, this use remains cautious and concealed, significantly influenced by cultural attitudes and fear of academic repercussions. The analysis indicated that students' acceptance of AI is positively correlated with their perception of its effectiveness. Moreover, a strong correlation was found between students' willingness to use ChatGPT and their previous experiences with AI.

Based on these results, the study recommends a shift in academic culture to embrace AI as a transformative tool for teaching and learning processes. Specific recommendations include the development of guidelines for ethical and effective use of AI in the classroom, promote teacher tolerance and encouragement of AI use, and address ethical concerns related to AI.

Keywords: Acceptance of AI · Students · Innovation in Education · Morocco

1 Introduction

The rapid advancement of Artificial Intelligence (AI) technologies has revolutionized various sectors, and education is no exception. AI tools, particularly language models like ChatGPT, are increasingly being integrated into educational environments to enhance

Ł. Tomczyk (Ed.): NMP 2024, CCIS 2537, pp. 248–263, 2025.
https://doi.org/10.1007/978-3-031-95627-0_17

learning experiences, facilitate academic tasks, and support students and educators alike. In higher education, AI has the potential to transform traditional teaching methods by providing personalized learning experiences, improving accessibility to resources, and assisting students in tasks such as research, writing, and language translation.

In Morocco, the Faculty of Letters and Human Sciences at the University of El Jadida offers a unique context for examining AI acceptance due to its diverse student population in the Department of English Studies. With a total of 2,129 students, the department provides an ideal setting for investigating how students perceive and engage with AI tools, particularly ChatGPT. The adoption of AI in education, however, is influenced by various factors, including cultural attitudes, institutional support, teacher acceptance, and students' familiarity with the technology. Understanding these factors is crucial to assessing how AI can be effectively integrated into educational practices.

This study aims to explore the impact of AI acceptance, specifically ChatGPT, on the learning experiences of students in the Department of English Studies. Through a mixed-methods approach that combines quantitative data from a survey with qualitative insights from student interviews, the study seeks to identify the key factors influencing the use and acceptance of AI tools in the classroom. By focusing on variables such as teacher attitudes, student familiarity, and perceived usefulness, this research provides valuable insights into the dynamics that shape AI adoption in the educational context. Ultimately, the goal is to contribute to the ongoing discussion of AI's role in education and inform strategies for fostering a positive and ethical learning environment that embraces technological advancements by answering one main problematic: How can we evaluate students' acceptance of using ChatGPT in the classroom?

2 Literature Review

2.1 The Use of AI in Education

Artificial intelligence (AI) has become a transformative force in various fields, including education, and is increasingly integrated into higher education (HE) systems. In recent years, the number of publications on AI in higher education has surged [6, 26, [29, 32. [7] conducted a systematic review of 138 studies published from 2016 to 2022, showing a sharp increase in publications in 2021 and 2022. They found that AI research in HE has expanded globally, with China now leading the field in the number of publications, surpassing the United States. This growing body of research highlights the shifting trends in AI's application in education, with a particular focus on undergraduate students and language learning. The study also categorized the ways in which AI is used in HE, identifying five primary areas: assessment and evaluation, predictive analytics, AI assistants, intelligent tutoring systems (ITS), and managing student learning. These trends emphasize AI's expanding role in enhancing the educational experience, particularly in areas such as personalized learning and assessment.

AI's potential to personalize learning has been a major area of focus. [8] discuss how AI technologies, such as intelligent tutoring systems and AI-powered learning platforms, have the capacity to create tailored learning environments that meet the individual needs of students. AI's ability to engage in human-like processes, such as learning, adapting, and synthesizing complex data, allows it to offer personalized feedback and support, which can significantly enhance both teaching and learning in higher education. These advancements are particularly valuable for students who require more personalized attention, as they help address the challenges posed by large class sizes and limited teacher-student interaction.

The role of AI in supporting inclusive learning is also gaining attention. [14] conducted a study on the use of chatbots as a means of facilitating equity in learning. Their research demonstrated that AI-driven chatbots could offer accessible, interactive, and confidential support to students from diverse backgrounds, including those facing socioeconomic challenges and varying learning styles. This study aligns with the broader goal of using AI to bridge gaps in educational access and ensure that all students have equal opportunities to succeed. The ability of chatbots to provide instant, personalized feedback makes them a valuable tool in fostering an inclusive learning environment where students receive the support they need at any time.

AI's applications are not limited to improving student outcomes alone. In Latin America, [30] conducted a systematic review of AI applications in higher education institutions, highlighting how AI is used to address key educational challenges such as student retention and academic success. They found that AI technologies such as predictive modeling, intelligent analytics, and assistive technologies have been applied to monitor student progress and detect those at risk of dropping out. These AI tools help educators intervene early and provide targeted support, ensuring that students remain engaged and succeed in their studies. Moreover, the study underscored the importance of AI in enhancing administrative processes, further streamlining educational operations and allowing faculty to focus on teaching and student interaction.

While AI holds immense promise for education, its ethical implications must be carefully considered. [8] note that as AI technologies become more integrated into educational settings, ethical issues such as data privacy, algorithmic bias, and fairness must be addressed. Ensuring that AI systems operate transparently and without discrimination is crucial for their effective and responsible use in education. The ethical concerns surrounding AI must be balanced with its potential to enhance learning, creating a framework for responsible implementation that safeguards student data and promotes equity.

As AI technologies continue to evolve, future research directions are likely to explore more sophisticated applications in education. [35] emphasize the need for interdisciplinary collaboration to advance AI in education and address current challenges. They highlight the importance of AI-powered intelligent tutoring systems and personalized learning platforms that can adapt to students' evolving needs. The future of AI in education will rely on continued innovation and the development of tools that are both effective and ethically sound, ensuring that AI contributes positively to the educational experience.

2.2 Factors Influencing the Acceptance of AI, Particularly Focusing on Technology Acceptance Models like TAM and UTAUT

The exploration of factors influencing the acceptance of AI across various contexts highlights a range of key variables that shape individuals' willingness to adopt new technologies. In the area of AI-assisted learning, [34] identify performance expectancy, effort expectancy, and social influence as critical factors in students' adoption of AI-driven academic tools, while also pointing out the moderating role of perceived risks, such as concerns about data privacy. These insights align with the findings from [17], who, using the Technology Acceptance Model (TAM), demonstrate that perceived usefulness and ease of use are essential in driving Thai students' adoption of generative AI tools like ChatGPT, though barriers such as digital literacy must be addressed for broader acceptance.

This trend continues with [18], whose systematic review of 60 studies reveals that perceived usefulness and trust are consistent predictors of AI adoption across various domains, from education to healthcare. Interestingly, their analysis also highlights cultural differences, suggesting that users in collectivist societies are more influenced by social factors than those in individualist cultures. Similarly, [31] emphasize the role of subjective norms and perceived enjoyment in consumer acceptance of AI products, proposing that emotional factors are often underexplored in traditional acceptance models, yet they significantly impact user behavior.

Further expanding on the emotional dimensions, [3] explores consumer acceptance of AI in e-commerce, emphasizing the importance of trust and perceived control. This emotional engagement mirrors the findings of [22], who extend TAM to the K-12 education sector, incorporating factors such as AI motivation and AI anxiety. Their study suggests that addressing emotional concerns, such as anxiety, can improve student engagement with AI curricula, reinforcing the need for a more holistic approach to AI adoption that includes emotional and cognitive factors.

In a broader context, [19] argue that addressing knowledge gaps, cultural resistance, and infrastructural challenges is vital for improving AI adoption across industries. This interdisciplinary approach complements the insights of [23], who note that facilitating conditions, such as technical support and infrastructure, are often underestimated but crucial for sustained AI use. These findings are also echoed in studies like that of [21], who highlights the importance of addressing concerns such as anxiety and job security among professionals in creative fields when adopting AI tools.

Finally, the integration of frameworks like TAM and the Technology-Organization-Environment (TOE) model, as seen in [27], provides more understanding of organizational AI adoption, emphasizing the need for targeted training and addressing resistance to change. This approach is further illustrated in the context of the Moroccan banking sector, where [11] adapt UTAUT to explore chatbot adoption, focusing on the significance of user interface design and interactive tutorials in enhancing engagement. Likewise, [2] examine the acceptance of ChatGPT among university students, reinforcing the importance of promoting ethical AI use to foster academic integrity. Collectively, these studies illustrate the multifaceted nature of AI acceptance, demonstrating that technological, emotional, and cultural factors all play crucial roles in shaping individuals' adoption of AI across different sectors.

2.3 Ethical Implications and Challenges of Artificial Intelligence in Education

The use of artificial intelligence (AI) in education brings significant ethical concerns, many of which relate to fairness and the impact on students from diverse backgrounds. One of the most pressing issues is algorithmic bias. Studies, such as those by [33], highlight that AI systems can perpetuate existing biases, particularly when these systems are trained on biased datasets. This can result in discriminatory practices that unfairly affect marginalized groups, influencing key decisions such as admissions, assessments, and learning outcomes. Furthermore, [10] and [9] emphasizes the unintentional reinforcement of stereotypes, particularly through the use of technologies like facial recognition, which may fail to account for cultural or contextual differences when assessing students' emotions or behaviors. These biases pose serious ethical challenges, especially in education settings where equity is essential.

Closely tied to the issue of bias is the growing concern over data privacy and security. As AI tools in education collect vast amounts of student data, including learning patterns, behaviors, and even emotional states, the potential for misuse or mishandling increases. [28] discuss how AI-driven educational tools may compromise student privacy if this data is not properly safeguarded. The unauthorized sharing of this information or its use beyond educational purposes could lead to violations of students' personal privacy. In response, [20] argue that robust data protection protocols and adherence to ethical standards for data usage are necessary to mitigate these risks and protect students' privacy.

Another significant challenge is the potential erosion of student autonomy. [16] express concern that AI, by taking on more decision-making roles in education, may reduce students to passive recipients of learning experiences. This could diminish opportunities for critical thinking and problem-solving, as AI systems often offer tailored solutions based on predetermined algorithms. This shift also threatens to undermine the essential human aspect of education, reducing the quality of teacher-student interactions that foster creativity, motivation, and social development.

Transparency and accountability in AI systems further complicate the ethical context. Many AI models operate as "black boxes," meaning their decision-making processes are not easily understood by users, including educators, students, and even developers. [33] argue that transparency is crucial, stressing the need for educators and students to understand how AI tools make decisions and recommendations. Without this transparency, AI could be misused in ways that conflict with educational objectives or ethical standards. [1] also warn that a lack of accountability could lead to harmful consequences, where errors or biases in AI systems may not be traceable to a responsible party, complicating efforts to address problems when they arise.

Academic integrity is another area where AI presents ethical dilemmas. The use of AI tools in assessments and grading could facilitate cheating or plagiarism, undermining the authenticity of student work. As [13] note, AI-generated content makes it easier for students to pass off machine-created essays or projects as their own. This challenges not only academic integrity but also the value of education itself. To maintain academic standards, it is crucial that AI tools are seen as complementary to, rather than a replacement for, human judgment.

To address these concerns, ethical principles such as fairness, privacy, transparency, accountability, autonomy, and beneficence have been proposed as guiding frameworks for AI in education. [28] suggest that fairness should be prioritized, ensuring equal access to educational opportunities for all students, regardless of their backgrounds. Privacy protections must be in place to prevent the misuse of sensitive student data, while accountability frameworks must be established to ensure responsible use of AI tools. The principle of beneficence, which focuses on using AI to improve student outcomes, should drive the development of AI tools that enhance, rather than hinder, learning.

Although AI offers the potential to transform education, its ethical implications must be carefully managed. The challenges of algorithmic bias, data privacy, transparency, autonomy, and academic integrity require ongoing attention. Through establishing frameworks based on key ethical principles, we can ensure that AI technologies are used responsibly, promoting fairness and protecting students' rights while supporting the advancement of education.

2.4 Use and Acceptance of Artificial Intelligence in Education in Morocco

The integration of Artificial Intelligence (AI) in education is reshaping traditional pedagogical and administrative practices, and Morocco is no exception. Over recent years, AI has begun to make its mark in various educational sectors, especially within higher education. AI is being used to personalize learning experiences, automate tasks, optimize educational resources, and improve academic outcomes. In Moroccan higher education, AI tools support both educators and students, providing research processes and enhancing academic delivery. As [25] note, AI holds the potential to significantly improve efficiency in educational settings, particularly through automated grading systems and virtual learning environments, which can reduce administrative burdens on teachers and allow for more student-focused teaching [12].

However, while the benefits of AI in education are widely acknowledged, acceptance of these tools among educators and students in Morocco varies. [12] conducted a study to explore Moroccan teachers' perspectives, revealing that though many teachers are open to AI integration, their technical expertise remains a significant barrier. The acceptance of AI among educators is influenced by factors such as academic level, with higher-level educators more likely to embrace AI. In contrast, factors such as age, gender, and years of teaching experience showed little to no effect on their attitudes toward AI. Similarly, students' perceptions are shaped by their familiarity with technology and ethical concerns, with those more exposed to AI being more receptive to its use in educational contexts. [24] suggest that bridging the knowledge gap is key to fostering broader acceptance, especially among students who have limited prior exposure to AI.

Despite its potential, the integration of AI in Moroccan education faces several challenges. Key obstacles include limited technological infrastructure, a lack of sufficient teacher training, and concerns regarding data privacy and security. [15] highlights the risks posed by relying on foreign technology platforms, which could undermine Morocco's educational sovereignty and raise issues related to data control. Furthermore, the absence of a national framework to manage AI's implementation complicates efforts to ensure its responsible and ethical use in education. These concerns emphasize the need for a solid digital ecosystem and comprehensive data privacy laws to safeguard student information and ensure the ethical deployment of AI tools in schools and universities.

Looking ahead, the future of AI in Moroccan education holds considerable promise, yet it requires careful planning and implementation. Other authors like [36] emphasize the growing role of generative AI tools, such as ChatGPT, in enhancing academic writing and supporting student learning. These tools are increasingly recognized as effective means to boost student engagement, personalize learning experiences, and improve academic performance. However, the full transformative potential of AI in Moroccan education can only be realized with systematic efforts to improve digital literacy among both educators and students.

For AI to succeed in Moroccan education, there is also a pressing need for policy development at the government and educational authority levels. Policies must address not only ethical concerns, such as data privacy and security, but also practical considerations, including promoting digital equity and AI literacy across the educational system. Through creating supportive policies and frameworks, Morocco can ensure that its educators and students are well-prepared to adapt to the changing educational landscape.

AI offers great potential to improve Morocco's education system, but for it to succeed, the country needs to address challenges related to technology, training, and ethics. By investing in teacher training, upgrading infrastructure, and promoting digital literacy, Morocco can make the most of AI to enhance learning, streamline administrative tasks, and improve educational results.

3 Method

This study explores the impact of Artificial Intelligence (AI) acceptance, particularly ChatGPT, on the learning experiences of students in the Department of English Studies at the Faculty of Letters and Human Sciences in El Jadida, Morocco.

The selection of the Department of English Studies is motivated by the fact that students are easily accessible on campus, and the researchers maintain direct contact with them. The department comprises a total of 2,129 students.

To collect data, the primary method used was a questionnaire, which yielded 1,900 responses, representing an 89% response rate and a substantial proportion of the target population. In addition, in-depth interviews were conducted with 20 groups of 32 students each, accounting for approximately 30% of the studied population.

The quantitative data obtained from the questionnaire were analyzed using Principal Component Analysis (PCA), which helped identify the key factors influencing the use and acceptance of AI tools.

This mixed-methods approach provided a comprehensive and nuanced understanding of students' perceptions and behaviors regarding AI tools, while considering the cultural and academic dynamics influencing their adoption. The questions incorporated in the questionnaire were as follows (Table 1):

Table 1. The questions incorporated in the questionnaire.

Variables	Possible answers
Gender	Male, Female
Age	[17 – 20 [, [20 – 23[, [23–26], [>26]
Level of Familiarity with AI	Strongly Disagree, Disagree, Neutral, Agree, Strongly Agree
Perceived Ease of AI Use	Strongly Disagree, Disagree, Neutral, Agree, Strongly Agree
Perceived Effectiveness of AI	Strongly Disagree, Disagree, Neutral, Agree, Strongly Agree
Perceived Usefulness of AI	Strongly Disagree, Disagree, Neutral, Agree, Strongly Agree
Access to AI Tools	1: Only one tool, 2: Two tools, 3: Three tools, 4: Four or more tools
AI Training Experience	Yes, No
Perceived Knowledge Growth in AI	Strongly Disagree, Disagree, Neutral, Agree, Strongly Agree
Frequency of AI Use	Never, Rarely, Sometimes, Often, Always
Satisfaction with AI Tools	Strongly Disagree, Disagree, Neutral, Agree, Strongly Agree
Acceptance of AI as a Permanent Tool	Strongly Disagree, Disagree, Neutral, Agree, Strongly Agree
Support from Institution for AI	Strongly Disagree, Disagree, Neutral, Agree, Strongly Agree
Teacher Encouragement of AI Use	Never, Rarely, Sometimes, Often, Always
Level of Teacher Tolerance for AI Use	Never, Rarely, Sometimes, Often, Always
Perception of ChatGPT Users	Very positive, Somewhat positive, Neutral, Somewhat negative, Very negative

The determination of the research variables was based on an adapted positivist approach. This conclusion is drawn from the fact that the research variables were derived from both the literature review and the research field.

Variables such as Perceived Usefulness and Perceived Ease of Use (TAM theory) were identified from studies addressing AI in education, such as the works of Wu el al (2024) and [18], among others. Meanwhile, the variable Familiarity with AI was sourced from the research of [24]. The variable Teacher Tolerance and Acceptance of AI originated from the study by [12].

Variables like Perceived Knowledge Growth in AI, Frequency of AI Use, and Satisfaction with AI Tools were derived from the works of [4] and [5]. Additional variables were identified from the research field during the development of the research model through interviews with academic staff from the Department of English Studies.

4 Results

To assess the feasibility of Principal Component Analysis, several tests were conducted and interpreted, including the KMO test, and Bartlett signification. The results are as follows (Table 2):

Table 2. Model derived from SPSS (PCA)

Tests performed	Results
KMO	0.690
BARTLETT	*0.000*

After analyzing the statistical model's feasibility, we find that the KMO test value is above 0.5 and the significance level of the Bartlett test is below 5%. Based on this analysis, we can conclude that it is feasible to conduct a PCA of the different factors impacting the acceptance of AI in the classroom. This analysis allows us to identify and present the dimensions defined by the PCA. Table 3 provides insights into the percentage of information explained by each component.

Table 3. Total variance explained: AI Acceptance Among Students

Components	Total	% of Variance	Cumulative %
1	5.692	40.661	40.661
2	2.907	20.763	61.423
3	1.827	13.048	74.472
4	1.107	7.905	82.376
5	0.836	5.973	88.349
6	0.441	3.148	91.497
7	0.292	2.083	93.580
8	0.259	1.846	95.427
9	0.219	1.566	96.992
10	0.163	1.166	98.158
11	0.116	0.827	98.985
12	0.077	0.547	99.532
13	0.056	0.403	99.935
14	0.009	0.065	100.000

Eigenvalues greater than 1 are associated with Components 1, 2, 3, and 4, which together account for more than 82% of the variance and, therefore, the information contained in the model. This is why we retain the first four components, representing four dimensions, resulting in a loss of approximately 18% of the information. The components are defined as follows (Table 4):

Table 4. Component matrix

	1	2	3	4
Bachelor/Master	0.048	−0.111	−0.387	−0.236
Level of Familiarity with AI	0.347	0.068	0.189	0.118
Perceived Ease of AI Use	0.159	0.053	−0.026	0.163
Perceived Effectiveness of AI	0.151	0.114	−0.027	0.024
Perceived Usefulness of AI	0.138	0.136	-0.038	0.160
Access to AI Tools	0.063	−0.289	0.140	0.031
Perceived Knowledge Growth in AI	0.028	0.224	0.276	−0.348
Frequency of AI Use	0.148	−0.072	−0.067	−0.170
Satisfaction with AI Tools	0.192	0.018	−0.077	−0.091
Acceptance of AI as a Permanent Tool	0.618	0.186	-0.088	0.166
Support from Institution for AI	0.035	−0.159	0.384	0.152
Teacher Encouragement of AI Use	0.083	−0.110	0.273	-0.404
Level of Teacher Tolerance for AI Use	0.681	-0.200	−0.033	0.528
Perception of ChatGPT Users	0.319	0.204	0.148	0.019

Acceptance of AI as a Permanent Tool is included in Component 1, encompassing the following variables: Level of Teacher Tolerance for AI Use, Level of Familiarity with AI, Perceived Effectiveness of AI, Satisfaction with AI Tools, and Perception of ChatGPT Users. It can be concluded that these variables exhibit correlated variances. In other words, influencing one of these variables will have an impact on the others.

To explain this observation, it can be stated that students' acceptance of AI use is strongly correlated with teachers' tolerance for it. This finding is logical, as classrooms are managed by teachers. Another key factor is the Level of Familiarity with AI, as the more familiar individuals are with a technology, the more likely they are to favor it. Additionally, Perceived Effectiveness of AI and Satisfaction with AI Tools are crucial in determining the acceptance of AI. If the results are satisfactory and ChatGPT's assistance is reliable, students are more likely to accept and use it during their academic journey.

Interviews conducted with students supported the statistical findings. Students confirmed that ChatGPT is mainly used for translating from French to English, paraphrasing passages from books and lectures for report or assignment writing, and explaining complex concepts.

However, students linked the use of ChatGPT to the tolerance of teachers, noting that some teachers do not allow its use. Furthermore, students themselves perceive ChatGPT's assistance as potentially unethical, which influences their explicit acceptance of its use.

5 Discussion

The Acceptance of AI as a Permanent Tool was included in Component 1, encompassing variables such as Teacher Tolerance for AI Use, Familiarity with AI, Perceived Effectiveness of AI, Satisfaction with AI Tools, and Perception of ChatGPT Users. It was found that these variables exhibited correlated variances, indicating that influencing one of these variables impacts the others. For instance, students' acceptance of AI use is strongly correlated with teachers' tolerance for AI, which is logical given that teachers manage classrooms. Furthermore, the Level of Familiarity with AI plays a significant role: the more familiar students are with a technology, the more likely they are to embrace it. Perceived Effectiveness of AI and Satisfaction with AI Tools are also crucial in determining AI acceptance. When the results are satisfactory and the assistance provided by tools like ChatGPT is reliable, students are more likely to use AI during their academic journey.

Interviews with students corroborated the statistical findings, with students confirming that they primarily use ChatGPT for translation from French to English, paraphrasing passages from books and lectures when writing reports or assignments, and explaining complex concepts. However, students also associated the use of ChatGPT with teachers' tolerance. Some teachers prohibit its use, and many students perceive ChatGPT's assistance as unethical, which affects their explicit acceptance of it.

In contrast to the findings of [34] and [18], where perceived ease of use and perceived usefulness were directly linked to AI acceptance, our study found that AI acceptance among students was not directly related to these two variables. This suggests that factors beyond ease and usefulness, such as cultural perceptions and institutional support, play a more significant role in AI adoption within the educational context.

Cultural resistance, as noted by [19], is confirmed by our study, particularly with respect to the representation of AI users and the institutional support provided. These elements are deeply rooted in cultural attitudes toward technology and influence how AI tools like ChatGPT are perceived and utilized by students.

Our study also supports the findings of [2] and [25], who assert that students' acceptance of AI is influenced by feedback from AI usage and the effectiveness of the software. The feedback provided by AI tools and the effectiveness of their application were key factors in shaping students' attitudes and their willingness to adopt AI in their learning processes.

In line with [4], our study confirms that Satisfaction with AI is a significant factor influencing students' acceptance of AI in the classroom. If students are satisfied with their experiences using AI tools, they are more likely to continue using them in their academic activities. Similarly, Teacher Acceptance of AI is a critical determinant of student acceptance, as proposed by [12]. If teachers are open to using AI in the classroom, students are more likely to follow suit.

Finally, our study also supports the work of [24], who state that Familiarity with AI is a key factor in determining students' acceptance of AI. The more familiar students are with AI tools, the more likely they are to accept and integrate them into their academic practices.

6 Recommendations

Based on the findings of this study, several recommendations can be made to improve the acceptance and integration of AI tools, particularly ChatGPT, into the educational environment at the Faculty of Letters and Human Sciences in El Jadida, Morocco:

Increase AI Familiarity through Training and Awareness Programs.

Given the strong correlation between students' familiarity with AI and their willingness to use AI tools, it is crucial to enhance training programs. These programs should aim to familiarize students with the various applications of AI, focusing on practical and ethical usage. By providing workshops, tutorials, and hands-on training, students can develop the necessary skills to use AI effectively and confidently in their academic work.

Promote Teacher Tolerance and Encouragement of AI Use

Teacher acceptance of AI tools plays a critical role in student adoption. Therefore, it is essential to encourage faculty to integrate AI into their teaching practices. Workshops or seminars should be organized for teachers to explore the potential benefits of AI in the classroom, address ethical concerns, and equip them with strategies to manage AI usage among students. Teachers should also be trained on how to incorporate AI as a tool for improving learning outcomes rather than viewing it as a threat to traditional teaching methods.

Address Ethical Concerns Related to AI

Many students perceive the use of ChatGPT as potentially unethical, which may hinder its widespread acceptance. Educational institutions should engage in discussions and provide clear guidelines regarding the ethical use of AI tools. These guidelines should focus on ensuring that AI is used as an aid for learning rather than a means to bypass academic integrity. Promoting responsible usage and educating students on the ethical implications of AI can help mitigate concerns about its misuse.

Enhance Institutional Support for AI Tools

As the study found that students' acceptance of AI is influenced by the support provided by the institution, it is recommended that the university invest in more accessible AI tools and resources. This could include providing students with access to multiple AI platforms and ensuring the tools are user-friendly. Additionally, the institution should create a support system for students, such as a helpdesk or online forums, where they can ask questions and resolve issues related to AI use.

Focus on AI Feedback Mechanisms

The effectiveness of AI tools, such as ChatGPT, greatly influences students' satisfaction and continued use. To improve the feedback process, AI tools should be designed to provide constructive and meaningful feedback. Institutions should also collect student feedback on AI usage to identify areas for improvement and ensure that the AI tools meet students' needs.

Encourage Peer Learning and Collaboration

To facilitate the adoption of AI tools like ChatGPT, students could be encouraged to collaborate and share experiences with their peers. Peer-to-peer learning can create a supportive environment where students can exchange tips on effectively using AI in their studies. This could be facilitated through student-led workshops, online discussion groups, or collaborative projects involving AI tools.

Cultural Sensitivity in AI Adoption

The study highlights that cultural perceptions play a significant role in AI acceptance. To address this, the institution should be mindful of cultural differences when introducing AI technologies and ensure that the implementation process is culturally sensitive. Workshops should acknowledge cultural attitudes toward technology and provide space for open dialogue about how AI can fit within the cultural context of Moroccan education.

Regular Evaluation and Updates

As AI technology evolves rapidly, it is important for the university to continuously assess and update the AI tools and strategies employed. Regular evaluations of AI tools' effectiveness, coupled with student and faculty feedback, should guide future improvements. This will ensure that AI tools remain relevant and useful for students' academic growth.

7 Conclusion

This study aimed to explore the impact of Artificial Intelligence (AI) acceptance, particularly ChatGPT, on the learning experiences of students in the Department of English Studies at the Faculty of Letters and Human Sciences in El Jadida, Morocco. Through a mixed-methods approach combining quantitative data from a survey with qualitative insights from student interviews, the research provided a comprehensive understanding of how students perceive and use AI tools in their academic journey.

The findings revealed that the acceptance of AI, including ChatGPT, is primarily influenced by a range of factors, including teachers' tolerance for AI use, students' familiarity with AI, the perceived effectiveness of AI tools, and their satisfaction with the tools. Teacher attitudes play a pivotal role, as students are more likely to embrace AI tools if teachers are supportive or open to their use. Additionally, students' familiarity with AI technologies significantly affects their willingness to adopt them, as does the perceived effectiveness and satisfaction with AI tools like ChatGPT.

While perceived ease of use and perceived usefulness—two critical factors highlighted in previous studies—were not found to have a direct impact on students' AI acceptance in this study, it was evident that cultural perceptions and institutional support are crucial elements in shaping students' attitudes toward AI adoption. The study also demonstrated that AI's role in academic activities, such as translating texts, paraphrasing, and clarifying concepts, was influenced by the broader educational and cultural context, with some students perceiving AI use as potentially unethical due to its association with cheating or bypassing traditional learning methods.

The research contributes to the growing body of literature on AI adoption in education by emphasizing the importance of institutional support, teacher attitudes, and student familiarity in shaping AI acceptance. It also underscores the need for a cultural shift towards greater openness and understanding of AI's potential in enhancing educational practices.

In conclusion, while AI tools like ChatGPT hold promise in transforming the learning experience, their successful integration into the classroom hinges on a combination of factors, including supportive teachers, increased student familiarity with the technology, and the creation of an environment that fosters positive perceptions of AI. As educational institutions move forward with AI integration, these factors must be carefully considered to ensure the effective and ethical use of AI tools in academic settings.

References

1. Akgun, S., Greenhow, C.: Artificial intelligence in education: addressing ethical challenges in K-12 settings. AI Ethics **2**(3), 431–440 (2021). https://doi.org/10.1007/s43681-021-00096-7
2. Almogren, A.S., Al-Rahmi, W.M., Dahri, N.A.: Exploring factors influencing the acceptance of ChatGPT in higher education: a smart education perspective. Heliyon **10**(11), e31887 (2024). https://doi.org/10.1016/j.heliyon.2024.e31887
3. Bou-Ghanem, D.: Factors that influence the acceptance of artificial intelligence technology by the consumer. In: The Tenth International Conference on Engaged Management Scholarship (2020). https://doi.org/10.2139/ssrn.3687765
4. Bouziane, A., Bouziane, K.: NICT acceptance among teachers and students in the context of higher education reform in Morocco. In: Tomczyk, Ł. (ed.) New Media Pedagogy: Research Trends, Methodological Challenges, and Successful Implementations (2024)
5. Bouziane, A., Tahri, W., Bouziane, K.: Satisfaction and acceptance of ICT in learning activities during Covid19: the case of Moroccan students. In: Tomczyk, Ł. (ed.) New Media Pedagogy: Research Trends, Methodological Challenges and Successful Implementations. NMP 2022, CCIS, vol. 1916, pp. 100–115. Springer, Cham (2023). https://doi.org/10.1007/978-3-031-44581-1_18
6. Chu, J., Xi, L., Zhang, Q., Lin, R.: Research on ethical issues of artificial intelligence in education. In: Yang, J., et al. (eds.), Resilience and Future of Smart Learning, pp. 1–12. Springer, Cham (2022). https://doi.org/10.1007/978-981-19-5967-7_12
7. Crompton, H., Burke, D.: Artificial intelligence in higher education: the state of the field. Int. J. Educ. Technol. High. Educ. **20**(22) (2023). https://doi.org/10.1186/s41239-023-00392-8
8. Crompton, H., Song, D.: The potential of artificial intelligence in higher education. Rev. Virtual Univ. Católica Del Norte **62**, 1–4 (2021). https://doi.org/10.35575/rvucn.n62a1
9. Douali, L., Selmaoui, S., Bouab, W.: Artificial intelligence in education: Fears and faiths. Int. J. Inf. Educ. Technol. **12**(7), 1666 (2022). https://doi.org/10.18178/ijiet.2022.12.7.1666
10. Du Boulay, B.: Artificial intelligence in education and ethics. In: Zawacki-Richter, O., Jung, I. (eds.) Handbook of Open, Distance and Digital Education, pp. 1–14. Springer, Heidelberg (2023). https://doi.org/10.1007/978-981-19-2080-6_6
11. Elkhatibi, Y., Guelzim, H., Benabdelouahed, R.: Factors influencing the adoption of AI-powered chatbots in the Moroccan banking sector: an extended UTAUT model. J. Logist. Informatics Serv. Sci. **11**(7), 559–585 (2024). https://doi.org/10.33168/JLISS.2024.0730
12. Fakhar, H., Lamrabet, M., Echantoufi, N., El Khattabi, K., Ajana, L.: Artificial intelligence from teachers' perspectives and understanding: Moroccan study. Int. J. Inf. Educ. Technol. **14**(6), 2111 (2024). https://doi.org/10.18178/ijiet.2024.14.6.2111
13. Foltynek, T., Bjelobaba, S., Glendinning, I., Khan, Z.R., Santos, R., Pavletic, P.: ENAI recommendations on the ethical use of artificial intelligence in education. Int. J. Educ. Integrity **19**, 12 (2023). https://doi.org/10.1007/s40979-023-00133-4
14. Gupta, S., Chen, Y.: Supporting inclusive learning using chatbots? A chatbot-led interview study. J. Inf. Syst. Educ. **33**(1), 98–108 (2022). https://aisel.aisnet.org/jise/vol33/iss1/11
15. Hajji, S.: Educational sovereignty and artificial intelligence challenges: the case of Morocco. In: Roumate, F. (Ed.), Artificial Intelligence in Higher Education and Scientific Research, pp. 145–162. Springer, Singapore (2023). https://doi.org/10.1007/978-981-19-8641-3_8
16. Holmes, W., et al.: Ethics of AI in education: towards a community-wide framework. Int. J. Artif. Intell. Educ. **32**, 504–526 (2022). https://doi.org/10.1007/s40593-021-00239-1

17. Kanont, P., et al.: Generative-AI, a learning assistant? Factors influencing higher-ed students' technology acceptance. Electron. J. e-Learn. **22**(6), 18–33 (2024). https://doi.org/10.34190/ejel.22.6.3196
18. Kelly, S., Kaye, S.-A., Oviedo-Trespalacios, O.: What factors contribute to the acceptance of artificial intelligence? A systematic review. Telemat. Inform. **77**, 101925 (2023). https://doi.org/10.1016/j.tele.2022.101925
19. Khanfar, A.A., Kiani Mavi, R., Iranmanesh, M.: Determinants of artificial intelligence adoption: Research themes and future directions. Inf. Technol. Manag. (2024). https://doi.org/10.1007/s10799-024-00435-0
20. Kousa, P., Niemi, H.: Artificial Intelligence Ethics from the Perspective of Educational Technology Companies and Schools. In: Niemi, H., Pea, R.D., Lu, Y. (eds.), AI in Learning: Designing the Future, LNCS, pp. 1–14. Springer, Cham (2023). https://doi.org/10.1007/978-3-031-09687-7_17
21. Li, W.: A study on factors influencing designers' behavioral intention in using AI-generated content for assisted design. Int. J. Hum.–Comput. Interact. (2024). https://doi.org/10.1080/10447318.2024.2310354
22. Li, W., Zhang, X., Li, J.: An explanatory study of factors influencing engagement in AI education at the K-12 level: an extension of the classic TAM model. Sci. Rep. **14**, 13922 (2024). https://doi.org/10.1038/s41598-024-64363-3
23. Marikyan, D., Papagiannidis, S.: Unified Theory of Acceptance and Use of Technology: A Review. In: Papagiannidis, S. (ed.) TheoryHub Book. ISBN 9781739604400 (2023)
24. Mohamed, K., Zineb, E., Zineb, M., & Bouchra, E.: AI in Moroccan education: Evaluating student acceptance using machine learning classification models. Indones. J. Electr. Eng. Comput. Sci. **37**(1), 452–462 (2025). https://doi.org/10.11591/ijeecs.v37.i1.pp452-462
25. Moukhliss, G., Lahyani, K., Diab, G.: Revolutionizing academic inquiry: artificial intelligence's influence on higher education in Morocco. In: Mejdoub, Y., Elamri, A. (eds.) Proceeding of the International Conference on Connected Objects and Artificial Intelligence (COCIA2024), LNSS, vol. 1123, pp. 100–115. Springer, Cham (2024). https://doi.org/10.1007/978-3-031-70411-6_6
26. Mumtaz, S., Carmichael, J., Weiss, M., Nimon-Peters, A.: Ethical use of artificial intelligence-based tools in higher education: are future business leaders ready? Educ. Inform. Technol. (2024). https://doi.org/10.1007/s10639-024-13099-8
27. Na, S., Heo, S., Han, S., Shin, Y., Roh, Y.: Acceptance model of artificial intelligence (AI)-based technologies in construction firms: applying TAM and TOE frameworks. Build. **12**(2), 90 (2022). https://doi.org/10.3390/buildings12020090
28. Nguyen, A., Ngo, H.N., Hong, Y., Dang, B., Thi Nguyen, B.: Ethical principles for artificial intelligence in education. Educ. Inform. Technol. **28**, 4221–4241 (2023). https://doi.org/10.1007/s10639-022-11316-w
29. Popenici, S.A.D., Kerr, S.: Exploring the impact of artificial intelligence on teaching and learning in higher education. Res. Pract. Technol. Enhanced Learn. **12**(22) (2017). https://doi.org/10.1186/s41039-017-0062-8
30. Salas-Pilco, S. Z., & Yang, Y.: Artificial intelligence applications in Latin American higher education: a systematic review. Int. J. Educ. Technol. High. Educ. **19**(21) (2022). https://doi.org/10.1186/s41239-022-00326-w
31. Sohn, K., Kwon, O.: Technology acceptance theories and AI-based intelligent products. Telemat. Informat. **47**, 101324 (2020). https://doi.org/10.1016/j.tele.2020.101324
32. Taibi, M.: The Critical Role of Artificial Intelligence in Enhancing Higher Education. PRSM: Changing Paradigms & Future Directions in Higher Education, vol. 7 (2023)
33. Tang, L., Su, Y.-S.: Ethical implications and principles of using artificial intelligence models in the classroom: a systematic literature review. Int. J. Interact. Multimed. Artif. Intell. **8**(5) (2023). https://doi.org/10.9781/ijimai.2024.02.010

34. Wu, W., Zhang, B., Li, S., Liu, H.: Exploring factors of the willingness to accept AI-assisted learning environments: an empirical investigation based on the UTAUT model and perceived risk theory. Front. Psychol. **13**, Article 870777 (2022). https://doi.org/10.3389/fpsyg.2022.870777
35. Zhang, K., Aslan, A.B.: AI technologies for education: recent research and future directions. Comput. Educ. Artif. Intell. **2**, 100025 (2021). https://doi.org/10.1016/j.caeai.2021.100025
36. Zubaidi, K., Jaafari, M., Touzani, F.Z.: Impact of ChatGPT on Academic Writing at Moroccan Universities. Arab World English Journal Special Issue on ChatGPT, (2024). SSRN: https://ssrn.com/abstract=4814268

A Preliminary Study on Higher Education Students' Usage, and Attitudes Towards AI

Andreja Klančar[1] (✉) and Aleksander Janeš[2]

[1] Faculty of Education, University of Primorska, 6000 Koper, Slovenia
andreja.klancar@pef.upr.si
[2] Faculty of Management, University of Primorska, 6000 Koper, Slovenia
aleksander.janes@fm-kp.si

Abstract. This contribution examines and compares undergraduate students' views of the Faculty of Education, University of Primorska regarding their usage and attitudes towards Artificial Intelligence (AI).

105 full-time undergraduate students participated in the survey. The research on the students' views reveals constructs regarding use, attitude, and ethical aspects and their intercorrelations. The normality of the data, the mean values, and the interpretation of the constructs, as well as the validity and correlations between the constructs, are analyzed.

Also, students are recognized for their curiosity and positive attitude toward integrating AI technologies into their everyday practice and learning. Although, on average, students can relatively easily become acquainted with new AI tools, they encounter challenges when using these technologies in decision-making.

The findings of the correlation analysis between constructs of usage and attitudes, conducted on undergraduate students, indicate that attitudes towards integrating AI in their everyday practice to a certain extent predict future attitudes and usage towards AI.

Keywords: Artificial Intelligence · Attitudes · Usage · Preference · Awareness · Students

1 Introduction

Beginning in the 1950s with John McCarthy, artificial intelligence (AI) is a multidisciplinary field of study that integrates the advances of computer technology, cognitive science, and logic. It seeks to replicate and improve the human mind's processes to address complicated issues outside the purview of straightforward algorithms. One of the distinguishing features of AI-based algorithms is their capacity to recognize patterns and apply that understanding to improve and expand their functioning [8]. Losing human control over external AI agents appears to be the biggest worry in this situation. The emergence of augmented intelligence, a theory that holds that AI is a component supporting the activities of human beings, could be one solution to this worry [23, p. 439].

Integrating artificial intelligence (AI) within higher education (HE) has transformed educational practices and students' experiences. As AI advances from basic automation

Ł. Tomczyk (Ed.): NMP 2024, CCIS 2537, pp. 264–279, 2025.
https://doi.org/10.1007/978-3-031-95627-0_18

to sophisticated generative and augmented intelligence systems, its applications in HE encompass personalized learning, administrative efficiency, and enhanced engagement tools. However, the adoption and acceptance of these technologies hinge on user attitudes, digital competencies [14], and the perceived benefits of AI integration [12, 24].

Recent studies have highlighted the dual-edged nature of AI's potential in education. While AI promises greater accessibility and individualized support, it also raises ethical concerns and practical challenges, including privacy issues, algorithmic bias, and over-reliance on automation [23]. Understanding how students perceive and interact with AI tools is critical for fostering a responsible and effective educational environment. This preliminary study explores HE students' usage patterns and attitudes toward AI, contributing to the ongoing discourse on the future of technology-enhanced learning environments.

The research aims to evaluate the benefits and limitations of AI from the student perspective. It seeks to inform institutional strategies for integrating AI in ways that enhance learning while addressing ethical and pedagogical concerns.

Research Question: How are students using, preferring, trusting, and aware of AI?

2 Literature Review

Despite the growing integration of AI tools in educational settings, there is a notable gap in research concerning students' sustained usage and attitudes towards these technologies. Previous studies have primarily focused on the initial acceptance and adoption of AI tools, leaving the factors influencing their continued use relatively unexplored. Understanding these factors is crucial for leveraging the full potential of AI in HE and ensuring that students can effectively utilize these technologies and enhance learning outcomes [7].

Insights from research on student perception can therefore be used to influence educational policies and practices regarding the incorporation of AI in HE [23].

2.1 Use of AI

According to a study [7], students' attitudes towards and trust in generative artificial intelligence (GenAI) directly impacted their intention to continue using it for learning. Their attitude towards GenAI, on the other hand, was based on social influence, effort anticipation, and facilitating circumstances. Also, faith in GenAI, as a result of these factors, was established.

The author [6, p. 37] found that higher education students are more likely to intend to use GenAI in their learning if they perceive it easy to use and beneficial for their daily studies. For instance, students are less likely to employ new technology for learning if they find it easy to use yet it does not improve their learning outcomes. According to [2, 15], students are more inclined to embrace new technology if they believe that minimal effort would be required to use it. When people interact with AI, perceived risks and possible threats may be linked to ease of usage [15].

Students who understood AI and could describe GenAI showed a greater comprehension of how to use it correctly. However, many students failed to understand how to use GenAI appropriately, underscoring the need to include AI instruction in the curriculum [13, p. 673].

According to [9], students acknowledge the effectiveness of AI but express concerns about how it may affect academic integrity and learning quality. This highlights the necessity for a responsible and balanced integration of AI in education to provide long-lasting results. The findings showed that most students use AI technologies, albeit the frequency of use varies depending on the student's academic level and topic of study.

2.2 Preference and Trust in AI-Attitude

The study findings [12, p. 387] show that perceived benefits and adoption of AI in HE in the Arab world are positively and significantly correlated with adopted attitude, digital proficiency, and openness to experience. AI tools, such as voice recognition, visual aids, and translation services, can help students with special needs.

According to [3], students' attitudes and impressions of a technological innovation such as GenAI, including their thoughts, concerns, and experiences with the technology, can affect their preparedness to use the tool in an educational setting. Students are more likely to show a strong intention to continue using GenAI when they retain a positive attitude, defined as a favorable emotional disposition and a sense of satisfaction with their technology interactions, according to [7]. On the other hand, a negative attitude characterized by discontent or annoyance may discourage students from using GenAI anymore. Thus, students' attitudes regarding GenAI have a big impact on how committed they are to continuing to use the platform as a useful tool for their academic endeavors.

General awareness and familiarity with AI technologies have a beneficial impact on formal training and integration, worries about AI, perceived utility, and positive attitudes toward AI [20]. Moreover, positive attitudes, formal training and integration, and perceived utility all significantly improve the frequency of using AI tools. On the other hand, worries about AI which could harm positive attitudes and perceived utility. According to indirect effects, good attitudes and formal training raise general awareness, which in turn raises usage frequency. The broad acceptance and successful integration of AI can be facilitated by raising students' understanding, providing them with access to AI technologies, resolving their worries, and improving academic experiences and outcomes. A transformative learning experience can result from embracing technology with an open mind and a willingness to investigate its potential, enabling students to more successfully and efficiently accomplish their academic objectives [6].

2.3 Ethical Aspects and Awareness-Raising

Researchers [7, 11] have suggested that trust in AI can result in positive outcomes and continuous usage.

Incorporating GenAI into a master's-level instructional design course improved students' comfort level with the technology and their comprehension of its ethical implications. According to the AI-Ideas, Connections, Extensions (AI-ICE) Framework, most students were at the initial engagement stage and becoming more conscious of the ethical concerns and limitations of GenAI. A possible way to improve learning outcomes, spark ethical discussion, and encourage a more involved and thoughtful teaching methodology is to incorporate GenAI into educational settings [24]. Among the drawbacks, the research [20] raises issues with data security, ethical concerns, possible job loss, and psychological impacts. Teachers and students should get sufficient training and assistance to guarantee the ethical and successful AI application. Without training programs, which appear to be few and could lead to skills shortages and reluctance to change, the adoption and use of AI technologies may not go as planned or desired [5].

3 Methodology

The study focuses on descriptive, inferential, regression, and correlational statistical analysis to give a thorough and nuanced picture of various university students' views and usage of AI, as outlined in [21, p. 2]. The sample comprised 105 full-time undergraduate students of the Faculty of Education, University of Primorska in the 2023–24 academic year. Of these, 6 were male (5.71%) and 99 were female (94.28%), which is similar to the gender distribution of all students at the Faculty of Education, University of Primorska in the 2023–24 academic year, where 6.79% were male and 93.21% were female. The data were processed using IBM SPSS Statistics.

3.1 Methods

The study used descriptive, Spearman correlation, and causal non-experimental methods of pedagogical research. A five-point Likert-type scale (ranging from 1: Strongly disagree to 5: Strongly agree) and open-ended and optional questions were included in the online questionnaire, using application 1ka, utilized for the study. The questionnaire was developed and tested by the authors at the University of Primorska.

We used closed-ended questions to obtain demographic and AI use, attitude, and ethic frequency data, using a five-point Likert-type scale of views, and the remaining questions were open-ended. These issues were thematically divided into three constructs: usage and future usage (USE), preferences and trust in AI-attitude (ATT), and Ethical aspects and awareness-raising (ETHIC). Combining Usage and Future Usage into a single construct is supported by theoretical models that conceptualize technology adoption as a continuous and interdependent process. The Technology Acceptance Model [27], Unified Theory of Acceptance and Use of Technology [25], and Theory of Planned Behavior [26] provide a theoretical framework for integrating present and future usage into a unified construct. These frameworks highlight that adopting technology is an ongoing process in which previous and current usage behaviors significantly influence future intentions and sustained implementation.

Cronbach's Alpha was used as a measure of internal consistency or validity (Table 1). Cortina [4, p.102] stated that if the number of construct's items exceeds 10, Cronbach's Alpha greater or equal to 0.7 is preferred. If the number of construct items is smaller than 10, Cronbach's Alpha greater than 0.5 is preferred. KMO (0.816) And Bartlett's test (Chi-Square = 421.317; Sig. < 0.001) were used for sampling adequacy.

Normality tests were performed and data on variables and constructs were non-normal distributed. Furthermore, the variance inflation factor (VIF) was calculated for all variables USE, ATT, and ETHIC ranging from 1.316 to 2.488. The modified Breusch-Pagan statistic indicates that the error term is about the same across all values of the independent variables (sig. = 0.085) and there is homoscedasticity. Cook's distance was calculated as less than 1 (0.000 for minimum, 0.287 for maximum, and 0.015 for mean).

4 Empirical Findings and Discussion

This paper presents data and findings from selected Faculty of Education in Slovenia. The gender imbalance in the sample (94.28% female) likely influences correlations between AI adoption variables, as prior research shows gender-related differences in AI knowledge, attitudes, and behavioral intention. The study by [28] found that the attitude-intention relationship was stronger among males ($\beta = 0.670$) than females ($\beta = 0.363$), while [29] reported a significant gender correlation in AI tool knowledge ($r = 0.513$, $p < 0.001$). Additionally, research by [30] demonstrated that gender moderates the relationship between AI anxiety and perceived ease of use ($p = 0.018$). In contrast, the field of study had minimal impact on AI perceptions ($p > 0.05$), suggesting that while the findings are applicable across teacher education, they may not be fully generalizable to more gender-balanced populations.

4.1 Cronbach Alpha

Cronbach's Alpha (Table 1) was used to measure the internal consistency of the questionnaire. The results were found to be sufficient to conduct further statistical analyses. This is viewed as the most appropriate measure of reliability when applying Likert-scale statements [17].

Table 1. Comparison of the Cronbach Alpha.

Construct	Cronbach's Alpha
USE (4 items)	0.849
ATT (3 items)	0.464
ETHIC (3 items)	0.577

Note: Acceptable Cronbach Alpha values range from 0.577 to 0.849. A low Cronbach Alpha value may be due to a few questions, poor item intercorrelations, or heterogeneous constructs

4.2 Usage and Future Usage of AI

Findings (Table 2) highlight a significant disparity between respondents' expectations for AI's future role in education and their current experiences and usage of AI. Most respondents use AI occasionally at 35.2%, monthly at 24.8%, weekly at 20% and regularly at 10%. 9.5% never used AI.

Students graded that AI has impacted educational experiences with study aids so far with moderate impact (35.2%), minimal impact (22.9%), some impact (20%), and significant impact (20%). With the grade of maximum impact (1.9%).

Table 2. Usage and future usage-USE Construct.

Construct variables	Average (SD)
Q4 How often have you actively used any AI technology in your academic or personal life?	2.87 (1.16)
Q5 How has AI influenced your educational experiences so far?	2.58 (1.11)
Q8 How often do you intend to use AI in your academic life?	2.82 (1.09)
Q9 To what extent do you think AI will impact education over the next decade?	3.93 (0.71)

Note: SD-Standard Deviation

The frequency of intention to use AI in academic life is as follows: 46.7% rated it with occasionally, 21% with weekly, 19% with a monthly, 8.6% with regularly (several times a week or daily), and 4.8% with never.

The representation of the role of AI in education in the next decade is estimated: at 60% with significant impact, 20% with moderate impact, 18.1% with maximum impact, 1% with minimal impact, and 1% with some impact.

In the set of questions about the analysis of Usage and future usage (USE, Table 2), students chose the highest values for the statement "To what extent do you think AI will impact education over the next decade?", (3.93 (0.71), with lower SD. Students mostly expect AI to have a significant impact on education.

As shown in Table 3, USE is a better indicator for the respondents' reported future use when compared with the average of the construct reporting on the respondents' preferences and trust in AI-attitude (ATT) and Ethical aspects and awareness (ETHICS).

Table 3. Comparison of the constructs.

Construct	Average (SD)
USE (4 items)	3.05 (0.857)
ATT (3 items)	2.819 (0.588)
ETHIC (3 items)	2.425 (0.753)

Note: USE-usage and future usage of AI; ATT-preferences and trust in AI-attitude; ETHIC-Ethical aspects and awareness-raising

In the following, we also explored which fields or subjects students believe AI could enhance learning. Students' answers to the open-ended question show that mathematics (35 mentions) is the most frequently identified subject, followed by technology-related fields (25), natural sciences (20), languages (15), and social sciences (10). Many students also emphasized AI's potential for general use across all subjects, particularly in preparing seminar papers, notes, and clarifying content. Students view AI as a tool that can: (1) enhance explanations of complex concepts tailored to individual needs; (2) increase interactivity and engagement through visual aids and animated content; (3) facilitate administrative tasks like writing and organizing learning materials; and (4) improve knowledge accessibility by quickly clarifying challenging concepts. The study sought to gain further insight by including an open-ended question that asked students to describe the purposes for which they use AI technologies in their everyday lives and to provide specific examples. The responses reveal that students most commonly use AI for information retrieval and clarification, mentioned in more than 50% of cases. This includes quickly obtaining answers, clarifying unknown concepts, and accessing additional explanations. Educational purposes account for approximately 30% of responses, where students reported using AI to write seminar papers, solve mathematical problems, search for literature, and check for grammatical errors. Around 15% of responses relate to idea generation and creative uses, such as drafting written content, proposing activities, or creating meal plans. Practical applications of AI in everyday life, such as assistance with cooking, navigation, and travel planning, were mentioned in approximately 10% of responses. Additionally, about 15% of students reported either not using AI or using it very rarely.

To further understand students' perspectives on AI, the study included an open-ended question asking them to identify specific AI applications or technological advancements they would like to see in the future to enhance their academic experiences. The analysis reveals that ChatGPT is the most frequently mentioned AI tool (25% of responses), highlighting its current popularity among students. Key areas for future AI advancements include research support (20%), such as reliable literature searches and source summaries, language and writing tools (15%) for grammar correction and essay writing, and interactive learning applications (15%) featuring visual aids, quizzes, and tailored explanations. Students also expressed the need for affordable and accessible tools, particularly in the Slovenian language.

The results align with research [23], which asserts that most students support using GenAI in the classroom and that many believe AI improves their learning efficiency. Nearly all of the respondents are familiar with GenAI, especially ChatGPT (95%), and over a third of them regularly use it (albeit typically not with other chatbots). According to findings in [23], students frequently utilize and are aware of other AI language tools, particularly language translation systems. Several authors stress that we still don't fully understand how AI affects and will continue to affect HE in the future, both positively and negatively, and point to the lack of empirical research [1, 10].

4.3 Preferences and Trust in AI-Attitude

A portion of students agreed or moderately agreed with the construct's statements, while a smaller portion entirely accepted or rejected them (Table 4).

The potential of AI to create employment opportunities or perhaps pose a threat to employment in the future is estimated as: 49.5% somewhat threatening, 28.6% neither nor, 14.3% good opportunity, 6.7% mostly a threat, and 1% mostly an opportunity.

The use of AI technology in everyday life is rated: easy 40%, mostly easy 25.7%, somewhat easy 21%, very easy 11.4% and not easy 1.9%.

Table 4. Preferences and Trust in AI-ATT Construct.

Construct variables	Average (SD)
Q12 How do you perceive the potential of AI to create employment opportunities, or perhaps pose a threat to employment in the future?	2.53 (0.856)
Q13 Indicate to what extent you agree with the statement: "The use of artificial intelligence technology seems easy in everyday life.“	3.24 (0.976)
Q14 Define the level of trust in the decisions of AI systems?	2.69 (0.684)

Note: SD-Standard Deviation

Students also provided diverse examples of how AI applications and tools have personally benefited them in their academic and daily lives. Answers to open-ended questions show that students primarily use AI to enhance efficiency and productivity in both academic and personal contexts. The tools are particularly effective for information retrieval, content generation, and resolving complex questions. However, a segment of respondents remains hesitant due to perceived limitations or a lack of familiarity with AI tools. The analysis reveals several key areas of usage: (1) Information retrieval and problem-solving (60%): The majority of responses highlight the use of AI for quick access to information, resolving academic or everyday questions, and understanding complex concepts. (2) Support in academic work (40%): Many students use AI for assistance in writing seminar papers, creating presentations, and generating ideas for projects or essays. Specific examples include proofreading, grammar correction, and suggesting content organization. According to their opinion, AI is valued for explaining difficult concepts, suggesting examples, and providing additional materials for better understanding, particularly in subjects like mathematics and social sciences. It has also been instrumental in helping students prepare for exams and structure their assignments. (3) Efficiency and time-saving (25%): Students frequently mention how AI helps them save time by providing fast and concise responses, streamlining their work processes, and reducing the effort required to gather resources. Students appreciate the speed and ease of obtaining information or ideas, which allows them to focus on other aspects of their work. (4) General and creative use (15%): Some students noted using AI to improve the quality of written content, such as crafting emails or formal letters, and brainstorming ideas for creative tasks or personal projects. Examples include e.g., generating meal plans, organizing schedules, and drafting emails or formal requests. AI's ability to simplify tasks and present information in a structured manner was frequently highlighted.

Some students do not use AI tools (10%) - a smaller proportion of respondents reported minimal or no use of AI, citing a lack of trust in its accuracy or unfamiliarity with how to effectively access and apply it.

The level of trust in the decisions of AI systems (Table 4) is estimated: as moderate trust 52.4%, somewhat distrust 37.1%, mostly trust 7.6%, not at all trust 1.9%, and with highly trust 1%.

The responses to the open-ended question, which asked students to identify specific AI applications or technological advancements they would like to see in the future to enhance their academic experiences, also revealed a need for tools with greater accuracy and reliability to effectively support their educational needs.

Findings highlight that while respondents are generally comfortable using AI in their daily lives, there is limited trust in its decision-making and significant concerns regarding its potential impact on employment. In the set of questions about Preferences and Trust in AI (Table 4), students chose the highest values for the statement "The use of artificial intelligence technology seems easy in everyday life.", (3.24 (0.976)). This is encouraging but there can be noticed higher SD.

The data indicate a lower level of acquittance with AI employment opportunities and trust in the decisions of AI systems.

These findings suggest the need for further education and awareness on how to effectively integrate AI into learning and daily activities, addressing trust issues and providing guidance on its potential applications.

The survey's findings are consistent with those of several authors, who have found that teacher education still shows a general lack of knowledge and abilities among students regarding how to use AI in a pedagogical and didactic manner [19, p. 253; 22]. According to the respondents there is still much room for awareness, use, and attitude improvement e.g., the need to integrate AI more effectively into educational practices to align with student expectations and maximize its potential. According to [23] more than half of the students are worried about how chatbots will affect education in the future; they are far less concerned about other kinds of AI-language tools.

There is a need for targeted educational initiatives to bridge the knowledge gap, foster a deeper comprehension of AI technologies, and enhance students' ability to engage critically and responsibly with AI systems. The HE has not fully embraced digital transformation literacy, as is widely recognized [17].

4.4 Ethical Aspects and Awareness-Raising

According to the results of the measurement of the ETHIC construct, there were both advantages and disadvantages of using AI practice (Table 5).

Table 5. Ethical Aspects and Awareness-raising-ETHIC Construct.

Construct variables	Average (SD)
Q16 To what extent are you familiar with regulations and/or guidelines in the field of AI?	2.24 (1.05)
Q17 How well do you understand the capabilities and limitations of AI?	2.00 (0.82)
Q18 To what extent would you be interested in learning more about AI and its applications as part of your academic curriculum?	3.04 (1.17)

Note: SD-Standard Deviation

In the set of questions about the Ethical Aspects and Awareness-raising (Table 5), the students chose the highest values (3.04 (1.17)) for the statement "To what extent would you be interested in learning more about AI and its applications as part of your academic curriculum?".

The statement "To what extent are you familiar with regulations and/or guidelines in the field of AI?" has a somewhat lower agreement (2.24 (1.05)) but has a higher standard deviation. This implies a large dispersion in the responses.

The lowest score (2.00 (0.82)) students agreed with is the statement "How well do you understand the capabilities and limitations of AI?".

Findings highlight that while respondents show a strong interest in learning more about AI and its applications in their academic curriculum, their familiarity with regulations and understanding of AI's capabilities and limitations remain low.

The responses to the open-ended question, which asked students to reflect on the ethical considerations they believe should be taken into account in the development or use of AI technologies, reveal that students are both aware of and concerned about the ethical dimensions of AI technologies. The key issues—data privacy, transparency, intellectual property, accuracy, and human oversight—underscore the importance of integrating ethical considerations into AI development and use. Out of the 105 surveyed students, 30 students did not provide a response. Among the 75 responses, the most frequently mentioned issue was data privacy and security, mentioned by 35% of respondents. Students emphasized the importance of protecting personal and sensitive data, and ensuring AI systems do not collect, misuse, or share information without consent. Related to this, transparency and accountability (20%) were also highlighted, with many students advocating for AI systems to be understandable, transparent, and responsible for their actions. Other significant concerns include intellectual property and authorship (15%), where respondents raised issues about proper attribution and the ethical use of copyrighted materials. Accuracy and reliability (12%) were also noted as crucial, as students stressed the need for AI systems to provide trustworthy and verifiable information, avoiding the spread of false or misleading data.

Additionally, human oversight and autonomy (10%) emerged as an important theme, with respondents cautioning against over-reliance on AI and underscoring the need to maintain human control to protect critical thinking and independence. Some students (8%) also mentioned the importance of bias and inclusivity, emphasizing the need to design AI systems that include diverse perspectives and avoid reinforcing stereotypes or discriminatory practices. The qualitative insights provide further depth to these quantitative findings. Students frequently expressed the necessity of maintaining a balance between human and AI collaboration, ensuring that AI serves as a tool to assist humans without replacing critical human judgment. Concerns about intellectual property reflect a broader awareness of the ethical implications of using AI to generate content. Transparency was also viewed as essential for fostering trust in AI systems, with students urging for clarity about how algorithms operate and make decisions.

The results are in line with previous studies [5, 20, 23, 24], which assert that to improve familiarity with regulations and understanding of AI's capabilities and limitations, enhance ethical discussion, and encourage involvement and thoughtful teaching methodology is to incorporate GenAI into educational settings [24]. Teachers and students should get sufficient training and assistance to guarantee the ethical and successful application of AI. The adoption and usage of AI technologies may not go as expected in the absence of training programs, which seem to be few and may result in a lack of skills and resistance to change [5]. One in four students expressly states that their institution has no regulations or standards about the safe use of AI, while most students are unaware of whether their institution has any [23].

These findings highlight the need for educational efforts to raise awareness of ethical AI practices, equipping students with the knowledge to engage critically and responsibly with these technologies.

4.5 Correlations Between Constructs

The study employed the Spearman correlation coefficient to investigate potential relationships between usage and future usage (USE), preferences and trust in AI-attitude (ATT), and Ethical aspects and awareness-raising (ETHIC) (Table 6).

The highest correlation is between USE and ATT constructs which is moderate (0.589). Correlations between USE and ETHIC (0.465) and ATT and ETHIC (0.488) are weak. All the correlations are positive and statistically significant at the 0.01 level.

The correlation analysis suggested that the USE construct is primarily associated with ATT and is somewhat less related to the ETHIC constructs.

Table 6. Correlations between Constructs.

Construct	USE	ATT	ETHIC
USE	-	0.589**	0.465**
ATT	0.588**	-	0.488**
ETHIC	0.465**	0.488**	-

Note: ** Significant at the 0.01 level (2-tailed). Usage and future usage (USE), preferences and trust in AI-attitude (ATT), Ethical aspects and awareness-raising (ETHIC)

The results (see Table 6) are consistent with several research projects [2, 6, 15], which suggests that HE students are more likely to want to use GenAI for their learning if they think it will be simple to use and helpful for their regular coursework. According to research [23], a large number of students see the use of GenAI in education favorably and believe that they can improve their educational experiences. Alongside these favorable opinions, there are, nevertheless, serious reservations and ambiguities about the development of regulations and the long-term effects of GenAI in the classroom. Many respondents link AI to other technical developments, such as calculators, the internet, and Google, and say that the education system should adapt and "modernize" itself to accommodate the usage of AI [23].

4.6 Standardized Multiple Linear Regressions Analysis

The results of the linear regression analysis (Table 7) indicate that all regression models show a lower explanation power of 28.6% to 40.1%. That is, the models do not include all variables that would explain a larger proportion of the dependent variables. This is due to the sample size and the majority of respondents from the 1st year of B1 studies. This fact suggests the conclusion that there must be external factors that are not covered by the model used. External factors could, for instance, be policy, requirements, beliefs, cultural background, and external expectations.

Table 7. Standardized multiple linear regression analysis (Stepwise).

Predictors	Dependent variable	S.C.B.	Adjusted R-Squared
	ATT		0.389
ETHIC		0.246	
USE		0.474	
	ETHIC		0.286
USE		0.325	
ATT		0.288	
	USE		0.401
ATT		0.465	
ETHIC		0.273	

Note: Significant at the 0.01 level (2-tailed). S.C.B. is the standardized coefficient of the variable. Constructs: Usage and future usage (USE), preferences and trust in AI-attitude (ATT), Ethical aspects and awareness-raising (ETHIC)

Regarding the explanatory power of the regression coefficients (S.C.B.), we can summarize that in the case studied, the ATT coefficient has the highest explanation power (Table 7). USE construct is mostly predicted by Attitude with stronger S.C.B. (0.465) and partly by ETHIC (0.273). Model is explained with 40.1%.

So, preferences and trust in AI-attitude (ATT) remain the main construct that impacts students' current and future use of AI in their academic and private practice.

Authors [18] also noted that trust is one of the key factors influencing students' attitudes and intentions to use AI. Their study examined university students' attitudes and behaviors towards AI in higher education and highlighted that AI awareness, trust, and social influence have a significant impact on students' attitudes and intentions to use AI. Trust emerged as a key factor shaping positive attitudes and driving behavioral intentions, while social influence highlights the role of peer and social norms in the acceptance of AI. Their findings suggest that strengthening AI literacy and building trust are essential for greater integration of AI in educational contexts. Despite their strong predictive power, their study also finds that external factors such as policy and cultural influences may also play a role, emphasizing the need for broader systemic considerations.

The suggestions for incorporating GenAI into classrooms mainly mirror tried-and-true teaching methods, highlighting the value of conventional teaching methods despite technological advancements. These strategies include providing students with learning support systems, employing scaffolding to progressively increase task difficulty as students become proficient, and ensuring that learning experiences are genuine to boost engagement and relevance. Besides that, encouraging experiential learning allows students to apply knowledge in real-world situations, and creates collaborative learning environments where students can benefit from each other's knowledge. However, the focus on moral issues and appropriate technology use distinguishes these suggestions when applied to GenAI. This means teaching students how to use GenAI technologies efficiently and understanding the broader implications of their use, including bias, privacy, and the potential for misuse [24].

5 Conclusion

This study investigates attitudes towards AI technology in the educational setting. To address the research question: How are students using, preferring, trusting, and aware of AI?

Results indicate that, according to the respondents, there is still much room for awareness, use, and attitude improvements:

- the need to integrate AI more effectively into educational practices to align with student expectations and maximize its potential,
- the need for greater transparency, education, and ethical considerations to address trust and employment-related fears surrounding AI, including raising students' awareness about guidelines for the ethical use of AI at the university level, national level, and beyond, and
- the need for targeted educational initiatives to bridge the knowledge gap, foster a deeper comprehension of AI technologies, and enhance students' ability to engage critically and responsibly with AI systems.

Recommendations for using AI in the educational setting:

- Primarily reflect tried-and-tested teaching strategies, emphasizing the importance of traditional teaching methods improved with the integration of digital technologies.
- These strategies include developing collaborative learning environments where students can benefit from each other's knowledge and ensuring authentic learning experiences to increase engagement and relevance.
- Support systems should be available to aid in their learning and gradually increase the complexity of tasks as students gain proficiency.
- When applied to the field of artificial intelligence, these recommendations differ in their emphasis on ethical considerations and responsible use of technology. This includes teaching students how to use AI technologies effectively and helping them to understand broader applications such as ethics, privacy, and bias issues.
- Enhance AI Literacy by equipping students with the skills to utilize AI technologies efficiently. This involves practical applications like leveraging AI for research and problem-solving, as well as developing a critical awareness of broader topics such as ethics, privacy, and biases within AI systems. By enhancing AI literacy, students will acquire technical expertise while also gaining the capacity to critically analyze the societal and ethical impacts of AI in various settings.

- Encourage interdisciplinary use, where AI is not limited to specific subjects but is integrated into different fields of study. This approach helps students see the relevance of AI in their field and develop transferable skills that can be applied in real-life scenarios.
- Enable continuous professional development for educators to equip them with the knowledge and skills needed to effectively incorporate AI into their teaching practices. This training should cover the use of AI tools, approaches to addressing ethical concerns, and methods for adapting teaching strategies to align with AI functionalities.
- Ensure accessibility and inclusivity also by providing tools and resources to support students with diverse needs.
- Regular evaluation of the effectiveness of the integration of AI in educational settings is crucial. Student feedback, together with teacher observations, should be used to improve the educational process using AI tools and to ensure that this is in line with pedagogical objectives and ethical standards.

The research is limited by a single measurement, a small sample size, and the involvement of only one Slovenian Faculty of Education, which may lead to gender imbalance.

Future research focuses on extending the survey to students from different faculties and disciplines, which could improve the generalizability of the results. Prospects for future research include focus groups in the design of the assessment instrument and in the process of developing and validating the pedagogical digital competency model. Limited research has been conducted on the effects of all significant constructs on students' future efficiency and effectiveness in the classroom and future workplace, including developmental and diagnostic evaluations.

Disclosure of Interests. The authors have no competing interests to declare that are relevant to the content of this article.

References

1. Adiguzel, T., Kaya, M. H., Cansu, F.K.: Revolutionizing education with AI: Exploring the transformative potential of ChatGPT. Contemp. Educ. Technol. **15**(3), ep429 (2023). https://doi.org/10.30935/cedtech/13152
2. Alyoussef, I.Y.: Acceptance of a flipped classroom to improve university students' learning: an empirical study on the TAM model and the unified theory of acceptance and use of technology (UTAUT). Heliyon **8**(12), e12529 (2022). https://doi.org/10.1016/j.heliyon.2022.e12529
3. Chan, C.K.Y., Hu, W.: Students' voices on generative AI: perceptions, benefits, and challenges in higher education. Int. J. Educ. Technol. High. Educ. **20**(1), 43–18 (2023). https://doi.org/10.1186/s41239-023-00411-8
4. Cortina, J.M.: What is coefficient alpha? An examination of theory and applications. J. Appl. Psychol. **78**(1), 98–104 (1993). https://doi.org/10.1037/0021-9010.78.1.98
5. Denecke, K., Glauser, R., Reichenpfader, D.: Assessing the potential and risks of ai-based tools in higher education: results from an eSurvey and SWOT analysis. Trends Higher Educ. **2**(4), 667–688 (2023). https://doi.org/10.3390/higheredu2040039

6. Duong, C.D., Bui, D.T., Pham, H.T., Vu, A.T., Nguyen, V.H.: How effort expectancy and performance expectancy interact to trigger higher education students' uses of ChatGPT for learning. Interact. Technol. Smart Educ. **21**(3), 356–380 (2024). https://doi.org/10.1108/ITSE-05-2023-0096
7. Duong, C.D.: Modeling the determinants of HEI students' continuance intention to use ChatGPT for learning: a stimulus–organism–response approach. J. Res. Innov. Teach. Learn. **17**(2), 391–407 (2024). https://doi.org/10.1108/JRIT-01-2024-0006
8. Ertel, W.: Introduction to Artificial Intelligence. Springer, Weingarten (2017)
9. Fošner, A.: University students' attitudes and perceptions towards AI tools: implications for sustainable educational practices. Sustainability **16**, 8668 (2024). https://doi.org/10.3390/su16198668
10. García-Peñalvo, F.J.: The perception of artificial intelligence in educational contexts after the launch of ChatGPT: disruption or panic? Educ. Knowl. Soc. **24**, e31279 (2023). https://doi.org/10.14201/eks.31279
11. Gkinko, L., Elbanna, A.: Designing trust: the formation of employees' trust in conversational AI in the digital workplace. J. Bus. Res. **158**, 113707 (2023). https://doi.org/10.1016/j.jbusres.2023.113707
12. Hazaimeh, M., Al-Ansi, A.M.: Model of AI acceptance in higher education: arguing teaching staff and students perspectives. Int. J. Inf. Learn. Technol. **41**(4), 371–393 (2024). https://doi.org/10.1108/IJILT-01-2024-0005
13. Iwasawa, M., Kobayashi, M., Otori, K.: Knowledge and attitudes of pharmacy students towards artificial intelligence and the ChatGPT. Pharm. Educ. **23**(1), 665–675 (2023). https://doi.org/10.46542/pe.2023.231.665675
14. Janeš, A., Madsen, S.S., Saure, H.I., et al.: Preliminary results from norway, slovenia, portugal, turkey, ukraine, and jordan: investigating pre-service teachers' expected use of digital technology when becoming teachers. Educ. Sci. **13**, 783 (2023). https://doi.org/10.3390/educsci13080783
15. Lim, W.M., Gunasekara, A., Pallant, J.L., Pallant, J.I., Pechenkina, E.: Generative AI and the future of education: Ragnarök or reformation? A paradoxical perspective from management educators. Int. J. Manag. Educ. **21**(2) (2023). https://doi.org/10.1016/j.ijme.2023.100790
16. Malmström, H., Stöhr, C., Ou, A. W.: Chatbots and other AI for learning: a survey of use and views among university students in Sweden. Chalmers, Sweden (2023). https://doi.org/10.17196/cls.csclhe/2023/01
17. Martzoukou, K., Fulton, C., Kostagiolas, P., Lavranos, C.: A study of higher education students' self-perceived digital competences for learning and everyday life online participation. J. Doc. **76**(6), 1413–1458 (2020). https://doi.org/10.1108/JD-03-2020-0041
18. Obenza, B. N., Caballo, J. H. S., Caangay, R. B. R. et al.: Analyzing university students' attitude and behavior toward ai using the extended unified theory of acceptance and use of technology model. Am. J. Appl. Stat. Econ. **3**(1), 99–108 (2024). https://doi.org/10.54536/ajase.v3i1.2510
19. Røkenes, F.M., Krumsvik, R.J.: Prepared to teach ESL with ICT? A study of digital competence in Norwegian teacher education. Comput. Educ. **97**, 1–20 (2016). https://doi.org/10.1016/j.compedu.2016.02.014
20. Sova, R., Tudor, C., Tartavulea, C.V., Dieaconescu, R.I.: Artificial Intelligence tool adoption in higher education: a structural equation modeling approach to understanding impact factors among economics students. Electronics **13**, 3632 (2024). https://doi.org/10.3390/electronics13183632
21. Stöhr, C., Ou, A.W., Malmström, H.: Perceptions and usage of AI chatbots among students in higher education across genders, academic levels and fields of study. Comput. Educ. Artif. Intell. **7**, 100259 (2024). https://doi.org/10.1016/j.caeai.2024.100259

22. Urrea-Solano, M., Hernández-Amorós, M.J., Merma-Molina, G., Baena-Morales, S.: The learning of E- sustainability competences: a comparative study between future early childhood and primary school teachers. Educ. Sci. **11**, 644 (2021). https://doi.org/10.3390/educsci11100644
23. Wójcik, M.: Augmented intelligence technology: the ethical and practical problems of its implementation in libraries. Library Hi Tech **39**(2), 435–447 (2021). https://doi.org/10.1108/LHT-02-2020-0043
24. Wood, D., Moss, S.H.: Evaluating the impact of students' generative AI use in educational contexts. J. Res. Innov. Teach. Learn. **17**(2), 152–167 (2024). https://doi.org/10.1108/JRIT-06-2024-0151
25. Elkefi, S., Tounsi, A., Kefi, M.A.: Use of ChatGPT for education by engineering students in developing countries: a mixed-methods study. Behav. Inf. Technol., 1–19 (2024). https://doi.org/10.1080/0144929x.2024.2354428
26. Wang, C., Wang, H., Li, Y., Dai, J., Gu, X.: Factors influencing university students' behavioral intention to use generative artificial intelligence: integrating the theory of planned behavior and AI literacy. Int. J. Hum.-Comput. Interact., 1–21 (2024). https://doi.org/10.3390/bs14100956
27. Davis, F.D.: Perceived usefulness, perceived ease of use, and user acceptance of information technology. MIS Q. **13**(3), 319–340 (1989). https://doi.org/10.2307/249008
28. Bayaga, A.: Leveraging AI-enhanced and emerging technologies for pedagogical innovations in higher education. Educ. Inf. Technol. Off. J. IFIP Techn. Committee Educ. **30**, 1045–1072 (2024). https://doi.org/10.1007/s10639-024-13122-y
29. Lamrabet, M.: AI-based tools: exploring the perceptions and knowledge of Moroccan future teachers regarding ai in the initial training—a case study. Int. J. Inf. Educ. Technol. **14**(11), 1493–1505 (2024). https://doi.org/10.18178/ijiet.2024.14.11.2180
30. Zhang, C., Schießl, J., Plößl, L., Hofmann, F., Gläser-Zikuda, M.: Acceptance of artificial intelligence among pre-service teachers: a multigroup analysis. Int. J. Educ. Technol. High. Educ. **20**(49) (2023). https://doi.org/10.1186/s41239-023-00420-7

Artificial Intelligence Metaphors for Students as a Fundament for Developing AI Literacy

Michal Černý(✉)

Faculty of Art, Masaryk University, Arne Nováka 1, 602 00 Brno, Czech Republic
mcerny@phil.muni.cz

Abstract. Metaphors are a form of abstraction of a particular model of reality, which is usually more complex and complicated. However, through metaphors, a person - a student - can get hold of complex phenomena and work with them. This abstraction is, at the same time, a form of cognitive shortcut, which always departs from specific details and characteristics of the phenomenon and, at the same time, can provide new insights into it. These insights can be inspiring but also misleading and simplistic. The study uses data from university students reflecting on their perceptions of what AI means to them and how they think about it. The study identifies four fundamental metaphors representing a student structuring of the AI phenomenon and offering specific educational strategies: Enkidu, Politics before the elections, Goddess Gaia and Extensions of the cognition.

Keywords: Metaphors · Artificial Intelligence · Philosophy of Education · Tacit Knowledge · Qualitative Analysis · University Students · Analysis of Metaphors · Conceptual Metaphors

1 Introduction

From 2022 onwards, we can see the development of artificial intelligence in all areas of human life, and it is only natural that it also affects the field of education [1–3]. The development of large language models allows many activities to be performed differently than before [4, 5] and enables a dialogue with the user [6, 7]. Dialogue is seen in the philosophical tradition as a specific manifestation of thinking [8–10] on which the Turing test is based. [11–13]. After an incredible fascination with and ignorance of the technological possibilities of large-scale language models, we are now in a situation where most undergraduate learners have active experience with AI, working with it, reflecting on its limitations, or conversely considering its possibilities [14, 15]. Therefore, our aim in this study will not be to define artificial intelligence as a phenomenon or technology [16, 17] nor to trace its social implications [18–20]. However, these are also implicit in the perception of artificial intelligence, and we will try in this study to trace students' perceptions of this phenomenon through the analysis of their metaphorical statements.

Research using metaphors to conceptualise various phenomena is relatively common, even in educational contexts [21–24]. As such, the exact definition of metaphor is

Ł. Tomczyk (Ed.): NMP 2024, CCIS 2537, pp. 280–292, 2025.
https://doi.org/10.1007/978-3-031-95627-0_19

complex and inconsistent. In our study, we will view it through a dual lens. The first is an implicit understanding of metaphor in terms of the assignment for students ("create a metaphor that…"), in which we have deliberately not gone into a deeper description of what a metaphor is. I expect students to draw on common school knowledge describing metaphor as a linguistic construction that transfers meaning based on external similarity, i.e., specific linguistic ornamentation [25].

As Lakoff and Johnson point out, this linguistic structure has long received insufficient attention and was thought to constitute only the aesthetic structure of language [25]. Our analysis is based on the beliefs of pragmatist philosophy [26] that the meaning of metaphors is much deeper, namely that, based on reflection on the environment and work in it, meanings are formed which can then be deconstructed and analysed, creating a specific conceptual-content structure that allows (through the unity of thought and action) to understand how students think about AI [25, 27]. Both authors demonstrate that the exploratory power of such metaphorical models enables us to understand the lived experience differently than conventional research methods [25, 28].

It is crucial for our research that we can use learners' metaphors to construct tailored foundational metaphors, i.e., prototypes through which it is possible to analyse how learners relate to the phenomenon of artificial intelligence. This knowledge forms the fundamental premise for subsequent education, which, on the one hand, must be based on the conceptualisation of AI literacy [29–32]. On the other hand, it must be based on the experience that learners manifest through the metaphor since different metaphors can (and will) lead to different educational strategies [23, 33].

2 Methodology

As the introduction indicates, the research searches for fundamental metaphors central to students' engagement with AI. At the same time, research on metaphors is relatively standard in pedagogy [21–24], at the same time methodologically inconsistent and can focus on different actors or structures of educational interactions with varying strengths of interpretation [34]. At the core of the research is the question:

What metaphors do learners use to describe their relationship with AI?

This is then followed by the discussion we have at the end of the study, namely, what educational approaches and concepts we should approach in the light of these metaphors [34] to develop AI literacy in learners [31].

2.1 Research Sample

The research sample was 58 students enrolled in the CORE100 AI Revolution: Artificial Intelligence as an Opportunity and Threat to Society course taught at Masaryk University in the fall semester of 2024. This course is offered to all pressure undergraduate students at the university, allowing them to gain a foundation in a particular scientific field or discipline. This course specifically focuses on using artificial intelligence and its impact on society. It combines hands-on activities focused on prompt creation and using various tools with critical analysis of selected social phenomena related to artificial intelligence. Thus, learners have a systematic experience with artificial intelligence during the semester and by thinking about their impact. Having a developed and shaped expertise is crucial to the research methodology.

The most significant number of students is from the Faculty of Arts (29), followed by the Faculty of Law (8), the Faculty of Economics and Administration (6), the Faculty of Informatics (5), the Faculties of Education and Science and the Faculty of Social Studies have 3 students each. One student is from the Faculty of Medicine. There are two students each in the seventh and ninth semesters.

2.2 Data Collection

Data collection took place between September 25 and December 20, 2024. As one of the assignments in the course, students were asked to write and explain a metaphor that expresses their perception of AI in any form - a short text, poem, essay, image, video, animation, or anything else. Students turned in assignments as files to the course submission room.

2.3 Data Analysis

Data analysis can be divided into two steps. In the first, we retrieved files from the university repository from students and combined these into one large document. This also performed anonymisation - no assignment was analysed with the presence of the student's name. This file was then uploaded to Taguette, where the metaphor analysis occurred.

The data processing was a combination of closed and open coding. For closed coding, we needed to know what media form the learners chose (picture, song, poem, simile, story, description - we gradually expanded this range as we encountered objectively existing forms of communication). We were also interested in learners' attitudes toward AI (positive, ambivalent, or negative). While the forms sometimes overlapped for the assessment, we always leaned towards the most likely option.

But the key step is the actual search for fundamental metaphors. We have methodologically drawn on the pedagogical approach of Švec [23, 33], except that, unlike him, we are working with the interview and pure language method but with fixed learner statements. In particular, Lakoff and Johnson [25, 28] noted that we were looking for metaphors in the same way they were looking for them to describe political structures or language. We eventually arrived at four fundamental metaphors (corresponding partly to [25]) by repeatedly counting the responses, coding, and restructuring the codes. These are subsequently presented in the results.

2.4 Ethics and Limits of Research

In terms of research ethics, this was ensured by fully anonymising the outputs at the level of data aggregation. The research was conducted over the data of Czech and Slovak learners, with the metaphors submitted in their native languages. The result presented in the study is a translation, so even with knowledge of the learner's specific lexicon, deanonymisation is not possible. If the output was a poem, we used ChatGPT-4 to translate the English translation. However, the original language texts were used for the actual analysis.

There are four limitations of the research, and all of them are related to the methodology used. The advantage of metaphors is that it is easy to access deeper mental structures and to understand meaningfully what respondents are thinking and experiencing [22, 23, 26, 27]. At the same time, however, it highlights the limitations of a qualitative approach - the sample is, in some ways, specific. For broader application in education, it would be helpful to consider the extent to which the metaphors found are transferable to other settings. It can be expected that the way metaphors are constructed will depend strongly on one's experience of the environment in which one finds oneself [26, 35]. For younger and older learners alike, the structuring of metaphors will likely need to be sought in different ways. The second limitation is finding fundamental metaphors that will be influenced by the researcher's knowledge and experience field. A third limitation typical of qualitative research is the sample size, although it appears that since task 30, the sample has been saturated, and new metaphors have not emerged.

The fourth limitation may be that students cannot accurately express their AI metaphor. They can work with AI and use it for many activities, but they may not have the creativity or insight to make the metaphor robust and accurate. In this study, we expect that such learners exist but that the choice of fundamental metaphors is, by its qualitative nature, such that (a) if they are expressed inaccurately, there is no distortion of the fundamental metaphor, and (b) we do not perform a quantitative analysis so that if a metaphor is misclassified, it should not affect the formulation of the fundamental metaphor per se concerning (a).

3 Results and Analysis

All 54 metaphors were analysed (11 poems, three pictures, one song, three stories, 12 descriptions, and 27 similes - some metaphors have more than one component). Positive discourse dominates (25 metaphors), followed by ambivalent (12) and negative (8). The images, music, and one poem were AI-generated, based on student input. Not all of them could be classified or did not contain a value sentiment.

We structure the individual metaphors into standard metaphorical fields that tell us how learners relate to AI. We will refer to these fields as foundational metaphors and capture them in Table 1, including their essential characteristics.

3.1 Artificial Intelligence as Enkidu

In analysing the metaphors that the learners expressed through the poems, we can focus on a reasonably clearly demarcated area, which is characterised by the fact that AI can have the character of something creative and close:

"AI is a quiet aide, steadfast and true,
In class and at work, always near you.
It helps us tackle what once caused dismay,
And organizes our plans in a seamless way."

Table 1. The table shows the basic metaphors that emerged about AI among the learners.

Fundamental metaphor	The position of the human	Characteristics of AI	AI personalisation	Human evaluation of AI
Enkidu	Human AI is in complete control and determines the modes of interaction	A powerful actor with a wide range of options	Strong	Positive
Politics before the elections	Humans are being manipulated and threatened by AI	A liar, a deceiver, an element seeking to manipulate a person	Strong	Negative
Goddess Gaia	Humans are in an environment shaped by AI that they can do nothing about	The omnipresent transcending entity	Weak	Ambivalent
Extensions of the cognition	Humans need to take a clear stance towards AI. This position he freely chooses for himself	A tool that expands the possibilities of thinking and acting	Strong	Positive or negative

"You accelerate the pace of everyday life,
A nurse, a mother, a grandmother's strife.
You take their roles, their tasks you replace,
Supporting each with tireless grace."

"To take or to leave?
Birth good, progress grieve?
Will I shape it? Will you?
Questions fall silent,
Answers: both fearful and true."

"In the world of ideas, the fog runs deep,
Chaos thrives where the wild weeds creep.
AI, the gardener, with net in hand,
Prunes the thoughts, lets the flowers stand."

"It sorts the seeds, it plucks the weeds,

Gathers the notions the garden needs.
Now blooms a space, both bright and pure,
Where darkness reigned, life's scents endure."

It is typical of the poems used by the students that they anthropomorphise artificial intelligence and at the same time seem to overestimate the role and freedom of man, who in these poems acts as a kind of autonomous sovereign who can easily decide for himself who the artificial intelligence will be for him. There is a specific "unearthly power" typical of the latter, as well as a plane of proximity; it seems as if, for some of the scholars using this metaphor, the artificial intelligence is the Enkidu of the Epic of Gilgamesh - an unbridled and powerful friend whose possibilities far exceed those of the ordinary man who has inculturated himself, whose friendship is earned by man's own decision. In other forms of metaphor, however, this Enkidu-like model does not occur or occurs only to a minimal extent, which may lead us to suppose that poetry enables precisely the constitution of such a thought model.

3.2 Artificial Intelligence as a Politician Before the Elections

Typologically, at first glance, the opposite group is metaphors, for which the essential connection of artificial intelligence with something explicitly negative, with personalised evil, often wrapped in a marketing-attractive package. As in the previous cases, the AI is personalised so that it has the characteristics of a person, but in this case, carried by its moral profile.

Examples of such conceptualisations include "AI is like a politician's promise before an election," "AI is like that, a brilliant, good-hearted, unguarded criminal on the loose." or "a child prodigy… Who others idealise *and trust what he says."*

All three examples have in common that they try to create a certain impression that is patently false. As another student writes: "*To me, AI is a bit like Clever Hans - a horse that could count. (…) But neither AI nor Clever Hans are capable of thinking for themselves. Hans didn't learn arithmetic like children in school, and AI didn't learn to think like children in life."* This significant conclusion sets up an important discourse on artificial intelligence among some learners.

On the one hand, it is untrustworthy. It does not speak the truth. It only imitates thought and speech. It is a sophisticated confidence game that can have immeasurable consequences, just as when one believes the promises of politicians or thinks that Hans the horse can count. It is a cognitive fallacy, but one that can have serious consequences. The cognitive fallacy is that the generative AI accentuates what we want to hear, saying (like a politician or a child prodigy) precisely the expected things that are conventional to the pre-existing thought structure of the one interacting with them. Another essential aspect of the metaphor is that the AI can do or think something to believe people want it to. And it does so strongly that it loses any critical distance. The seamless interpretation of the world is replaced by the adherents of this metaphor with the associated banality.

At the same time, the politician is the one who has the power, so he is the "*Arbiter of human fate*".

3.3 Artificial Intelligence as the Goddess Gaia

Another group of metaphors about artificial intelligence situates it in the natural world, either as part of it or linking it to some natural element.

> *"It is spring, and the tree is awakening. It is branching out and expanding its crown of artificial intelligence with more and more branches. The older it gets, the stronger its roots become and the easier it can withstand the possible winds of the internet. It can withstand the storm of viruses and adapt to the sunlight of monitors and the different seasons. However, the tree is still young, and its flowers are slowly budding. They find their place on the tree and in a garden full of ones and zeros. More and more young trees are joining it."*

> *"A river always starts somewhere, but it never ends. It keeps flowing, on and on, without end. The imaginary place of ending is the sea or the ocean, but it does not begin anywhere, so it cannot end. I see the same thing with information, which we can now draw on virtually without limit thanks to AI."*

> *"AI is a fire that can both warm and burn."*

> *"Artificial intelligence is a normal part of my life, expressed in the first person: it has become as natural to me as the air I breathe. It is a ubiquitous but often unnoticed force that integrates seamlessly into my daily existence. Just as oxygen sustains my body, artificial intelligence sustains the digital structure that powers my modern life on the fly."*

It is evident from the statements that artificial intelligence is understood here as an element shaping the environment, as something that is everywhere and cannot be avoided, that becomes part of nature both in the sense of natural as permanent and solid, as the cornerstone of reality, and also natural in the sense of natural. If artificial intelligence is fire, air, river, tree or sun, it can be said to become part of the order of the world. Such a model does not allow for distance or critical analysis. These metaphors are often ambivalent because it makes no sense to evaluate nature, which is neither good nor bad but only is.

At the same time, it is interesting that they move away from the model of the persona to an impersonal, in a sense, a transcending concept that permeates everything. Through the embedding of artificial intelligence in the space of nature, a structure is thus created that is unregulatable and independent of man, which, following the example of Greek mythology, becomes an arché (αρχη), an element that permeates everything, the basis of all reality. It is a "*living tapestry,*" complex, woven, constantly growing, and connected to everything.

3.4 Artificial Intelligence as an Extension of Cognition

A special group is metaphors that personalise artificial intelligence with art but which are not done with sufficient quality, an example being:

> *"AI sculptor: from a chaotic block of data, AI begins to carve a sculpture, as in marble stone on laptop screens."*

> *"AI is an automated brush in the hands of a painter; it renders a painting quickly, but if you use it all the time, your brushstrokes can lose subtlety and depth."*

In these examples, it is clear that AI can generate digital objects very efficiently ("*Once* [Cinderella] *even had to write a bachelor's thesis for one of her sisters, but fortunately, thanks to the help of ChatGPT, it wasn't a big problem for her, and she spent a fraction of her time on it*"). Still, the result is not genuinely creative and profound, it is essentially superficial, banal, and lacks depth. In counterpoint to this metaphor are those that make AI a second brain:

> *"For me, AI is like a second brain. I used it most for studying when I needed to look up some information or just needed it to be worded differently. I sometimes discuss information with the chatbot to get feedback and see if I understand it correctly."*
>
> *"AI is like a silent partner in the thought process. It's like a trusted friend who quietly listens and offers new perspectives I might not have thought of alone. It's a partner that doesn't get in the way but supports - like an invisible hand that directs the flow of thoughts and helps find new connections and answers. AI is not there to guide, but to gently complement and expand my thinking."*
>
> *"Artificial intelligence is nowadays a tool that has already simplified and accelerated work in many areas. AI can be compared to a potter's wheel, making work easier."*
>
> *"AI is like Tom Raddle's diary from Harry Potter - every time you confide in it, the answer appears as if written in invisible ink. It listens to you, responds to your thoughts, and even though it looks like an ordinary page, there's much more to it than meets the eye."*

Although these two metaphors form opposite structurations of reality at first glance - the banal artist vs. the second brain, the silent friend - they refer to the same structure. Artificial intelligence is seen as an extension of the self, allowing a person to be faster, more efficient, and think better. Of course, this goes back to how we relate to this extension, whether we perceive a trivialisation or a higher performance and discrete support. What is shared, then, is a connection to the extended mind, however polarising its evaluation, sharpening the dilemma of how we relate to such an extension - the technology is there. It is impossible not to relate to it.

4 Discussion

If we analyse the concepts presented in the results section, we can summarise their pros and cons (with a degree of generalisation) in Table 2. We know that the individual learners' accounts do not all form equally central prototypical representatives for the fundamental metaphors, which aligns with Lakoff's research [27, 36]. Nevertheless, the table may be a good starting point for considering an educational strategy to develop AI literacy.

As for the first structural metaphor, which we refer to as Enkidu, it can be said to be closely related to the idea of technology as a form of implicit religion [37, 38] in

Table 2. The table captures the main advantages and disadvantages of metaphors concerning AI literacy and educational perspectives of working with a given metaphor.

Fundamental metaphor	The pros of metaphor	The cons of metaphor
Enkidu	Emphasis on the person's activity and ability to use the tool	Uncritical approach to technology, lack of reflection on AI's social and ethical implications
Politics before the elections	Critical evaluation of AI, distance, and emphasising the ethical and social dimensions of working with AI	Possible rejection of AI as such, risk of falling into the digital abyss
Goddess Gaia	AI is part of our space, absent the fascination with technology	Absence of critical distance, impossibility of ethical evaluation, and possible reflection on the phenomenon
Extensions of the cognition	The obligation to take a stand, the emphasis on the tool's usefulness, and its reflection in the individual's situation	Simplistic (either/or) evaluation scheme, one-sidedness, lack of context

which a discourse of the power of man controlling technology is present, but which, in the context of the broader discussion, gives a romantic impression rather than a reality corresponding to reality [39–41]. In the case of working with these learners, it is essential to seek ways of reflecting more broadly and challengingly on the role of technology in society and to work consistently to analyse the impact of AI on society, for example, through social media [42, 43]. Educationally, on the other hand, we can take advantage of the distinct anchoring in our own experience and the fact that people inhabiting this metaphorical field with technology have a powerful experience that they can gradually transform into their actions [44].

In some ways, the opposite is the position of the 'politician before the election,' who is sufficiently critical and working at a distance to reflect on the need to reconceptualise specific policies and strategies for the operation of AI [41, 45]. These vital skills are essential to reap here and framing the entire field in information literacy [46, 47]. It is necessary to look for ways to maintain a critical perspective while encouraging the framing of experience and working with AI tools where beneficial [48]. It is Floridi's emphasis on the absence of real intelligence [48] represents an essential feature of working with this group of students if AI literacy education is to be credible.

Perhaps the most educationally challenging group is the people using the "Goddess Gaia" metaphor. Its decisive advantage over the previous two concepts is the low level of AI personalisation [48], which makes it possible to remove some essential misconceptions. For this group, it is crucial to identify themes that can be the subject of concrete critical discussion [40, 49], which will allow for at least a partially critical approach to the topic [30]. It is essential to look for ways that will lead to the empowerment of learners [45, 50].

In the last group, working with the metaphor of the extension of cognition, one can see an easy continuity with the philosophical concept of the extended mind [51, 52], a distinct concept with implications for educational strategies. The approach to education in this area is fundamental in removing the dualistic reasoning model - either/or [53, 54], which reduces thinking to a choice between two options. The gradual removal of this dualism [27] also in other areas of education can lead to positive results in the development of AI literacy.

Our research demonstrates that some conceptualisations of AI literacy [55]that emphasise only rationalist positions and imagine it as a strictly logical and rational matter are educationally unsustainable and, above all, do not correspond to psychological findings [56] nor the social reality [28]. Education needs a more balanced and comprehensive system that can integrate the learner's experience well while allowing for critical distance that can change over time and knowledge [57].

5 Conclusion

The study identified four fundamental metaphors learners use to understand AI: Enkidu, Politician before Election, Goddess Gaia, and Cognition Extension. Each of these metaphors carries certain biases or limitations but also contains good reasons why the learners may hold them. It demonstrates that the topic of artificial intelligence, through its novelty, enters the experiential field and requires a certain metaphorical (and thus mental, conative, and value) structuring that is not easy yet necessarily occurs. We see it as a significant educational challenge to find ways to help different groups of learners whose needs (and biases and strengths) are differentiated to overcome misconceptions. Given the nature of technological change, metaphor research (arguably) suggests deeper thought structures that can be worked with more long-term and systematically.

References

1. Abdullah, M., Madain, A., Jararweh, Y.: ChatGPT: fundamentals, applications and social impacts. In: 2022 Ninth International Conference on Social Networks Analysis, Management and Security (SNAMS), pp. 1–8. IEEE, Milan (2022). https://doi.org/10.1109/SNAMS58071.2022.10062688
2. Baidoo-Anu, D., Owusu Ansah, K.: Education in the era of generative artificial intelligence (AI): understanding the potential benefits of ChatGPT in promoting teaching and learning (2023). https://papers.ssrn.com/sol3/papers.cfm?abstract_id=4337484 (2023)
3. Balmer, A.: A sociological conversation with ChatGPT about AI ethics, affect and reflexivity. Sociology, 00380385231169676 (2023)
4. Aydin, Ö.: Google Bard Generated Literature Review: the Metaverse. J. AI. 7, 1–14 (2023). https://doi.org/10.61969/jai.1311271
5. Murphy, P.: Writers and writers of writers: creativity and authorship in the first AI Novel by Paula Murphy, Kritikos, Vol. 19, Fall/Winter 2022/2023. Krikos Int. Interdiscip. J. Postmod. Cult. Sound Text Image. 2022/2023 (2023)

6. Vestrucci, A.: Introduction: five steps toward a religion-Ai dialogue. Zygon® **57**, 933–937 (2022). https://doi.org/10.1111/zygo.12828
7. Aboelmaged, M., Bani-Melhem, S., Ahmad Al-Hawari, M., Ahmad, I.: Conversational AI Chatbots in library research: an integrative review and future research agenda. J. Librariansh. Inf. Sci. 09610006231224440 (2024). https://doi.org/10.1177/09610006231224440
8. Heidegger, M.: Being and Time. Blackwell (1967)
9. Heidegger, M.: What Is Called Thinking? HarperCollins (1976)
10. Andrade, J.A.: The ethics of autonomous vehicles: levinas and naked streets. South Afr. J. Philos. **2**, 124–136 (2021)
11. Brynjolfsson, E.: The turing trap: the promise & peril of human-like artificial intelligence. In: Augmented Education in the Global Age, pp. 103–116. Routledge (2023)
12. Pinar Saygin, A., Cicekli, I., Akman, V.: Turing test: 50 years later. Minds Mach. **10**, 463–518 (2000). https://doi.org/10.1023/A:1011288000451
13. Sejnowski, T.J.: Large language models and the reverse turing test. Neural Comput. **35**, 309–342 (2023)
14. Ali, M.H., Kainat, M., Maqsood, M., Fernandez, S.F., Ali, S., Ahmad, M.: Chatbots in academic literacy exploring AI in education: In: Demir, Ş.Ş. and Demir, M. (eds.) Advances in Higher Education and Professional Development, pp. 37–59. IGI Global (2024). https://doi.org/10.4018/979-8-3693-1666-5.ch002
15. Abbas, N., Whitfield, J., Atwell, E., Bowman, H., Pickard, T., Walker, A.: Online chat and chatbots to enhance mature student engagement in higher education. Int. J. Lifelong Educ. **41**, 308–326 (2022). https://doi.org/10.1080/02601370.2022.2066213
16. Cobb, P.J.: Large Language models and generative AI, oh my!: archaeology in the time of ChatGPT, midjourney, and beyond. Adv. Archaeol. Pract. **11**, 363–369 (2023). https://doi.org/10.1017/aap.2023.20
17. Kublik, S., Saboo, S.: GPT-3: Building Innovative NLP Products Using Large Language models. O'Reilly Media Inc, Sebastopol (2022)
18. Eloundou, T., Manning, S., Mishkin, P., Rock, D.: GPTs are GPTs: An Early Look at the Labor Market Impact Potential of Large Language models (2023). http://arxiv.org/abs/2303.10130. https://doi.org/10.48550/arXiv.2303.10130
19. Hui, X., Reshef, O., Zhou, L.: The short-term effects of generative artificial intelligence on employment: evidence from an online labor market (2023). https://papers.ssrn.com/abstract=4527336. https://doi.org/10.2139/ssrn.4527336
20. Kőkuti, T.: Artificial intelligence in a transforming labour market-new skills are needed? J. Recycl. Econ. Sustain. Policy **2** (2023)
21. Fábián, G.: The application of improved metaphor analysis in education research. Procedia - Soc. Behav. Sci. **93**, 1025–1029 (2013). https://doi.org/10.1016/j.sbspro.2013.09.323
22. Lynch, H.L., Fisher-Ari, T.R.: Metaphor as pedagogy in teacher education. Teach. Teach. Educ. **66**, 195–203 (2017). https://doi.org/10.1016/j.tate.2017.03.021
23. Švec, V., Nehyba, J., Svojanovský, P.: Student Teachers Between Tacit and Explicit Knowledge. Masaryk University, Brno (2016)
24. Leino, A.-L., Drakenberg, M.: Research Bulletin 84 (1993)
25. Lakoff, G., Johnson, M.: Metaphors we Live By. The university of Chicago press, Chicago (2003)
26. Johnson, M.: The Meaning of the Body. University of Chicago Press, Chicago (2007)
27. Lakoff, G.: Women, Fire, and Dangerous Things: What Categories Reveal About the Mind. University of Chicago press, Chicago (2008)
28. Lakoff, G., Johnson, M.: Philosophy in the Flesh: the Embodied Mind and its Challenge to Western Thought. Basic Books, New York (1999)

29. Černý, M.: AI literacy in higher education: theory and design. In: Tomczyk, Ł. (ed.) New Media Pedagogy: Research Trends, Methodological Challenges, and Successful Implementations, pp. 364-379. Springer, Cham (2024). https://doi.org/10.1007/978-3-031-63235-8_24
30. Yi, Y.: Establishing the concept of AI literacy: focusing on competence and purpose. JAHR **12**, 353–368 (2021). https://doi.org/10.21860/j.12.2.8
31. Ng, D.T.K., Leung, J.K.L., Chu, S.K.W., Qiao, M.S.: Conceptualizing AI literacy: an exploratory review. Comput. Educ. Artif. Intell. **2**, 100041 (2021). https://doi.org/10.1016/j.caeai.2021.100041
32. Ng, D.T.K., Leung, J.K.L., Su, J., Ng, R.C.W., Chu, S.K.W.: Teachers' AI digital competencies and twenty-first century skills in the post-pandemic world. Educ. Technol. Res. Dev. **71**, 137–161 (2023). https://doi.org/10.1007/s11423-023-10203-6
33. Šíp, R., Švec, V.: The concept of tacit knowledge in the unified field paradigm. Pedagog. Orient. **23**, 664–690 (2013)
34. Weller, M.: Metaphors of Ed Tech. Athabasca University Press (2022). https://doi.org/10.15215/aupress/9781771993500.01
35. Johanns, B., Dinkens, A., Moore, J.: A systematic review comparing open-book and closed-book examinations: evaluating effects on development of critical thinking skills. Nurse Educ. Pract. **27**, 89–94 (2017)
36. Lakoff, G.: Cognitive Models and Prototype Theory. Core Readings, Concepts (1999)
37. Latzer, M.: The digital trinity-controllable human evolution-implicit everyday religion: characteristics of the socio-technical transformation of digitalization. KZfSS Cologne. Z. Für Soziol. Sozialpsychologie. **74**, 331–354 (2022). https://doi.org/10.1007/s11577-022-00841-8
38. Biana, H.T.: Feminist re-engineering of religion-based AI chatbots. Philosophies **9**, 20 (2024). https://doi.org/10.3390/philosophies9010020
39. Heidegger, M.: Die Frage nach der Technik; Wissenschaft und Besinnung ; Überwindung der Metaphysik ; Wer ist Nietzsches Zarathustra? Neske, Pfullingen (1967)
40. Bridle, J.: New Dark Age: Technology and the End of the Future. Verso Books (2018)
41. van Dijck, J.: Governing digital societies: private platforms, public values. Comput. Law Secur. Rev. **36**, 105377 (2020)
42. Berghel, H.: Malice domestic: the Cambridge analytica dystopia. Computer **51**, 84–89 (2018)
43. Hellemans, J., Willems, K., Brengman, M.: The new adult on the block: daily active users of TikTok compared to Facebook, Twitter, and Instagram during the COVID-19 crisis in Belgium. In: Digital Marketing & eCommerce Conference, pp. 95–103. Springer, Cham (2021)
44. Johnson, M.: Embodied Mind, Meaning, and Reason. University of Chicago Press, Chicago (2017)
45. Latour, B.: Down to Earth: Politics in the New Climatic Regime. Polity Press, Cambridge (2018)
46. Scott-Branch, J., Laws, R., Terzi, P.: The intersection of AI, information and digital literacy: harnessing ChatGPT and other generative tools to enhance teaching and learning (2023)
47. Li, H., Zhu, S., Wu, D., Yang, H.H., Guo, Q.: Impact of information literacy, self-directed learning skills, and academic emotions on high school students' online learning engagement: a structural equation modeling analysis. Educ. Inf. Technol. **28**, 13485–13504 (2023). https://doi.org/10.1007/s10639-023-11760-2
48. Floridi, L.: AI as agency without intelligence: on ChatGPT, large language models, and other generative models. Phil. Technol. **36**, 15 (2023)
49. George, A.S., George, A.S.H., Martin, A.S.G.: The environmental impact of AI: a case study of water consumption by chat GPT. Partn. Univ. Int. Innov. J. **1**, 97–104 (2023). https://doi.org/10.5281/zenodo.7855594

50. Wallerstein, N., Bernstein, E.: Empowerment education: freire's ideas adapted to health education. Health Educ. Q. **15**, 379–394 (1988). https://doi.org/10.1177/109019818801500402
51. Clark, A., Chalmers, D.: The extended mind. Analysis **58**, 7–19 (1998)
52. Rupert, R.D.: Cognitive Systems and the Extended Mind. Oxford Univ. Press, Oxford (2010)
53. Šíp, R.: Why Education and its Actors are Failing. Masaryk University (2019)
54. Kahneman, D.: Thinking, Fast and Slow. Farrar, Strauss and Giroux, New York (2011)
55. Lin, C.-H., Yu, C.-C., Shin, P.-K., Wu, L.Y.: STEM based artificial intelligence learning in general education for non-engineering undergraduate students. Educ. Technol. Soc. **24**, 224–237 (2021)
56. Damasio, A.R.: Descartes' Error: Emotion, Reason, and the Human Brain. Putnam, New York (1994)
57. Latour, B.: Reassembling the Social: An Introduction to Actor-Network-Theory. Oup, Oxford (2007)

Ensuring Quality in AI-Generated Multiple-Choice Questions for Higher Education with the QUEST Framework

Martin Ebner(✉), Benedikt Brünner, Noel Forjan, and Sandra Schön

Graz University of Technology, Münzgrabenstr. 36/I, 8010 Graz, Austria
martin.ebner@tugraz.at

Abstract. With the rise of generative AI models, such as large language models (LLMs), in educational settings, there is a growing demand to ensure the quality of AI-generated multiple-choice questions (MCQs) used in higher education. Traditional quiz development methods fall short in addressing the unique challenges posed by AI-generated content, such as consistency, cognitive demand, and question uniqueness. This paper presents the QUEST framework, a structured approach designed specifically to evaluate the quality of LLM-generated MCQs across five dimensions: Quality, Uniqueness, Effort, Structure, and Transparency. Following an iterative research process, AI-generated questions were assessed and refined using QUEST, revealing that the framework effectively improves question clarity, relevance, and educational value. The findings suggest that QUEST is a viable tool for educators to maintain high-quality standards in AI-generated assessments, ensuring these resources meet the pedagogical needs of diverse learners in higher education.

Keywords: assessment · prompting · AI generated content · multiple choice · quiz · technology-enhanced learning · massive open online courses generative AI

1 Introduction

In recent years, generative AI models like large language models (LLMs) have increasingly been applied in educational settings, particularly in higher education, to create various learning resources such as quizzes, summaries, and interactive content [1, 2]. At Graz University of Technology for example we produced complete online course [3] edited videos with AI help [4], produced multilingual online courses [5, 6]. The capacity to generate personalized educational materials presents new opportunities to enhance learning efficiency and accessibility for a diverse range of learners [7]. However, despite the potential of generative AI, the quality and reliability of AI-generated resources, especially quizzes used for knowledge assessment, require careful consideration [8]. This paper examines how a structured approach to quality assurance can be applied to AI-generated quizzes, using the QUEST framework developed in a bachelor's thesis [9] as the foundation. The primary focus is to establish a robust assessment method that educators can rely on to ensure that quizzes meet high-quality standards.

Ł. Tomczyk (Ed.): NMP 2024, CCIS 2537, pp. 293–303, 2025.
https://doi.org/10.1007/978-3-031-95627-0_20

2 Developing and Evaluating Quizzes and Their Quality in Traditional Way and the Challenge of Using Generative AI

Traditionally, quiz development in educational settings has involved careful planning and rigorous quality assessment. Educators typically follow established guidelines to ensure that each question is relevant, well-structured, and aligned with learning objectives [10]. Standard practices for quality assurance in quizzes focus on factors such as question clarity, relevance to the topic, and the appropriateness of difficulty levels. Techniques include manual review and peer assessment, where questions are reviewed by experts or colleagues to identify potential biases, ambiguities, or issues in complexity [11].

In multiple-choice question (MCQ) development, particular attention is given to distractors, or incorrect answer options, which are designed to assess a learner's critical thinking. Effective distractors are plausible but incorrect answers that reveal common misconceptions [12]. Such quality criteria ensure that the quiz serves as an effective assessment tool, accurately reflecting the learner's understanding of the content and providing meaningful feedback. However, manually developing and evaluating quizzes is resource-intensive, prompting the need for AI-based solutions that can create quizzes at scale while maintaining quality.

AI-generated quiz questions present – compared with human-developed quizzes - challenges that traditional quality standards do not fully address. Unlike human-crafted questions, large language models (LLMs) such as ChatGPT generate content based on training data and prompts, which can lead to unpredictable outputs. These machine-generated questions therefore require systematic evaluation to ensure not only factual accuracy but also clarity, appropriate structure, and sufficient cognitive challenge. Additionally, AI-generated questions can often suffer from content repetition and lack creative distractors (incorrect answer options), which can undermine quality. The developed QUEST framework provides a specialized tool that addresses these specific demands, ensuring that AI-generated questions meet reliable quality standards and are valuable for educational use.

3 Research Approach

To assess the feasibility of using generative AI for quiz creation, an approach called the QUEST framework was developed in a bachelor's thesis [9] and applied to evaluate AI generated MCQs and enhancing the prompts. QUEST provides a structured assessment of MCQs created by LLMs. This research involved generating multiple-choice questions from online course content and evaluating them through QUEST to measure their quality, uniqueness, cognitive demand, structure, and transparency. So, the presented research work is not already a full circle of developing an assessment scheme (QUEST) and evaluating it as this is typically done in psychology, so we did not yet evaluate QUEST's validity and reliability in details. We utilized the QUEST framework as an apparently valid instrument for evaluating multiple-choice questions, while acknowledging its limitations, to derive improved prompts for the generation of multiple-choice questions in a specific application context. We additionally use insights from using the QUEST framework to use it in prompting MCQ from another bachelor's thesis [13]. Within this third part, we will present differences of human-based and results of the used AI using the QUEST framework to evaluate a set of MCQ. All results are not publicly available yet.

Figure 1 illustrates the approach presented in this paper.

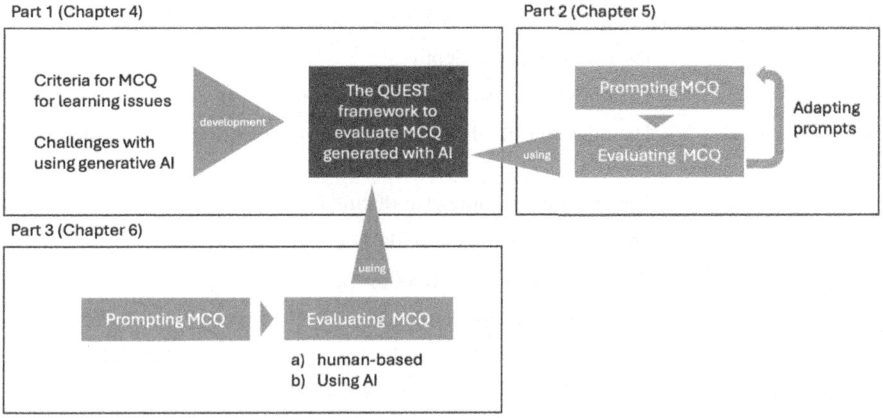

Fig. 1. Research approach

4 Development of the QUEST Framework

In our initial tests with AI-generated test questions, we observed specific issues that are less common in human-generated questions, such as the occurrence of identical answer options within the same question. Drawing on established literature on the quality of learning assessments [8, 10–12], we identified and adapted key aspects that we believe are particularly relevant for evaluating AI-generated test questions. These aspects were chosen to address the unique challenges posed by AI question generation and to provide a structured approach for improving the overall quality and reliability of the outputs. So, the QUEST framework is a quality assessment model specifically designed to evaluate multiple-choice questions generated by AI. So, QUEST uses five key criteria: Quality, Uniqueness, Effort, Structure, and Transparency: "Quality" ensures each question is relevant and covers important concepts, while "Uniqueness" checks that questions do not repeat topics unnecessarily. "Effort" measures the cognitive demand needed to answer, aiming for a balanced challenge, while "Structure" assesses clarity and consistency in the presentation of questions and options. Finally, "Transparency" ensures that questions and answers are clear and easily understood, minimizing confusion for the learner. The QUEST model (see Table 1) tries to support the evaluation of a single multiple-choice question, so we hopefully encompass a large part of that makes such a question "good". Each of the categories helps to gauge a question's overall value for a specific learning task, i.e. target group and learning objectives.

Table 1. The QUEST framework to assess quality of quizzes

Category	Score	Description
Quality	4	The question explores a significant concept / topic
	3	Explores a relevant concept/topic but could go more in depth
	2	The question is somewhat meaningful, but it could be more specific
	1	The question lacks depth
	0	The question is irrelevant to the content
Uniqueness	4	The question stands out, content focus is different from other questions
	3	The question is somewhat distinctive
	2	The question is not particularly distinctive
	1	The question lacks distinction
	0	The question is not distinct at all
Effort	4	The question requires significant effort and critical thinking, and is on the same effort level as other questions
	3	The question requires significant effort and critical thinking but is harder/takes more effort than other questions
	2	The question requires some effort
	1	The question demands minimal effort (can be answered without much critical thinking)
	0	The question requires no effort or critical thinking to answer (can be answered using logic)
Structure	4	Question and answers are well-organized and presented in a clear format (structure and format stays the same as with other questions)
	3	The structure and format of the question are mostly clear
	2	The question and answers may be somewhat disorganized or unclear
	1	The structure and format of the question get in the way of understanding
	0	The question and answers are entirely disorganized / presented in an unclear format
Transparency	4	The question is clear, easily understandable
	3	The question can be further clarified to aid comprehension
	2	The question is somewhat confusing / requires additional clarification
	1	The question is hard to understand
	0	The question is completely unclear

5 Using the QUEST Framework to Evaluate AI Generated Quizzes

To evaluate the quality of AI-generated multiple-choice questions (MCQs), selected course materials were utilized as the basis for question generation. Specifically, content was drawn from the iMooX.at course [14] on digital competences of university student beginners by Ebner and Hohla-Sejkora [7]. This resource provided comprehensive and relevant material for generating educational questions in a structured, digital literacy-focused context.

The multiple-choice questions were generated using the GPT-3.5 model from OpenAI, facilitated by the *langchain* Python library. This tool allowed for seamless communication with the LLM, enabling automated processing of educational content to produce questions. To handle the output formatting and storage, a Python script was developed to organize the questions and answers in JSON format, ensuring consistency and ease of further analysis.

5.1 Prompting Several Quizzes

The prompts went through many different versions before the one that was best was created. The process was iterative, meaning that for each prompt a few questions were generated and assessed. The requirements for the string were designed in such a way that the output and its structured form can be reused immediately, e.g. in a learning management system. If the questions could be improved the prompt was changed to generate better questions. A total of 9 prompts were created and tested. The best results were produced with the following: "Given a text input, generate {q_a} multiple choice questions from it along with the correct answers. Make sure that there is a possibility of multiple answers. If there is only one answer, make sure it is not always option 'a', but also 'b' or 'c' or 'd'. Output for multiple answers should not always be'a','b','c', but something like 'a', 'b', 'd'; or 'b', 'c', 'd'. Output it as a JSON string, with the format from the following example, where the correct answers are a, b, and c: {{"questions": [{{"question": "?","options": {{"a": "Answer a", "b": "Answer b", "c": "Answer c", "d": "Answer d"}}, "answer": ["a", "b", "c"]}}],... {user prompt}".

5.2 Framework Application

All quizzes and so each generated question was assessed by one expert in the field of our case using the QUEST framework. Each question of each 9 prompt results received a score for these dimensions, guiding the iterative improvement process.

5.3 Iterative Improvement of Prompts

The iterative improvement process involved revising the prompts and questions based on their QUEST scores. For example, if a question scored low in "Structure" due to unclear formatting or wording, adjustments were made to the prompt to ensure more concise outputs. Through multiple iterations, the prompts were refined, resulting in higher-quality questions that aligned better with educational goals.

5.4 Evaluation of the Generated Quizzes

The application of QUEST demonstrated that the last prompt (see Sect. 5.1) AI-generated MCQs could reach high levels of quality, particularly in terms of topic relevance, clarity, and structure. For this, 52 questions were assessed using the QUEST model. The results using the QUEST are shown in Table 2 and Fig. 2.

Table 2. Assessement of generated quiz with QUEST, example with 52 questions [9].

Category	Value	Std. Dev.
Quality	3.87	0.35
Uniqueness	3.96	0.28
Effort	3.52	0.75
Structure	3.38	0.87
Transparency	3.87	0.35

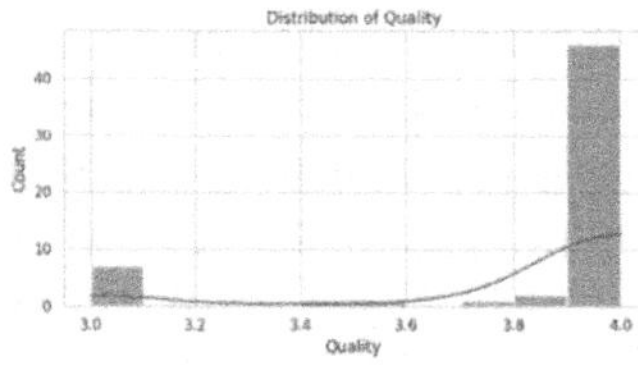

(a) Distribution of Quality

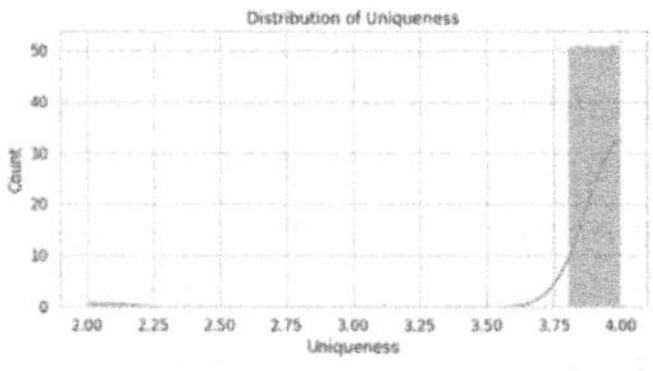

(b) Distribution of Uniqueness

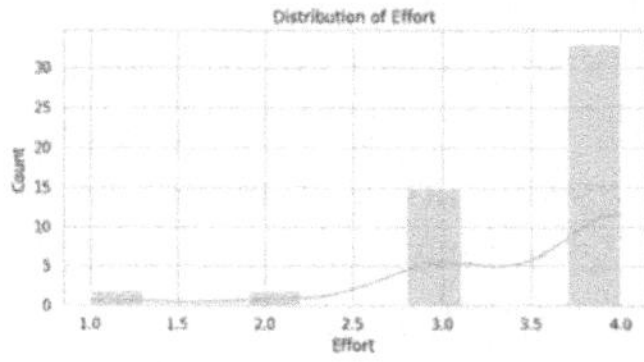

(c) Distribution of Effort

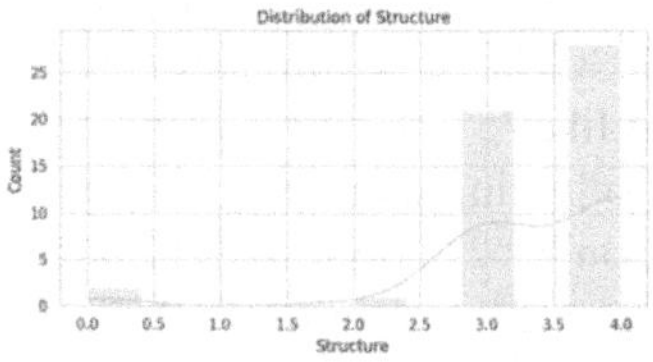

(d) Distribution of Structure

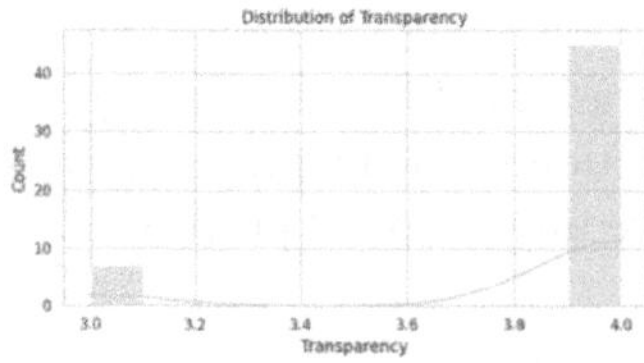

(e) Distribution of Transparency

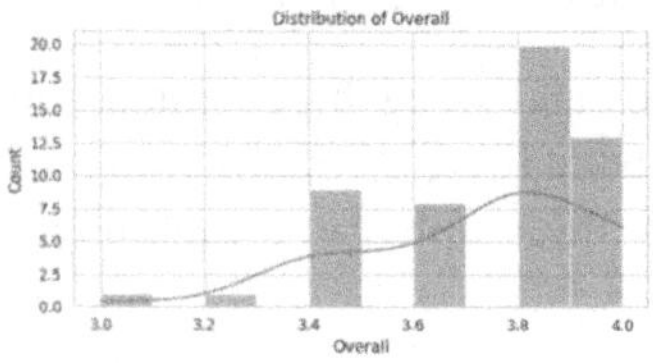

(f) Distribution of Overall

Fig. 2. Distribution of ratings across individual QUEST dimensions (Quality, Uniqueness, Effort, Structure, and Transparency) as well as the overall score

So, the application of the QUEST framework revealed both strengths and weaknesses in AI-generated multiple-choice questions (MCQs). While the overall quality of the generated questions was high, some recurring issues were identified that impacted specific QUEST dimensions.

Most of the questions covered relevant and significant concepts from the source material. However, some lacked depth or specificity, leading to a superficial assessment of knowledge. The AI also tended to generate overly simple or general questions, which did not always align with the intended level of cognitive demand.

Most questions were distinct, ensuring that different aspects of the course content were covered. However, an observed issue was the occasional duplication or near-duplication of questions, where the same concept was tested multiple times with slightly varied wording. This redundancy reduced the effectiveness of quizzes, as learners were not sufficiently challenged with new material. For example, two questions assessing nearly the same concept were generated, so got a low rating in uniqueness (see Fig. 3).

What is the primary benefit of open-book exams?	Which type of exam allows the use of external materials and is more realistic than a closed-book exam?
A) Increased realism	A) Open-book exam
B) Reduced stress	B) Timed assessment
C) Higher accessibility	C) Weekly performance evaluations
D) More time for responses	D) Oral examination

Fig. 3. Example of two questions with low uniqueness (translated from German).

Another issue was the presence of weak distractors, meaning that incorrect answer choices were often too obvious or implausible, reducing the cognitive challenge of the question. In extreme cases, distractors could be eliminated through simple logic, making prior knowledge unnecessary for selecting the correct answer. Figure 4 shows an example where distractors were clearly incorrect, making the question too easy.

What is one advantage of cloud storage?
A) Files can be shared easily ☑
B) Files can only be stored locally ✕
C) Files must be sent via physical mail ✕
D) Files can only be accessed from one device ✕

Fig. 4. Example of a multiple-choice question with weak distractors (translated from German).

So, overall the QUEST framework provided valuable insights into the strengths and limitations of the exemplarily AI-generated MCQ.

6 Using QUEST Framework as Base for MCQ Evaluation from the AI Compared with Human-Based Results

In the following, we present the results of the bachelor's thesis [13], which utilized scripts to generate multiple-choice questions (MCQs) from four learning videos with GPT-4o. The prompt used for the generation was "You are a helpful assistant. You generate well-structured multiple-choice questions in JSON format. Each question should include a 'q' key for the question text, 'a1' to 'a4' keys for the answer options, and a 'correct' key indicating the correct answer in an array (e.g., '[2, 3]' for the second and third answer). The output should be a JSON object with these keys."

Two different video scripts from were taken as base, 10 MCQ were requested, and two runs were done for each. Then, the generated MCQs with 10 questions were subsequently evaluated by the AI itself using the QUEST framework. Simultaneously, a human expert provided their own assessment of the MCQs, and these results are compared. In Table 3, results for two different MCQ sets developed on base of one video script were assessed by a human and genAI.

Table 3. The QUEST to ensure quality of quizzes. Please note: Detailed results are available online [15]

MCQ evaluated	QUEST category	human-based	AI generated
MCQ from Script 1 - first run	Quality	3,6	3,8
	Uniqueness	2,5	2,8
	Effort	2,5	2,4
	Structure	4,0	4,0
	Transparency	4,0	4,0
	Overall	3,3	3,4
MCQ from Script 2 - second run	Quality	3,0	3,4
	Uniqueness	2,5	2,6
	Effort	2,5	2,7
	Structure	4,0	4,0
	Transparency	4,0	4,0
	Overall	3,2	3,3

The comparison of human-based and AI-generated evaluations concerning the QUEST framework revealed discrepancies across multiple categories, with variations in both directions. The AI consistently assigned higher scores in the "Uniqueness" category, which can be attributed to its evaluation method focusing primarily on linguistic differences between questions rather than deeper conceptual overlap. This sometimes led to overestimation of the distinctiveness of similar questions, particularly when they were phrased differently but tested the same concept.

In contrast, the results for "Structure" and "Transparency" were nearly identical between human and AI evaluations. This alignment suggests that AI is capable of reliably assessing formal aspects such as grammatical correctness, clarity, and logical consistency of the questions. However, for more nuanced criteria, such as "Effort", discrepancies emerged. AI evaluations tended to rate effort either higher or lower than human evaluators, likely due to its inability to fully grasp the cognitive challenge required from a learner's perspective. For instance, questions that demanded deeper reasoning or cross-topic connections were sometimes undervalued by AI, whereas questions that appeared complex due to wording but were conceptually simple were occasionally overrated.

An illustrative example highlights this divergence: AI-evaluated as high effort: "What year did the TCP/IP protocol become the standard for ARPANET communication?" While precise, this question is mainly factual recall, which does not necessarily require deep reasoning. In contrast, human-evaluated as high effort: "How did the adoption of the TCP/IP protocol influence the expansion of the internet?" This question requires analytical thinking and contextual understanding, making it more challenging despite a similar topic. Please note, that questions are translated from German in both cases.

These findings underscore the importance of human oversight in AI-driven assessment processes, particularly when evaluating higher-order cognitive demands. While genAI offers efficiency in standardized assessments, its ability to differentiate between superficial complexity and genuine cognitive challenge remains a limitation that requires further refinement through iterative prompt engineering and hybrid evaluation approaches.

Discussion

The QUEST framework proved effective for quality assessment of AI-generated quizzes, offering a systematic method to ensure MCQ reliability in educational contexts. While LLMs present a promising avenue for large-scale quiz creation, challenges remain in achieving consistent cognitive demand and structural quality across questions. Implementing iterative improvement cycles and diversifying prompt structures could enhance quality further. Of course, the presented applications and examples for individual videos and MOOCs are merely an initial attempt, and the results could vary depending on the content, language, and difficulty of the assessment—requiring further investigation.

Integrating AI in educational resource creation holds transformative potential for personalized learning, enabling automated, scalable quiz generation. However, maintaining rigorous quality control remains crucial to prevent over-standardization and ensure that AI complements, rather than replaces, human expertise in educational design [3, 6].

Critically, we see a potential need to adapt the framework for other topics where the use of generative AI in multiple-choice question development might include ethical challenges and require evaluation concerning reliability and validity. Furthermore, a limitation of our study is that the MCQs were assessed by only one expert. To strengthen the reliability of the evaluation, future research should involve multiple raters and inter-rater reliability analysis.

7 Conclusion and Outlook

Concerning our first experiences, the QUEST model provides a valuable framework to assessing the quality of AI-generated MCQs and to further develop prompting. This ensures in a longer run that quizzes are effective tools for learning and assessment. By maintaining a balance between human oversight and AI efficiency, educational institutions can leverage generative models to enhance learning while upholding high standards of question quality. A simple next step could be to use the QUEST framework itself while prompting MCQ to already automatically assess and results through generative AI (see Fig. 5).

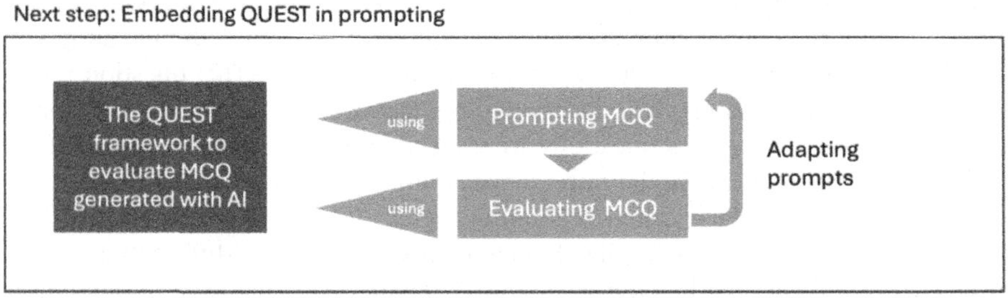

Fig. 5. Future potential usage of the QUEST framework

Besides this, we are aware that the QUEST model itself still needs to be critically assessed if it valid and reliable or if missed to add criteria. For example, we are not sure if ethical aspect might occur for some MCQ topics that should be supervised and used in evaluation critically as well. Additionally, to improve the reliability of assessments, it is recommended to involve multiple evaluators and calculate inter-rater agreement metrics, such as Cohen's Kappa coefficient.

References

1. Jahic, I., Ebner, M., Schön, S.: Harnessing the power of artificial intelligence and ChatGPT in education – a first rapid literature review. In T. Bastiaens (ed.), Proceedings of EdMedia + Innovate Learning, Vienna, Austria: Association for the Advancement of Computing in Education (AACE), pp. 1462–1470 (2023). https://www.learntechlib.org/primary/p/222670/
2. Jahic, I., Ebner, M., Schön, S., Edelsbrunner, S.: Exploring the use of generative AI in education: broadening the scope. In Learning and Collaboration Technologies, pp. 283–304 (2024). https://doi.org/10.1007/978-3-031-61691-4_19
3. Edelsbrunner, S., Gritsch, P., Ebner, M., Lanzinger, M., Schön, S.: "MOOCing ohne Mensch" Fallstudie zum KI-generierten MOOC "Societech". In: Accepted for GMW 2024 Proceedings (2024)
4. Nußbaumer, D., Mair, B., Schön, S., Edelsbrunner, S., Ebner, M.: Evaluating the efficacy of automated video editing in educational content production: a time efficiency and learner perspective study. In: Zaphiris, P., Ioannou, A., Ioannou, A. (eds.) Learning and Collaboration Technologies - 11th International Conference, LCT 2024, Held as Part of the 26th HCI International Conference, HCII 2024, Proceedings, Lecture Notes in Computer Science, vol.

14722, pp. 234–246. Springer, Heidelberg (2024). https://doi.org/10.1007/978-3-031-61672-3_15
5. Unite! University: Unite! pioneers open science and multilingual OER courses (2024). https://www.unite-university.eu/unitenews/unite-pioneers-open-science-and-multilingual-oer-courses
6. Schön, S.; Brünner, B., Ebner, M., Edelsbrunner, S.; Hohla-Sejkora; Uhl, B.: Early findings from pilots in AI-driven education: effects of AI-generated courses and videos on learning and teaching. In: Auer, M.E., May, D. (eds.) 2024 Yearbook Emerging Technologies in Learning, Learning and Analytics in Intelligent Systems Series, vol. 44. Springer, Heidelberg (2025). https://doi.org/10.1007/978-3-031-80388-8_2
7. Ebner, M., & Hohla-Sejkora, K.: Digitale Kompetenzen für Studienanfänger (2023/24). Retrieved from imoox.at (2023)
8. Thomas, M.: Developing and Validating Multiple-Choice Test Items. Lawrence Erlbaum Associates (2004)
9. Forjan, N.: Ensuring Quality in LLM-Generated Multiple-Choice Questions with the QUEST Model [Bachelor's thesis, unpublished]. Graz University of Technology (2024)
10. Clay, B.: Is This a Trick Question? A Short Guide to Writing Effec-tive Test Questions. Kansas State University. (2001)
11. Tobin, M.A.: Guide to Item Analysis. Schreyer Institute (2018)
12. Haladyna, T.M.: Developing and Validating Multiple-Choice Test Items. Lawrence Erlbaum Associates (2004)
13. Kusonjić, I.: Creating Quality Multiple-Choice Questions from Learning Videos with Large Language Models. [Bachelor's thesis, unpublished]. Graz University of Technology (2024)
14. Ebner, M.: iMooX - a MOOC platform for all (universities). In: 2021 7th International Conference on Electrical, Electronics and Information Engineering (ICEEIE), pp. 1–5 (2021). https://doi.org/10.1109/ICEEIE52663.2021.9616685
15. Kusonjić, I.: Gitlab Repository data. https://gitlab.tugraz.at/ed-tech/2024/quality-mcq/-/tree/main/output?ref_type=heads. Accessed 07 Mar 2025

Bridging Scientific Research and AI: How Indonesian Teacher Candidates Perceive Emerging Technologies in Education

Elisabeth Desiana Mayasari[1,2(✉)], Khofidotur Rofiah[3], and Muchamad Irvan[4]

[1] Faculty of Educational Sciences, University of Łódź, Łódź, Poland
elisabeth.mayasari@edu.uni.lodz.pl
[2] Faculty of Teacher Training and Education, Universitas Sanata Dharma, Yogyakarta, Indonesia
[3] Disability Innovation Center, Universitas Negeri Surabaya, Surabaya, Indonesia
[4] Faculty of Education, Universitas Negeri Malang, Malang, Indonesia

Abstract. The competencies and attitudes towards scientific research are crucial for teacher candidates as one of the basic requirements for professional teachers. Moreover, the power of AI (artificial intelligence) is massively used in many aspects, especially in the academic sector. However, in the Indonesian context, there is still a lack of studies focused on exploring these variables. This paper aims to identify teacher candidates' attitudes towards scientific research and the relationship between their knowledge and familiarity with AI. The current research involved 268 teacher candidates from various Indonesian universities through the use of both closed-ended and open-ended surveys. The results indicate that teacher candidates exhibit consistently positive attitudes across most dimensions of the research inventory, as well as a high level of knowledge regarding AI; however, exhibit a moderate level of familiarity with the application of AI in education. A significant correlation exists between their attitudes towards scientific research and their knowledge and familiarity with using AI in education. Thematic analysis was then conducted on the open-ended responses, revealing dual perceptions and beliefs about the use of AI in education, which were categorized into two emerging themes: AI as (1) a wonderful tool for research, and (2) dangerous and unethical tools for research. This research suggested the importance of emphasizing research knowledge, attitudes, and skills for Indonesian teachers' education curriculum, focusing on theoretical and practical competencies, including the use of AI wisely.

Keywords: attitudes towards scientific research · knowledge of AI · familiarity of AI · teachers candidates · Indonesia

1 Introduction

Scientific research is a systematic process that entails the testing and development of knowledge through a variety of methodologies, activities, and theoretical frameworks [1]. It follows a sequential approach, including problem identification, method selection, data collection and processing, and formulating conclusions [2]. Scientific research

Ł. Tomczyk (Ed.): NMP 2024, CCIS 2537, pp. 304–327, 2025.
https://doi.org/10.1007/978-3-031-95627-0_21

equips students with theoretical, technical, practical, and methodological knowledge in education, empowering them to address future challenges and drive societal transformations [3]. Students should be encouraged to engage in research experiences [4], as it can positively impact their development [5]. Strategies to enhance students' research skills include participation in academic conferences [6] and improving their understanding of project execution and research methodologies [7].

While the importance of scientific research in education is widely acknowledged, the perception of science education varies across different cultures. For instance, in Bhutan, science is often perceived as abstract and complex [8]; in contrast, students in countries such as Cyprus, Australia, Canada, and South Korea generally hold more favorable views of science [9]. These cultural differences highlight the need for tailored science education and research approaches across different regions. This is related to the importance of research skills in various professional fields. Although, each profession has a different scope and approach to research.

Therefore, teachers are essential in connecting scientific research with education, as they facilitate transformations in the learning process, instructional design, and problem-solving strategies [10]. Their involvement in research can enhance their content understanding, pedagogical expertise, critical thinking skills, and ability to reflect deeply [11]. Teachers who engage in research are better positioned to design effective curricula, serve as knowledge drivers in education, and enhance their self-confidence in the classroom [12].

For teacher candidates, developing a research culture, scientific perspective, and positive attitude toward research is essential [13]. These qualities can influence their future students' attitudes towards science, affecting the science learning process [14]. By fostering a strong research orientation in teacher candidates, educational institutions can create a ripple effect that enhances scientific literacy and research skills among future generations of students.

Despite the acknowledged significance of research skills, students frequently view research methodology courses as challenging and anxiety-provoking [15]. While recognizing the significance of students' positive attitudes towards research, several challenges persist. Many students shy away from research activities, not identifying themselves as researchers, which leads to a belief in their inability to comprehend and conduct studies effectively [16, 17]. Furthermore, a common misconception among students is the equation of research with statistics. This misunderstanding often leads students to believe that their perceived lack of mathematical proficiency will hinder their research capabilities. Such beliefs can have long-lasting effects on their learning process and future professional development [17, 18]. This anxiety can negatively impact students' self-efficacy and attitudes towards research [19]. A study of teacher candidates in the US and Canada revealed that many consider research difficult and complex [20–22]. These perceptions highlight the necessity for innovative teaching approaches in research methodologies that can mitigate student anxiety and cultivate a more favorable attitude toward research.

In response to the rising demand for research skills, education faculties need to ensure that pre-service teachers are well-equipped with the necessary aptitude and proficiency for success [23]. Further investigation is essential to comprehend the factors that influence teacher candidates' attitudes toward scientific research, which will provide valuable insights into the interplay between educational factors and perspectives on scientific research. By addressing these challenges and fostering a positive research culture among teacher candidates, educational institutions can enhance their preparation of future educators by integrating research skills into their teaching practices and inspiring scientific curiosity in their students.

Integrating technology and artificial intelligence (AI) in education has rapidly transformed the teaching and learning landscape. As emerging technologies evolve, their impact on educational practices becomes increasingly significant. This paradigm shift necessitates thoroughly examining how teacher candidates perceive and adapt to these technological advancements. Utilizing technology and AI in education has proven effective in improving learning outcomes, personalizing instruction, and boosting educational efficiency [24]. AI-driven tools have the potential to create adaptive learning experiences, streamline administrative tasks, and give students real-time feedback, fundamentally revolutionizing traditional educational approaches [25]. For instance, intelligent tutoring systems have demonstrated the ability to tailor instruction to individual student needs, potentially bridging achievement gaps and promoting equitable learning opportunities [26].

Previous research on technology and AI in education has highlighted the potential advantages and obstacles linked to their implementation. A study by Luckin and Holmes [27] emphasized the importance of developing AI literacy among educators to leverage these tools in the classroom. Similarly, Roll and Wylie [28] explored the role of AI in supporting collaborative learning environments, highlighting the need for careful integration of technology with pedagogical practices.

Nonetheless, there are notable gaps in our understanding of how prepared teacher candidates are to embrace technological advancements. The first gap concerns their readiness to leverage technology for professional development. While research has shown that technology integration can enhance teacher effectiveness [29], there is limited information on how Indonesian teacher candidates perceive and prepare for this technological shift in their future careers. This gap is further highlighted by recent research by Werdiningsih et al. [30], which explored Indonesian EFL students' experiences and strategies when using ChatGPT in their writing. The study revealed both the potential and the limitations of AI tools in education. The study found that ChatGPT often provides overly complex suggestions and lack cultural sensitivity. These findings underscore the importance of comprehensive training programs for both teachers and students on responsible AI integration. The second gap concerns the readiness of teacher candidates to integrate AI and research-based practices in shaping Indonesia's future education. With the ongoing evolution of AI, its ability to transform educational research and practice is rapidly growing. However, there is a lack of insight into how Indonesian pre-service teachers view the convergence of AI and scientific research in their prospective roles as educators.

Another important aspect to consider is the impact of AI on research methods in education. AI-powered tools can significantly enhance data collection, analysis, and interpretation processes, potentially revolutionizing educational research [31]. For instance, machine learning algorithms can identify patterns in large datasets that might not be visible through conventional statistical methods, providing new insights into learning processes and educational outcomes [32]. Moreover, AI can facilitate more efficient literature reviews, automate data coding in qualitative research, and even generate research hypotheses based on existing knowledge [33]. These advancements can potentially accelerate the pace of educational research and provide more robust evidence for pedagogical decision-making. However, incorporating AI into research methods presents important ethical challenges. Careful attention must be given to data privacy, algorithmic bias, and the interpretability of AI-generated results to safeguard the integrity and validity of educational research [24].

As Indonesian teacher candidates prepare to enter a rapidly evolving educational landscape, it is crucial to understand their perceptions and readiness to engage with these emerging technologies. This understanding will inform the development of teacher education programs that effectively prepare future educators to leverage the power of AI and scientific research in their professional practice. Future research should explore Indonesian teacher candidates' attitudes, knowledge, and skills regarding AI and its applications in education and research. By bridging the gap between scientific research and AI in teacher education, institutional education can better prepare future educators to navigate the complex interplay of technology, pedagogy, and research in the 21st-century classroom. This integration could significantly elevate the quality of education in Indonesia and play a vital role in the global dialogue regarding the future of learning in the age of artificial intelligence.

2 Literature Review

2.1 Definition of Scientific Research

Scientific research is a systematic and methodical process that involves testing and building knowledge through various activities, methods, and theories [1]. It follows a sequential approach, encompassing problem identification, method selection, data collection, data processing, and formulating conclusions [2]. This process is crucial for advancing knowledge and understanding in various fields, including education. Scientific research in education is crucial for equipping students with the necessary theoretical, technical, practical, and methodological knowledge. It enables them to face future challenges and drive societal transformations [3]. Engaging in research experiences enables students to cultivate their critical thinking, communication, and problem-solving skills [34, 35].

2.2 Definition of Attitudes Towards Research

Bolin et al. [21] stated that attitudes toward research are emotional responses or feelings associated with the research process. These responses encompass various attitudes frequently discussed in the literature, such as negativity, anxiety, fear of failure, inadequate preparation or ability to succeed, and a lack of interest. Korkmaz et al. [13] emphasize that developing a research culture, scientific perspective, and positive attitude toward research is essential for teacher candidates. These attitudes can influence their future students' approaches to science and learning [14]. However, research methodology courses are often perceived as challenging and anxiety-inducing by students [15]. This anxiety can negatively impact students' self-efficacy and attitudes towards research [19].

2.3 Definition of Artificial Intelligence (AI) in Education

The AI technique is a developmental tool that creates an innovative learning environment, categorized into several areas. It centered on the development of algorithms, such as classification, matching, recommendation, and deep learning to support and improve the learning and teaching processes. In the extraction dimension, AI techniques, primarily grounded in algorithms, were utilized to deliver feedback, facilitate reasoning, and enable adaptive learning for students. The application aspect included elements such as affective computing, role-playing, immersive learning experiences, and gamification. AI techniques incorporated human factors as essential variables in the integration dimension to assess and examine the unique characteristics of learners. These studies employed human-computer interaction to promote creativity, accountability, and critical thinking, which, in turn, affected learners' performance and their perceptions [36].

Another description stated by Cardona et al. [37] is that AI is an "automation driven by associations." When computers automate reasoning based on patterns found in data or insights derived from expert knowledge, two key transformations essential to AI take place, pushing computing beyond traditional educational technology. These shifts include (1) moving from simply collecting data to identifying patterns within it and (2) transitioning from merely offering access to instructional resources to automating decisions related to instruction and other educational processes. The ability to detect patterns and make automated decisions represents a significant advancement in the responsibilities entrusted to a computer system.

2.4 The Importance of AI Proficiency for Teacher Candidates

Mastery of AI by teacher candidates is a strategic effort to realize an education system that is relevant and responsive to the dynamics of technological developments. AI can analyze large datasets, identify intricate patterns, and offer recommendations through predictive analysis, which contributes to increasing the efficiency and effectiveness of the learning process. Within the educational context, AI opens up opportunities for implementing more personalized, efficient, and innovative teaching strategies, such as adaptive learning systems that dynamically adjust to the specific needs of students [38].

However, implementing AI also presents challenges that require a deep understanding from both technical and ethical perspectives. AI has potential risks, including data privacy violations, algorithmic bias, and over-reliance on technology that can reduce teachers' pedagogical autonomy [39]. Therefore, teacher candidates need to develop critical competencies in evaluating and utilizing AI technology wisely. These skills involve grasping the principles of AI operation, evaluating the accuracy and relevance of outcomes produced by AI, and recognizing the social and ethical implications linked to the use of this technology.

Within this framework, the education of teacher candidates should be designed to include a curriculum and training oriented towards mastering AI. Teachers are expected to not only be users of technology but also facilitators who are able to optimally integrate AI into learning without sacrificing the interpersonal relationship aspect that is the core of education. Thus, mastery of AI by teacher candidates can support them in becoming competent agents of transformation in facing the challenges of education in the digital era and maximizing students' potential holistically [40].

2.5 The Scope of AI in Education

The integration of artificial intelligence (AI) in education covers various aspects that can be grouped into five main categories: administrative, assistive technology, inclusion and accessibility, educational development and innovation, and policy and ethics [41, 42]. This grouping illustrates the broad scope of AI in supporting holistic educational transformation. AI has a significant role in increasing the efficiency of educational management. Technologies such as learning analytics and prediction systems enable real-time monitoring of student progress and early identification of the risk of learning failure. Automating administrative tasks, such as automatic assessment or report generation, helps teachers save time and focus on learning. In addition, AI supports data-driven curriculum design and evaluation relevant to future needs.

In the educational process, AI enhances personalized and effective teaching and learning by utilizing adaptive learning systems and AI-powered tutors [43]. Virtual assistants and learning chatbots provide students with direct feedback and additional guidance, especially in self-paced learning. So far, learning materials have also been widely developed by integrating AI. Virtual reality (VR) and AI-based gamification create interactive learning environments, increasing student motivation and understanding. In the same context, accessible learning support has also grown significantly along with strengthening the topic of inclusivity in Education. For example, assistive technology that helps students learn, such as layer readers and voice-to-text converters, have been widely used.

2.6 The Use of AI in Inclusive Education

Advances in artificial intelligence (AI) technology are significantly impacting inclusive education, enabling unprecedented personalization of learning. In this context, AI assists in identifying the specific requirements of students, particularly those with learning challenges, through data analysis and the provision of tailored learning pathways. Studies such as that by Kohnke and Zaugg [44] highlight the capability of AI to assist students with disabilities in STEM disciplines, opening up wider access to science and technology education. In addition, AI-based tools have been developed and specifically designed to support the social and emotional growth of children with autism [45, 46]. This shows how AI can help with academic aspects and support the holistic dimension of education. On the other hand, applications such as "GLaM-Sign" allow deaf students to access learning through multimodal lip reading and sign language technology.

However, significant challenges remain. Research by Festus and Emmanuel [47] highlights social and cultural barriers to AI adoption, such as a deficiency in understanding the technology and the digital divide. Additionally, according to a study by Muralidhar et al. [48], ethics in AI implementation is a major concern, including the risk of algorithmic bias that could exacerbate inequalities in education. Infrastructure issues are also a barrier, especially in areas with limited access to technology. While there is a connection between teacher candidates' perceptions of inclusive education and digital competencies [49], however, Almaki et al. [50] found that teachers' resistance to new technologies is often due to a lack of training and support. AI holds significant promise for transforming inclusive education by offering more equitable and accessible learning opportunities. However, successful implementation requires collaboration across multiple stakeholders to overcome existing social, cultural, and technological barriers.

3 Research Questions

The intersection of scientific research and emerging technologies, such as artificial intelligence (AI), presents a critical area of exploration in contemporary education. This study investigates the attitudes of teacher candidates regarding scientific research and their perceptions of how AI could impact teaching and learning practices.

Three research questions guide the study:

RQ1: What are teacher candidates' attitudes toward scientific research as measured by the Teacher Candidates' Attitudes Toward Scientific Research Inventory?

RQ2: What are Indonesian teacher candidates' knowledge and familiarity with AI?

RQ3: What is the relationship between teacher candidates' attitudes toward scientific research and their perceptions of AI in education? Is there a statistically significant relationship between teacher candidates' attitudes towards scientific research and AI.

The corresponding hypotheses posit that:

H1: Teacher candidates have a generally positive attitude toward scientific research as measured by the Teacher Candidates' Attitudes Toward Scientific Research Inventory.

H2: Teacher candidates have a generally positive knowledge and familiarity with AI in education.

H3: A significant positive relationship exists between teacher candidates' attitudes toward scientific research and their perceptions of AI's impact on education.

By addressing these questions, the study aims to contribute to the academic discourse on the role of scientific research and emerging technologies in shaping the attitudes and preparedness of future educators within a rapidly evolving educational landscape.

4 Research Method

We used an exploratory research quantitative approach, utilising both closed and open-ended surveys to comprehensively investigate the Indonesian teachers' candidates' attitudes towards scientific research and their knowledge and familiarity with using AI (Fig. 1). This method enabled effective data aggregation from various participants across Indonesia, yielding important insights into their attitudes and perceptions.

4.1 The Questionnaires

Attitudes Toward Scientific Research Inventory. Attitudes Toward Scientific Research inventory by Mayasari [51] aims to measure teacher candidates' attitudes toward scientific research. The inventory themes include critical thinking, self-efficacy, feelings toward research, practice-based elements, and reinforcement. These themes are categorized into three main factors: cognitive, affective, and behavioral. The cognitive factor includes critical thinking and self-efficacy, the affective factor pertains to attitudes toward research, and the behavioral factor encompasses practice-based elements and reinforcement. Critical thinking is represented by seven statements; self-efficacy is represented by eight statements; feelings toward research (emotion) are represented by seven statements; seven statements represent practice-based; reinforcement is represented by eight statements. Based on the present study's dataset, a reliability scale test was performed, resulting in an internal consistency coefficient of 0.923.

Familiarity and Experiencing with AI instruments. The Familiarity and Experiencing with AI instruments by Petricini et al. [52] aims to assess the familiarity and experiences of faculty and college students with AI instruments, particularly generative AI tools like ChatGPT. The instruments aimed to gather insights into students' perceptions of AI's usefulness, effectiveness, and ethical considerations within educational contexts. It included questions designed to gauge respondents' awareness of generative AI technologies, their confidence in utilizing these tools for pedagogical purposes, and their overall attitudes towards AI's impact on learning and teaching. The Familiarity and Experiencing with AI instruments are represented by eight statements. Based on the present study's dataset, a reliability scale test was performed, resulting in an internal consistency coefficient of 0.773.

Evaluating Attitudes Toward AI Instruments. The Evaluating Attitudes toward AI instruments by Petricini et al. [52] aims to systematically assess the perceptions of faculty and students regarding the use of generative AI tools, such as ChatGPT, in higher education. This comprehensive survey included scaled items, open-ended responses, and targeted inquiries to capture a variety of attitudes and experiences. The instrument covers the participants' familiarity with AI technologies, confidence in utilizing these tools for educational purposes, and views on the ethical implications of AI integration in academic settings. Additionally, the instrument included specific questions that evaluated respondents' experiences with AI in practical scenarios, such as using AI for research assistance or writing support. The Evaluating Attitudes toward AI instruments are represented by fourteen statements. Based on the present study's dataset, a reliability scale test was performed, resulting in an internal consistency coefficient of 0.726.

Figure 1 represents a research instrument exploring teacher candidates' attitudes, perceptions, and experiences related to research and the use of artificial intelligence (AI). It is divided into two main sections: closed-ended surveys and open-ended surveys. The closed-ended survey section examines two primary areas: the attitudes of teacher candidates toward research and their perceptions of AI usage. Attitudes toward research are further divided into categories such as reinforcement, practice-based approaches, feelings toward research, self-efficacy, and critical thinking. Perceptions of using AI include familiarity and experiences, as well as the benefits and risks of AI. The open-ended survey section focuses on teacher candidates' experiences, encompassing their experiences with research and their experiences using AI specifically for research purposes. The diagram visually connects these themes, demonstrating the relationships between survey type and research focus areas.

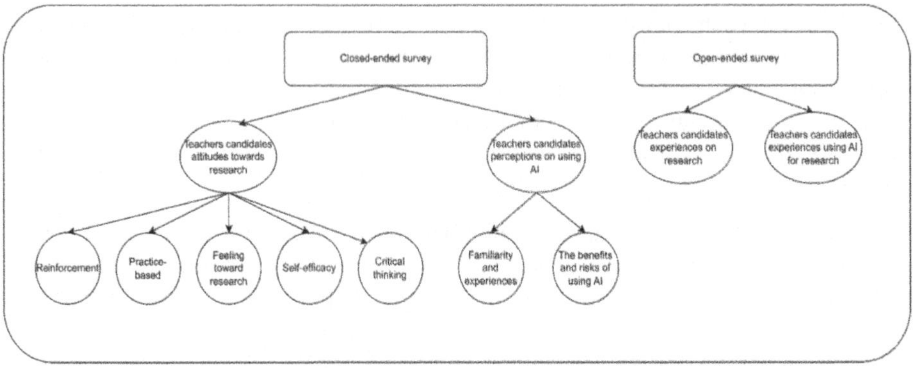

Fig. 1. Research Instrument

4.2 Data Analysis

The analysis of the closed-ended survey data involved utilizing the 27.0 version of IBM SPSS software to detect and understand patterns, trends, and correlations. The open-ended responses underwent thematic analysis [50] to uncover the participants' key themes, subthemes, perspectives, and opinions. This approach provided a thorough understanding of the data. Table 1 below details the demographics of the participants.

Table 1. Participants Characteristics

		N = 268	%
Gender	Male	47	17.5
	Female	222	82.5
Field of expertise	Natural science	12	4.5
	Social science	257	95.5
Study years	1st	101	37.5
	2nd	92	34.2
	3rd	11	4.1
	4th	60	22.3
	>5th	5	1.9

The participants involved in this study are 268 bachelor students joining teacher education programs in Indonesian universities. According to Statistical Power by Cohen [53] regarding sample size, to reach a medium or large effect size requirement with 95% confidence level, the sample in this study was enough and representative with 65% response rate. Most participants were female students, while 17.5% were male. They are 100% in a full-mode study program, which is a four-year study, 95% in social sciences and only 4,5% in natural science. In terms of study year, 37.5% came from the first year,

34.2% in the second year, 4.1% in the third year, 22.3% in their fourth year, and 1.9% more than five years.

5 Results

Non-parametric tests were performed on the dataset (see Table 2), which demonstrates that the distribution adheres to a non-normal distribution.

5.1 RQ 1: What are Teacher Candidates' Attitudes Toward Scientific Research as Measured by the Teacher Candidates' Attitudes Toward Scientific Research Inventory?

The overall analysis indicates that teacher candidates exhibit positively high attitudes across most dimensions of the research inventory (Table 2), including *Reinforcement*, *Practice-based Attitudes*, *Self-efficacy*, and *Critical Thinking*. However, the dimension of *Feelings Toward Research* reflects a moderate attitude, suggesting the need for targeted interventions to enhance teacher candidates' emotional engagement and intrinsic motivation toward scientific research. This study presents essential insights into teacher candidates' attitudes toward research, which can assist in shaping teacher education programs that promote a vibrant research culture.

Table 2. The summary Indonesian teacher candidates' attitudes toward scientific research

	N	Min	Max	Mean	Std. Deviation	Interpretation
Reinforcement	268	18	47	37.84	4.171	Positively high
Practice-based	268	14	42	33.76	4.216	Positively high
Feeling toward research	268	16	42	29.77	4.729	Moderate
Self-efficacy	268	16	48	33.22	5.227	Positively high
Critical thinking	268	14	42	33.59	4.613	Positively high

5.2 RQ2: What are Indonesian Teacher Candidates' Knowledge and Familiarity with AI?

The findings demonstrate that teacher candidates perceive their knowledge of AI positively high (Mean: 35.75), indicating confidence in their conceptual understanding of the subject. However, their familiarity with AI was rated as moderate (Mean: 54.58), indicating less direct interaction or experience with AI technologies in real-world educational contexts (Table 3). These results highlight the need for professional development initiatives and teacher education programs that emphasize experiential learning with AI tools and applications to connect theoretical knowledge with practical experience.

Table 3. The summary Indonesian teacher candidates' knowledge and familiarity with AI

	N	Min	Max	Mean	Std. Deviation	Interpretation
Knowledge of AI	268	16	48	35.75	5.828	Positively high
Familiarity with AI	268	24	78	54.58	6.885	Moderate

Table 4. Differences in Indonesian teacher candidates' knowledge and familiarity between the gender

	Knowledge of AI	Familiarity with AI
Mann-Whitney U	4347.000	4224.000
Z	−1.757	−2.012
Asymp. Sig. (2-tailed)	.079	.044

a. Grouping Variable: GENDER

Differences in knowledge and familiarity with AI across teacher candidates of different genders (male and female) were analysed using the Mann-Whitney U test (Table 4).

A significant difference was found in teacher candidates' familiarity using AI between male and female (Mann-Whitney, $U = 4224.000$, $Z = -2-012$, $p < 0.05$), with a mean rank of 113.87 for males and 138.89 for female teacher candidates, meaning that female participants had significantly higher scores on the familiarity with AI than male counterparts. The possible explanation for this specific result came from Armutat, et al. [54] which concluded in previous research that women perceived knowledge as key to generating more interest in AI. In addition, they want more practical examples, better communication of the advantages and disadvantages of AI, and a more democratic and transparent decision-making process. Furthermore, differences in knowledge and familiarity with AI among teacher candidates across different academic years (1st, 2nd, 3rd, 4th, and 5th year and beyond) were examined using the Kruskal-Wallis test (see Table 5).

Table 5. Differences analysis on Indonesian teacher candidates' knowledge and familiarity based on their study years

	Knowledge of AI	Familiarity with AI
Kruskal-Wallis H	24.393	17.031
df	3	3
Asymp. Sig	.000	.001

a. Kruskal Wallis Test
b. Grouping Variable: YEAR

The findings reveal significant differences in both AI knowledge (Kruskal-Wallis, $H = 24.393$, $p < 0.001$) and familiarity with AI for research purposes (Kruskal-Wallis, $H = 17.031$, $p < 0.001$) among the various academic year groups. This necessitates further analysis using post hoc tests to pinpoint specific group differences (see Table 6).

Table 6. Multiple comparisons of Indonesian teacher candidates' knowledge and familiarity based on study years

Dependent Variable	(I) YEAR	(J) YEAR	Mean Difference (I-J)	Std. Error	Sig	95%Confidence Interval	
						Lower Bound	Upper Bound
Knowledge of AI	1	2	2.384*	.800	.026	.19	4.58
		3	1.522	1.767	.911	−3.33	6.38
		4	−2.497	.917	.053	−5.02	.02
		> 5	3.158	2.550	.729	−3.85	10.16
	2	1	−2.384*	.800	.026	−4.58	−.19
		3	−.862	1.775	.989	−5.74	4.01
		4	−4.881*	.931	.000	−7.44	−2.32
		> 5	.774	2.555	.998	−6.25	7.79
	3	1	−1.522	1.767	.911	−6.38	3.33
		2	.862	1.775	.989	−4.01	5.74
		4	−4.019	1.831	.185	−9.05	1.01
		> 5	1.636	3.002	.982	−6.61	9.88
	4	1	2.497	.917	.053	−.02	5.02
		2	4.881*	.931	.000	2.32	7.44
		3	4.019	1.831	.185	−1.01	9.05
		> 5	5.655	2.595	.191	−1.47	12.78
	> 5	1	−3.158	2.550	.729	−10.16	3.85
		2	−.774	2.555	.998	−7.79	6.25
		3	−1.636	3.002	.982	−9.88	6.61
		4	−5.655	2.595	.191	−12.78	1.47
Familiarity with AI	1	2	−.811	.952	.914	−3.43	1.80
		3	−.822	2.103	.995	−6.60	4.96
		4	−5.184*	1.091	.000	−8.18	−2.19
		> 5	1.778	3.035	.977	−6.56	10.11

(continued)

Table 6. (*continued*)

Dependent Variable	(I) YEAR	(J) YEAR	Mean Difference (I-J)	Std. Error	Sig	95%Confidence Interval	
						Lower Bound	Upper Bound
	2	1	.811	.952	.914	−1.80	3.43
		3	−.011	2.112	1.000	−5.81	5.79
		4	−4.373*	1.108	.001	−7.42	−1.33
		> 5	2.589	3.041	.914	−5.76	10.94
	3	1	.822	2.103	.995	−4.96	6.60
		2	.011	2.112	1.000	−5.79	5.81
		4	−4.362	2.178	.268	−10.35	1.62
		> 5	2.600	3.573	.950	−7.21	12.41
	4	1	5.184*	1.091	.000	2.19	8.18
		2	4.373*	1.108	.001	1.33	7.42
		3	4.362	2.178	.268	−1.62	10.35
		> 5	6.962	3.087	.163	−1.52	15.44
	> 5	1	−1.778	3.035	.977	−10.11	6.56
		2	−2.589	3.041	.914	−10.94	5.76
		3	−2.600	3.573	.950	−12.41	7.21
		4	−6.962	3.087	.163	−15.44	1.52

***. The mean difference is significant at the 0.05 level.**

Tukey's HSD post-hoc analysis showed that Indonesian teacher candidates in their fourth year of education had significantly higher knowledge of AI than those who are in the second year of study (Tukey's HSD, $\Delta = 4..881$, $p < 0.001$), while first-year study teachers candidates revealed significantly higher knowledge of AI than second-year students (Tukey's HSD, $\Delta = 2.384$, $p < 0.05$). Similar to their familiarity with AI, Tukey's HSD post-hoc analysis revealed that fourth-year teachers candidates had significantly higher scores on familiarity with AI than those who are first-year (Tukey's HSD, $\Delta = 5.184$, $p < 0.001$) as well as those in second-year (Tukey's HSD, $\Delta = 4.373$, $p = 0.001$).

5.3 RQ3: What is the Relationship Between Teacher Candidates' Attitudes Toward Scientific Research and Their Knowledge and Familiarity with AI in Education?

The research examined the connection between teacher candidates' attitudes toward scientific research and their perceptions of AI in education. A Spearman correlation analysis was conducted to determine the strength and significance of the relationships between the five dimensions of attitudes toward scientific research (*Reinforcement, Practice-based, Feelings Toward Research, Self-efficacy*, and *Critical Thinking*) and the two dimensions of AI perceptions (*AI Knowledge* and *AI Familiarity*).

The analysis reveals several statistically significant relationships between teacher candidates' attitudes toward scientific research and their perceptions of AI in education. In particular:

AI Knowledge. The dimensions of *Reinforcement, Practice-based Attitudes, Self-efficacy,* and *Critical thinking* were significantly correlated with AI knowledge, indicating that teacher candidates who hold more positive attitudes toward scientific research are likely to perceive themselves as having a greater understanding of AI.

AI Familiarity. While weaker, significant correlations were observed for *Reinforcement* and *Practice-based Attitudes*, suggesting some link between these research attitudes and familiarity with AI technologies. However, dimensions such as *Feelings Toward Research* and *Self-efficacy* demonstrated minimal or no significant correlations with AI familiarity, suggesting that emotional and confidence-related aspects of research attitudes may not directly influence engagement with AI tools.

Table 7. Correlation of candidate teachers' attitudes towards research and their knowledge and familiarity with artificial intelligence.

		A	B	C	D	E	F	G
Reinforcement (A)	Correlation Coefficient	1	0.644**	0.468**	0.484**	0.521**	0.272**	0.167**
	Sig. (2-tailed)		0.000	0.000	0.000	0.000	0.000	0.006
Practice-based (B)	Correlation Coefficient	0.644**	1	0.584**	0.593**	0.713**	0.312**	0.165**
	Sig. (2-tailed)	0.000		0.000	0.000	0.000	0.000	0.007
Feeling toward research (C)	Correlation Coefficient	0.468**	0.584**	1	0.725**	0.524**	0.087	-0.015
	Sig. (2-tailed)	0.000	0.000		0.000	0.000	0.157	0.801
Self-efficacy (D)	Correlation Coefficient	0.484**	0.593**	0.725**	1	0.524**	0.135*	0.031
	Sig. (2-tailed)	0.000	0.000	0.000		0.000	0.027	0.615
Critical thinking (E)	Correlation Coefficient	0.521**	0.713**	0.524**	0.524**	1	0.282**	0.1
	Sig. (2-tailed)	0.000	0.000	0.000	0.000		0.000	0.102
Knowledge of AI (F)	Correlation Coefficient	0.272**	0.312**	0.087	0.135*	0.282**	1	0.351**

(*continued*)

Table 7. *(continued)*

		A	B	C	D	E	F	G
	Sig. (2-tailed)	0.000	0.000	0.157	0.027	0.000		0.000
Familiar with AI (G)	Correlation Coefficient	0.167**	0.165**	-0.015	0.031	0.1	0.351**	1
	Sig. (2-tailed)	0.006	0.007	0.801	0.615	0.102	0.000	

** *p < 0.001; * p < 0.05.*

The correlation analysis (Table 7) showed a significant correlation between several variables. Reinforcement had the strongest correlation with practice-based learning (Spearman rho, $\rho = 0.644$, $p < 0.001$) and critical thinking (Spearman rho, $\rho = 0.521$, $p < 0.001$). Practice-based learning also had a significantly strong relationship with critical thinking (Spearman rho, $\rho = 0.713$, $p < 0.001$). Feelings towards research are the most strongly correlated to self-efficacy (Spearman rho, $\rho = 0.725$, $p < 0.001$). Critical thinking demonstrated significant strong relationships with practice-based learning and self-efficacy (Spearman rho, $\rho = 0.524$, $p < 0.001$ for both). Additionally, Indonesian teachers' candidates' knowledge of AI had a significant correlation with familiarity with AI (Spearman rho, $\rho = 0.351$, $p < 0.001$). However, it had no significant or weaker correlations with other variables. The results indicated that practice-based learning and critical thinking are essential for enhancing self-efficacy and attitudes toward research.

5.4 The Analysis of Open-Ended Questions

Additionally, the open-ended questions were analysed using thematic analysis by [55] to understand more comprehensively. The final thematic map illustrates the primary themes and subthemes related to teacher candidates' perceptions and experiences of using AI for research (see Fig. 2).

The thematic map (Fig. 2) highlights the essential elements based on the experiences of Indonesian teacher candidates in utilizing AI for research. The primary themes identified were (1) The wonderful tools for research and (2) Dangerous and unethical tools for research.

Theme 1: The Wonderful Tools for Research. The first theme that emerged was 'the wonderful tools for research', with two subthemes: (1) gather ideas and (2) enhance productivity. This theme reflects the positive aspects of teacher candidates' perceptions regarding the use of AI in conducting research.

Gather ideas. The first subtheme in the first main theme is 'gather ideas'. Interestingly, many Indonesian teacher candidates think of AI as a tool to gather ideas related to their academic path, including research. The statement below (made by Indonesian teachers' candidates) illustrates their perceptions.

AI is very good at using research [context] for students.

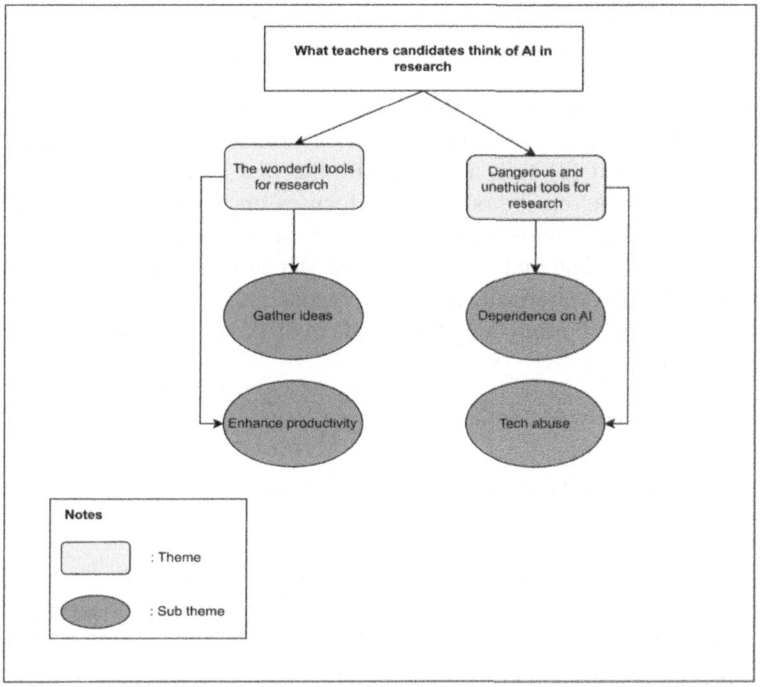

Fig. 2. Thematic map of teachers candidates toward research and AI

Basically, AI is made to make it easier for humans, and as students, we should also use AI as it should be, just to help, not to complete the entire task [research].

The use of AI in the context of education is very helpful for lecturers and students; more precisely, it adds a very broad insight and makes it easier for students to dig up information [related to study].

The use of AI in the context of education is very helpful for lecturers and students; more precisely, it adds a very broad insight and makes it easier for students to dig up information [related to study].

Enhance Productivity. The second subtheme in the first main theme is 'enhance productivity'. The participants shared their experiences of utilizing AI in education to improve their research and study productivity, highlighting their positive encounters with the technology. Nonetheless, they expressed concerns about the need for responsible usage.

The existence of AI is certainly very helpful in doing all tasks and work, but keep in mind that we also need to sharpen our writing skills even without AI's help.

AI is considered good and helpful for students and lecturers as long as AI is used positively and does not violate the rules that apply in higher education.

AI is a tool that can improve efficiency, make work easier, and provide innovative solutions to other complex problems.

> *I always use AI to improve my sentences. Then I read the sentence words according to the research so that I can understand the reading of composing sentences.*

Theme 2: Dangerous and Unethical Tools for Research. The second theme that emerged was 'dangerous and unethical tools for research', with two subthemes: (1) dependence on AI and (2) tech abuse. While the first theme emphasized the positive aspects, this theme, on the other hand, focuses on the negative perceptions and apprehensions of teacher candidates related to the use of AI in research.

Dependence on AI. The first subtheme in the second main theme is 'dependence on AI'. It explores the perception among teacher candidates regarding their reliance on AI when it is not utilized appropriately. Participants voiced their concerns regarding their dependence on AI usage.

> *Using AI can actually add broad insights, but students can also be dependent on using AI.*
>
> *If students depend on AI, then the integrity of a university's academic graduates is questionable.*

The use of AI is a form of technological adaptation that cannot be abandoned therefore our attitude towards technology needs to be considered so as not to lead to the negative side, for example in the use of AI ChatGPT, students can use AI to develop sentences that have been compiled independently before so that AI is only a tool that does not replace the obligations as a student in completing assignments.

Tech Abuse. The second subtheme in the second main theme is 'tech abuse'. This sub-theme centers on participants' perceptions of the misuse of AI technology and unethical practices in research. The statements reflected participants' beliefs about the implications of tech abuse when using AI in research.

> *Many students are now misusing AI for assignments and even for their research. In this case, of course, there is a need for further action.*
>
> *The use of AI for students to complete coursework can lead to a decline in academic integrity at universities.*
>
> *AI helps students to find some references so many children feel helped by the AI policy. In research, AI also helps with the procedures for compiling research. However, the unwise use of AI can create problems for children, especially if it is misused.*

6 Discussion

6.1 The Link Between Scientific Research Attitudes and AI Perceptions in Teacher Education

This study offers important insights into the connection between teacher candidates' attitudes toward scientific research and their perceptions of AI's role in education. Several dimensions of research attitudes, including Reinforcement, Practice-based Attitudes, Self-efficacy, and Critical Thinking, are significantly correlated with AI knowledge. This indicates that teacher candidates with positive research-oriented attitudes are more likely to perceive themselves as knowledgeable about AI. These results align with prior research suggesting that engagement with scientific inquiry fosters a deeper understanding of technological advancements, including AI [56, 57].

However, the relationship between research attitudes and familiarity with AI reveals a more complex scenario, with weaker correlations noted between Reinforcement and Practice-based Attitudes and AI familiarity. At the same time, dimensions such as Feelings Toward Research and Self-efficacy demonstrated limited or no significant relationships with AI familiarity. This finding suggests that although confidence and emotional disposition toward research may enhance perceptions of AI knowledge, they do not necessarily translate into practical familiarity with AI tools [58].

The distinction between AI knowledge and familiarity underscores the importance of adopting a dual approach. Teacher education programs should cultivate positive attitudes toward scientific research and integrate practical, hands-on experiences with AI technologies. Research emphasizes that authentic learning experiences, such as workshops or simulations that incorporate AI in real classroom settings, effectively connect theoretical knowledge with practical application [24]. These strategies can enhance familiarity with AI tools and the confidence to use them effectively in professional settings [59].

6.2 Insights and Implications Research Attitudes in Teacher Education

The findings of this study reveal that most teacher candidates exhibit positive attitudes toward research in the dimensions of Reinforcement, Practice-based Attitudes, Self-efficacy, and Critical Thinking. The result suggests their cognitive readiness to understand and apply research methods. However, moderate attitudes in the dimension of Feelings Toward Research reflect emotional barriers, which may stem from fear or scepticism toward technology, including AI, perceived as a threat or unethical tool.

The concerns surrounding AI identified in this study underscore stereotypes that depict it as "dangerous" and "unethical." According to qualitative data, some teacher candidates believe that using AI in academic tasks may diminish the originality of their work. These concerns align with findings by Lo [60], who noted that generative AI could impact students' motivation and creativity while posing misconduct risks, such as the unsupervised use of AI-generated content. The phenomenon of technological dependence can also explain moderate attitudes toward the dimension of Feelings Toward Research. As highlighted by Wiederhold [61], reliance on AI technology can negatively impact mental health, leading to emotional stress, sleep disturbances, and weakened interpersonal relationships. For instance, teacher candidates may struggle to balance the use of technology with the development of traditional research skills.

Although AI offers various benefits, such as rapid and accurate data analysis, concerns about ethical issues and potential dependency can hinder the development of positive attitudes toward research. This paradox is evident in generative AI, where teacher candidates find it helpful in expediting research processes but are also concerned about its long-term effects on creativity and critical thinking skills. Ajani et al. [62] suggest that teacher education programs should integrate AI literacy training that emphasizes ethics and responsible usage to bridge the gap between research attitudes and perceptions of AI. For example, workshops on the ethical application of AI in research can provide teacher candidates with guidelines on how to utilize AI to enhance productivity without compromising academic integrity.

According to Butson and Spronken-Smith [63], it falls upon educators to navigate this technological transformation while upholding academic values. Through support, skepticism, or alternative strategies, their decisions today will define the educational framework for future generations. Therefore, maintaining an adaptive and ongoing dialogue is essential to continually reassess and redefine humanity's relationship with AI as it evolves. This is not merely a technological imperative but also an ethical, epistemological, and existential one. However, this effort is certainly not only the responsibility of individuals. Teacher trainers have a crucial role in taking an approach to introduce and guide students about the ethics of using AI.

6.3 Teacher Candidates' AI Knowledge and Familiarity Through Experiential Learning

Attitudes toward research and perceptions of AI use in education are closely related, although both can align or show tension depending on the approach used. Based on the research findings, teacher candidates' positive perceptions of their knowledge about AI (average: 35.75) reflect their confidence in understanding the theoretical concepts of AI. However, their familiarity with AI (average: 54.58) indicates their direct experience with this technology in real educational contexts remains limited. This points to a gap that needs to be addressed through professional development initiatives and educational programs that emphasize the practical integration of AI into educational practices.

AI has the potential to improve teaching and learning outcomes, as highlighted by Luckin and Holmes [27], its analytical capabilities enable the development of adaptive learning systems designed to address the unique needs of each student. In the context of educational research, AI allows for more efficient analysis, such as simulating learning interventions and assessing teaching effectiveness. Therefore, a positive attitude toward research that is open to new technologies often aligns with the acceptance of AI as a tool that can expand educational understanding and enhance efficiency.

Nevertheless, incorporating AI into education introduces notable ethical challenges. Selwyn [64] warns that excessive reliance on technology, including AI, may undermine more humanistic educational goals, such as developing critical thinking and social interaction. AI can reduce human interaction in the learning process and may exacerbate biases embedded in algorithms, which can lead to injustice, particularly concerning race, gender, and socio-economic status. This could potentially conflict with the inclusivity values of educational research, particularly in areas concerning equality and social justice.

Furthermore, challenges related to oversight, privacy, and autonomy in AI use in education add to the complexity of integrating this technology. According to Pedro et al. [38], reliance on biased AI data can hinder inclusive educational research goals. Therefore, it is essential to ensure that AI is used with ethical considerations that involve fairness and equality. In this regard, the TPACK framework [65] provides guidance on using AI to complement pedagogy, emphasizing human interaction and humanistic principles.

Social and cultural aspects are also important in technology use, where gender gaps in access to technology highlight the need for more inclusive policies [66]. A UNESCO [67] reveals that women are less involved in technology, including data and AI. Thus, policies that encourage women's access to technology and ensure their participation in AI development are needed. This is also supported by findings from UNICEF [68], which emphasize the importance of education in bridging the gender digital gap, thereby reinforcing equality in the technology sector.

Recent research by Nikoula and Caroni [69] underscores the importance of education in equipping teacher candidates with the skills and knowledge necessary to navigate the evolving landscape of AI technology. They found that first-year students showed greater familiarity with AI-based devices. This familiarity stemmed from introducing this technology during secondary education. Nikoula and Caroni [69] findings further reveal that senior students showed greater familiarity with and use of AI for complex tasks across various subjects. This indicates that early exposure to AI can increase the use and understanding of this technology among students in higher education and their future careers as educators. Therefore, teacher candidates should gain direct experience with AI tools early on to prepare them for the challenges and opportunities presented by this technology in education.

The findings from this study suggest that teacher preparation programs should balance theoretical and practical learning approaches. By fostering positive attitudes toward scientific research and providing opportunities for practical engagement with AI technologies, these programs can ensure that teacher candidates are knowledgeable about AI and skilled in its application within their professional practice. Addressing this dual need is critical for equipping future educators to meet the demands of 21st-century education [59].

7 Conclusion

The results indicate that teacher candidates exhibit positively high attitudes across most dimensions of the research inventory and possess knowledge and familiarity with AI in educational settings. A significant correlation exists between their perceptions of scientific research and their knowledge and familiarity with using AI in education. In complementing the survey result, the open-ended questions were conducted which concluded that there is still dual perception and belief on how AI is used in education. There are two emerging themes based on thematic analysis: AI as (1) a wonderful tool and (2) a dangerous and unethical tool for research.

8 Limitation

However, a limitation of this study is its reliance on self-reported data and its focus on a specific Indonesian context, which may limit its generalizability. Future research should consider comparing teacher candidates (preservice) and in-service in including AI in research and teaching strategies to find the best practices using AI. In addition, the efforts and approaches of teacher trainers in adapting AI are also important to study. Furthermore, the comprehensive research should also focus on the dual perceptions of using AI in research.

Acknowledgement. The authors express their deepest gratitude to all Indonesian teacher candidates who participated in this research.

Declaration of Interest. The authors report no potential conflict of interest.

Informed Consent Statement. Respondents provided informed consent for participation in accordance with the approval of the review board.

Data Availability Statement. The datasets generated and/or analysed during the current study are available from the corresponding author upon reasonable request. Due to privacy concerns, some data cannot be publicly shared.

Declaration of Ethics. This project was carefully reviewed and received positive feedback from the Institutional Review Board Universitas Negeri Malang, Indonesia, No. Reff: 5.12.9/UN32.14/PB/2024.

References

1. Melo, A.F., da Costa, W.P., Rodrigues, R.R., Nunes, L.de A.C.B., Noll, P.R.E.S., Noll, M.: Panorama of undergraduate research in Brazil: profile, scientific production, and perceptions. Publications **11**(2), 30 (2023). https://doi.org/10.3390/publications11020030
2. Llewellyn, D.: Inquiry within: Implementing inquiry- based science standarts. Inc. A Sage Publications Company, USA, Corwinn Pres (2002)
3. Heras, M., Ruiz-Mallén, I.: Responsible research and innovation indicators for science education assessment: how to measure the impact? Int. J. Sci. Educ. **39**(18), 2482–2507 (2017). https://doi.org/10.1080/09500693.2017.1392643
4. Russell, S.H., Hancock, M.P., McCullough, J.: Benefits of undergraduate research experiences. Science **316**(5824), 548–549 (2007)
5. Cone, J.D., Foster, S.L.: Dissertations and theses from start to finish: psychology and related fields. Am. Psychol. Assoc. (1993)
6. Mabrouk, P.A.: Survey study investigating the significance of conference participation to undergraduate research students. J. Chem. Educ. **86**(11), 1335–1340 (2009). https://doi.org/10.1021/ed086p1335
7. Russell, S.H., Hancock, M.P., McCullough, J.: Benefits of undergraduate research experiences. Science **316**(5824), 548–549 (2007). https://doi.org/10.1126/science.1140384
8. Rinchen, S.: Bhutanese girls' perceptions of science and the impact of science on career choice. RABSEL: the CERD Educ. J. **III**, 17–46 (2003)
9. Papanastasiou, C., Papanastasiou, E.C.: Major influences on attitudes toward science. Int. J. Phytorem. **21**(1), 239–257 (2004). https://doi.org/10.1076/edre.10.3.239.30267
10. Fareh, S., Saeed, A.T.: The teacher as researcher in the context of language teaching. Procedia Soc. Behav. Sci. **15**, 153–159 (2011). https://doi.org/10.1016/j.sbspro.2011.03.066
11. McBee, M.T.: The classroom as laboratory: An exploration of teacher research. Roeper Rev. **27**(1), 52–58 (2004). https://doi.org/10.1080/02783190409554288
12. Ballenger, C., Rosebery, A.S.: What counts as teacher research? investigating the scientific and mathematical ideas of children from culturally diverse backgrounds. Teach. Coll. Rec. **105**(2), 297–314 (2003). https://doi.org/10.1111/1467-9620.00241
13. Korkmaz, Ö., Şahin, A., Yeşil, R.: Study of Validity and Reliability of Scale of Attitude towards Scientific Research Bilimsel Araştırmaya Yönelik Tutum Ölçeği Geçerlilik ve Güvenirlik Çalışması **10**(3), 961–973 (2011)

14. Perkins, K.K., Adams, W.K., Pollock, S.J., Finkelstein, N.D., Wieman, C.E.: Correlating student beliefs with student learning using the colorado learning attitudes about science survey. In: Marx, J., Heron, P., Franklin, S. (eds.) 2004 Physics Education Research Conference, pp. 61–64. American Institute of Physics (2005). https://doi.org/10.1142/9789812813787_0100
15. Onwuegbuzie, A.J., Leech, N.L., Murtonen, M., Tähtinen, J.: Utilizing mixed methods in teaching environments to reduce statistics anxiety. Int. J. Mult. Res. Approaches **4**(1), 28–39 (2010). https://doi.org/10.5172/mra.2010.4.1.028
16. Lodico, M.G., Spaulding, D.T., Voegtle, K.H.: Methods in Educational Research from Theory to Practice. Jossey-Bass, San Francisco (2006)
17. Mayasari, E.D., Pasikowski, S.: Teachers' and students' attitudes toward science and research methodology. In: Chiou, V., Geunis, L., Holz, O., Ertürk, N.O., Ratkowska-Pasikowska, J., Shelton, F. (eds.) Contemporary Challenges in Education: Paradoxes and Illuminations, vol. 3, pp. 300–3012. Waxmann (2023)
18. Papanastasiou, E.C.: Revised-attitudes toward research scale (R-ATR); a first look at its psychometric properties. J. Res. Educ. **24**(2), 147–159 (2014). https://doi.org/10.1037/t35506-000
19. Lei, S.A.: Factors changing attitudes of graduate school students toward an introductory research methodology course. Education (Chula Vista) **128**(4), 667–685 (2008)
20. Secret, M., Ford, J., Rompf, E.L.: Undergraduate research courses?: a closer look reveals complex social work student attitudes. J. Soc. Work. Educ. **39**(3), 411–422 (2003). https://doi.org/10.1080/10437797.2003.10779146
21. Bolin, B.L., Glen Maye, L.F., Lee, K.H., Yoon, D.P.: Impact of research orientation on attitudes toward research of social work students. J. Soc. Work. Educ. **48**(2), 223–243 (2012). https://doi.org/10.5175/JSWE.2012.200900120
22. Maschi, T., Wells, M., Yoder Slater, G., MacMillan, T., Ristow, J.: Social work students' research-related anxiety and self-efficacy: research instructors' perceptions and teaching innovations. Soc. Work. Educ. **32**(6), 800–817 (2013). https://doi.org/10.1080/02615479.2012.695343
23. Bhargava, A., Paty, M., Sambalpur, P.: Quintessential competencies of a teacher: a research review. Int. J. New Trends Educ. Implications **1**(1), 1–13 (2010). https://www.semanticscholar.org/paper/QUINTESSENTIAL-COMPETENCIES-OF-A-TEACHER%3A-A-Review-Bhargava-Paty/efcc87dcd46cab4f5633d0757b874d12f370da4d
24. Zawacki-Richter, O., Marín, V.I., Bond, M., Gouverneur, F.: Systematic review of research on artificial intelligence applications in higher education–where are the educators? Int. J. Educ. Technol. High. Educ. **16**(1), 1–27 (2019)
25. Holmes, W.: Artificial intelligence in education: Promises and implications for teaching and learning. Center for Curriculum Redesign (2019)
26. VanLehn, K.: The relative effectiveness of human tutoring, intelligent tutoring systems, and other tutoring systems. Educ. Psychol. **46**(4), 197–221 (2011)
27. Luckin, R., Holmes, W., Griffiths, M., Forcier, L.B.: Intelligence Unleashed: An Argument for AI in Education. Pearson, London (2016)
28. Roll, I., Wylie, R.: Evolution and revolution in artificial intelligence in education. Int. J. Artif. Intell. Educ. **26**, 582–599 (2016)
29. Tondeur, J., Scherer, R., Siddiq, F., Baran, E.: A comprehensive investigation of TPACK within pre-service teachers' ICT profiles: Mind the gap!. Australas. J. Educ. Technol. **33**(3) (2017)
30. Werdiningsih, I., Marzuki, Rusdin, D.: Balancing AI and authenticity: EFL students' experiences with ChatGPT in academic writing. Cogent Arts Humanit **11**(1) (2024). https://doi.org/10.1080/23311983.2024.2392388

31. Popenici, S.A.D., Kerr, S.: Exploring the impact of artificial intelligence on teaching and learning in higher education. Res. Pract. Technol. Enhanc. Learn. **12**(1), 22 (2017)
32. Shaun, R., De Baker, J., Inventado, P.S.: Chapter 4: Educational Data Mining and Learning Analytics. Springer (2014)
33. Garg, A.X., et al.: Effects of computerized clinical decision support systems on practitioner performance and patient outcomes: a systematic review. JAMA **293**(10), 1223–1238 (2005)
34. İnce, H., Çenberci, S., Yavuz, A.: The relationship between the attitudes of mathematics teacher candidates towards scientific research and their thinking styles. Universal J. Educ. Res. **6**(7), 1467–1476 (2018). https://doi.org/10.13189/ujer.2018.060707
35. Zydney, A.L., Bennett, J.S., Shahid, A., Bauer, K.W.: Faculty perspectives regarding the undergraduate research experience in science and engineering. J. Eng. Educ. **91**(3), 291–297 (2002). https://doi.org/10.1002/j.2168-9830.2002.tb00706.x
36. Zhai, X., et al.: A Review of Artificial Intelligence (AI) in Education from 2010 to 2020. Hindawi Limited (2021). https://doi.org/10.1155/2021/8812542
37. Cardona, M.A., Rodríguez, R.J., Ishmael, K.: Artificial intelligence and the future of teaching and learning insights and recommendations artificial intelligence and the future of teaching and learning (2023). https://tech.ed.gov
38. Pedro, F., Subosa, M., Rivas, A., Valverde, P.: Artificial intelligence in education: Challenges and opportunities for sustainable development. UNESCO (2019)
39. Miao, F., Cukurova, M.: AI competency framework for teachers. UNESCO (2024)
40. Hollands, F.M., DiPaola, D., Breazeal, C., Ali, S.: AI mastery may not be for everyone, but AI literacy should be. In: Proceedings of the 2024 on ACM Virtual Global Computing Education Conference, V. 1, pp. 60–66 (2024)
41. Katsamakas, E., Pavlov, O.V., Saklad, R.: Artificial intelligence and the transformation of higher education institutions: a systems approach. Sustainability **16**(14), 6118 (2024)
42. Zdravkova, K.: The potential of artificial intelligence for assistive technology in education. In: Handbook on Intelligent Techniques in the Educational Process: Vol 1 Recent Advances and Case Studies, pp. 61–85. Springer (2022)
43. Rane, N., Choudhary, S., Rane, J.: Education 4.0 and 5.0: Integrating artificial intelligence (AI) for personalized and adaptive learning. SSRN 4638365 (2023)
44. Kohnke, S., Zaugg, T.: Artificial intelligence: an untapped opportunity for equity and access in STEM education. Educ. Sci. (Basel) **15**(1), 68 (2025)
45. Vanaja, D.S., Raj, J.A.: AI-Enhanced IoT tool for emotional and social development in children with autism. Int. J. High Speed Electron. Syst. 2540148 (2025)
46. Irvan, M., Junaidi, A.R., Dewantoro, D.A., Puspitasari, E.P., Pramesti, Y., Ramadhani, V.W.: Emotional expressions recognize ability in children with autism: Intervention using emotion recognition assistance application. In: 8th International Conference on Education and Technology (ICET), pp. 87–90. IEEE (2022)
47. Festus, O., Emmanuel, O.B.: Sociocultural and digital communication challenges in AI adoption for classroom communication: insights from Nigerian colleges of education. Lang. Technol. Soc. Media **3**(1), 30–45 (2025)
48. Muralidhar, L.B., Sathyanarayana, N., Kumar, V.L., Santhosh, Y.: AI learning and talent strategies in transnational education: driving global leadership with agility. In: Innovative Approaches to Staff Development in Transnational Higher Education, pp. 245–276. IGI Global Scientific Publishing (2025)
49. Rofiah, K., Ngenge, R.T., Kholidya, C.F., Ainin, I.K.: Digital literacy and perception of inclusive education of preservice teachers at Indonesian universities, pp. 24–43 (2024). https://doi.org/10.1007/978-3-031-63235-8_2
50. Almaki, S.H., Mafarja, N., Al Mansoori, H.M.S.: Teacher well-being and use of artificial intelligence applications and tools: moderation effects of leadership support in inclusive classroom. STEM Educ. 5(1), 109–129 (2025)

51. Mayasari, E.D.: Tools construction to measure phenomena in university education. In: 4th International Perspectives in Education (IPiE) Conference, University of the Aegean, Mytilene, Greece (2024)
52. Petricini, T., Wu, C., Zipf, S.: Perceptions about generative AI and ChatGPT use by faculty and college students (2023). https://doi.org/10.35542/osf.io/jyma4
53. Cohen, J.: A power primer. Psychol. Bull. **112**(1), 155–159 (1992). https://doi.org/10.1037/0033-2909.112.1.155
54. Armutat, S., Wattenberg, M., Mauritz, N.: Artificial Intelligence – gender-specific Differences in perception, understanding, and training interest. In: Proceedings of the 7th International Conference on Gender Research,**7**(1), 36–43. Academic Conferences International Ltd, Barcelona (2024). https://doi.org/10.34190/icgr.7.1.2163
55. Braun, V., Clarke, V.: Using thematic analysis in psychology. Qual. Res. Psychol. **3**(2), 77–101 (2006). https://doi.org/10.1191/1478088706qp063oa
56. Hopcan, S., Türkmen, G., Polat, E.: Exploring the artificial intelligence anxiety and machine learning attitudes of teacher candidates. Educ. Inf. Technol. (Dordr) **29**(6), 7281–7301 (2024). https://doi.org/10.1007/s10639-023-12086-9
57. Yue, M., Jong, M.S.-Y., Ng, D.T.K.: Understanding K–12 teachers' technological pedagogical content knowledge readiness and attitudes toward artificial intelligence education. Educ. Inf. Technol. (Dordr) **29**(15), 19505–19536 (2024). https://doi.org/10.1007/s10639-024-12621-2
58. Alwaqdani, M.: Investigating teachers' perceptions of artificial intelligence tools in education: potential and difficulties. Educ. Inf. Technol. (Dordr) (2024). https://doi.org/10.1007/s10639-024-12903-9
59. AI and the Future of Skills, Volume 1. OECD (2021). https://doi.org/10.1787/5ee71f34-en
60. Lo, C.K.: What Is the impact of chatgpt on education? A rapid review of the literature. Educ. Sci. (Basel) **13**(4), 410 (2023). https://doi.org/10.3390/educsci13040410
61. Wiederhold, B.K.: 'Alexa, are you my mom?' The role of artificial intelligence in child development. Cyberpsychol. Behav. Soc. Netw. **21**(8), 471–472 (2018). https://doi.org/10.1089/cyber.2018.29120.bkw
62. Ajani, O.A., Gamede, B., Matiyenga, T.C.: Leveraging artificial intelligence to enhance teaching and learning in higher education: promoting quality education and critical engagement. J. Pedagogical Soc. Psychol. **7**(1), 54–69 (2024). https://doi.org/10.33902/JPSP.202528400
63. Butson, R., Spronken-Smith, R.: AI and its implications for research in higher education: a critical dialogue. High. Educ. Res. Dev. **43**(3), 563–577 (2024). https://doi.org/10.1080/07294360.2023.2280200
64. Selwyn, N.: Should Robots Replace Teachers?: AI and the Future of Education. Wiley (2019)
65. Mishra, P., Koehler, M.J.: Technological pedagogical content knowledge: a framework for teacher knowledge. Teach. Coll. Rec. **108**(6), 1017–1054 (2006)
66. Bray, F.: Gender and technology (2007). https://doi.org/10.1146/annurev.anthro.36.081406.094328
67. Unesco: Unesco Call to Action: Closing the Gender Gap in Science (2024)
68. United Nations Children's Fund: Bridging the Gender Digital Divide: Challenges and an Urgent Call for Action for Equitable Digital Skills Development. New York (2023)
69. Nikoulina, A., Caroni, A.: Familiarity, use, and perception of AI-poweredtools in higher education. Int. J. Manage. Knowl. Learn. **13** (2024). https://doi.org/10.53615/2232-5697.13.169-181

Not All Bodies are Created Equal: Use of Generative AI in Physical Education

Stuart Evans(✉) and Alexia Maddox

La Trobe University, Melbourne, VIC, Australia
Stuart.evans@latrobe.edu.au

Abstract. Physical Education (PE) is a process that uses physical activity to help people acquire skills, fitness, knowledge, and attitudes that contribute to their optimal development and well-being. Curriculum-based PE provides children with a planned, sequential and standards-based program of curricula and instruction designed to develop motor skills, knowledge and behaviours for active living, physical fitness, self-efficacy and emotional intelligence. Enhancing a child's motor skill and physical abilities in the absence of generative AI involves the implementation of various conventional methods and strategies. Due to difficulties with children's attendance and engagement in PE combined with varying levels of teachers' teaching ability and knowledge of the scientific principles of human movement, the knowledge and skills that children learn in PE can be limited. Children can spend a lot of time and energy on physical exercise, but if professional theory and understanding is lacking, the final exercise effect may not be satisfactory and even may cause harm. The integration of generative AI in physical activity and sports-specific training in education has emerged as a possible approach to enhancing a child's development in PE, optimizing training strategies and providing personalised insights for both children and the teacher. The strategic use of generative AI can empower both teacher and children through a 'learner as a leader' paradigm. There has been limited attention to meaningful pedagogy PE learning in the generative AI community so far, which is likely due to the lack of appropriate technological support available for movement detection at low cost and with low intrusion. Despite this, generative AI-powered tools could significantly enhance meaning and engagement with both PE and physical activity by identifying patterns and correlations within the data, allowing for the personalized creation of training plans and optimized lesson schedules. This article looks at the rapidly evolving technological resource of Generative AI and how it can be used effectively and ethically within a physical educator's role and the overall teaching profession.

Keywords: digital pedagogy · health and physical education · generative AI · PE pedagogy

1 Introduction

Sports, physical activity and exercise have long occupied an important place in the physical education (PE) curriculum. Regular physical activity in childhood and adolescence is important for promoting lifelong health and well-being and preventing various

Ł. Tomczyk (Ed.): NMP 2024, CCIS 2537, pp. 328–342, 2025.
https://doi.org/10.1007/978-3-031-95627-0_22

health conditions. Schools are in a unique position to help children attain the recommended 60 min or more of moderate-to-vigorous physical activity daily. Recommendations by the World Health Organization [1] suggest children should be exposed to activities that develop musculoskeletal tissue and improve movement control at least three times weekly. Furthermore, PE provides cognitive content and instruction designed to develop motor skills, knowledge, and behaviors for physical activity and physical fitness. Thus, PE is a process that uses physical activity to help children acquire skills, fitness, knowledge, and attitudes that contribute to their optimal development and well-being.

The academic subject of PE is the foundation of many comprehensive school physical activity programs. In the quest to combat youth physical inactivity, health, physical education, exercise, fitness and physical activity, physical literacy has emerged as a key concept that synthesizes these key variables. Supporting schools to establish PE daily can provide children with the ability and confidence to be physically active for a lifetime. The subject of PE is characterized by a planned, sequential curriculum that is generally based on a respective country's national standards for physical education. Today's PE landscape demands more than just traditional teaching methods – it requires that physical educators to be pedagogically adaptable and resourceful.

Physical education can be divided into four sub-disciplines: physical education training, sports humanities, exercise biology, and traditional ethnic sports [2]. Unlike sports training, which is oriented towards skill enhancement and competitive performance, PE focuses on students' holistic growth and lifelong participation in physical activities [3]. Emerging technologies, including artificial intelligence (AI), machine learning (ML), and other digital tools, such as educational robots, are increasingly being introduced into PE, though their integration and impact remain in early stages and require further research and development to realize their full potential [4]. The applications of AI in education are rapidly evolving, reshaping the overall teaching and learning landscape [5]. While conversations around generative AI systems such as ChatGPT and other AI instances being adopted and misused by students remains a hot topic among the education community, with ever-increasing teacher workloads, could the emerging prevalence of AI, and particularly generative AI technology, present an opportunity for physical education teachers to increase student engagement and overall physical activity levels? AI is a rapidly evolving technological resource that has and will continue to impact all areas of education and teaching, so its role must be thoroughly understood. If utilized in PE, it must be done with a clear understanding of how it can be used effectively and ethically within an educator's role and the overall teaching profession.

This chapter looks at the rapidly evolving technological resource of Generative AI and how it can be used efficiently and ethically within a physical educator's role and the overall teaching profession. As the integration of generative AI in physical activity and sports-specific training in education has emerged as a possible approach to enhancing a child's development in PE, it is important to optimize training strategies that provide the PE teacher with personalized. From here, the strategic use of generative AI can empower both teacher and children through a 'learner as a leader' paradigm. Given the limited attention to meaningful PE pedagogy in the generative AI community so far, which is likely due to the lack of appropriate technological support available for movement detection at low cost and with low intrusion, the remaining sections unpack different realms and how Generative AI could be beneficial.

2 What is Generative AI and AI?

The Organisation for Economic Co-operation and Development (OECD) defines AI as, "a machine-based system that can, for a given set of human-defined objectives, make predictions, recommendations, or decisions influencing real or virtual environments. AI systems are designed to operate with varying levels of autonomy." [6]. While AI computing has been around since the 1950s, it has only been since the 2000's that the broad population has started seeing advances in the AI-related areas of computer vision, graphics processing and speech recognition technology. Among the emerging trends, generative AI, a subset of AI, has shown potential in reshaping industries, among them education. But how does it differ from traditional AI?

Traditional AI centers on executing a specific task intelligently. It refers to systems intended to respond to a particular set of inputs. These systems have the capacity to learn from data and make decisions or predictions based on that data. Essentially, the computer knows the rules – it can predict moves and makes its own move based on a pre-defined strategy. In comparison, generative AI can be thought of as the next generation of artificial intelligence and is a form of AI that can create something original.

Generative AI models are trained on a set of data and learn the underlying patterns to generate *new* data that mirrors the training set. Thus, the main difference between traditional AI and generative AI lies in their corresponding capabilities and application. For instance, conventional AI approaches are primarily used to analyze data and make predictions, while generative AI goes a step further by generating novel data like its training data. While many education leaders understand that, at a high level, new skills are required to work with generative AI, the sense of how these changes might create value and benefit can be vague and underinformed. Furthermore, in many instances the possibilities of using generative AI to improve PE teacher efficiency is not always front of mind.

Generative AI has many application fields and research themes [7] while physical educational technology falls under the sports, education, computer science, and other fields [8]. Yet dialogue on the future of PE has long highlighted the significance of progressing skills and ongoing professional development. The growth of ChatGPT is, perhaps, a proof point. Most students and teachers agree that ChatGPT is just another example of why the education sector cannot keep doing things the old way in the modern world.

Generative AI's capabilities relative to PE include computer vision for movement analysis, pattern recognition for skill development, and predictive modeling for performance optimization. These systems use deep learning networks trained on vast amounts of movement data to understand, analyze, and provide feedback on physical activities. Unlike traditional AI systems that simply classify movements as correct or incorrect, generative AI can create detailed feedback, suggest modifications, and even generate personalized training programs based on individual student data [9]. The technology can process multiple data streams simultaneously - from video analysis of movement patterns to biometric data from wearable devices - creating comprehensive insights for both teachers and students. However, this sophisticated data processing also raises important considerations around privacy, data security, and ethical use of student information [10], particularly in educational settings where the protection of student data is paramount. In the context of PE, generative AI's ability to create personalized content and analyze complex movement patterns represents both opportunities and challenges. While the technology offers unprecedented possibilities for individualized instruction and real-time feedback, it requires careful integration with existing pedagogical practices and consideration of student privacy and safety [10]. Understanding these technical capabilities and limitations is crucial for physical educators seeking to leverage generative AI effectively in their teaching practice.

3 What is Physical Activity?

Physical education is an important school subject that promotes physical activity, exercise and fitness modalities through an array of interactive and game-based pedagogical activities. Physical activity is a subset of physical education. The World Health Organization (WHO) defines physical activity as any bodily movement produced by skeletal muscles that requires energy expenditure [1]. Physical activity refers to all movement including during leisure time, for transport to get to and from places, or as part of a person's work or domestic activities. Essentially, this can be classified as deliberate and incidental physical activity. Both moderate- and vigorous-intensity physical activity are known to improve health and can include walking, cycling, wheeling, sports, active recreation and play, and can be achieved by most children regardless of skill level.

Exercise is described as structured or planned physical activity, such as going to the gym, a swim or a jog each day [1]. The five components of fitness are the blueprint for the American College of Sports Medicine (ACSM) physical activity guidelines and serve as

Fig. 1. WHO [1] infographic based on physical activity guidelines.

a helpful tool for organizing and executing a well-balanced workout routine [11]. The five components of fitness as stated by the ACSM are cardiovascular endurance, muscular strength, muscular endurance, flexibility, and body composition. The WHO Global guidelines on physical activity and sedentary behaviour provide recommendations for children (age 5 and up), adolescents, adults, older adults, pregnant and post-partum women, and people living with chronic conditions and disabilities (see Fig. 1) [1].

Despite the recommended physical activity guidelines, in many Western countries the national report on children's physical activity shows both young children and adolescents are not moving enough [1], with experts concerned that sedentary living patterns established in childhood will increase the risk of poor health outcomes in later life. Broadening physical activity options for children and young people may increase activity levels and bring associated health and wellbeing benefits.

4 Physical Education and Digital Literacy

Digital technology continues to grow in popularity in the PE teaching and learning process. Technology usage, including generative AI, within contemporary PE theoretically can enrich educational content, alter perceptions of education, and effects changes to traditional physical education models and pedagogy. Generative AI also has the potential to improve the practicability of education for learners, reconstruct PE, and promote continuous development [12].

While science-oriented research, for example, tends to meet this challenge openly, in discussions regarding PE, digital technology has typically been linked to topics such as lack of exercise [13]. To this end, the use of digital media in PE that is informed by the physical, cognitive, social, affective, and applied within a school framework matched by appropriate pedagogical remains a challenge for many physical educators. In this context, the role and responsibility of a PE teacher requires an innovative response matched by integrative foci. This is where the physical nature of physical education can be utilized and matched with the digital realm.

Digitally mediated literacy practices require competencies specific to the online environment [14]. This incorporates skill sets that may also be denoted to as computer literacy, ICT literacy, data literacy, or data fluency. The incorporation of generative AI and AI literacy into digital literacy and how it should be dealt with is currently a dominant topic in the PE discourse. Since it is usually not taught as a separate subject, generative AI education can be included as part of an informed and practically based physical education pedagogical strategy. Nonetheless, there is ongoing debate regarding the evidence of its impact on teaching and learning in PE. With increasing use of generative AI in education, digitally competent physical educators are necessary to the success of its integration, if indeed generative AI's integration is as predicated.

With increasing use in PE, teachers who possess digital competence are necessary to the success of its integration [13] given that technology works best in supporting student achievement when the technology is in the hands of the teacher [15]. Yet such research has generally been applied to classroom-based learning which does not necessarily transfer to the practical demands of PE. For instance, the systematic review of Sargent and Calderón [16] showed that most of the technology-enhanced interventions are not using digital technology in transformative ways (allowing for the enactment of learning tasks that are inconceivable without the use of technology), but 'just' as a direct tool substitute of the teacher, with no functional change. Two of the reasons that can potentially explain those findings that require more research are: (i) teacher digital competency; (ii) and a misunderstanding of the dichotomy pedagogy-technology mainly based on technological or pedagogical determinism [17]. Yet a perceived conflict between the physical and digital worlds exists. One of the priorities of physical education is to promote an active and healthy lifestyle, supporting an autonomous climate, social interaction and comprehensive participation during class [18], with some [19] suggesting that inactive children and adolescents are mainly due to the increasing use of digital technology. Consequently, disengagement in PE, physical activity and the construct of digital literacy is the purported result. As Moore et al. [20] highlights, this disengagement is caused by a new trend based on spending time on computer games (sometimes called e-sports), TV and social media.

An alternative relevant barrier is the negative experience that some students underwent in previous sports and/or physical activity program. But paradoxically, new technologies can have a relevant role in motivating and engaging these students in physical education classes. For that reason, a teacher's personal digital competence is conceived as a highly relevant 21st-century capability. Nonetheless, barriers to integrative physical education and technology do not only come from students. For example, when it comes to practical barriers to teachers' use of digital technology and the uptake of generative AI, time, expense, the teacher's digital competence, teacher burden as well as a certain level of resistance to change and use of digital technology are mooted as factors.

5 Digital Competence Frameworks and Entangled PE Pedagogy

In a fast and ever-changing world, a physical educator's role is continually being altered to adapt and teach according to modern educational challenges. Specifically, there are expectations placed on both primary and high school teachers that require them to obtain new skills via professional development. It is generally required that PE complete a designated set of hours per annum of professional development, of which practically based pedagogy and frameworks, new trends, workshops and additional education initiatives are offered by education providers and associations. Notwithstanding decades of efforts to incorporate technology into physical education, many teachers remain unprepared for online learning as suggested by the recent body of literature on the impact of the COVID-19 pandemic on education [21]. The possibilities of teaching physical education with generative AI are being questioned. Educational technologies are also being reframed as an issue rather than a silver bullet for resolving various educational challenges [22]. Therefore, the integration of generative AI into teaching and learning and the need to integrate digital pedagogy remains a contentious issue in physical education.

Existing digital competence frameworks are built based on an amalgamation of technological and pedagogical determinism. This is where technology and teachers are considered drivers of change [17], and their digital skills are defined by their agency in choosing and using methods and tools to use technology in the classroom [23]. The entanglement that exists between the traditional classroom and the external environment that both physical education and physical activity occur differs from that of traditional subjects such as mathematics, science, and humanities. Arguably, blending digital tools with classroom-based pedagogical approaches is somewhat easier when the environment is predictable (i.e., static) compared to the dynamic nature of physical activity and the game-based pedagogies that are often applied. While research indicates that the use of digital technology in a classroom environment has provided numerous benefits for teaching and learning, for example, an encouraging influence on student motivation and engagement in classwork due to the enactment of digital technology in the teaching and learning process [24]. Further, others discuss how digital technology can improve student collaboration with their peers [25].

6 Applications of AI in Physical Education

A fundamental aim of PE is to improve students' physical fitness but also emphasize students' comprehensive development in cognitive, social, and psychological aspects of physical education. A recent systematic review of generative AI implementation in PE has identified three primary application areas that support these aims: data-driven optimization of teaching and training, computer vision-based motion behavior recognition, and virtual technology innovation for assessment [10]. Through these applications, AI has presented novel ways to enhance learning and teaching in practical classes.

Some researchers have found generative AI to improve and innovate PE methods through technical means to enhance teaching effectiveness and personalization [26] while others have seen improved personalized feedback, optimization of teaching resources, and enhancement of the overall student learning experience [27] due to deepened generative AI applications in PE [10]. However, implementation faces several challenges. Technical reliability and accuracy remain concerns, particularly for complex movement analysis and real-time feedback systems. Data privacy and security considerations are paramount, especially when collecting and analyzing student performance data. Additionally, teacher training and support needs must be carefully considered, as studies show that pre-service PE teachers often lack confidence in applying generative AI technologies despite recognizing their potential benefits [10]. As generative AI technology continues to evolve, the specific details and applications are undergoing continuous refinement and updates, with no current unified standard.

The successful implementation of generative AI requires careful attention to teacher preparation and professional development. Studies indicate that pre-service physical educators face unique challenges when integrating generative AI technologies, including gaps between theoretical knowledge and practical application, limited experience with technical tools, and concerns about maintaining pedagogical quality while adopting new technologies [10]. To address these challenges, strategies should focus on three key areas: structured technical training that builds confidence with generative AI tools, mentorship programs that pair experienced technology users with novice teachers and continuing professional development opportunities that help teachers stay current with evolving technologies. This should be complemented by clear guidelines for data privacy and security, ensuring teachers understand both the technical and ethical dimensions of AI implementation.

The integration of generative AI into sport, notably extra-curricular sporting activities, involves utilizing cameras to capture athletes' data, analyzing and assessing them through video-based human motion recognition algorithms, and drawing informed conclusions [28]. This approach permits athletes to obtain intuitive awareness into their training shortcomings and deficiencies, permitting them to receive higher-quality training plans through coach guidance and analysis. For generative AI to be applied and customized for PE classes, teacher knowledge provision, learner evaluation, and learner methods are needed for PE teachers. The practical implications and relevance to PE need to be explicitly defined. Fan and Jiao [29] propose three paradigms for understanding the evolution of AI in education.

- Paradigm One (AI-Directed, Learner-as-Recipient), AI systems primarily direct the learning process, with learners having limited control.
- Paradigm Two (AI-Supported, Learner-as-Collaborator) introduces more interaction between learners and AI systems, with learners having increased input
- Paradigm Three (AI-Empowered, Learner-as-Leader) represents the most advanced stage - AI acts as a supportive tool empowering learners to take primary agency over their learning.

Although many contemporary personalised and adaptive learning systems align more closely with Paradigms One and Two, the field is evolving towards Paradigm Three. This evolution involves increasing learner agency, more sophisticated AI that can handle complex, open-ended interactions, and a shift towards AI as a tool that empowers learners rather than directs them. Strengthening the research of AI's main theory system in PE might offer a foundation for the evolution of the modern PE field. For learning to be effective and meaningful in PE, the characteristics of each children's interests and aptitude must be addressed.

7 Personalised Learning

Personalised learning is an educational approach that aims to provide children with customized learning experiences that are constituted by tailoring instruction, content, and pacing to the needs, preferences, interests, and abilities of each student [30]. The transition from early automated systems to more adaptive and learner-centered approaches is demonstrated by key developments in personalised learning technologies and pedagogies. In the 1970s and 1980s, Fred Keller's 'Personalized System of Instruction' (PSI) introduced self-paced, mastery-based learning [31, 32]. The personalized system of instruction is a student-centered approach to learning which consists of five principles, namely that:

- Learning is self-paced.
- Students must meet certain performance criteria for each component before proceeding to the next level of learning.
- Content is delivered through written text (the contemporary approach uses mobile applications such as applications).
- The use of "proctors" assesses students on individual components of the course and provide support

- Instruction is focused on motivation rather than content delivery

The amalgamation of generative AI into personalised learning represents a possible evolution in physical educational technology, building upon the PSI approach and adaptive learning systems and data analytics. Recent research has shown that this integration can particularly benefit physical education by supporting both individual skill development and group dynamics [10]. Zawacki-Richter et al. [33] highlight how generative AI can process and interpret vast amounts of learner data, offering more nuanced and dynamic personalisation than previous systems. This generative AI-enhanced approach provides real-time, individualised learning experiences that adapt to a learner's knowledge state, engagement level, and contextual factors. Generative AI-powered systems can offer sophisticated automated assessment and feedback, creating customized learning pathways and recommending personalized content. The fusion of generative AI with existing physical education practices and pedagogies has the potential to significantly enhance the responsiveness and effectiveness of personalised learning environments. This integration is particularly valuable in physical education settings where students' abilities and learning can vary significantly. Research indicates that such technology-enhanced personalization can improve intrinsic motivation and motor skills development while supporting cooperative learning approaches [10]. This reflects a continuous effort to leverage advancing technology in pursuit of more effective, individualized learning experiences for all students while simultaneously informing and improving institutional processes.

Despite this, personalized learning and the use of generative AI is not a panacea for in the curriculum-oriented physical education environment as it faces numerous key implementation challenges. For instance, Shemshack and Spector [34] identify fundamental issues including the lack of agreement on essential components and the challenge of balancing personalisation with standardised curriculum requirements. Evaluates by Zhang et al. [35] and Walkington and Bernacki [36] highlight how contextual factors affect implementation, particularly when scaling across classrooms with varying resources and support levels. Looking ahead, the assessment by Shemshack and Spector [34] suggests several directions for future research, including developing a common framework and definition, examining the effectiveness of different personalised learning components, incorporating higher-order thinking skills development, and exploring the use of emerging technologies such as generative AI in personalised learning environments. These challenges are particularly relevant in physical education settings where the need to balance individual progress with group dynamics and cooperative learning approaches requires careful consideration.

8 Marginalization

Compared to traditional academic subjects, PE is often viewed as a marginal subject within respective curriculums. Unfortunately, many secondary schools actively reduce physical education time to make way for what are deemed more "serious" or "important" subjects [37]. Marginalization occurs when school structures prioritize traditional cognitive subjects like science, mathematics, and language. Consequently, subjects that require physical effort and creativity, such as physical education, art, and music, are considered less important and, therefore, marginalized. Marginalization is maintained by various factors, such as uncertain teacher–coach roles, large class sizes and inadequate facilities [38], a lack of clear program goals in the profession and insufficient teacher preparation and professional development for real-world situations and a lack of mentorship [39]. While physical educators are often fighting against marginalization in schools, the strategic and meaningful use of generative AI give the physical education teacher avenues to lead educational initiatives while building relationships with their colleagues.

The use of generative AI in the physical educational landscape has the promise to reduce the notion of marginalization. For instance, an emerging sports training approach rooted in AI is referred to as the intelligent sports training system [40]. In the current PE technology landscape, intelligent teaching systems predominantly rely on preset teaching lesson plans and pedagogical models that can lack flexibility to adapt to individual differences and specific needs of students in physical activity. This limitation happens from the systems' emphasis on predetermined teaching strategies, overlooking the dynamic progress and distinct needs of students. Moreover, these systems often lack adaptableness in reacting to the complex dynamics of the physical education teaching process, hindering timely adjustments based on student performance and feedback.

In addressing these challenges and recognizing the individual differences that occur in physical activity and the unique context of PE, this the use of generative AI offers an intelligent-assisted PE teaching model based on high-order complex networks to enhance existing technology. Additionally, with teacher input, generative AI can monitor students' physical activity and overall fitness progress in real-time, offering timely advice and insights for the teacher, the students and the parents (see Fig. 2).

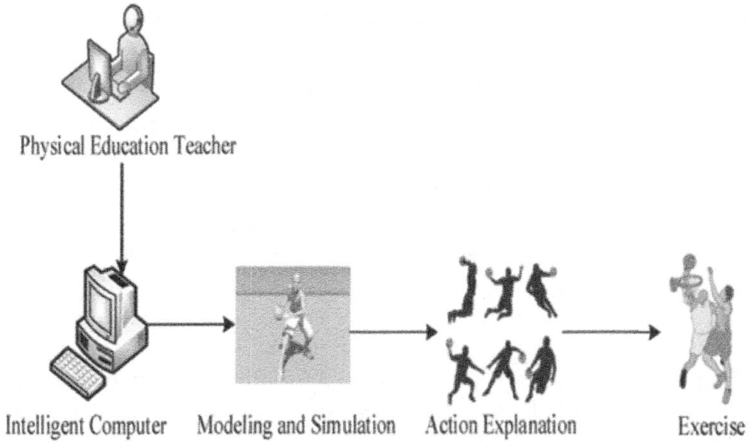

Fig. 2. Model of teacher learner as leader

9 Examples of Applied and Practical Uses of Generative AI in Physical Education

Integration of generative AI in sports-specific training in education has emerged as a possible approach to enhancing individual performance, optimizing training strategies and providing personalized insights for student as athlete and teacher. Adaptive learning is often used interchangeably with personalised learning, especially when referring to technology-enhanced approach [34]. Generative AI-powered systems can give real-time feedback on form and technique, which may help reduce the risk of injury and improve performance and motor skill development. While not an exhaustive list, additional examples of how generative AI can be applied during PE are listed in Table 1.

Table 1. Practical uses and descriptors of generative AI in physical education.

Practical usage	Descriptor
Diversify the curriculum	Adapt to students' preferences and skill levels while promoting meaningful and active participation and learning
Analyze data	Provide teacher recommendations for lesson content, ensuring that activities align with educational standards and cater to individual needs
Support	Provide teacher support in teaching motor skills, simplifying complex movements; may help students achieve mastery
Real-time feedback	Offers real-time feedback and guidance to enhance the learning experience, helping students refine their physical abilities
Personalisation	Tailor programs for students with disabilities, ensuring inclusivity and access for all
Customized modifications	Helps teachers meet the unique needs of each student
Theoretical improvements	Potential to continue developing PE, given that a basic theoretical system suitable for this purpose is developed along with convergence with other fields
Multifaceted integration	Considers individual learners' physical condition, physical activity achievement level, psychological characteristics, and home environment

In a PE setting, generative AI offers potential for providing personalized instruction (for students) and real-time feedback and assessment in diverse learning environments. Concerns have also been raised that the usage and possible integration of generative AI into a PE context could reinforce biomedical approaches to health and lead, for example, to a focus on increasing fitness through technology alone [9]. It is therefore important that the fundamental parameters of exercise and physical activity programming is retained and monitored, this is particularly important when manipulation of training volume and load (resistance) intensity are considered given the propensity for injury if done incorrectly. While there appears to be limited awareness of how generative AI could be applied to create a meaningful pedagogical experience for student learning, this is likely due to the lack of appropriate technological support available for movement detection at low cost and with low intrusion. But generative AI-powered tools could enhance a student's engagement and interest in physical education by the teacher identifying patterns and correlations within generative AI produced data to subsequently create and deploy personalized lessons plans and optimized schedules. From here, students who follow these generative AI-guided lessons could experience improvements in their physical capabilities, such as increased strength, speed, agility, and endurance with direct instruction and monitoring provided by the teacher (Fig. 3).

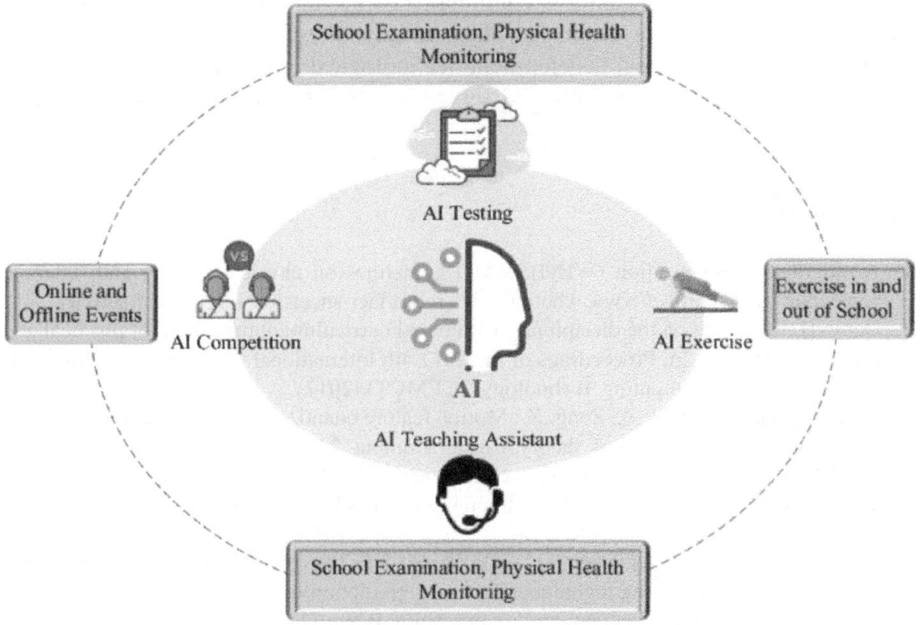

Fig. 3. Primary applications of AI in physical education.

10 Conclusion

Looking ahead, the development of generative AI in PE must balance technological innovation with pedagogical effectiveness and teacher empowerment. Research suggests that future developments should focus on several key areas: enhancing the accuracy and reliability of movement recognition systems, developing more sophisticated personalization capabilities, and improving the integration of virtual and augmented reality tools [10]. However, equally important is the need to build teacher capacity and confidence. This includes developing comprehensive pre-service training programs that prepare new PE teachers for generative AI-enhanced environments, creating sustainable professional development pathways, and establishing communities of practice where teachers can share experiences and best practices.

Teacher education programs focused on physical education must work to better infuse technology throughout their curriculum, moving beyond treating technology as a standalone entity. To address the contemporary needs of physical educators and the stagnant levels of physical activity, physical educators can lead by example and learn how generative AI can be used to support novel ways of teaching and learning. Additionally, more attention must be paid to developing frameworks for measuring the impact of generative AI implementations on student learning outcomes, ensuring that technological innovation truly serves educational goals. It is no longer possible to think about health and physical literacy solely as a linguistic or movement-based accomplishment. Tomorrow's PE teachers need to comprehend, respond to, and compose multimodal texts in diverse forms, where meaning is communicated through dynamic combinations of two or more modes. This evolution of physical education teaching requires a systematic approach to professional development, technological integration, and pedagogical innovation, ensuring that generative AI serves as a tool for empowerment rather than replacement.

References

1. World Health Organization (WHO): WHO guidelines on physical activity and sedentary behaviour. (2024) https://www.who.int/news-room/fact-sheets/detail/physical-activity
2. Dong, H.: Research on the disciplinary nature and curriculum optimization of physical education and training. In: Proceedings of the 2017 4th International Conference on Education, Management and Computing Technology (ICEMCT) (2017)
3. Leng, X., Jiang, H., Zou, X., Zeng, X.: Motion feature quantization of athletic sports training based on fuzzy neural network theory. Cluster Comput. **22**, 4631–4638 (2019)
4. Van Mechelen, M., et al.: Emerging technologies in K–12 education: a future HCI research agenda. ACM Trans. Comput. Hum. Interact. **30**(3), 47(2023). https://doi.org/10.1145/3569897
5. Costa, E.B., Fonseca, B., Santana, M.A., de Araújo, F.F., Rego, J.: Evaluating the effectiveness of educational data mining techniques for early prediction of students' academic failure in introductory programming courses. Comput. Hum. Behav. **73**, 247–256 (2017)
6. Popenici, S.A., Kerr, S.: Exploring the impact of artificial intelligence on teaching and learning in higher education. Res. Pract. Technol. Enhanced Learn. **12**(1), 1–13 (2017)
7. Organisation for Economic Co-operation and Development. (OECD). What is AI? Can you make a clear distinction between AI and non-AI systems? - OECD.AI (2024)
8. McCabe, A., Trevathan, J.: Artificial intelligence in sports prediction. In: Proceedings of the Fifth International Conference on Information Technology: New Generations (itng 2008), Las Vegas, NV, USA, 7–9 April, pp. 1194–1197, (2008)
9. Hu, Z., Liu, Z., Su, Y.: AI-driven smart transformation in physical education: current trends and future research directions. Appl. Sci. **14**(22), 10616 (2024)
10. Zhou, T., Wu, X., Wang, Y., Wang, Y., Zhang, S.: Application of artificial intelligence in physical education: a systematic review. Educ. Inf. Technol. **29**(7), 8203–8220 (2024)
11. Ferguson, B.: ACSM's Guidelines for Exercise Testing and Prescription 9th Ed. 2014. J Can Chiropr Assoc, **58**(3), 328 (2014)
12. Lee, H.S., Lee, J.: Applying artificial intelligence in physical education and future perspectives. Sustainability **13**, 351 (2021)
13. Jastrow, F., Greve, S., Thumel, M., et al.: Digital technology in physical education: a systematic review of research from 2009 to 2020. Ger. J. Exerc. Sport Res. **52**, 504–528 (2022)

14. Silvhiany, S.: Critical digital literacies in education 4. Preparing Students for the Uncertainties of Post-Truth World. LINGUA, **19**(2), 102–109 (2019)
15. Instefjord, E.I., Munthe, E: Educating digitally competent teachers: a study of integration of professional digital competence in teacher education. Teach. Teach. Educ. **67**, 37–45 (2017)
16. Sargent, J., Calderón, A.: Technology-enhanced learning physical education? A critical review of the literature. J. Teach. Phy. Educ. (2021)
17. Fawns, T.: An entangled pedagogy: Views of the relationship between technology and pedagogy. https://open.ed.ac.uk/an-entangled-pedagogy-views-of-the-relationship-between-technology-and-pedagogy. University of Edinburgh
18. Ryan, R.M., Deci, E.L.: Intrinsic and extrinsic motivation from a self-determination theory perspective: definitions, theory, practices, and future directions. Cont. Edu. Psy. **61**, 101860 (2020)
19. Kerres, M.: Bildung in a digital world: The social construction of future in education. Bildung in the Digital Age. Routledge (2022)
20. Moore, R., Edmondson, L., Gregory, M. Griffiths, K., Freeman, E.: Barriers and facilitators to physical activity and further digital exercise intervention among inactive British adolescents in secondary schools: a qualitative study with physical education teachers. Front. Public Health, **11** (2023)
21. Howard, S.K., Tondeur, J., Fazilat Siddiq, F., Scherer, R.: Ready, set, go! Profiling teachers' readiness for online teaching in secondary education. Tech, Pedagogy Educ. **30** (2020)
22. Selwyn, N.: Digital degrowth: toward radically sustainable education technology. Learn. Media Technol. 186–199 (2024)
23. Redecker, C.: European framework for the digital competence of educators: DigCompEdu. Publications Office of the European Union (2017)
24. Østerlie, O.: Can flipped learning enhance adolescents' motivation in physical education? An intervention study. J. Res. Arts Sports Educ. **2**, 1–15 (2018)
25. Eyyam, R., Yaratan, H.: Impact of use of technology in mathematics lessons on student achievement and attitudes. Soc. Behav. Pers. **42** (2014)
26. Yang, D.P., Oh, E.S., Wang, Y.C.: Hybrid physical education teaching and curriculum design based on a voice interactive artificial intelligence educational robot. Sustainability **12**, 8000 (2020)
27. Guo, Q., Li, B.: Role of AI physical education based on application of functional sports training. J. Intell. Fuzzy Syst **40**, 3337–3345 (2021)
28. Bamunif, A.O.A.: Sports information & discussion forum using artificial intelligence techniques: a new approach. Turk. J. Comput. Math. Educ, **12**(11), 2847–2854 (2021)
29. Fan, O., Jiao, P.: Artificial intelligence in education: the three paradigms. Comput. Educ. Artif. Intell. **2**, 100020 (2021)
30. Baidoo-Anu, D., Owusu Ansah, L.: Education in the era of generative artificial intelligence (AI): understanding the potential benefits of ChatGPT in promoting teaching and learning. J. AI **7**(1), 52–62 (2023)
31. Keller, F.S.: Good-bye, teacher. J. Appl. Behav. Anal. **1**(1), 79–89 (1968)
32. Keller, F.S., Sherman, J.G.: The Keller Plan Handbook. W. A. Benjamin, Menlo Park, CA (1974)
33. Zawacki-Richter, O., Marín, V.I., Bond, M., Gouverneur, F.: Systematic review of research on artificial intelligence applications in higher education – where are the educators? Int. J. Educ. Tech. Higher. Educ. **16**(1), 39 (2019)
34. Shemshack, A., Spector, J.M.: A systematic literature review of personalized learning terms. Smart Learn. Env. **7**(1), 33 (2020)
35. Zhang, L., Basham, J. D., Yang, S.: Understanding the implementation of personalized learning: a research synthesis. Educ. Res. Rev. **31** (2020)

36. Walkington, C., Bernacki, M.L.: Appraising research on personalized learning: Definitions, theoretical alignment, advancements, and future directions. J. Res. Technol. Educ. **52**(3), 235–252 (2020)
37. Sprake, A., Palmer, C.: Physical education: the allegory of the classroom. J. Qual. Res. Sports Stud. **12**(1), 57–78 (2018)
38. Barroso, C.S., McCullum-Gomez, C., Hoelscher, D.M., et al.: Self-reported barriers to quality physical education by physical education specialists in Texas. J. School Health **75**(8), 313–319 (2018)
39. Evans, S.: Maintaining skill development of newly qualified physical education teachers: mentorship after graduation. GILE J. Skills Dev. **4**(3) (2024)
40. Song, X.: Physical education teaching mode assisted by artificial intelligence assistant under the guidance of high-order complex network. Sci. Rep. **14**, 4104 (2024)

Academic Use of Artificial Intelligence Tools by University Students

Andrea Ibieta(✉), Samuel Aguilera, María Constanza-Medina, María Ignacia-Sepúlveda, and Luis Mario Castellanos-Alvarenga

Facultad de Ciencias Sociales y Comunicaciones, Escuela de Psicología, Universidad Santo Tomás, Santiago, Chile
aibieta@santotomas.cl

Abstract. Integrations of generative Artificial Intelligence (Gen AI) technologies in higher education have transformed teaching and learning. The accelerated transformation comes after the Covid-19 pandemic, which allowed the adoption of these tools. This study inspects the use of Gen AI by social science students in their academic contexts, addressing a gap in research predominantly focused on STEAM education. From a qualitative approach, with a phenomenological design, this study aims to explore types of use of Gen AI through semi-structured interviews of 10 university students in Temuco, Chile. Results reveal three types of use: as an information repository, an editing tool, and a cognitive aid. Students used these types of activities for tasks such as information retrieval, enhancing writing quality, and supporting cognitive processes like brainstorming and problem-solving.

Results demonstrate that Gen AI tools provide unique applications within social sciences, such as generating therapeutic techniques and adapting content to individual needs, underscoring the tools' versatility. However, challenges include risks of misuse, overconfidence, and ethical concerns, emphasizing the need for structured training and policy frameworks.

This study refines the understanding of Gen AI's role in education by offering a detailed framework of usage patterns. It calls for further research into its cognitive and psychological impacts, exploring its potential to enhance critical thinking, creativity, and professional preparedness across disciplines.

Keywords: Generative Artificial Intelligence (Gen AI) · Higher Education · Social Science · types of use

1 Introduction

The advent of generative Artificial Intelligence (AI) technologies introduces a transformative dimension to university education, which has already undergone significant changes due to the COVID-19 pandemic. This global crisis necessitated an abrupt transition to online education, as noted by [18] compelling institutions to adopt information and communication technologies (ICT) and AI tools at an unprecedented rate.

Ł. Tomczyk (Ed.): NMP 2024, CCIS 2537, pp. 343–353, 2025.
https://doi.org/10.1007/978-3-031-95627-0_23

Before 2020, applications of AI in student learning processes were not widespread as it is now, despite the evidence supporting student openness for such innovations [25]. Even though AI tools were used for purposes such as adaptive learning strategies, teaching evaluation, virtual classroom, feedback and adaptative learning, among others [13, 30] the pandemic accelerated the integration of these technologies in the daily basis use, prompting an evolution in pedagogical strategies and fostering enhanced digital engagement [7].

Specifically, generative AI through tools such as chatbots and Generative Pre-trained Transformers (GPTs), has emerged a significant innovation in this context. These technologies work as conversational agents able to interact with users to deliver instant responses, providing educational support. GPTs have enabled the creation of "human-like" text or responses based on specific instructions or contextual information, have demonstrated applicability across various natural language processing tasks, including text completion, conversational generation, and translation [5, 10]. In the educational domain, GPTs have shown the potential to revolutionize learning by offering personalized educational experiences, automating routine processes, and fostering creativity [16].

Empirical studies reveal that students predominantly employ AI tools as writing assistants, personalized learning aids, research and analysis support systems, and instruments for creative and artistic exploration [23, 24, 29]. For instance, Chan and Hu (2023) discovered that generative AI technologies were primarily used by undergraduate students to enhance writing skills, particularly for grammar correction and paraphrasing [8]. Similarly, Ziebell and Skeat (2023) found that postgraduate students were more inclined to use AI tools for learning support, content generation for academic assignments, and even submitting AI-generated material as part of their coursework [31].

Complementarily, Ruiz-Rojas et al. (2024) show that using Gen AI like Chat PDF and YOU COM improves critical thinking competencies in university students. In fact, 64% of participants report that using these tools to analyse and summarize complex data improve their evaluative and synthetic capabilities. The use of other tools like Canva and Tome AI enables students to foster out-of-the-box thinking, and the use of Google Docs enhances student communication and collaboration, improving motivation, teamwork, and communication skills in 60% of the participants [26].

Correspondingly, literature argues that confidence in using GenAI tools increases with experience; however, this confidence varies across disciplines and students. Many students tend to overestimate their abilities, leading to potential misuse [10]. Moreover, students also emphasize the importance of continuous training and support to ensure that AI tools are used effectively and ethically [9]. As noted by Barret and Pack (2023), there is a lack of preparedness for integrating GenAI into the learning process, highlighting a significant gap in its proper use [6].

According to Yang (2023), Gen AI can be utilized in education as a virtual tutor, providing personalized learning experiences and answering student questions, enhancing student engagement and motivation, and it can integrate into game-based learning, promoting active learning and knowledge retention across various subjects [28]. Farrelly and Baker (2023) argued that Gen AI can be utilized to support non-English speaking students by providing content and resources in multiple languages, enhancing accessibility, and understanding, and this is important like is argued in previous studies [15, 29].

Other authors explain that systems such as ChatGPT serve as virtual tutors, providing systematic explanations of complex concepts and answering students' questions, which is particularly beneficial for struggling learners [5]. These systems cater to diverse learner needs by adapting content and pace to individual abilities [15] and, when integrated with UDL principles, offer multiple means of representation, engagement, and expression, fostering inclusivity by addressing diverse learning styles [27]. Among other benefits, researchers argue that AI use can support collaborative learning by creating distinct scenarios for group problem-solving, fostering a sense of community among students [17, 19]. Furthermore, research suggests that AI enhances critical thinking by fostering analytical, problem-solving, and creative skills. Additionally, AI promotes collaborative learning and increases student engagement, motivation, and self-efficacy [24].

In Latin America, Molina et al. (2024) report that AI adoption positively impacts educators by streamlining the development of customized instructional content and reducing administrative burdens [23]. For students, AI facilitates personalized learning through adaptive tutoring systems and immediate feedback mechanisms. In administrative contexts, AI optimizes curriculum management, student support services, and resource allocation. This evidence underscores how AI integration within the educational sector not only transforms teaching and learning methodologies but also contributes to significant improvements in educational quality [1, 3].

However, while generative AI tools present promising opportunities, careful implementation strategies are essential to maximize benefits and minimize risks [26]. Concerns about privacy and security in the collection of personal data [29] risks to academic integrity [2] and overconfidence in the technology, which may hinder critical thinking and creativity [8]. These concerns encourage policymakers, educational institutions, and technology experts to provide clear guidelines to address these risks and ensure responsible and effective use in educational settings to harness all promising opportunities provided by AI to improve educational outcomes.

The integration of Gen AI into the educational context has demonstrated significant potential to enhance student learning [4, 11, 22]. However, the effective use of these technologies is not without challenges, underscoring the importance of user confidence, adoption types, and adequate training. Moreover, there is limited understanding of its applications in social sciences, particularly in identifying discipline-specific usages and challenges.

Addressing these elements is critical to ensuring effective use and incorporation of Gen Ai in learning environments. In this context, this study aims to describe usage patterns of Generative AI tools by university students in a social sciences program for their academic assignments.

Consequently, its relevance becomes essential considering the lack of empirical studies in this field of social sciences. This study will contribute a deep understanding of how students use generative artificial intelligence tools, where such comprehension would allow the identification of usage patterns, potential misunderstandings, or improper uses. Furthermore, analyzing the specific needs of students based on their disciplines could help personalize the integration of these tools into the learning process and design AI tools and use policies that better cater to the needs of these students.

2 Method

2.1 Research Design

This study adopts a qualitative approach with a phenomenological design and a descriptive scope [20]. The objective is to provide an in-depth, objective description of the phenomenon under study, authentically reflecting the participants' experiences, perceptions, environments, and circumstances without bias [14]. The descriptive scope further emphasizes the importance of providing a detailed account of participants' perceptions, environments, and circumstances to generate a holistic understanding of the phenomenon under study. To achieve this, a voluntary sampling method was employed, allowing participants to self-select based on their willingness and relevance to the study.

Participants
The sample consists of 10 university students from Temuco, Chile, selected based on specific inclusion and exclusion criteria.

The inclusion criteria were 1) Participants must be enrolled in a university program, 2) They must have completed their first year of study, 3) Maintain an active academic status during the first semester of 2024 and 4) participants should actively use artificial intelligence tools in their academic activities.

2.2 Data Collection Instrument

The primary data collection instrument was a semi-structured individual interview. This approach employs a pre-designed set of flexible questions, allowing for spontaneous reformulation or the creation of additional questions to explore participants' narratives in greater depth [20]The interview focusses on general use of artificial intelligence tools by the participants for academic purposes.

2.3 Procedure

2.4 Data Analysis

For data analysis, the systematic analysis was employed following a conventional content analysis[12]. The conventional content analysis is an inductive category development process and is appropriate when theories or research of a phenomenon is limited. Researchers refrain from employing predetermined categories, instead allowing these categories to arise naturally from the data. By thoroughly engaging with the data, researchers can discover fresh insights, a process referred to as inductive category development. This technique is frequently utilized in various qualitative designs.

Initially, the recordings of the individual semi-structured interviews were transcribed verbatim and imported into the ATLAS.ti analysis software [21]. Subsequently, the researchers reviewed each transcript to identify excerpts that aligned with the objective of characterization, thereby initiating the open coding process. Simultaneously, a triangulation of the results was conducted based on the individual analyses performed by each researcher, adhering to the comparative nature of qualitative analysis.

During the analysis, central codes and categories were identified, addressing the characterization of perceptions regarding the use of AI, self-efficacy, and learning. In this phase, units of analysis related to how students use AI were identified, including the types of academic situations in which it is employed—such as exams, assignments, or studying—the frequency of its use, among other factors. Additionally, the analysis explored students' perceptions of learning during and after using AI, their perceived self-efficacy, and how AI usage impacted it.

Finally, these findings were visually represented through a conceptual map, facilitating a clearer understanding of the data obtained.

3 Results

According to the interviews conducted, it was observed that students perform three types of activities supported by Gen AI tools. The first is as an information repository; the second involves using these tools as an editing tool; and finally, albeit in fewer cases, as a cognitive tool.

As can be seen in Fig. 1, each of these broader categories includes sub-categories that will be explained in detail.

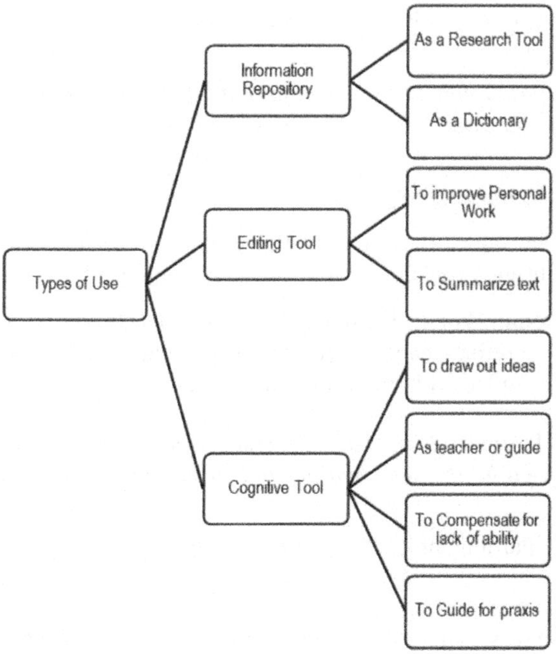

Fig. 1. Categories Three

3.1 Information Repository

This category describes the role of AI as a facilitator of knowledge acquisition, where students use AI tools, such chat GPT to efficiently retrieve, organize and access information for academic purposes. AI is perceived as a "knowledge mediator".

Research Tool: Composed of 15 citations that refer to the use of AI as a primary source for searching academic information, basic and complex. Chat GPT helps students to identify theories, methodologies, and research approaches, enhancing information accessibility and self-directed learning, as can be seen in the following quotes:

> Fragment 4:24. Participant 4: *"I try sometimes to look for information for my thesis project same then for example the types of approaches in psychology how I could apply them in my project".*
>
> Fragment 3:8. Participant 3: *"I feel that it has made me more autonomous by the fact that in the way I use chat gpt it helps me to look for information scientific study in a faster way then that allows me to feel that I have more access, I have faster access to information".*

Dictionary for Concept Clarification: Composed of 6 quotes, refers to the use as a lexical and conceptual aid, helping students to decipher academic jargon or understand theoretical constructs. As pointed out by participants 5 and 2:

> Fragment 5:25. Participant 5: *"I feel that I have learnt a bit more, it's that sometimes the meaning of words, so I feel that it has made it a bit easier for me on certain points".*
>
> *Fragment 2:2. Participant 2: "Some word that I don't understand that you explain it to me in a different way".*

3.2 Editing and Refining Tool

In this subgroup are codes highlighting the use of AI for enhancing the quality of academic output, through revision, synthesis, and coherence building.

To Improve Personal Work: Composed of 5 quotes, this type of use is based on students using AI to refine academic reports or presentations to achieve better clarity and coherence, as is reflected in the following quotes:

> Fragment 8:21 Participant 7: *"For University work such as reports and presentations, to help guide the information and to be able to write in a better way (...)".*
>
> Fragment 1:10. Participant 1: *"To correct my writing, to answer some research questions".*

To Summarize Text: Composed of 5 quotes, this use refers to students using AI tools to synthesize large amounts of information they need to study or to write academic papers or reports, this activity makes study material more concise and digestible for students. As shown in the following quotes:

Fragment 2:21 Participant 2: *"Any word that I don't understand, explain it to me in another way, or any paragraph that I ask you to explain it to me in a clearer way or in other words".*

Fragment 1:16. Participant 1: *"Yes I have used, I have used ChatGPT, another one called [unintelligible] that does like works, summaries... I have also used another one that transcribes recordings that I don't remember the name...".*

3.3 Cognitive Tool

This subgroup describes the use of AI tools to improve thinking processes, problem solving, or learning by supporting cognitive processes. This type of use is primarily to facilitate information processing and cognitive tasks that would otherwise be much more demanding.

To Draw Out Ideas: Students use AI as a source of inspiration to integrate into different academic activities, being an aid that complements personal knowledge, acting like a cognitive scaffold in exploratory phases of academic tasks. As reflected in the testimonies of participants 6 and 9:

Fragment 7:1. Participant 6: *"Well, I have mainly used it to generate ideas like brainstorming, I don't know, for example, the other time I used it to ask it to give me ideas for questions".*

Fragment 10:9. Participant 9: *"In the thesis I remember that at one point I didn't know what more information could be included in the theoretical framework and then I asked her for ideas on how to go deeper into it, for example".*

As a Teacher or Guide: Composed of 11 quotes, students use AI tools customized tutor, making the information more accessible and dynamizing the learning process, reducing learning barriers by adapting content complexity. As stated by participants 2 and 5:

Fragment 2:6. Participant 2: *"If I have a job, ehh I can, I don't know how to put a part of the guideline and I say, explain me a bit about this... And from there, like, as it is, as it is a chat I talk to the chat, I ask more things or later I say, develop the idea a bit more, things like that (...)".*

Fragment 5:9. Participant 5: *"When they send us books to read and certain paragraphs to read that I don't understand very well, and I don't know, I tell the AI to explain it to me in other words so that I can understand it and maybe if it gives me information that is clearer, I can understand it better".*

Compensate For Lack of Ability: Students use AI tools when they feel that demands exceed their perceived cognitive abilities or their knowledge. As indicated by participants 1 and 9:

Fragment 1:4. Participant 1: *"Yes, in fact if there is a job first I see I do what I can do but if I see that it is too difficult or I am in a hurry I use it".*

Fragment 10:17. Participant 9: *"In a diploma work I had to do an essay and I was half sick and a lot of things happened and I felt like I was blocked and I asked the AI for guidance on how I could do it, like it told me the step by step and I used it the truth, it was like a good base and obviously I looked for bibliography and other things and also like with my knowledge but the truth is that it saved me a lot and it was good for me".*

As a Guide for Praxis: Composed of 4 quotes, this refers to the use of AI to address specific needs of the degree specialization, such as generating ideas or techniques for professional scenarios.

Fragment 4:18. Participant 4: *"Yes, it has helped me a lot with the issue of patient care, for example, when I sometimes have a patient with issues of self-esteem, for example, I ask him I don't know ehh, can you give me techniques for self-esteem, how to work on it or self-concept, self-knowledge, etc. and he gives me, he gives me the shot, so I think it has helped me a lot in that respect".*

Fragment 10:1 Participant 9: *"Emm for all in general I have used it as for example for ideas of patients as that it gives me some activity or for works that orient me a little in what I have to do emm that generally".*

As can be seen in the data, using artificial intelligence for academic purposes go through a wide range of complexity. In this sample, AI use goes from refine, understand knowledge, and retrieve basic information to a set of complex cognitive activities. AI work as an information repository, research assistant, and conceptual clarifier, allowing students to navigate academic material independently and fostering autonomy. Beyond retrieving data, AI helps students refine and organize their work, acting as an editorial assistant to polish ideas and enhance written expression. AI's deepest engagement is as a cognitive aid, supporting higher order thinking and problem-solving, where it becomes an intellectual collaborator, guiding students through complex thought processes and enhancing their ability to construct and apply knowledge. This dynamic interaction strengthens various levels of use, enabling students to refine comprehension through repeated questioning and critical reflection. AI acts as a cognitive scaffold, advancing from speeding information retrieval to enhancing cognitive abilities, transforming learning into a more autonomous and engaging experience, and becoming essential to student cognition and professional development.

4 Discussion

The results show that students use Artificial Intelligence tools in their academic activities mainly as an information repository and as an editing tool. In addition, students use AI tools as a cognitive tool to facilitate thinking and problem solving. In general, these types of activities match with those proposed in the literature, however, results show new insights and refine the understanding of how university students from a social science program use generative AI tools in their academic assignments.

Regarding the use as an information repository, in this sample, students frequently use generative AI tools to retrieve and understand information efficiently, for example, to find data and concepts for academic tasks, thesis projects, or written assignments [23, 24, 29] or to quickly grasp the meaning of unfamiliar terms [10]. These results show rich and granular descriptions, which uncover detailed ways of students interacting with AI tools.

In relation to the use of AI tools as an editing tool, results support evidence which highlights that AI tools have the potential to automate routine tasks [16] and to improve personal work [8]. However, these results, on the one hand, go under the purposes of using the tools (focusing on improving personal work) and on the other, go beyond the opportunities and potential use, showing real integration for academic purposes that highlight real use and opportunities to generate proper instruction for social sciences students, according to this discipline-specific usages.

Finally, participating students use AI tools as a cognitive tool, on the one hand, to facilitate thinking processes [5, 28], such as a brainstorming partner, to expand and clarify guidelines, and as a cognitive aid in cases where demands are perceived as overwhelming or exceed perceived students' capacities. On the other hand, AI tools are used as a professional aid, where they show the adaptability of AI tools to support students in generating therapeutic techniques.

These findings are in line with the theoretical framework by illustrating how generative AI tools improve learning, assist with academic tasks, and cater to disciplinary requirements. The wide range of applications (like information retrieval, editing, and cognitive support) showcases AI's adaptability, but also underscores the need for organized training to avoid misuse, as previous studies [6, 23].

In summary, the study refines the understanding of how students use generative AI, by grouping activities into three categories. This categorization offers a structured framework, that goes beyond general descriptions and potential use, going deep and identifying subcategories and practical applications. These detailed applications are rarely documented in prior research, adding depth to the newly comprehension scenarios.

The study also presents empirical evidence about the use among social sciences students, in a context where most studies come from STEM education, offering a contextual insight into a less frequently explored discipline. Showing, for example, how AI tools act as a cognitive enhancer, expanding cognitive capabilities and as a personalized tutor by adapting content and pace to individual abilities [15].

Regarding to limitations this study is that the study focuses on students from a single social sciences program, limiting its applicability to other disciplines. The voluntary sampling method may have introduced a bias toward participants with prior interest in AI tools, potentially affecting the results. Furthermore, the rapid evolution of generative AI tools could impact the relevance of the findings over time, as new features and functionalities emerge.

Future research could adopt a mixed-methods approach, combining qualitative insights with quantitative measures to explore the frequency, depth, and impact of AI tool usage on academic performance and cognitive development. Longitudinal studies would also provide valuable insights into how students' use of AI tools evolves over time, particularly as they transition from academic to professional settings.

Finally, given the findings on the use of AI tools as cognitive enhancers and personalized tutors, future studies could investigate the psychological and cognitive effects of AI usage on learning processes, such as improvements in critical thinking, problem-solving, and metacognitive skills, and generate insights about the role of cognitive and digital competences needed to improve the use of Artificial Intelligence.

References

1. Al-Zahrani, A.M.: Unveiling the shadows: beyond the hype of AI in education. Heliyon. **10**(9), e30696 (2024)
2. Ali, O., Murray, P.A., Momin, M., Dwivedi, Y.K., Malik, T.: The effects of artificial intelligence applications in educational settings: challenges and strategies. Technol. Forecast. Soc. Chang. **199**, 123076 (2024)
3. Almasri, F.: Exploring the impact of artificial intelligence in teaching and learning of science: a systematic review of empirical research. Res. Sci. Educ. **54**(5), 977–997 (2024)
4. Bahroun, Z., Anane, C., Ahmed, V., Zacca, A.: Transforming education: a comprehensive review of generative artificial intelligence in educational settings through bibliometric and content analysis. Sustainability **15**(17), 12983 (2023)
5. Baidoo-Anu, O., Ansah, L., D.: Education in the era of generative artificial intelligence (AI): understanding the potential benefits of ChatGPT in promoting teaching and learning. J. AI. **7**(1), 52–62 (2023)
6. Barrett, A., Pack, A.: Not quite eye to A.I.: student and teacher perspectives on the use of generative artificial intelligence in the writing process. Int. J. Educ. Technol. High. Educ. **20**(59) (2023)
7. Capone, R., Lepore, M.: From distance learning to integrated digital learning: a fuzzy cognitive analysis focused on engagement, motivation, and participation during COVID-19 pandemic. Technol. Knowl. Learn. **27**, 1259–1289 (2021)
8. Chan, C.K.Y., Hu, W.: Students' voices on generative AI: perceptions, benefits, and challenges in higher education. Int. J. Educ. Technol. High. Educ. **20**(43) (2023)
9. Darvishi, A., Khosravi, H., Sadiq, S., Gašević, D., Siemens, G.: Impact of AI assistance on student agency. Comput. Educ. **210**, 104967 (2024)
10. Farrelly, T., Baker, N.: Generative artificial intelligence: implications and considerations for higher education practice. Educ. Sci. **13**(1109) (2023)
11. Giannakos, M. et al.: The promise and challenges of generative AI in education. Behav. Inf. Technol. 1–27
12. Hsieh, H.F., Shannon, S.E.: Three approaches to qualitative content analysis. Qual. Health Res. **15**(9), 1277–1288 (2005)
13. Huang, J., Saleh, S., Liu, Y.: A Review on artificial intelligence in education. Acad. J. Interdisc. Stud. **10**(3), 206 (2021)
14. Johnson, R.B., Christensen, L.: Educational Research: Quantitative, Qualitative, and Mixed Approaches. SAGE Publications Inc, Thousand Oaks (2019)
15. Kannadhasan, M.: The function of artificial intelligence in inclusive English language teaching: strategies for diverse learners. Int. J. Teach. Learn. Educ. (2024)
16. Kelly, A., Sullivan, M., Strampel, K.: Generative artificial intelligence: university student awareness, experience, and confidence in use across disciplines. J. Univ. Teach. Learn. Pract. **20**(6), 12 (2023)
17. Kim, J., Lee, H., Cho, Y.H.: Learning design to support student-AI collaboration: perspectives of leading teachers for AI in education. Educ. Inf. Technol. **27**(5), 6069–6104 (2022)
18. Leiva, M., Benavides, M.: Aprendizaje y buenas prácticas sobre la pandemia en educación superior en Chile BT - Educación superior y pandemia: Aprendizajes y buenas prácticas en Iberoamérica (2021)

19. Marzuki, W.U., Rusdin, D., Indrawati, I.: The impact of AI writing tools on the content and organization of students' writing: EFL teachers' perspective. Cogent Educ. **10**(2), 2236469 (2023)
20. Merriam, S.B., Tisdell, E.J.: Qualitative Research: A Guide to Design and Implementation, 4th edn. Jossey Bass, San Francisco (2016)
21. Miles, H.A.M., Saldaña, J.M.B.: Qualitative Data Analysis: A Methods Sourcebook. SAGE Publications (2020)
22. Mohamed, A.M., Shaaban, T.S., Bakry, S.H., Guillén-Gámez, F.D., Strzelecki, A.: Empowering the faculty of education students: applying AI's potential for motivating and enhancing learning. Innovative High. Educ. (2024)
23. Molina-Cobo, E., Pineada, J.: La revolución de la IA en Educación: Lo que hay que saber. Innovaciones Digitales de Educación (2024)
24. Patiño-Mardones, R., Garcés, L., Valencia, A., Arango, D., García, R., J.: Tendencias investigativas frente al uso de inteligencia artificial en contextos universitarios. Revista Ibérica de Sistemas e Tecnologias de Información. **59** 245–260 (2023)
25. Romero-Alonso, R.E., Tejada-Navarro, C.A., Núñez-Barrera, O.: Actitudes hacia las TIC y adaptación al aprendizaje virtual en contexto COVID-19: Alumnos en Chile que ingresan a la educación superior. Perspectiva Educacional. **60**(2), 99–120 (2021)
26. Ruiz-Rojas, L.I., Salvador-Ullauri, L., Acosta-Vargas, P.: Collaborative working and critical thinking: adoption of generative artificial intelligence tools in higher education. Sustainability **16**(5367) (2024)
27. Saborío-Taylor, S.. Rojas-Ramírez, F.: Universal design for learning and artificial intelligence in the digital era: fostering inclusion and autonomous learning. Int. J. Prof. Dev. Learners Learn. **62** (2024)
28. Su, J., Yang, W.: Unlocking the power of ChatGPT: a framework for applying generative AI in education. ECNU Rev. Educ. **6**(3), 355–366 (2023)
29. Wang, T., Lund, B.D., Marengo, A., Pagano, A., Mannuru, N.R., Teel, Z.A., Pange, J.: Exploring the potential impact of artificial intelligence (AI) on international students in higher education: generative AI, chatbots, analytics, and international student success. Appl. Sci. **13**(16716) (2023)
30. Zhai, X., et al.: A review of artificial intelligence (AI) in education from 2010 to 2020. Complexity **2021**, 1–18 (2021)
31. Skeat, J. Ziebell, N.: How is generative AI being used by university students and academics? (2023)

Author Index

Ł. Tomczyk (Ed.): NMP 2024, CCIS 2537, pp. 355–356, 2025.
https://doi.org/10.1007/978-3-031-95627-0

The manufacturer's authorised representative in the EU is Springer Nature Customer Service Centre GmbH, Europaplatz 3, 69115 Heidelberg, Germany. If you have any concerns regarding our products, please contact ProductSafety@springernature.com

Printed and bound by CPI Group (UK) Ltd, Croydon, CR0 4YY
30/09/2026
02225566-0014